LA PINTA

LA PINTA

CHICANA/O PRISONER LITERATURE, CULTURE, AND POLITICS

B. V. OLGUÍN

University of Texas Press | Austin

Requests for permission to reproduce material from this work should be sent to:
Permissions
University of Texas Press
P.O. Box 7819
Austin, TX 78713-7819
www.utexas.edu/utpress/about/bpermission.html

♾The paper used in this book meets the minimum requirements of ANSI/NISO
Z39.48-1992 (R1997) (Permanence of Paper).

Library of Congress Cataloging-in-Publication Data

Olguín, B. V., 1965–
    La pinta : Chicana/o prisoner literature, culture, and politics /
B.V. Olguín.
        p. cm.
    Includes bibliographical references and index.
    ISBN 978-0-292-71960-6 (cloth : alk. paper) — ISBN 978-0-292-71961-3
(pbk. : alk. paper)
    1. Mexican American prisoners.   2. Mexican American prisoners—Political
activity.   3. Prisoners—Civil rights—United States.   4. Mexican Americans
in popular culture—United States.   5. Prisoners in popular culture—United
States.   I. Title.
    HV9466.O54 2009
    365'.608968073—dc22
                                                                2009014307

For my brothers Anthony and Adrian,
mis tíos Nick y Quique,
y toda La Raza with numbers for names

Pintos are at the intersection of our colonial
reality and our revolutionary potential.

—*Raúl Salinas (1996)*

Contents

Preface

THIS IS PERSONAL. A FIGHT IS ALWAYS PERSONAL. IT IS ALSO POLITI-
cal. Too many people I know, and millions of people I do not know, have
endured much worse than my own encounters with corrupt and brutal
police, lawyers, jailers, and judges for me to engage in an exercise of
scholarly revenge. Someone is in prison tonight and will be tomorrow,
and they need our solidarity.

While this is, fundamentally, a scholarly book, the indictments and
insights are culled from experience: incessant police harassment of me and
friends in the lower east-side Houston barrio of Magnolia for suspicion
of one thing or another; a father beaten by White cops in Fort Worth for
having a photograph of a White girlfriend in his wallet; women relatives
subject to double standards and domestic violence who found the courage
to fight back and rebuild lives for themselves and their children; uncles
caught in the crimes of poverty who served time with convict intellectuals
who became famous behind the walls and beyond; personal friends and
mentors who turned a life of crime into revolutionary praxis.

Yet I cannot, nor do I wish to, simplistically celebrate any and all
criminal acts. Rather, I seek to historicize the racialized and gendered
nature of criminalization in the United States, and the broader effect this
exercise of juridical power has on extended families and communities,
specifically my own Chicana/o community. I seek to responsibly map the
constructions of Chicana/o criminality, from the petty to the pathological,
to the immanently as well as maturely revolutionary. My overarching goal
is to situate Chicana/o criminality in relation to broader constructions
of crime and the exercise of punishment in the broad history of U.S.
imperialism. I also seek to humanize prisoners even as I critique them
alongside the political economy that often overdetermines their crimes
and, even more so, their punishment.

This book is an attempt to examine the construction of crime as an
organizing principle for society, and, as such, to some this very book
itself will seem criminal. At a time when civil liberties and the essential
humanity of dark brown men and women are under siege yet again—this

time Muslims—any attempt to critique institutions of power is seen as aberrant. I want to be this type of deviant. At the same time, this book represents many negotiations of power and privilege. I am, after all, a college professor.

This textual performance of privilege nevertheless has come at a heavy price. My refusal to compromise on the integrity of the stories, and my active solidarity with the people who are the focus of this study have led to attacks on me in the otherwise privileged academic institution where I earn a relatively comfortable living. I dared to treat the voices of dark people as legitimate, and subsequently was marked as an illegitimate academic by Euro-centric and outright racist ideologues. This book's decade-long publication delay was in large part due to persistent uncollegiality and gross bias of the retrograde elements within the Department of English, Classics, and Philosophy at the University of Texas at San Antonio. Those who were silent in the face of the persecution and differential treatment of me and other faculty are equally complicit. *J'accuse!*

Indeed, if this book has any value at all, it arises from my attempt to attack institutions and the complex processes of institutionalization that render otherwise decent people complicit in abusive power relations. Yet this study is not just about bigotry. It is about boys and girls, men and women, and also legions of elders who have learned about themselves and, more importantly, about the true nature of our society by enduring its prisons. This is about them, and it is an attempt to learn from them.

Still, as a book, it certainly is not enough of an intervention to disrupt the prison industrial complex to the degree necessary for us to herald a new order. After all, it is just a book. In many respects, this study is overly textual and burdened by academic jargon and esoteric vocabulary. I did my best to make it accessible to the people on whom it is based, many of whom have not had the opportunity of a college education, but I felt compelled to use the tools of vocabulary necessary for the issues and concepts at hand. Sometimes a hammer is called for; other times a sickle is the best tool for the job. I nevertheless apologize for being didactic and elitist in my language.

This is a book about people who ran, fought, spoke back, and wrote against attempts to contain, occupy, and oppress them. It is about criminalized people who became something else in the balance of the doing and the writing. There are murderers and sadists, but also bandits and *sediciosos*, hustlers and true Pinta and Pinto revolutionaries. Some I am happy never to have met. Yet I also count myself honored to have had the opportunity to know and write about some of the most brilliant and righteous rebels this world has ever known. May we all continue to transgress against injustice. *¡Hasta la victoria, siempre!*

Acknowledgments

MANY, ESPECIALLY MY FAMILY, HAVE SHARED THE TRAUMAS AND any triumph that completion of this book may represent. My *compañera* Bernadette Andrea and son Ross have provided the love, support, and grounding necessary to realize that a book can never fully explain or supercede the interpersonal nature of our humanity. My parents, Antonia Valdez Olguín and Ben Montez Olguín, as well as my brothers Anthony and Adrian, have provided the greatest incentive to finish this project by their humbling pride at having a "doctor" in the family and their understanding that I am somehow trying to do something for the family. My uncles Nicanor "Nick" Valdez and Enrique "Quique" Valdez lived what I have tried to write about, and shared the insights necessary to get it right. My maternal grandfather Nicanor, "Nico" Valdez, was the first person to ever take me onto the grounds of a university when he worked as a custodian at the University of Houston. His tolerance of my childish scribbling on the chalkboard he had just cleaned opened a world of discourse that was closed to him, my maternal grandmother, Eduarda "Lala" Loredo Valdez, and my paternal grandparents. This piece of chalk *es para ustedes también*. My *primo* Alfred "Freddy" Porras Jr. kept me honest and humble with his reminders to always remember the next seven generations.

I have many friends who contributed to this project and my own intellectual and political growth. I am especially grateful to Louis G. Mendoza and Sandra "Sandy" Soto. Raúl Salinas, Ricardo Sánchez, Alvaro Hernández Luna, and Johnny V. Martinez were always *camaradas* whose insights, born of their own painful lessons in *la pinta*, are embedded throughout the manuscript. Benjamin Ortiz, Jesús Rosales, Gabriela Gutierrez Muhs, and Francis Morales of the Stanford University Centro Chicano gave me the most important help of all: a hug, a meal, and an occasional place to sleep. *Un saludo fraternal* to all the Centro Chicano *locos* and vision questers.

Colleagues at the University of Texas at San Antonio were instrumental in helping me complete this project. I am very grateful to Sonia Saldívar-Hull, Rodolfo "Rudy" Rosales, Arturo Vega, and Rubén Martinez. A special thanks to Ray Garza, who supported me and this project from the start. My former dean, Alan Craven, and department chair, Linda Woodson, deserve recognition for never failing to treat me with the respect that my other White colleagues felt so free to deny me and other minorities on a daily basis. I am very grateful to neighbor and fellow writer Gregorio Barrios Jr. for sharing his primary materials and insights on Fred Gómez Carrasco. I especially appreciate the research assistance provided by UTSA graduate students Marco Cervantes and Roberto Macias. René Valdez and Lilia Rosas also helped with research.

Arte Público Press's Recovering the Hispanic Literary Heritage Project provided partial funding for portions of the research. The UTSA College of Liberal and Fine Arts also provided summer research grants, a well-earned faculty development leave, and funding for the cover art. The Tomás Rivera Center Dissertation Completion Project, run out of UTSA by Ray Garza, also provided the necessary nourishment and feedback to develop preliminary studies into a viable book project. Barbara Cox provided important early copyediting. The National Research Council provided me with a Ford Foundation Postdoctoral Fellowship to expand the dissertation into a book. The National Endowment for the Humanities selected me for a Human Rights Summer Seminar run by Andrew Nathan—a true scholar-activist—at Columbia University in 2004. I also received financial support from the Hispanic Scholarship Fund, the League of United Latin American Citizens (LULAC) of Houston, and the Boys Club of Houston. Every dollar made a difference because it came from the purses and wallets of poor people who trusted these organizations to transform community love into an opportunity for members of our community to compound the benefit. The University of Houston's Mexican American Studies Program—expertly led by Tatcho Mindiola and Lorenzo Cano—remains the single most important site of my personal, intellectual, and political development. The University of Houston's Honors Program, and especially its director, Bill Monroe, further enabled my early research on Chicana/o authors.

Nicolás Kanellos is undoubtedly the most important intellectual influence in my life. He mentored me from an angry undergraduate to a still angry professor while always supporting my efforts each step of the way. Mary Louise Pratt also deserves special thanks for taking a chance on me as a graduate student. Tomás Ybarra-Frausto convinced his colleagues to accept me into the Department of Spanish and Portuguese, and subsequently changed my life. Yvonne Yarbro-Bejarano, Ramón Saldívar, Maria Herrera-Sobek, Lauro Flores, and Luís Leal provided the mentoring and friendship everyone needs to get through a Ph.D. program. José David Saldívar, José Limón, Barbara Harlow, and David Montejano generously helped from other institutions. At Cornell University, Helena María Viramontes, Bedoin Jeyifu, Reeve Parker, Satya Mohanty, and Phil Lewis were genuine colleagues as I tried to make may way and make a difference as a new assistant professor. Paula M. L. Moya's enthusiasm for my activism and scholarship helped give me the opportunity to develop it further at Cornell. She also introduced me to my life partner, wife, and intellectual companion, for which I am eternally grateful. Juan Mah y Busch, Ami Ongiri, Eliza Rodriguez y Gibson, Sean Teuton, Vera Palmer, and all the students of the Writing Resistance: U.S. Minority and Third World Prisoner Literatures class helped me realize the importance, and inherent limits, of this type of work. I am especially grateful to Tim Mitchell, an expert in Theater of the Oppressed, for guiding me towards new ways to teach in prison. Above all else, I thank the prisoners who trusted me enough to tell their stories and keep challenging me to do more than simply telling stories for an academic audience. *Aquí les va . . .*

LA PINTA

La Pinta

History, Culture, and Ideology in Chicana/o Convict Discourse

> The production of the terrorist as a figure in the American imaginary reflects vestiges of previous moral panics as well, including those instigated by the mass fear of the criminal and the communist. Willie Horton is the most dramatic example of the former. Anti-communism successfully mobilized national—perhaps I should say nationalist—anxieties, as does the so-called war on terrorism today. None of these figures are entirely new, although the emphasis has been different at different historical conjunctures.
>
> —*Angela Davis (2005)*

I. CRIME, TERRORISM, AND THE WAR ON DARK BROWN MEN

THE SPECTACULAR SEPTEMBER 11, 2001, ATTACKS ON THE PRINCIPAL symbols of U.S. economic and military might in New York City and Washington, D.C., are transforming U.S. society like no other time in history. Yet some of the ongoing transformations were foreseen by critics of the draconian 1994 Omnibus Crime Bill, who warned against the erosion of civil liberties—especially for ethnic and racial minorities—under the guise of yet another war on crime that extended and intensified former President Reagan's "war on drugs" in the 1980s and former President Nixon's "crusade against crime" in the 1960s.[1] The 1994 Omnibus Crime Bill dedicated over $28 billion for law enforcement, including increased prison construction, fifty thousand new police officers, an expanded list of death penalty offenses, a circumscribed death row appeals process, and mandatory sentencing guidelines for select offenses. Ironically, the war on terror—ostensibly inaugurated to combat international terrorism—has had an even more severe impact on domestic law enforcement than the Omnibus Crime Bill. In the relatively short time since the September 11 attacks, the country has been transformed into a carceral apparatus by the 2002 passage of the "USA PATRIOT Act" (the Orwellian acronym for "Uniting and Strengthening America by Providing Appropriate Tools Required to Intercept and Obstruct Terrorism") and subsequent

PATRIOT Act II as well as the 2006 Military Commissions Act. These laws collectively curtail constitutional freedoms of speech, association, and information; infringe on constitutional rights to legal representation, a timely public trial, and protection from unreasonable searches; and allow for the use of extrajudicial imprisonment and secret military tribunals for citizens and noncitizens accused of aiding or abetting terrorism. PATRIOT Act II initially included provisions that made it easier for law enforcement surveillance and even allowed for review of a person's library book-use record. These initiatives were complemented by the establishment of the Information Awareness Office, charged with collecting and processing surveillance data in search of potential threats to U.S. security. Its inaugural motto was "*scientia est potentia*," or "knowledge is power," and its logo featured an all-seeing eye atop a pyramid spying upon the figure of a globe in the foreground; it was later changed following public outcry over its totalitarian overtones. Worse, within a year of the September 11 attacks, a new office—the Terrorism Intelligence Prevention System, or TIPS—was created to serve as a nationwide surveillance network that effectively would have deputized civil servants and ordinary citizens as domestic spies. The plan was to have neighbors watching neighbors.[2]

Under the USA PATRIOT Act I and II, as well as related 2006 legislation extending their provisions, anyone in the United States or abroad is susceptible to government surveillance, arrest, interrogation, and indefinite detention without legal representation or access to U.S. or international courts. Predictably, in the first year after the September 11 attacks, more than a thousand "foreigners" studying or working in the United States—primarily Arab, South Asian, and African Muslim males—had been detained and held incommunicado in U.S. prisons. Most of the detainees were arrested on visa violations but later were imprisoned under suspicion of having terrorist links. The U.S. Department of Justice, which conducts the detentions through its various subordinate agencies, refuses to release the names of most past and current detainees, and also occludes details surrounding their alleged offenses from the public, legal representatives, and even detainee family members. In the first two years of this pogrom, at least fourteen U.S. citizens were caught in the dragnet and detained in civilian prisons and military brigs with limited or no access to legal representation. All but one were racial minorities. The demographics of this subversion of habeas corpus—a foundational U.S. legal right guaranteeing a defendant access to the courts—not only confirms that the country is at war, but also reveals how the country's leaders initially constructed this war as a battle against a perceived "enemy within": he is a home-grown (or immigrant) "religious radical" who is overdetermined by law enforcement practices and mass media reportage as a Muslim male with dark brown skin.

The racial and religious profile of this twenty-first-century villain demands a broader meditation on racialized constructions of difference in the history of crime and punishment in the United States. Indeed, September 11 introduced not only a new enemy—the dark-skinned Muslim male—but a new way of understanding the old racial minority "menace to society" who, historically, has been figured as a Black male and/or, with increasing frequency, a Latino male. Today, the two villains—the international and the domestic—have become indistinguishable. The convergence of the new specter in the war on terrorism and the old antagonist from four decades of the wars on crime is underscored by the differential treatment of U.S. citizens detained and classified as "enemy combatants" for their alleged membership in al-Qaida, the organization that the U.S. government holds responsible for the September 11 attacks. This new classification is unique in U.S. jurisprudence because it situates its designee in the interstices of domestic and international law. Enemy combatants are denied access to U.S. courts and international tribunals precisely because they are American citizens accused of engaging in or planning bellicose actions against U.S. civilian or military targets. They are enemies of the United States, yet have no formal nation-state patron, which would make them eligible for international protection. An "enemy combatant" is distinct from an "unlawful combatant," who is a foreigner charged with engaging in combat for a third party that is not recognized as a legitimate combatant by the U.S. government. (The U.S. detainees from the wars in Afghanistan and Iraq, as well as the broader war on terror that spans the globe, have been classified as "unlawful combatants" as well as "enemy combatants" and denied legal representation, even though most nations throughout the world—including U.S. allies Britain and France—maintain they should be eligible for international protections as guaranteed by the Geneva Conventions. In response to this worldwide outcry, new U.S. president Barack Obama issued an executive order on January 22, 2009, closing all U.S. prisons in foreign territory and also ordered a hearing on the legal status of detainees previously classified as "enemy combatants." However, while he pledges to discontinue the use of this category, President Obama still has not eliminated the practice of "extraordinary rendition" by which these formerly classified "enemy combatants" are hunted, captured, and transported to a third country for unrestricted interrogation, which includes the possibility of torture.) Regardless of their new classification, the treatment afforded these detainees continues to be distinct from that of prisoners of war, who are afforded the rights outlined by the Geneva Conventions and have access to legal defense by military attorneys. Even a person charged with sedition or espionage is allowed access to legal representation. Guantanamo Bay detainees, on the other hand, exist in a legal limbo as new "anti-citizens" of the world.

The fourteen U.S. citizens detained as enemy combatants in the first two years following the September 11 attacks came from vastly different ethnic backgrounds: Arab, East Asian, African, African American, (mixed-race) Latina/o, and even one White American. They also included one woman, the African American wife of an accused al-Qaida cell leader in Oregon. Rather than diversify the image of the new twenty-first-century menace to society, however, the circumstances surrounding the detention and prosecution of these U.S. (anti)citizens further reinforces the prejudicial racialization of this new antithetical American. John Walker Lindh is a case in point. Born into a White upper-middle-class family in upscale Marin County north of San Francisco, Lindh was captured in combat against U.S. troops in Afghanistan in December 2001. Despite being classified as an enemy combatant, Lindh gained access to a federal court in San Francisco with the assistance of his father, a wealthy corporate attorney. After accepting a plea bargain that enabled him to escape a possible death sentence in exchange for pleading guilty to lesser crimes than the initial charge of terrorism, the younger Lindh apologized for his actions and pledged to help the government capture his former al-Qaida colleagues. (Hearst Washington Bureau reporter Stewart M. Powell [2002] suggests that Lindh may have provided information to federal investigators that led to the arrest of six Yemeni Americans, all of whom received training at the same time as Lindh in a base in Afghanistan and therefore could be visually identified by Lindh.) Initially denigrated as a traitor in U.S. media reports, which dubbed him "Jihad Johnny" and "Johnny Taliban," Lindh symbolically reclaimed his White American identity by turning on his darker former allies and affirming "I love America" before a judge sentenced him to twenty years in prison, with the possibility of parole and early release for "good behavior."

In contrast, Yasser Hamdi, who was born in Louisiana to Saudi Arabian parents during his father's employment in the oil industry, was held incommunicado for three years in a U.S. Navy brig in Norfolk, Virginia, after his capture in the same Mazar al-Sharif battle against U.S.-

supported Afghan troops in which Lindh participated. Hamdi was released in 2005 after a U.S. Supreme Court ruled in *Hamdi vs. Rumsfeld* (2005) against the government's right to hold enemy combatants indefinitely and incommunicado.[3] The aforementioned six Yemeni Americans arrested in New York City in September 2002, along with four African Americans and one Saudi Arabian American arrested in October 2002, also remained in detention without access to legal representation or a courtroom hearing for over two years. Puerto Rican José Padilla—an ex-convict and reputed former gang member born in New York City and raised in a low-income Latina/o neighborhood in Chicago—was another U.S. citizen charged and detained as an enemy combatant. Several years after converting to Islam during a prison stint in Florida, Padilla was arrested in Chicago on May 8, 2002, on suspicion that he was scouting targets for a uranium-loaded "dirty bomb" attack on U.S. territory. Padilla was held incommunicado in a military brig for over four years. The U.S. government avoided the application of *Hamdi vs. Rumsfeld* by applying new charges to Padilla. He was convicted in 2007 and sentenced to seventeen years' imprisonment under domestic criminal statutes in 2008, with the potential for an enemy combatant war crimes trial still lingering.

These detentions suggest that not all enemy combatants are created equal. Indeed, while all the detained enemy combatants are Muslims, the only one who gained expedient and full access to federal civilian courts (without the threat of summary expulsion from the country) is a White American male. Furthermore, less than a month after Lindh's classification as an enemy combatant was superceded by his conviction and sentence in a civilian court, the classification of the remaining racial minority enemy combatants was upheld by a secret tribunal of federal judges and subsequently ratified in January 2003 by President George W. Bush. But this should come as no surprise. As critical race and legal studies scholars have long argued, both formal and informal legal practices in the United States are undergirded by prejudice against racial minorities. Data by the Sentencing Project, an independent criminal justice policy institute that advocates alternatives to mass incarceration in the United States, confirm that minorities, especially Black males, continue to receive prejudicial treatment from the police, courts, and prison officials.[4] The classification, extended detention, and differential judicial treatment of twelve racial minority males, and the African American wife of one of them, as enemy combatants is significant because it illustrates that race—further "darkened" by a religion deemed by some to be "foreign"—continues to undergird the construction of abjection in the United States. In the U.S.

war on terrorism, the quintessential, viscerally repulsive anti-citizen is an American with dark brown skin. As Angela Davis notes in the epigraph to this introduction, U.S. government foreign policy at the turn of the twenty-first century has rendered the local neighborhood, dark brown, American male into a villain of global proportions.

This convergence of the racialized domestic criminal of the war on crime with the new anti-American terrorist is enabled by the alarmist and racially coded reportage that has accompanied the detention of enemy combatants who are ethnic and racial minorities, especially Padilla. Following former U.S. attorney general John Ashcroft's initial proclamation that Padilla was a "dangerous terrorist," journalist Dan Freedman's syndicated report, ominously titled "Prison system could be terror breeding ground," added that the recent arrest of ex-convict Padilla "could be evidence that prison systems here and overseas have become inadvertent breeding grounds for militant Islamic terrorists" (2002: A19). Freedman cites Charles Colson, an aid to former president Richard Nixon, and the architect of the inaugural war on crime in the 1960s. (Colson later served a prison sentence for his role in the Watergate cover-up, and upon his release he founded the nonprofit evangelical Christian organization Prison Fellowship, which targets prisoners for conversion.) Colson observes that "alienated, disenfranchised people are prime targets for radical Islamists who preach a religion of violence, of overcoming oppression by Jihad" (2002: A27). After noting the growing numbers of disenfranchised racial minorities in prison, Colson warns that "it's no accident that Islam's influence is growing behind bars" (2002: A27). While Colson's alarmist report carries problematic racial and religious overtones, it does coincide with statistics indicating that Latina/os are the fastest growing population of Muslims. Hisham Aidi (2002: n.p.) suggests that this trend may be as much a political phenomenon as a religious one: "by embracing Islam, previously invisible, inaudible, and disaffected individuals gain a sense of identity and belonging to what they perceive as an organized, militant, and glorious civilization that the West takes very seriously." Aidi cites a Chicano ex-convict convert to Islam, who extends the political linkages: "the Palestinians had their homeland stolen and were oppressed in much the same way as Mexicans" (2002: n.p.).

Regardless of their varied ideological trajectories, such mass media reports accentuate the abjection of the U.S. prisoner population by invoking a neo-crusade discourse that pits the Christian West against a potentially expanding Islamic East—all of which is purportedly taking place within the borders of the United States. In the wake of September 11 attacks, the specter of the criminal masses reproducing their abjection in U.S. prisons is not just a domestic crisis; it has become a matter of national security. However hyperbolic this representation of a mass uprising of prisoners-cum–Islamic terrorists may be, it nonetheless foregrounds how domestic law enforcement practices and U.S. foreign policy have begun to converge at the site of the penitentiary. In fact, under provisions of the PATRIOT Act, the Bureau of Justice Statistics, the government agency responsible for compiling national crime data, is now under the purview of the same office responsible for fighting the new war on terror: the Office of Homeland Security.

The coup de grace in this linkage of the war on crime, the war on terror, and the American penitentiary appears in a June 24, 2002, *Time* magazine feature by Amanda Ripley titled "The Case of the Dirty Bomber: How a Chicago Street Gangster Allegedly Became a Soldier for Osama Bin Laden." The article is introduced by a full-page close-up of Padilla's darkened face framed by a checkered red and white kaffiyeh, enlarged from a photograph of him outside a Florida mosque.

The semiotics of this layout become even more significant given that editors of *The New Republic*, the purportedly liberal alternative to *Time*, admitted darkening Saddam Hussein's complexion and cropping

FIGURE 1.1. Alleged al-Qaida terrorist José Padilla. *Time*, June 24, 2002. Courtesy of *Time* magazine.

his mustache (reminiscent of Hitler's) during the first Gulf War to make him appear more ominous. *Time*'s photo of Padilla as a dark Muslim male "international terrorist" is framed by a smaller black-and-white mug shot of Padilla from a previous stint in jail after being convicted for firing a gun in a "road rage" incident. The substance of the story revolves around Padilla's evolution from petty thief to prisoner to alleged international terrorist:

> It must have been one of Jose Padilla's proudest moments. He had spent his life chasing respect but rarely earning it—marking a dreary passage from a Chicago gang to juvenile detention to grownup prison to a Florida fast-food job and, finally, to a new life as a Muslim in the Middle East. (Ripley 2002: 28)

Described as "unsophisticated" and even "ordinary," Padilla becomes a metonym for a new type of domestic-cum-international enemy: he could be as recognizable as a neighbor, yet his willingness "to kill his fellow citizens" with a nuclear weapon situates him beyond the pale of human decency. The term "dirty" thus not only serves as an adjective that describes the type of bomb Padilla is accused of preparing, but also modifies the noun "bomber." It identifies Padilla as a distinctly different type of dark and dirty American who is a danger to us all. He, in effect, is a postmodern permutation of the Latino *bandido*: the terrorist next door.

Bandidos and Terrorists, or Insurgents and Revolutionaries?

The post–September 11 linkage of Latina/o criminality to international terrorism is not new. There are historical antecedents dating to the early nineteenth century in which Latin American and U.S. Latina/o anti-imperialist insurgents were classified as common criminals, international terrorists, and sometimes both simultaneously. In *Prisoners of Colonialism: The Struggle for Justice in Puerto Rico* (1994), Ronald Fernandez provides extensive case studies of imprisoned Puerto Rican independence activists and insurgents, or *independentistas*, from the early twentieth century to the present. He demonstrates how each falls under the rubric of the United Nations definition of legitimate anticolonial "freedom fighters," despite the U.S. government's classification and prosecution of them as "terrorists." "It must be recognized," Fernandez writes, "that the label terrorist is as much a political term as it is a characterization of groups who violate internationally accepted moral and legal norms" (201). The prosecution and detention of *independentistas* as terrorists has enabled the U.S. government to obfuscate its neocolonial relationship with the island nation of Puerto Rico, a reality underscored by the fact that Puerto Ricans, who are U.S. citizens, cannot vote in federal elections unless they permanently reside in the continental United States. The ambiguous status of Puerto Rican prisoners was further complicated by the Special International Tribunal on the Human Rights Violations of Political Prisoners/POWs in the USA, held in New York in 1990, which recognized the political and military status of more than a dozen Puerto Rican prisoners who had been incarcerated since the 1980s; former president Bill Clinton pardoned and released most of them in 1999. A political prisoner, this tribunal noted, includes: (1) someone who has been imprisoned for overt political acts, or (2) someone already in prison for "common crimes" who subsequently is subjected to retribution for their political activities in prison. While this does not necessarily render all Puerto Rican and Latina/o detainees as political prisoners or prisoners of war, it raises the possibility of their development as such.

This reassessment of the nomenclature of criminology and penology has a salient resonance for Chicana/os, whose histories of crime and punishment share significant colonial legacies with Puerto Ricans despite distinct contemporary trajectories. Indeed, members of both groups became U.S. citizens (or residents) as a result of U.S. imperialist wars of conquest. In *Gringo Justice* (1987), Alfredo Mirandé provides a diachronic examination of primarily male nineteenth- and twentieth-century Mexican American and Chicana/o criminality to argue that their outlaw conduct must be historicized in relation to the disruption of the "pastoral economy" and attendant communitarian "world view" that followed the U.S. occupation and annexation of the Mexican northeast at the end of the U.S.-Mexico War in 1848. He argues that "Chicanos have been labeled bandits and criminals because they have not passively accepted their economic and political exploitation" (236). For Mirandé, Chicana/o criminality is always anticolonial agency, and all past and present Chicana/o prisoners are a priori political prisoners because of their status as colonial subjects.

Mirandé's linkage of nineteenth-century vigilantes Tiburcio Vásquez and Joaquin Murrieta with nationalist insurgents Juan Cortina and Catarino Garza—as well as members of modern prison-based drug cartels, the Mexican Mafia, Nuestra Familia (Our Family), and even ordinary street gangs—could be seen as nostalgic cultural-nationalist dogma. However, Mirandé's analysis remains useful for understanding the volatile political context of U.S. prisons in the 1970s, an era renowned for its prison uprisings. The competing characterizations of these prison rebellions as lawless or revolutionary is the subject of much debate. Yet no one disputes that many of the racial minority participants in these events were informed by the various domestic "power" movements and by third world liberation struggles outside the walls that, to a large degree, deemed the disproportionately high racial minority incarceration rates as symptoms of colonial oppression.

Mirandé's examination of the political status of Chicana/o prisoners even intersects with some government assessments of minority criminality, and together they raise important questions about crime and punishment in the United States that provide new opportunities for theorizing racial minority criminality. In a special California state legislative session on "Gang Violence in Penal Institutions" held in Los Angeles on March 15, 1974, for instance, witnesses reported that gangs in prisons run by the California Department of Corrections were "connected with revolutionary groups and are concentrating on the recruitment of inmates for radical purposes" (4). More alarming to these California state senators was the existence of Venceremos (which roughly translates as "we will win"), a Chicano-led prison group described as "a Third World revolutionary organization whose goal is to unite all prison gangs" (6). Its "Principles of Unity," which was read into the official record, proclaims:

> We are a small organization in the embryonic stages of a protracted
> war, waged by the peoples of the world, against a monstrous enemy.
> We have no long history with mounds of experience to speak from, but
> the significance of *Venceremos* is that it is a multi-national organization,
> collectively engaged in day-to-day practice and struggles. (83)

Venceremos, whose rank-and-file membership was largely Chicano and racial minority, is described as being particularly dangerous, and not merely for its alleged links to groups such as the American Indian Movement, Mexican Mafia, Black Liberation Army, Black Guerrilla Family, the Weathermen, and the ominously named Vanguard Suicide Squad. Venceremos is described as an imminent threat to the state and nation at large for its efforts to recruit membership from all "minority" groups, including "poor whites," "females," and even high school students (86). More threatening was the fact that Venceremos drew its membership from prisoners incarcerated for "common crimes," and theorized crime as a symptom of the a priori disenfranchisement, marginalization, and outright oppression experienced by the poor of all races, especially Chicana/os, Blacks, and women in general, all of whom they sought to organize into an insurgent army.

The California state legislature's alarmist characterization of this small prison group suspiciously coincided with the rise of a very profitable prison construction boom, which raises questions about potential ulterior motives. This hearing is especially suspicious since Venceremos apparently had become defunct several years before the proceedings. These facts notwithstanding, this report posits the radical potential—and also the persistent ambiguity—surrounding the definition of criminality in the United States, and especially Chicana/o criminality. In the California Senate testimony report, the Chicano prisoner leadership of Venceremos serves as a scapegoat (and economic opportunity) for capitalist profiteers at the dawn of the prison-industrial complex, while simultaneously functioning as an immanent challenge to a capitalist economy that relies on a surplus, permanently unemployable, criminal-cum-prisoner population. This is not to say that Venceremos, as well as the dozens of other multiracial and Chicana/o prisoner organizations, did not pose a significant challenge to the racist, sexist, capitalist status quo.[5] Alán Eladio Gómez (2006a, 2006b) and Louis Mendoza (2006) have presented concrete evidence of Chicana/o participation in prisoner revolutionary consciousness-raising activities, insurrections, and coordinated linkages to "freeworld" revolutionary organizations and political parties.

The liminal yet highly politicized nature of Chicana/o criminality is illustrated by Alvaro Hernandez Luna, who is classified by the U.S. Bureau of Prisons as a convicted murderer but recognized by grassroots and international nongovernmental organizations as a Chicano political prisoner. Beginning with an arrest as a youth for burning the police cars of abusive White officers in his hometown of Alpine, Texas, he later was convicted as an adult for a triple murder he claims he did not commit and served over a decade in the Texas Department of Corrections. While incarcerated, Hernandez Luna founded a Chicana/o cultural nationalist organization, the National Movement of La Raza, and used his considerable rhetorical and artistic skills to form alliances with various student, civil rights, and even revolutionary organizations in prison and out. He subsequently was accused of being a member of the Mexican Mafia and subjected to extrajudicial punishment that included solitary confinement and physical attacks by guards. With the assistance of community activists, he nonetheless succeeded in his effort to gain parole in 1990. He was incarcerated anew in 1996 after being involved in a shootout with the same Alpine Police officers who had participated in his earlier persecution. These police confronted him during a visit to his mother's home in Alpine and sought to arrest him, with charges never specified. As he withdrew into the house, the police began firing at him and accidentally inflicted a nonlethal wound on their own sheriff. Hernandez Luna was subsequently charged with attempted murder of a "peace" officer. Prior to his 1996 reincarceration, Hernandez Luna was one of two Chicanos recognized as political prisoners by the Special International Tribunal on the Human Rights Violations of Political Prisoners/POWs in the USA, and he continues to be recognized as such. There is now an Alvaro Hernandez Defense Committee.

Hernandez Luna's early life, criminal case history, prison transformation, and continuing persecution thus complicate the conventional image of Chicana/o and other racial minority criminals and prisoners, which has been largely shaped by the proliferation of prime time television crime programming and media saturation coverage of notorious figures throughout U.S. history. One contemporary subject of this legacy of sensationalist media coverage is Ramsey Muñiz, the former Raza Unida Texas gubernatorial candidate convicted of drug smuggling in 1976 on dubious charges. Another is Richard Herrin, the Los Angeles barrio boy who murdered his White girlfriend in a fit of rage while both were students at Yale University, and who later became the subject of a true crime bestseller. Herrin is often compared to José Razo, the Los Angeles Chicano Harvard undergraduate who committed a string of armed robberies during visits home from school in the 1980s. They both have become, as one headline noted, "proof" that affirmative action is a "danger" to the country. Richard Ramirez, the infamous Los Angeles "Night Stalker" who committed a string of rapes and murders, serves as the quintessential Chicano villain, and his courtroom flash of a palm tattooed with a satanic pentagram remains an enduring and recurring image in popular television, print, and Internet accounts of "criminal monsters." Moreover, violent turf wars by prison-based gangs such as the Mexican Mafia, Nuestra Familia, and the Texas Syndicate, as well as spectacular shootouts by drug cartels on both sides of the Texas-Mexican border, frequently are represented in mainstream media as "confirmation" that the nation is under a state of siege from "Latino terrorists."

This mass media fetish on Latino, and especially Chicano, criminals-cum-potential terrorists is especially evident in the sensationalist coverage of Ricardo Chávez-Ortiz, an unemployed thirty-seven-year-old

Mexican American who made front-page headlines after his April 14, 1972, hijacking of a U.S. jetliner from New Mexico to Los Angeles. But Chávez-Ortiz's stated motives complicate the mass media fetish. Wearing the pilot's cap and waving a pistol from the cockpit of his commandeered jetliner, Chávez-Ortiz demanded airtime on two Spanish-language radio stations, from which he delivered a thirty-four-minute speech decrying the discriminatory treatment of "Mexican Americans and poor people everywhere."[6]

Chávez-Ortiz became a cause célèbre in the Chicana/o community, which raised his bail of $300,000 in an initiative led by CASA (Centros de Acción Social Autónomo [Centers for Autonomous Social Action]), a Marxist-Leninist immigrant rights organization that also set up defense committees for other Chicano political prisoners throughout the 1970s. In fact, such mass media preoccupation with purportedly drug addicted, diabolic, or "mentally disturbed" Chicano criminals also produces profound slippage that ultimately undermines itself: as revealed by the

FIGURE 1.2. Airline hijacker Ricardo Chávez-Ortiz. *Los Angeles Times*, Friday, April 14, 1972. Courtesy of the *Los Angeles Times*.

Chávez-Ortiz coverage and attendant mass mobilization for his defense, Chicana/o criminality—a "terrorist" airplane hijacking, no less!—can also be a catalyst for multiracial alliances, anticapitalist diatribe, and even insurrection.

Towards a Critical Chicana/o Criminology and Penology

Despite the complicated legacy of these and other Chicana/o "criminals," Chicana/o criminality, along with various representations of it, have been grossly undertheorized. Even though social scientists have long debunked the eugenicist impulse that inaugurates criminology in the late nineteenth century, many contemporary attempts to theorize Chicana/o criminality have inadvertently replicated racial binaries. Foundational studies of Chicana/o history such as Rodolfo Acuña's *Occupied America: A History of Chicanos* (2004); Américo Paredes's *With His Pistol in His Hand: A Border Ballad and Its Hero* (1958); Julian Samora, Joe Bernal, and Albert Peña's *Gunpowder Justice: A Reassessment of the Texas Rangers* (1979); and Mirandé's aforementioned *Gringo Justice* (1987)—as well as related cultural nationalist studies such as Pedro Castillo and Albert Camarillo's *Furia y muerte: Los bandidos Chicanos* (Rage and death: Chicano bandits) (1973)—all propose Chicano (and no Chicana) fugitives and prisoners as modern permutations of Eric Hobsbawm's "social bandits."[7] For these scholars, early Chicano lawbreakers were populist rebels fighting against prejudice, exploitation, and the unjust political order established during the U.S. imperialist occupation of northeast Mexico. Despite necessary and incisive critiques of the colonial context and racist exercise of police and judicial authority in the nineteenth- and twentieth-century United States, these studies ultimately fail to examine the more common and controversial forms of criminality such as rape, murder, and violent nonproperty offenses, which occur with alarming frequency among all demographic groups, including Chicana/os. These early Chicana/o historiography and criminology studies also neglect to provide a more candid assessment of the ideological limitations of social banditry, populist rebellions, and nationalist insurgencies. Hobsbawm himself observed that "social banditry, a universal and virtually unchanging phenomenon, is little more than endemic peasant protest against oppression and poverty: a cry for vengeance on the rich and the oppressors, a vague dream, of some curb upon them" (1969: 5). Social bandits are populist champions of the peasantry who emerge at times of intense pressure on their traditional life and economy. Hobsbawm situates them between common thieves, whom he characterizes as individualist opportunists, and revolutionaries who seek to transform an entire political economic order instead of simply seeking redress and reform.

These foundational studies in Chicana/o historiography and criminology also fail to differentiate the many types of criminal acts or provide a convincing general theory of Chicana/o criminality. Nor do they account for the reification of the Chicana/o lumpen segment for whom crime—from common property offenses to various types of vice and crimes of violence—forms an integral component of prisoner subcultures. These crime-based subcultures are not always empowering and, to be honest, rarely revolutionary. On the contrary, crime-as-subaltern agency can be as repressive as, and integral to, colonial domination. Frederick D. Homer (1984), a proponent of the state terrorism studies movement, notes how law enforcement neglect of minority-on-minority crime is part of a broader network of containment practices that limit the threat to middle-class, primarily White, Americans in stratified capitalist societies. He adds that the deliberate use of a containment policy is constitutive of government terror on the poor, who are disproportionately racial minorities. Crime, that is, can also be counter-revolutionary.

An alternative and growing body of literature about Chicana/o criminality has sought to explore the complex historical material context of crime as well as the equally complicated relationship between crime and incarceration in the articulation of new Chicana/o subjectivities. James Diego Vigil's *Barrio Gangs: Street Life and Identity in Southern California* (1988), a multigenerational survey of Chicana/o youth delinquency and gang activity as "a partial substitute for family" and identity formation in Los Angeles in the 1980s (12), is one of the most important contributions to this growing field. So, too, is Marie "Keta" Miranda's *Homegirls in the Public Sphere* (2003), which explores the highly gendered inflections of power in Chicana barrio kinship networks that function as organic feminist self-help organizations. Vigil's and Miranda's research was preceded by Joan Moore's *Homeboys: Gangs, Drugs, and Prison in the Barrios of Los Angeles* (1978) and subsequent follow-up study (*Going Down to the Barrio* [1991]). Moore's research is noteworthy for her collaboration with Chicana/o gang members and prisoners pursuant to collective explications of the contexts and contours of Chicana/o criminality. Martín Sánchez-Jankowski's *Islands in the Street: Gangs and American Urban Society* (1991) draws on field research with Irish, African American, Puerto Rican, Chicana/o, Dominican, Jamaican, and Central American members of thirty-seven gangs in Los Angeles, New York, and Boston in the late 1980s to argue that gang structures, and even illicit gang activity, essentially are "criminalized" vernacular analogues to modern American capitalism (312). Despite their different methodologies, these scholars collectively mark a profound shift in Chicana/o criminology away from nostalgic cultural nationalist diatribe, towards complex historical materialist analyses that have begun to map in-group conflicts and contradictions.

Moore's collaboration with the Chicano Pinto Research Project in the 1970s, based in Los Angeles (and later expanded to northern California), inaugurates Chicana/o penology. Her research is particularly significant because it recognizes the uniqueness of Chicana/o prisoner life and culture, even if her study only offers a preliminary assessment of the contours of this culture. Moore also collaborated with Chicana/o prisoners in developing alternative policy recommendations based on (primarily male) Chicano prisoner self-help organizational models that further distinguish her work from standard, detached sociological studies. Contemporaneous with, but separate from, this initiative, R. Theodore Davidson's *Chicano Prisoners: The Key to San Quentin* (1974) represents the first sustained study of Chicano life inside prison. Davidson's case study of Chicanos behind bars in San Quentin Prison in the 1970s provides a useful introduction to the vast prisoner lexicon and the attendant social values in Chicano prisoner culture. Davidson's emphasis on Chicano prisoner sexual mores and traffic in contraband, however, tends to pathologize this subgroup. He also privileges male prisoners and therefore is limited in his ability to provide comprehensive assessments of Chicana/o prisoner cultures. Even more troubling is Davidson's explicit admission that his research was conducted with prison administration support in exchange for a pledge to inform the warden if he discovered "that the prisoners were going to destroy the prison in some manner" (1). In her exploration of the disciplinary linkages between the academy and the penitentiary, Barbara Harlow critiques Davidson's pledge as a "complicit compromise" that enabled the prison administration to usurp his research (1992: 25).

As Harlow notes, academic complicity and the ever-present threat of co-optation by carceral regimes have transformed Chicana/o criminology and penology into a field wrought with contradictions, controversies, and conflict. It would be an overstatement to suggest a binary division, yet current scholarship illustrates a bifurcation. On one hand, there are studies apparently driven by less altruistic motives that fetishize prisoners and prisoner culture within preexisting (and, in some cases, neo-eugenicist) theoretical, cultural, and political agendas. Other scholars are inspired by an activist impulse to influence policy in solidarity with the populations from which most prisoners emerge. Prime examples of the latter include Yvette Flores-Ortiz's case studies mapping the social geography of Chicana incarceration patterns. In "Pintas: Policy Implications of Chicana Inmates" (1995a), she summarizes data from personal interviews with Chicana prisoners, all of whom report sexual abuse as girls and young women, and also domestic abuse as adults, to demonstrate that the incarceration of Chicanas oftentimes is presaged by their own victimization by men. She militates for alternative treatment programs, sentencing practices, and other forms of statutory and community interventions. Juanita Díaz-Cotto further substantiates Chicana claims of systematic abuse in her collection of *testimonios* and sociological analysis, *Chicana Lives and Criminal Justice: Voices from El Barrio* (2006). She also maps the cross-racial and highly gendered inter-institutional prisoner agency in her preceding work, *Gender, Ethnicity, and the State: Latina and Latino Prison Politics* (1996). Díaz-Cotto's research shifts attention from a pathological model of prisoners towards an assessment of the material context, cultural specificity, and political significance of Latina and Latino prisoner agency in the highly nuanced settings of male and female prisons.

Chicana/o criminality, as well as their prison-based agency, has undergone provocative revisionary treatments beyond pathological "culture of poverty" models, especially in more recent multidisciplinary cultural studies paradigms. Although I engage many of these scholars throughout this study, it is important to foreground a few salient issues and debates in prisoner literary and media studies. In *Rethinking the Borderlands: Between Chicano Culture and Legal Discourse* (1995), for instance, Carl Gutiérrez-Jones extends Mirandé's cultural nationalist theory of crime by surveying select contemporary Chicana/o literary and cinematic texts. He argues that these expose and contest the racist imperialist conceits inherent in the objectivist claims of the Euro-American jurisprudence that facilitated and consolidated U.S. imperialist designs on the Mexican northeast. Eclectically drawing upon critical race theory, critical legal studies, and postcolonial and cultural nationalist methodologies, Gutiérrez-Jones attempts to explicate the "process by which historical events and historiography itself are rewritten by Chicanos" (6). While Gutiérrez-Jones's characterization remains over-celebratory, it nonetheless succeeds in illustrating how legal discourse is rendered *sous rature*, under erasure and partially rewritten, by alternative Chicana/o narratives. This shift in attention to the creation of Chicana/o criminality as a network of contestatory discourses enables a broader and more incisive analysis of Chicana/o criminality as potential counterhegemonic agency. Despite this important contribution to the field, however, Gutiérrez-Jones fails to examine any prisoner-produced texts, resulting in an inadvertent effacement of the conflictive and contradictory dimensions of Chicana/o prisoner discourses.

Other scholars err by overinvesting in undertheorized profiles of select Pinta and Pinto authors. Juan Bruce-Novoa's early work on Raúl Salinas and Ricardo Sánchez, for instance, was important for identifying a potential subcategory—Chicana/o convict, or Pinta/o, literature—in the growing canon of Chicana/o literature, even as it was inspired by a New Criticism framework that failed to make broader historical materialist connections from the close readings of select poems. In *Chicano Timespace: The Poetry and Politics of Ricardo Sánchez* (2001), Miguel López Rojo presents a literary biography intent on resituating Sánchez within the Chicana/o and broader U.S. literary canon. Yet his celebratory genealogy of Sánchez's ancient and modern philosophical "influences," and mimetic restatements of previous scholarship of Sánchez's poetics, actually obfuscate the complexity of Pinta/o discourses by effacing Sánchez's highly controversial masculinist signifying practices, an issue I address in Chapter 3.

In contrast, Harlow (1992) resituates the highly local inflections of Judy Lucero's prison verse by locating this Chicana prison poet in broader postcolonial contexts, specifically women's cultural and political agency from prisons throughout the Western world. Harlow's linkage of the prison-industrial complex with the broader militarization of U.S. society (1991) informs my broader explication and contextualization of Lucero's entire corpus in Chapter 7. Ironically, while Harlow has since qualified the notion of "resistance literature"—a category she helped create with her eponymous book (1987)—Raúl Homero Villa proposes in "Of *Corridos* and Convicts: *Gringo* (In)Justice in Early Border Ballads and Contemporary *Pinto* Poetry" (1996) that Chicana/o and Latina/o prisoner poetry presents modern permutations of the anticolonial resistance that the epic heroic *corrido* performed in the southwestern United States in the late nineteenth and early twentieth centuries. While Villa's genealogy provides a compelling map of the overlapping oppositional tones in Pinta/o poetry, and the *corrido* form it allegedly mimics, this framework ultimately is too teleological in its insistence on the *corrido* as a "taproot," or master narrative. María Herrera-Sobek (1990) illustrates the limits of such readings by underscoring the neofeudal masculinist conceits of various *corrido* genres.

Adding to the dissensus in Pinta and Pinto literary studies, Cordelia Candelaria argues that despite the large corpus of Pinto poetry, its topical unity, and the recurrence of a unique Chicano prisoner patois, "it is a mistake to consider it a distinct, stylistic school identifiable by a unique poetics" (1986: 54). She further effaces the coherence of a subcategory or subgenre by proposing that "in style and theme, pinto poetry was like any other protest poetry" of the Chicano Movement in the 1960s and 1970s. In his contemporary analogue to Candelaria's survey of Chicana/o poetry, Rafael Pérez-Torres (1995) provides a more viable topography of the various themes in Chicana/o prisoner verse through short explications of familiar Chicana/o prisoner poets: Ricardo Sánchez, Judy Lucero, Jimmy Santiago Baca, and Luis Omar Salinas. While the virtue of Pérez-Torres's short section on Pinta and Pinto poets arises from its insistence on a mapping of the divergent trajectories in this body of verse instead of overdetermining a presumed "essence," he nonetheless concludes by privileging the various shifts from the declamatory aesthetic of Pinto poets of the 1960s and 1970s to the meditative asceticism of writers such as Jimmy Santiago Baca, whom he describes as exemplary, a position I contest in Chapter 2. Moreover, Pérez-Torres is far too introductory and leaves out too much of Chicana/o prisoner poetry and the vast number of other genres found within the Chicana/o prisoner population, which is renowned for its prolific production of prison-based newspapers, literary journals, magazines, and anthologies, as well as a vast corpus of multimedia artwork such as tattoos, embossed leather work, glossed envelopes, *paños* (handkerchiefs), and hand-drawn postcards.[8]

The most provocative of the literary-based studies of Latina/o and multiethnic U.S. prisoners is Michael Hames-García's *Fugitive Thought: Prison Movements, Race, and the Meaning of Justice* (2004). Hames-García examines the extratextual resonance of Latina/o prisoner literary agency beyond poetry by paying particular attention to manifestos, autobiographical essays, and mixed-genre anthologies of prison literature. This study historicizes prisoner agency by mapping how Latina/o prisoners have followed Black slaves and ex-prisoners such as Frederick Douglass and Martin Luther King Jr. to interject themselves into foundational debates in the nation's history. Hames-García argues for the centrality of the prison—and prisoners—in the articulation of U.S. notions of justice and broader epistemological concepts such as ethics and human freedom, thereby potentially raising the counterhegemonic resonance of Chicana/o prisoner discourses. In *Gang Nation: Delinquent Citizens in Puerto Rican, Chicano, and Chicana Narratives* (2002), Monica Brown extends this trajectory in Latina/o criminology and penology by examining the commodifications of Puerto Rican and Chicana/o gang life in Latina/o literature as well as in film. Brown proposes that the literature by former Latina and Latino gang members is the manifestation of an alternative "national symbolic," or counter-nation (xx). She argues that this corpus implicitly militates for Latina/o inclusion in the American polis and symbolically creates its own avenues for this inclusion in the wake of the increasingly more intense carceral apparatus that systematically targets Latina and Latino youth for exclusion. Unfortunately, Brown fails to examine the cultural production of prisoners, who, as I will show throughout this study, variously position themselves within and without the ideological state apparatus through complex extra-textual negotiations of culture and power.

Los Pintos de América: Recentering Chicana/o Prisoners

While the aforementioned studies provide crucial insights into juris-prudence, minority criminality, and the cultural economy of crime, they often suffer from their own virtues: they are circumscribed by disciplinary boundaries and localized case studies that yield limited data; are undergirded by undertheorized linkages between, and differences among, male and female subjects or different ethnic communities; or are hamstrung by omissions of prisoner art and culture. What is needed for the study of Chicana/o criminality and prisoner cultures are nuanced assessments of the local and global significance of their agency in prison and out. Several scholars point the way. José Luís Morín (2005) has provided concrete diachronic statistical analyses of Latina/os in the U.S. criminal justice system that conclusively link this justice system to imperialism, colonialism, and internal colonialism. Studies that further globalize the criminalization of Latina/o communities include David M. Hernández's research on the uses of immigrant detention centers to "disappear" Latina/os. Louis Mendoza (2006) chronicles the 1970s radical multiracial revolutionary prisoner movements in the United States, and Alán Gómez (2006a, 2006b) presents a broader expansion of prisoner revolutionary politics beyond the United States. Dylan Rodriguez (2006) presents provocative insights on the prison-industrial complex and prisoner challenges to it that also include Latina/o prisoners. David

Brotherton and Luis Barrios's *The Almighty Latin King and Queen Nation: Street Politics and the Transformation of a New York City Gang* (2004) provides an equally insightful case study of the potential for prisoners and gang members to become radicalized agents of revolutionary change, while still responsibly marking the failures of this particular movement.

These scholars reveal that prison research and activism today must be informed by the disciplinary frameworks unique to individual case studies, yet not bound by disciplines or master narratives that force a teleological reading of unique prisoner subcultures. This has been the goal of Chicana/o counter-criminology studies since the Chicana/o cultural nationalist and immanently internationalist journal *El Pocho-Che*, which is a fusion of a local and global model of Chicana/o identity—the betwixt and between cultural hybrid *Pocho* coupled with internationalist allusions to Che Guevara's internationalist *foco* model of revolution. The December 1970 special issue of the journal was dedicated to Chicana/o prisoners and temporarily retitled *El Pinto (Pocho) Che* *(Figure 1.3)*. It helped foreground the sociohistorical and culturo-political contexts of the Pinta/o situation through a blend of *testimonios*, poetry, sociological accounts, and urgent appeals for grassroots interventions into the neocolonial practice of imprisonment throughout Aztlán and beyond. This special issue, as well as the subsequent 1976 special issue of the Chicana/o interdisciplinary journal *De Colores* subtitled "Los Pintos de América," foregrounded a multigenre, multidimensional, and multinational—even internationalist—Pinta/o discourse. In *El Pinto (Pocho) Che*, this incipient discourse included meta-critical explications of prison culture and Chicana/o identity, including a special column called the "Convict Report" that discusses prison vocabulary among other issues that informed freeworld Chicana/o culture. Pinta/os and their "freeworld" Chicana/o community thus signaled the integrity of an entire subculture that, in many respects, also assumed the status as the "folk base" of Chicana/o culture.

In "What Is Cultural Studies Anyway?" (1987), Richard Johnson articulates a prescription for a materialist interdisciplinary cultural studies methodology that provides an appropriate critical framework for extending this meta-critical enterprise to the present. Johnson argues that one must interrogate the formal features of a text proper as well as the circumstances of its production and the highly subjective forms of consumption, which include an assortment of readings and "mis-readings" that often take lives of their own. Each moment of a text's life in this circuit, Johnson notes, is embedded with different and oftentimes

EL
PINTO (POCHO)
CHE

LO QUE TENEMOS

Francisco Mange — Introduction: Hermano, Forget Me Not.....I'm lost! 1

A Pinto from S.Q. — An Open Letter from a Pinto. 2

El Jopo Trejo — Cinco de Mayo en San Quentin. 4

Tomas Montoya — Mi Carnalas Lindas. 5

Poesia from Chino:

Paul Velarde — Movimiento. . , ... 6

Jerry Garcia — Lamento. 7

Rudy Alanis — A La Madre. . . . . . . : 7

Esteban Nuñez — Porque. 8

Francisco Estrada — Prison Culture y el Chicano. 9

Domingo Rivera — Portfolio of Art, Drawings in Jail. . . 20

Convict Report — The Word from los Pintos. 23

Prison Vocabulary. 49

Mario M. Alvarez — Poesia from San Bruno Jail. 55

Rudy Espihoza — A Word Para Los Pintos. 57

Pocket Lawyer of Legal First Aid. . . . 60

FIGURE 1.3. Table of contents from *El Pocho Che* 1: 3 (1970), *El Pinto (Pocho) Che* (special issue). Courtesy of Chicano Studies Library, University of California at Berkeley.

competing power relationships that must be seen in tandem to get the "big picture" of a text's cultural, political, and historical significance (46–47). I propose to complement and extend the scholarship on Latina/o and multiethnic criminality through a cultural studies examination of Chicana/o prisoner (and ex-prisoner) identity and culture across time, place, and genre. I offer case studies of the political and cultural economy of Chicana/o prisoners from the nineteenth century to the present alongside explications of renowned and little-known prisoner-produced and prisoner-themed literary, cinematic, and multimedia visual and aural texts. This focus on Chicanas and Chicanos enables me to ground the study in a specific community with its own history and cultural idiosyncrasies. Chicana/os are the largest subgroup of Latina/os in the United States, and their culture has been thoroughly explored and well-theorized by Chicana/o scholars. The wealth of secondary material provides an excellent resource and opportunity to ground the analysis of Chicana/o prisoner agency within an interdisciplinary Chicana/o cultural studies project that, as Angie Chabram-Dernersesian (1999) and José David Saldívar (1991) have demonstrated, eclectically adapts the Birmingham School of Cultural Studies to the unique vernacular context of the southwestern United States.

The evolution and inevitable reification of Chicana/o prisoner identity and culture is a complex process that is grounded in the racial economics of penology at different times in U.S. history, and also is informed by popular Chicana/o cultural forms and signifying practices. This study thus is grounded in prison or, more precisely, the political and cultural economy of the prison. But my attention to prisons and prisoners also is an attempt to map the intersections between the inside and outside. I am guided by Mary Pardo's *Mexican American Women Activists: Identity and Resistance in Two Los Angeles Communities* (1998), which examines several groups, including the Mothers of East L.A., a grassroots organization of primarily Mexican immigrant and Chicana women who initially formed to protest the construction of a jail in their neighborhood. They built upon their successes to take on broader social and political causes. As a central character in Edward James Olmos's 1992 prison film *American Me* notes, "the inside and outside go together."

Extending and problematizing Monica Brown's claim that Latina/o gang members express a "love/hate relationship" with the United States, I argue that Chicana/o criminal and prisoner agency is complex: it is hegemonic and counterhegemonic—and sometimes both simultaneously. Chicana/o criminality cannot be understood as simply a figural substitute (or mechanism) for Chicana/o inclusion in the polis. It is historically contingent and actually far less coherent than Brown, Mirandé, and others allow. There is a broad range of Chicana/o criminal conduct and prisoner agency, from revolutionary politics to problematic mimetic performances of the commodity fetish that involve everything from drug peddling to various types of assault. This study not only maps their complicated critiques of power but also their equally complex and problematic claims to power from the margins. Following the Latin American Subaltern Studies Group's recognition that scholars have not fully recognized or theorized the way that subaltern subjects from the margins have "spoken back" to the center (1995), I submit that any attempt to map the contours of Chicana/o prisoner culture inevitably must attend to the very vocabulary of the Chicana/o prison, which in the unique patois of Chicana/o prisoners is known as *la pinta*.

II. LA PINTA

La pinta is the Chicana/o vernacular Spanish term for prison. It is a truncated alliterative abbreviation for *penitencia*, the Spanish word for "penitentiary." Social and cultural linguists have argued that such

Chicana/o Spanish abbreviations or deliberate "misspellings" are complex signifiers that enable users to symbolically claim something as their own while simultaneously signaling how the object itself is transformed by this Chicana/o claim to it. This is especially true of the lumpen Chicana/o slang known as Caló, which was popularized by Pachucos and zoot suiters in the 1940s and is still widely practiced today among prisoners and other sectors of the Chicana/o community.[9] For example, Califas (Kah-lee-fahs), the Caló term for California, refers not so much to the southwestern state as to the Chicana/o experience in it and, more importantly, the symbolic Chicana/o ownership that enables them to rename the state. Similarly, the Chicana/o linguistic truncation and transformation of the U.S. penitentiary to *la pinta* also problematizes the original eighteenth-century Quaker idea that posits the penitentiary as a brutally "altruistic" institution that facilitates a prisoner's repentance and reformation.[10] *La pinta* is quite distinct from the "pen," the popular English abbreviation of "penitentiary." The "pen" preserves the etymological root of the standard English spelling of penitentiary—the penitent—thereby alluding to the problematic model of penology that reductively presumes prisoner pathology and guilt. In contrast, *la pinta* is part of a counterhegemonic Chicana/o prisoner linguistic system, culture, and worldview that arises from a uniquely racialized incarceration experience. This Chicana/o vernacular term also suggests the existence of a distinct Chicana/o outlaw subjectivity that challenges the authority of the penitentiary and the positivist theories of criminology and penology buttressing it.[11] That is, *la pinta* represents the prison as a site where coercive state authority confronts its antithesis.

Like most Caló terms, *la pinta* is dialogic: it is embedded with the political unconscious—specifically, the popular memory of past and present power struggles. Indeed, *la pinta* is a term whose meaning is defined at the intersection of competing historiographies of the U.S. penitentiary system. Noted scholar Luís Leal (1996) claims the first appearance of the term can be traced to a popular Mexican *corrido* in 1882 that decried the hardships of incarceration. But *la pinta* is best understood in relation to more recent reassessments of the history of U.S. criminology and penology. In fact, it forms the basis of a Chicana/o prisoner discourse on power that pressures Michel Foucault's (1979) archaeology of the prison in Western civilization. Foucault is recognized for mapping the role of the penitentiary in the exercise of state power across time and place, paying particular attention to Europe. Yet feminist, critical race studies theorists and critical legal studies scholars such as Monique

Deveaux (1996), Adrian Howe (1994), and Angela Davis (1998, 2005) have argued that Foucault's archaeology of penology is predicated on an androcentric body that dismisses the gendered and racialized subjectivity of prisoners and, subsequently, their differential status in prison and out. They note that nineteenth- and twentieth-century penological and criminological theories have facilitated the exercise of power through uniquely patriarchal and racist presumptions. Davis aptly notes that "the political economy of prisons relies on racialized assumptions of criminality" that raise the specter of racially marked abject bodies (1998: 1). I add that the Caló term for the penitentiary similarly signals the racial, cultural, and also gender difference of Chicana/o prisoners through the use of a unique linguistic register that is embedded with its own epistemology. *La pinta* thus serves as a racially nuanced nodal point in the wave of revisionist histories of U.S. penality that link early U.S. criminology and penology to U.S. colonialism and imperialism: it postulates that the construction of Chicana/o difference and subsequent criminalization and containment of this difference is inalienably linked to U.S. capitalist imperialist hegemony in the Southwest and beyond. That is, *la pinta* introduces an alternative global Chicana/o prisoner theory of crime and punishment as well as power and counterpower, from the eponymous margin.

Similar to other Chicana/o translations and transformations of institutional terms and discourses that scholars such as Rosaura Sánchez (1983) and Alfred Arteaga (1994) identify as fundamental to the evolution and definition of Chicana/o poetics, *la pinta* not only signals a Chicana/o prisoner discourse on power, but also suggests a coherent Chicana/o prisoner culture. One of the main objectives of this study is to illustrate how Chicana/o prisoners develop unique practices that illuminate what cultural anthropologist Américo Paredes (1979, 1993) has called the "folk base" of Chicana/o culture. Stripped to the bare essentials of human existence, all prisoners are forced to make due with limited resources, and Chicana/o prisoners are particularly accomplished in their vernacular, hybrid productions and performances of visual art, literature, and other forms of popular culture. They are renowned for their *rasquache* sensibility—that is, their ability to create coherent cultural artifacts out of scarce and disparate materials. This poetics of improvisation, as Tomás Ybarra-Frausto has argued in "Rasquachismo: A Chicano Sensibility" (1991), involves contestatory reclamations of Chicana/o subordination through an appropriation and aesthetic elaboration of their very lack of material resources:

> In an environment always on the edge of coming apart (the car, the job, the toilet), things are held together with spit, grit, and *movidas*. Movidas are the coping strategies you use to gain time, to make options, to retain hope. Rasquachismo is a compendium of all the movidas deployed in immediate, day-to-day living. Resilience and resourcefulness spring from making do with what is at hand (*hacer rendir las cosas*). This use of available resources engenders hybridization, juxtaposition, and integration. Rasquachismo is a sensibility attuned to mixtures and confluence, preferring communion over purity. (156)

The limited and even restricted access to art materials in prison does not stifle the production of art or the performance of unique cultural identity. Rather, these sparse conditions necessitate and ultimately distinguish Chicana/o prisoner art and subjectivity as oppositional and potentially counterhegemonic. As Frausto argues, "rasquachismo is an underdog perspective—a view from *los de abajo* [the underdogs], an attitude rooted in resourcefulness and adaptability, yet mindful of stance and style" (156).

This resiliency, however, does not necessarily imply that oppositional Chicana/o prisoner culture is revolutionary or fully actualized counterhegemonic agency. Following Antonio Gramsci (1971), Raymond Williams (1978) has identified "hegemony" as a social relation in which domination is exercised with the complicity of the ruled through a flexible absorption of dissent. The hegemonic incorporates its natural constituents along with its antithesis. Within this relationship, the dominant episteme, which is always already embedded with residual culture from the ancient to the more recent past (e.g., folk forms such as epic ballads), attempts to co-opt expressions of oppositional agency. The dominant simultaneously attempts to prevent this oppositional emergent culture from consolidating itself as a coherent paradigm that could develop into a new *counter*hegemony. Williams adds "the 'residual' and the 'emergent,' which in any real process, and at any moment in the process, are significant both in themselves and in what they reveal of the characteristics of the 'dominant'" (122).

Ramón Saldívar (1990) and José E. Limón (1992) have deployed Williams's notions of the "dominant," "residual," and "emergent" to argue that the epic heroic *corrido* both chronicles and contests the transformation of the semifeudal agrarian society of the southwestern United States by the incursion of capital in the mid-eighteenth century. This study seeks to map how Chicana/o prisoners use residual and emergent cultural forms to articulate a discourse on power and, moreover, propose contestatory, albeit inchoate, interpretations of and interventions into material history in the southwestern United States at the site of the prison. While the epic heroic *corrido* eventually lost prominence in the new hegemonic capitalist order (for which the bourgeois novel can serve as a metonym), I submit that Chicana/o prisoner culture persistently refuses to cede to the dominant despite its inevitable co-optations. Eclectic Chicana/o prisoner performances of culture through a polyphony of hybrid forms and genres illustrate the contours of the incessant struggle between the hegemonic and the incipient counterhegemonic in the southwestern United States and beyond. For instance, even as Chicana/o prisoner dress and style (e.g., cropped hair, baggy denim pants, and prison footwear such as Brogan boots or Converse All-Star sneakers) have become veritable fashion statements among working-class and middle-class youth, these garments continue to serve as emblems of marginality that can be seen as pre-critical forms of dissent by some bearers.[12] Chicana/o prisoner culture is always in a struggle against the dominant (as well as against its own conflicting trajectories), and towards the consolidation of a new counterhegemonic order, but this emergent episteme is not without its limits.

Despite being distinguished for its residual *rasquache* folk forms and emergent new critical consciousness, Chicana/o prisoner culture inevitably is inchoate and profoundly contradictory. Like much of prisoner discourse in general, Chicana/o prisoner culture—or rather, cultures—are inflected through highly gendered performances of power that sometimes are antithetical to each other. Much of the scholarship in Chicana/o studies over the past three decades has shown how Chicana/os occupy overlapping yet vastly different social locations, which inevitably undergird uniquely gendered performances of culture and negotiations of power. Angie Chabram-Dernersesian (1992), Norma Alarcón (1989), and Sonia Saldívar-Hull (2000), among many other feminist scholars, have noted how Chicana writers and artists problematize the masculinist conceits of Chicano cultural nationalism from the 1960s and 1970s. Chicanas rearticulate misogynist archetypes such as La Malinche, which is predicated on circumscribed models of women's sexuality and agency, and also reclaim symbolic spaces such as the "barrio" and the "family," which had been equally restrictive for women. While many Chicana artists are concerned with the same issues of racism and colonialism that motivate male writers of the era, Saldívar-Hull notes that Chicanas quite simply are speaking from different social locations and, accordingly, make different claims about power and different claims to power (27–29). Accordingly, this study not only seeks to attend to the similarities and differences between and among Chicana/o prisoners. It also seeks to map how these different inflections of an oppositional culture and identity—which are simultaneously embedded with residual norms and emergent new sensibilities—ultimately may illuminate the tensions in, and facilitate the potential transformations of, broader social and political relations. Williams has noted that "in our own period as in others, the fact of emergent cultural practice is still undeniable, and together with the fact of actively residual practice is a necessary complication of the would-be dominant culture" (1978: 126). I add that Chicana/o prisoner cultures mark the complex nature of power in modern society. Indeed, Chicana/o prisoner elaborations of their marginality enable them to emerge as contestatory, albeit ambiguous, subaltern agents who inevitably complicate the hegemonic and, equally as important, conventional theories about the counterhegemonic contours of Chicana/o cultural and political agency.

As I will show in the various case studies that comprise this book, Chicana/o prisoner culture extends across a wide range of discourses—from their advocacy of revolutionary violence to intensely misogynist and homophobic rituals to, ironically, the same commodity fetish that initially animated the modern penitentiary. For instance, the masculinist rituals of agency such as cross-racial rape by Chicano prisoners and the reproduction of hierarchical heterosexual family kinship networks by Chicana prisoners (which I will discuss in Chapters 3 and 7, respectively) inevitably problematize the "culture of resistance" paradigm that has been so prominent in Chicana/o Studies.[13] Despite its contributions to the study of the conflicted relationship between popular culture and capitalist power, the resistance paradigm simply is too ahistorical in its proposal that Chicana/o culture is inherently oppositional. This is especially so given the complex history of class in Chicana/o history and also because of the mimetic nature of *rasquachismo*. But neither is Chicana/o prisoner culture-of-improvisation simplistically reactionary. On the contrary, postcolonial and materialist feminist scholars such as Homi Bhabha (1984, 1994), Michael Taussig (1993), Luce Irigaray (1985), and Judith Butler (1990) have shown how mimesis demands a constant reassessment of the relationship between popular culture and the exercise of power and counterpower. While Bhabha's argument that pidgin speech disrupts the hegemonic narrative of nation is over-celebratory, Taussig, Irigaray, and Butler provide more plausible accounts of how mimesis enables subaltern subjects to negotiate power in ways that sometimes are as empowering as they are disempowering. "The very mimicry corrodes the alterity," Taussig notes, even as it continues to be mimicry (1993: 8). I submit that Chicana/o prisoner uses and transformations of root forms, paradigms, and broader tropes of intercultural communication demand and also enable a complex model for reassessing conventional theories of Chicana/o art and culture. Chicana/o prisoner cultural practices and related political agency reveal the provocative yet problematic nature of the exercise of Chicana/o *counter*power.

Towards a Pinta/o Ontology

The term *la pinta*, then, is part of a distinct Chicana/o prisoner vocabulary and culture that undergirds an ideologically ambiguous discourse on power. The term also implies the existence of an immanently counterhegemonic Chicana/o prisoner subjectivity. Davidson (1974) has offered a preliminary mapping of this subject in his discussion of prisoner nomenclature. He notes that those prisoners who conform to prison rules and regulations are viewed as subordinate and therefore earn the prison epithet "Inmate"—the official prison administration term for prisoners. Those who resist assume the vernacular accolade "Convict," which alludes to their criminal convictions and also their defiant refusal to being subordinated. These observations coincide with many contemporary prisoner accounts.[14] However, Davidson fails to recognize that the more popular terms for Chicana/o Convicts are "Pinta" and "Pinto." Some anecdotal etymologies posit that these unique nominatives refer to the striped prison uniforms that American prisoners were forced to wear in the early nineteenth century.[15]

These neologisms also have a more modern metaphysical and politically salient bilingual resonance that enables Chicana/os to reconfigure positivist (and incipiently eugenicist) definitions of criminality in general, and Chicana/o prisoner subjectivities in particular. The masculine noun "Pinto," as well as the corresponding feminine form, "Pinta," both function as a bilingual play on *penitencia* (penitentiary), as well as the Chicana/o colloquial past participle *pintao* (or *estar pintado*), which means to be painted, tainted, or otherwise marked (e.g., by skin pigmentation or a courtroom conviction). Like all Convicts, Pintas and Pintos are defined by their *convictions*: both their legally sanctioned imprisonment by a court of law, and the certainty undergirding their defiant attitude. Moreover, as the bilingual resonance of their unique nominative suggests, Pintas and Pintos are distinguished by their vernacular theorizing about the intersections between the broader social abjection of racial minorities and the oppositional agency this phenomenon ultimately predetermines. While Chicana/os share a more or less common experience with other racialized minorities in prison and out, Pintas and Pintos are constituted through their counterhegemonic appraisal of the source and significance of their uniquely racialized and gendered prison experiences, their various complex performances of counterpower, and, more importantly, their belligerence. Indeed, for many Pintas and Pintos, crime, incarceration, and resistance to authority constitute a unique individual and group identity. These specific nominatives thus function to indict the processes by which Chicana/os as a whole are figured as abject in a racist society, while also serving as defiant signifiers of their oppositional posture.

But not all Chicana/o prisoners seek to be identified as Pintos and Pintas. In the aforementioned 1970 special issue of *El Pocho Che* dedicated to Pintos, Chicano prisoner Rudy Espinosa makes an appeal to the journal's readers to send educational materials and supplies to the Chicano self-help organization EMPLEO (Work). He begins the piece "A Word Para Los Pintos" by first noting, "I am not a Pinto and I do not ever want to be one" (57), and then articulates a materialist critique of U.S. colonialism in which he argues that the prison functions as the last stage in the planned underdevelopment of the Chicana/o, Native American, and Black communities. The term "Pinto," Espinosa notes, marks a schism from the freeworld communities he wishes to rejoin, not only out of a desire to be released from prison, but also as an ontological need. The terms "Pinta" and "Pinto" thus are the subject of much debate.

Furthermore, even as these nominatives may connote a counter-hegemonic posture or, as with Espinosa, anomie, the subjects to whom these terms refer are part of a diverse and ideologically inchoate prisoner population that occupies a profoundly ambiguous space in the Chicana/o community and in society at large. As noted above, not all Pintas and Pintos are social bandits, and Hobsbawm reminds us that even those who are may in fact be counter-revolutionary. Pinta/os are comprised of a diverse group of Chicana/o Convicts who range from conscientious social bandits to internationalist revolutionaries, but also include petty property and drug offenders, rapists, murderers, and exploitative crime syndicate members. This broad range explains, in part, their ambiguous status: they are alternately the objects of shame, fear, resentment, and hatred, yet they also elicit feelings of desire, pride, and familial affection since they are fathers and mothers, uncles and aunts, brothers and sisters, sons and daughters, nieces and nephews, family friends. Sometimes they are celebrated as bad-man heroes, while at other times they are simply denigrated as very bad men or women.

Therefore, just like it would be inaccurate to characterize contestatory Chicana/o prisoner cultures as being uniformly opposed to capitalism or other forms of exploitation, so, too, would it be incorrect to situate Chicana/o prisoners simply as victims of coercive social and historical forces such as imperialism, racism, and sexism. Critical legal and critical race studies explications of the social and cultural construction of deviance—as well as feminist, postcolonialist, and Marxist accounts of the material conditions of crime—necessarily involve incisive critiques of exploitative acts such as rape or narcotics dealing, for example, which are destructive and antirevolutionary even if some may claim they are counterhegemonic. This qualification is clearly illustrated in feminist rebukes of Eldridge Cleaver's proposal in his infamous prison memoir, *Soul on Ice* (1968), that Black-on-White rape is an appropriate "revolutionary" praxis for subverting White power.[16] Yvette Flores-Ortiz (1995a, 1995b) and Juanita Díaz-Cotto (2006) underscore that many female offenders were victims of abuse by older men prior to their own lawbreaking activities. Joy James (2003) thus emphasizes that for "those who (continue to) prey on others in physical and sexual assaults on children, women, and men, 'political prisoners' would be an obscene register; for they do not manifest as liberatory agents but exist as merely one of many sources of danger to be confronted and quelled in a violent culture" (2003: 11). As shown in several chapters of this study, similar critiques apply to some Pintos.

A fundamental goal of this book is to historicize the use of the penal apparatus in the disenfranchisement of Chicana/os, while also assessing the different localized Chicana/o prisoner negotiations of power as part of the complex dialectical interplay between hegemony and counterhegemony. Several fundamental questions emerge. What, for instance, is the relationship between Pinta/o culture and power across time and place? Moreover, what is the significance of the differences and similarities between various Pinta/o performances of counterpower? What model of subjectivity is associated with Pinta/o cultural and political praxis? How are Pintas and Pintos functioning as vernacular Chicana/o permutations of Gramsci's (1971) model of the "organic intellectual," as well as various revisionist accounts of this figure, such as Bhabha's

(1984, 1994), Taussig's (1993), and Irigaray's (1985), and Butler's afore-mentioned "mimic" (1990), Gayatri Spivak's "subaltern" (1988), Renato Rosaldo's "vernacular interpreter" (1989), Gloria Anzaldúa's "mestiza/o intellectual" (1987), and Norma Alarcón's "interstitial" agent (1989 and 1990)? Even more precisely, where might Pintas and Pintos fit into Joy James's model of the "prisoner intellectual" in her study, *Imprisoned Intellectuals: America's Political Prisoners Write on Life, Liberation and Rebellion* (2003), which inexplicably excludes Chicana/o prisoners? What is the status of this Pinta/o intellectual in the history of the U.S. prison, the Western prison in general, and, more broadly, in post- and neocolonial history overall? Finally, how has September 11 changed the significance of Pinta and Pinto agency?

Pursuant to an exploration of these questions, this book is divided into four parts, each with two chapters. Part One, "Land and Liberty," historicizes Chicana/o criminality, especially the complicated link between incarceration, the loss of sovereignty, and competing land claims in the southwestern United States. In Chapter 1, I draw upon Lizbeth Haas's (1995) historiography of Mexican American identity formation in California following the U.S. colonization of the state to further explore the significance of Modesta Avila, a twenty-two-year-old Mexican American woman who was imprisoned for obstructing railroad tracks built across her family land without her permission. I reread the original court transcripts of Avila's two trials in 1889 to uncover the complex interplay between sexist gender norms, criminalization of racial minorities, and Mexican American peonization. I pair this performance of colonialism with the neo-imperialist opera by Hungarian-born and California transplant George Siposs titled "Modesta Avila: An American Folk Opera," which premiered at the Westminster Auditorium on October 10, 1989, as part of the Orange County Centennial Celebration. I close by mapping how Avila, who died in San Quentin Prison, subsequently became a touchstone in contrapuntal Chicana historiography. In Chapter 2, I examine how former prisoner Jimmy Santiago Baca's neo-picaresque corpus of poetry and prose further renders the prison, and the southwestern land upon which it is built, as contested liminal zones. I am particularly concerned with Baca's tropes of identity that replicate troubling racial and gender archetypes. While his lyrical meditations on Native American and Chicana/o dispossession introduce the figure of the counterhegemonic Pinto intellectual, I show how his use of hegemonic genres and archetypes simultaneously illuminates the limits of mimesis in Pinto discourse.

Part Two, "Embodied Discourses," re-centers the Chicana/o body in the practice of imprisonment and, indirectly, the Chicana body in masculinist models of Pinto "resistance" discourses. In Chapter 3, I explicate the masculinist conceits undergirding Ricardo Sánchez's unique declamatory prison poetry. While Sánchez's verse symbolically harnesses violence in order to prescribe a proto-revolutionary praxis for Chicana/o liberation, I show how his use of misogynist and homophobic rhetoric fails to synthesize the very contradictions he identifies, further rendering the Pinto intellectual as an incompletely actualized oppositional subject. In Chapter 4, I continue this examination of Pinto poetics by mapping how Raúl Salinas performs a complex Chicana/o claim to place and ontological space in his prison poetry and tattoo art. I show how Salinas and fellow prisoners use homosocial tattoo rituals in prison that involve the symbolic exchange of women to articulate a vernacular and collectivist poetic and political meditation on, and claim to, power in prison and out. Through his problematic though transgressive vernacular theories of praxis, Salinas ultimately comes to embody another model of the Pinto intellectual: the internationalist revolutionary.

Part Three, "Crime and Commodification," further explores consumptions of the Pinto as a "bad-man hero" and "social bandit." Chapter 5 focuses on the mass media commodifications of Pintos in Edward James Olmos's Chicano prison gang saga, *American Me* (1992). I show how this film attempts to revise the exoticist Hollywood "gangxploitation" and prison sagas by cultivating and exploiting various types of resistant and resistance spectatorship. The film uses didactic tattoo rituals and visceral verité cinematography to trope color as race, and race as sociopolitical critique. I close with a critique of the film's contradictory call for Pinta/o and homeboy self-erasure as necessary for Chicana/o self-actualization. Chapter 6 further examines the problematic yet contested mass media commodifications of Chicano prisoners, specifically Fred Gómez Carrasco, the notorious South Texas drug baron who in 1974 staged a bloody prison break attempt from the Walls Unit of the Texas Department of Corrections in Huntsville. While he became a negative reference point and catalyst for various prison staff and guard memoirs, as well as mainstream newspaper reporting, I show how Carrasco and his wife, Rosa, have been recuperated by the Chicana/o community through vernacular counterhegemonic forms such as the *narco-corrido*, declamatory poetry, *actos* (or agitprop drama), and grassroots journalism. Carrasco becomes a palimpsest in the South Texas permutation of the racialized culture wars.

Part Four, "Storming the Tower," focuses on institutions, institutionalization, and proposed counterhegemonic challenges to institutional containment. In Chapter 7, I show how Chicana prisoner Judy Lucero intervenes in the masculinist regime of prison and, more importantly, in the violent and misogynist Pinto forms of agency that have posed problematic challenges to it. Lucero's poetry not only anticipates foundational Chicana cultural nationalist gynopoetics and materialist feminism of the 1970s and 1980s, but also introduces a collectivist politics free of the violent overtones that undermine Pinto performances of counterpower. Lucero thus introduces an alternative to previous articulations of the Pinta/o intellectual. In Chapter 8, I explore how these prisoner interventions inform and challenge the problematic nature of "prison work"; that is, volunteer educational and social service activities by academics, activists, and former prisoners. I examine several Service-Learning projects I organized in juvenile detention facilities and maximum-security prisons in upstate New York in 1996, alongside other prison education projects in Canada and the United States. The goal of this chapter is to resist a celebratory treatment of prison research, including this study, by exploring the complicated power relationships that emerge from the workshop designs, selection of canonical versus noncanonical materials, and inadvertent instructor complicity with institutional regimens of control.

In the conclusion, I examine past and ongoing models of prisoner activism and advocacy, especially 1970s Chicana/o prisoner invocations of human rights discourses, to call for a new paradigm for prisoner advocacy. I show how the convergence of various wars on crime with the war on terror—a convergence accompanied by deliberate, legally justified subversions of international treaties and standards to which the United States is a signatory—ultimately demands and enables a recourse to human rights regimes and a relocation of U.S. prison work onto an international sphere.

PART ONE

Land and Liberty

CHAPTER I

Toward a Materialist History of Chicana/o Criminality

Modesta Avila as Paradigmatic Pinta

CHICANA/O HISTORY, TRAGIC ROMANCE NARRATIVES, AND PINTAS

IN THE FINAL ACT OF GEORGE SIPOSS'S *MODESTA AVILA: AN AMERICAN Folk Opera* (1986), the eponymous heroine lies emaciated on her death-bed in the stark minimalist stage re-creation of a late-nineteenth-century cell in San Quentin Prison. The morbid scene is set in 1891, two years after the real Modesta Avila—a twenty-two-year-old Mexican American woman—had been tried, convicted, and imprisoned for a felony offense: stringing her clothesline and laying other obstructions across the California Central Railroad tracks that crossed the three-acre San Juan Capistrano property she claimed as her own. Her conviction in Santa Ana, the Orange County seat, by an all-White, all-male jury for "willfully, maliciously and feloniously obstructing the railroad" was virtually assured by the defiant English-language note she allegedly left at the scene of the crime.[1] One witness recalls the note stating: "This land belongs to me; if the railroad company don't pay me $10,000, they can't pass."[2]

The trial began on October 22, and on the following day the jury returned a split 6–6 vote, resulting in a mistrial. A second trial began six days later. Avila was found guilty the next day, on October 29, 1889. Her appeals were dismissed and within a week she began serving a three-year sentence. Even though the California state legislature recently had reduced the penalty for obstructing a railroad from death to a maximum of five years in prison, Avila's conviction and imprisonment in the notoriously unhygienic women's ward of San Quentin Prison were, effectively, a death sentence. Opened in 1852, San Quentin included a women's ward until 1933, when the women's penitentiary at Tehachapi was built. By some accounts, female prisoners were coerced into prostitution by prison officials, guards, and even male prisoners. Avila died in San Quentin in September 1891 from an unknown illness, apparently tuberculosis, which she had contracted after serving only two years.

In the twentieth-century operatic rendition of Modesta Avila's life and death—conspicuously subtitled "An American Folk Opera"—the festive Mexican and rural Western American folk singing and clogging in the first three acts gives way in Act Four to a melodramatic final encounter between the dying Avila and her would-be lover Bill. Ironically, but predictably for an opera, Bill is a burly White American who works for Avila's nemesis, the California Central Railroad. Although there is no evidence that such an interracial romance existed in Avila's real life, Bill's presence in the opera buttresses the tragic romance plot and progress narrative subtext, which reaches its climax with this death scene. As the lighting fades to a ghoulish yellow, Bill enters stage left with a bouquet of flowers for their final duet: "Oh Modesta, I've been longing for you. Are you all right? Do you sleep well? Are you ill?" Between anguished coughs, Modesta responds, more somberly, "I can't sleep and I'm dying."

Staring straight into Bill's eyes as he holds her exhausted body, she adds a final pathos-laden query: "Why did you create such a great monster? Why did God break my heart?"

Modesta's subsequent death rattle is interspersed with Bill's melodramatic aria: "Modesta! Oh my God! Why did the train come between us? We could have lived life together." When she finally dies, all Bill can do is offer the audience a feeble canto that serves as the opera's crescendo: "She died. She died for her land."[3]

The love affair between the sultry and headstrong Mexican American woman and the strong and handsome White American male is never consummated. The curtain closes to the applause of the White-majority audience that has gathered to commemorate the centennial anniversary of the founding of the small southern California town of Santa Ana, in whose honor the opera was written.

The date of this little-known opera's "world premiere" (which only ran two nights in the eighty-seat Westminster Community Center and Museum) also coincided with a dramatic demographic shift in Orange County in the 1980s that was fueled by a wave of Asian and Latina/o immigration. This new population had rendered the opera's White-majority audience into a minority for the first time since the United States colonized the region more than a hundred years earlier. The opera spectacle thus resonates as a symbolic reassertion of an otherwise waning White hegemony. It heralds yet another chapter in the complex and already racialized and gendered struggle for land and power in the perennially contested region now known as the southwestern United States. As in the opera, both the railroad and the U.S. judicial system are at the center of this historical drama.

The railroad, such as the one that crossed the small Avila family plot, has always been the quintessential symbol of modernity and a key trope in the nationalist progress narratives that inform many Western national literatures. In contrast, the railroad oftentimes is personified as the embodiment of evil in nineteenth-century Mexican American literature, which emerges as a complex counter-discourse at the end of the U.S.-Mexico War in 1848, when Mexican American citizenship was formally codified through the Treaty of Guadalupe-Hidalgo.[4] One prominent example is Amparo Ruiz de Burton's 1885 historical romance novel, *The Squatter and the Don*, a thinly veiled semiautobiographical tale that traces the dispossession of the Alamar family of Spanish-descent, California-born landowners, also known as *criollos*, who are displaced first by White American squatters and then by the Central Pacific Railroad. While the novel deliberately attempts to serve as a critique of the encroachment of White American capital in the Mexican northeast, the story is complicated by a romance between Mercedes, an Alamar daughter, and Clarence Darrel, the eldest son of a White squatter who stakes an illegal claim to part of her family's land. What began as a critique of White American capitalist imperialist incursion thus evolves into an inadvertent admission of *criollo* complicity with it. This novel also suggests that the otherwise unlikely romance between Bill and Modesta in Siposs's opera is less implausible and dissonant, even if it did not actually occur.

The ill-fated romance between the nineteenth-century railroad's Mexican American opponent and its White American champion has a real-life analogue in Ruiz de Burton's own life. Ruiz de Burton's historical novel recalls her own marriage to a White U.S. Army officer, Captain Henry S. Burton, which is particularly problematic given that Captain Burton arrived in the region with the U.S. Army in 1848 as part of the U.S. invasion of Baja California. He later relocated to the newly annexed state of Alta California, where he met his future wife. While such unlikely love affairs are cliché devices in romance literature, Ruiz de Burton's own interracial marriage became a haunting specter in her futile life-long legal struggle to reclaim her family land (approximately 3,500 hectares) that were lost piecemeal after the United States formally annexed its newly conquered territory. Rosaura Sánchez and Beatrice Pita note in the introduction to the 1997 edition of *The Squatter and the Don* that Amparo Ruiz and Captain Henry Burton were the subjects of popular ballads and newspaper stories that represented them as "enemy lovers" (11).[5] Although Ruiz de Burton's upper-class *criolla* status enabled alliances with the emergent White capitalists, she was also caught in a liminal space where she, as a Mexican American woman in a newly conquered land, was pitted against the government legal apparatus that her White American husband had imposed upon Californio families by force of arms. Ruiz de Burton's novel and corresponding legal battles thus illustrate how the early Mexican-cum-Mexican American population is implicated, through commerce and marriage, in the encroaching White American capital heralded by the railroad's blaring horn, even as these culturally and racially marked *Mexican* American families attempt to challenge their resultant disempowerment in the new hegemonic order. Ironically, Ruiz de Burton would rely on the railroad to ferry her voluminous files and correspondence from coast to coast in her lawsuits and related appeals.

Although Modesta Avila and Amparo Ruiz de Burton came from vastly different class, social, and even racial backgrounds—the former having been a *mestiza* subsistence farmer, and the latter an upper-class *criolla* heir to prime real estate—they both serve as important frames of reference for this study on Pintas and Pintos. They complicate the conventional overdetermination of Pinta/os as male social bandits, and they also problematize related discourses on Chicana/o identity as unambiguously subaltern. For instance, whereas nineteenth-century Mexican American figures such as Gregorio Cortez continue to be celebrated for their failed attempts to outrun U.S. law and the railroad locomotives that ferried its officers, Avila was imprisoned for directly, defiantly, and deliberately challenging the railroad as a multilingual Mexican American woman. Moreover, Avila's conflict with the region's newly adopted U.S. legal system dramatizes the traumatic transformation of the region's semifeudal order. It also graphically illustrates how this historical process was facilitated by masculinist notions of female propriety. As I explicate below, Avila's acts of sabotage, her resultant prosecution, *and* defense are predicated upon her identity as a bilingual, bicultural, mixed-race, lower-class single woman who became infamous for daring to challenge the phallic-shaped metonym of modernity that comes to be known among displaced rural folk of all races as the "black monster."[6] As noted in the introduction, the imbrication of race and gender in the construction of contemporary Chicana and Latina criminality continues to be a critical lacuna in most Pinta/o studies. Modesta Avila, one of the earliest known Mexican American prisoners, therefore is indispensable to this study because she further historicizes the creation of a discourse about Mexican American criminality that is not only racialized but always already gendered.[7]

Equally important, Avila's acts were immediately reified through mass media in ways that anticipated the current Hollywood and mainstream media fascination with racial minority criminality. Her defiant criminalized conduct—from the apparently benign act of stringing her clotheslines to placing potentially lethal railroad ties and a wagon axle across the tracks—also place the issue of Mexican American resistance under erasure. After all, Avila's criminalized acts of resistance were profoundly complex. She experienced firsthand the mass dispossession of Mexican Americans following the U.S. annexation of the region. However, as was the case with Ruiz de Burton, the land that Avila claimed had been made available only through the previous Spanish and Mexican colonial dispossessions of local Native American tribes. Moreover, the three-acre plot in dispute technically no longer belonged to the Avilas since her brother had sold it to another Mexican American family without her consent.[8] Her brother's unauthorized sale of the land was never questioned by the authorities. This gender differential in the exercise of legal privilege also informs and distinguishes male and female relations to crime and punishment up to the present. Modesta Avila's dramatic and traumatic life story, and the related stories about her, thus foreground Pinta/o identity and agency as complex and highly problematic manifestations and negotiations of gender, race, class, and power.

Pursuant to a complex mapping of Pinta/o history, culture, and agency, this inaugural chapter examines the relationship between the Mexican loss of sovereignty, Mexican American incarceration, and competing Mexican American and White American claims to land and power in the southwestern United States. In her study of Mexican American identity formation in California in the two centuries following U.S. colonization of the state, Lisbeth Haas (1995) has shown how the ever-changing ecclesiastical and legal status of Native Americans and Mexican Americans in nineteenth- and twentieth-century California was inextricably linked to property rights and related privileges. I extend Haas's study by *re*reading the aforementioned court transcripts from Avila's 1889 trials to explicate how nineteenth-century legal discourse in the newly expanded U.S. empire was undergirded by sexist tropes of female propriety. I also further explicate the neo-imperialist imprints in the aforementioned opera about Avila vis-à-vis contemporary Chicana literary and dramatic reclamations of Avila as a Chicana feminist "foremother."

I am guided by several questions. How does the court case, which produced the first convicted felon in newly incorporated Orange County, California, introduce foundational tropes of Mexican American criminality? How are these tropes nuanced by gender and race? How does the criminalization of Avila enable imperialist White American claims to the former Mexican land now known as the southwestern United States? And how does the reification of Avila's criminality by Chicana feminists illustrate the counterhegemonic potential of Pinta agency?

PROPERTY AND FEMALE PROPRIETY IN *THE PEOPLE OF THE STATE OF CALIFORNIA VS. MODESTA AVILA* (1889)

Arguing that Modesta Avila became a touchstone in competing White American and Mexican American historical narratives, Haas notes how the English-language press expressed its intolerance for Avila through headlines such as "Modesta Again."[9] This story, I further note, becomes more revealing given that it is printed on the same page as boldface advertisements reading: "REAL ESTATE: for sale." Moreover, upon Avila's death the *Santa Ana Standard* printed an obituary that identified Avila as a "prostitute" even though no evidence suggests that she was one. The obituary was reprinted in Steve Emmons's August 22, 1988, retrospective feature on Avila in the *Orange County Register*:

> Modesta, a well-known favorite of the Santa Ana boys, died in the penitentiary this week at San Quentin. She had served two years of her time and was getting along finely when she was stricken down in the prime of her usefulness. (3)

In contrast, regional Spanish-language newspapers ran empathetic stories and editorialized Avila's case as another instance of White racism and the unjust disenfranchisement of long-time Mexican American residents by the emergent White American monopoly capitalism. Haas has observed that Avila's "indignation over the usurpation of the lot—a space that symbolized the intersection of culture and history, family and community—ran deep and was widely shared" (90). Avila had become the metonym for the turbulent historical transformations of the Mexican northeast into the southwestern United States.

Yet Avila's reification in the media is more complicated than the racial binaries in competing media representations of her. The courtroom transcripts of both her trials in October 1889 reveal that the prosecutor and his witnesses—as well as the defense attorney and his witnesses—relied upon racist tropes and sexist notions of female propriety. That is, she was directly and indirectly vilified in and out of court by her enemies *and* allies.

To her accusers, Avila represented the old feudal Mexican order that refused to give way to "progress." She is marked as being too anachronistically Mexican—and therefore a threat—to the new White capitalist hegemony. Avila embodied the recently repressed past that was always threatening to reassert itself in the present. The unique charges against Modesta foreground this colonialist fear. Although the law against obstructing a railroad uses only one adjective, "maliciously," Orange County district attorney Colonel E. E. Edwards, a Confederate Civil War veteran, added "wilfully" and "feloniously" to the complaint against her in the first trial.

This slightly, though significantly, amended charge prompted the judge to define the legal terminology in this case in such a way that it virtually overdetermined Avila's "guilt." Judge Towner notes:

> The Statute only uses the word "maliciously"; it does not use the words "wilfully" or "feloniously."

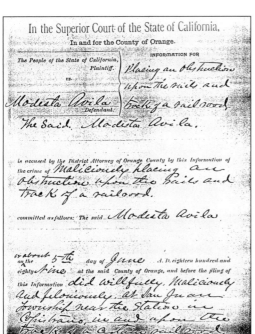

Figure 1.1. Original court transcript from *The People of the State of California vs. Modesta Avila* (1889a). Courtesy of the Santa Ana County (California) Library History Room.

The code defines the word "willfully" in this way: "When applied to the intent with which an act is done or committed, it implies simply a purpose or willingness to commit the act, or making the omission referred to. It does not require any intent to violate law, or to injure another, or to acquire any advantage." It simply means that the person does the act willingly, not under compulsion. (*The People . . .*, 1889a: 3)

In an era when Mexican American citizenship and land tenure were being undermined and transformed as illegitimate, Avila's counterhegemonic effort to reassert her agency as a Mexican American landowning woman profoundly unsettled the region's White citizens. Even before testimony began, the judge underscored the threat that Avila's agency represents to the new hegemonic order when he added:

Again, the word "Maliciously" implies "a wish to vex, annoy or injure another person, or an intent to do a wrongful act, established either by proof or presumption of law."

So there are two meanings to the word "maliciously," one of which confers the wish to hurt somebody, in short, to do some injury. The other, simply an intent to do a wrongful act; to do something that is wrong; that is, wherever that intent exists in the person meaning to do wrong. (1889a: 3)

The judge's convoluted—if not Kafka-esque—instructions to the jury on how to determine malice confirm that Avila's will to act was, in fact, more threatening than any act she was accused of perpetrating:

It is not absolutely indispensable, in order to prove malice, the existence of malice. . . . I say it is not necessary to show that the person had expressed malice, actual malice, against any person; and in all such cases malice may be inferred by the jury, if the wrong or the act is unlawful, it may be inferred from the means used to do the thing. . . . The evil intent may be inferred from the probable consequences of the act that was done, and upon that point, I will further say to you that it is not necessary in this State, or to establish this charge, that it should be shown that the act was done with the intent to injure life. It is not necessary to be shown by the prosecution in this case that it would have injured life. . . . Here, all that is necessary for the prosecution to show and establish this charge, is to show that the act was done, and was done with the intent to do a wrongful act; whether it would have injured life or not. (1889a: 4–5)

These qualifications apparently were necessitated by the fact that no one had been injured by Modesta Avila's clothesline or other obstructions.

As if performing on cue, the prosecuting attorney devoted most of his attention to the note Avila allegedly left nailed to a railroad tie forty yards from her small wood-frame house, which he cited as an admission of guilt. Max Mendelson, Avila's main accuser, was the only person who saw the alleged note. He claimed to have destroyed it, but the missing note still had a profound impact on the jury: allegedly written in English, it revealed Avila to be a bilingual, bicultural threat who could challenge the status quo in two languages.[10] Although several clauses in the Treaty of Guadalupe-Hidalgo signed after the U.S.-Mexico War in 1848 guaranteed that Mexican American land, language, and culture would be protected, Avila's English note and related oral boasts in Spanish marked her as simultaneously too Mexican and too American. The transcripts of both trials reveal that the prosecutor spent more time interrogating witnesses about Avila's writing and speech than her alleged act of sabotage. Avila's use of two languages to reassert the landownership that was her right under the previous Mexican government was seen as foreign yet unnervingly familiar. With the Treaty of Guadalupe-Hidalgo just fifty years old, everyone involved with the case knew what was at stake: nothing less than the right to claim legitimate ownership of the land now known as the southwestern United States. While the testimony contained in the trial transcripts lacks any overtly racist epithets, Avila's prosecution thus carries cryptic racial overtones. It facilitated the "ethnic cleansing"—both culturally and physically—of the region so the White colonist population could take possession.

The transcript of Avila's second trial also reveals how her prosecution was buttressed by sexist notions of female propriety. For instance, in addition to interrogating witnesses about Avila's alleged confessions, much of the prosecutor's cross-examination focused on the time and place witnesses saw her. He sought to link Avila to the scene of the crime on the date that Mendelson, the prosecution's star witness, claimed to have seen her there. The prosecuting attorney also sought to overdetermine Avila's criminality by parading a string of witnesses who all testified to seeing her dancing to Mexican music, drunk, in jail, or under arrest on several occasions. The coup de grace in the prosecutor's attempt to insinuate that Avila had a pattern of arrests for criminal conduct came when he questioned Charles S. McKelvey, justice of the peace for Santa Ana Township. The transcript of their exchange reads:

Q. Are you acquainted with the defendant, Modesta Avila?
A. I have had her before me a number of times.
Q. What time in the early part of June was she before you?
A. She was here before me the first time on the 8th day of June.
Q. What was that for?
A. For keeping a disorderly house. (1889b: 69)

Avila's arrest for "keeping a disorderly house" arose from the party she hosted to celebrate the windfall expected from the California Central Railroad for the use of her land.[11] The "offense" of "keeping a disorderly house"—the connotations of which extend from neglected housekeeping to sexual "excesses"—remains a cultural trope in Western legal and literary history that is inextricably linked to notions of female propriety. This notion of proper conduct—which in this late Victorian era was exemplified by the "conduct book" genre—was inextricable from Modesta Avila's land claims and the economic and personal independence they enabled.

The prosecutor concluded his depiction of Avila as a "bad woman" by noting that she had flamboyantly and dangerously claimed status as a landed Mexican American woman. He does so by situating her behind bars on several occasions before her arrest for railroad sabotage. Justice of the Peace McKelvey continues:

> She was brought before me, and on the 8th I fixed bail in $100 and she didn't have the bail, so she went to jail. . . . On the 17th day of June she was arrested—complaint was filed before me charging her with grand larceny. On the 18th she was arrested and brought before me and committed to jail in default of bail. On the 19th the district attorney appearing, withdrew the complaint charging her with grand larceny, and filed a complaint charging petit [sic] larceny. She was brought before me and plead [sic] guilty. I sentenced her to 30 days in the county jail at Los Angeles. (1889b: 71)

McKelvey subsequently made a crucial link between Avila's purported patterns of arrests, her outspoken nature, and her alleged act of sabotage when he testified:

> While she was in the court room waiting for the officer—I was making out a commitment—she did a great deal of talking. Among other things she said she was going to get $10,000. That same railroad—I can't say certainly whether it was the California Southern or California Central . . . running

through or past land that belonged to her. That they had to pay her for it; that she couldn't get the money out of them in any other way, so she blocked up the track. She didn't state what with—if she did, I didn't pay any attention. I was busy and she was talking—in fact she was doing a great deal of it. She said that while blocking the track, they had come to time. They had paid $10,000. (1889b: 71–72)

Not only is Modesta Avila portrayed as having been in jail before her main trial, but words attributed to her were used to confirm her unabashed criminality. After all, whereas most prisoners are renowned for maintaining their innocence from behind bars, Avila admitted to guilt even before being transported to jail. In response to the prosecutor's question "Was this statement voluntary at the time?" McKelvey responds, "It was most certainly!" (1889b: 72). Already convicted of "larceny" and "keeping a disorderly house," Modesta Avila was imprisoned—and symbolically re-housed—in the women's ward of San Quentin Prison on a charge that depicts her agency as a resolute, landowning, nineteenth-century Mexican American single woman as "willfully malicious."

Avila's defenders also relied on sexist notions of female propriety by attempting to "save" her from prison by figuratively re-housing her in the domestic space. Her father, José Avila, attempted to dispel courtroom insinuations about his daughter being a "loose woman" by reiterating that her house was located only three hundred yards from his. He emphasized that his daughter always visited his house whenever she was in town. However, his diligence in portraying Avila as a "good daughter" by emphasizing her relationship to the paternal home inadvertently located her outside the proper domestic home space: by recounting her frequent visits when she was in town, Avila's father unintentionally revealed that she was, in fact, frequently "out" (1889b: 62–63). His testimony accentuated the fact that she lived alone and traveled unescorted. Although he denied having any knowledge about the sabotage incident, his attempts to characterize her as a "good girl" only emphasized the fact that she was a single woman in her twenties, an age when most Mexican American and White American women were married mothers. The pressure on Modesta Avila's father in the second trial was intensified by the news that she was pregnant.[12] Her family's testimony thus added to Modesta Avila's gendered and racialized darkening (as in a woman's "blackened" reputation) in the eyes of the all-White, all-male judge, prosecutor, and jury. It also may have influenced her lukewarm reception among the Mexican American population. Haas notes:

Possibly because she was a woman who acted publicly in a defiant manner, she did not become part of the regional Spanish-language oral tradition, which interpreted similar acts admiringly as a form of banditry or resistance to the new forms of economic and political power. (1995: 102)

While male Mexican and Mexican social bandits have been celebrated from the nineteenth century to the present, Modesta Avila's agency was seen as improper by the patriarchs of both communities.

Even the defense attorney, Mr. Hayford, considered Avila's speech and flamboyant lifestyle to be distasteful and evidence of moral depravity. He also maintained that Avila's apparent boasting about her alleged act of sabotage, which had been entered into the courtroom testimony as an admission of guilt, was unreliable because she had been drinking at the time. Hayford even called Avila a chronic "liar"—a defense tactic so unusual that even the judge was incredulous, ignoring courtroom decorum to ask for clarification:

> THE COURT: It seems to me it is very unusual to undertake to impeach the character of the defendant by the defendant herself. . . . Here evidence has been given of an alleged declaration by the defendant in regard to a certain matter. Of course this evidence is against her. The weight of it can be determined by the jury. Now, you can show that that statement alleged to have been made by her was done at what time by promises, or it was made when she was drunk, or whether it was made when she was insane, or anything else; or that would impair its value to exclude it altogether. But to undertake what you propose doing ought not to be considered—that because she was not a person to tell the truth.
> MR. HAYFORD: I wish by this introduction—she becomes a witness virtually the same as though it was testimony. We certainly have the right to show that she is in the habit of telling lies, and for that reason we endeavor to bring this question for impeaching her veracity and her habit to tell them these identical things. (1889b: 40)

Modesta Avila's defense attorney then proceeded to recount how she had been drinking the day she made her boasts about sabotaging the railroad and about the windfall she expected to receive. The judge again expressed his surprise at the start of the second day of testimony, emphatically stating: "This is the first time in the course of my life or legal practice that I ever heard or knew of its being attempted—to show bad character of the defendant by the defense itself!" (1889b: 68). Testimony by Avila's defense attorney thus intersected with that of prosecution witnesses. One witness, Santa Ana resident George T. Insley, testified: "I don't think her reputation is extra good for anything that I heard of" (1889b: 39). Furthermore, not only does Avila's defense attorney attempt to silence her by refusing to call her as a witness, but he also attempts to undermine the only instance in which her voice is heard in the historical record. He dismisses her defiant and determined claim to personal and historical agency by depicting her exactly as the prosecution had: as a loud-mouthed, ill-mannered, and untrustworthy woman who was also a drunkard. She was so bad, he implied, that people should have expected the worst from her.

Luana Ross (1998) has argued that the criminalization and mass incarceration of Native American women in nineteenth-century Montana not only accompanied the White colonization of native lands, but facilitated it. She adds that this dialectic of abjection-and-dispossession continues to the present. I submit that a similar process of gendered and racialized abjection and dispossession governed the persecution of Modesta Avila by the prosecutor and the "defense" attorney in nineteenth-century California. The 1889 testimony in both trials—especially the second, in which she was convicted—confirms that Mexican American criminality in the nineteenth century was overdetermined by imperialist designs, racial prejudice, and sexist gender norms. It thereby introduced problematic tropes that continue to govern more contemporary representations of Mexican American criminality.

MODESTA AVILA: AN AMERICAN FOLK OPERA
AS NEO-IMPERIALIST NOSTALGIA

While Modesta Avila's prosecution in late nineteenth-century California was based on racist and sexist prejudices, contemporary attempts to recuperate her otherwise silenced voice have been even more problematic. George Siposs's 1986 opera and accompanying media reports demonstrate how the tropes figuring Avila as a racial menace and improper woman continue to resonate one hundred years after her persecution for asserting her personal, economic, and political agency. As noted above, the opera was performed in a context that gave it a racially charged significance even before the curtain opened: at a time when Santa Ana and adjoining municipalities had become minority-majority populations, this opera included only one Latino—wearing the obligatory sombrero—in a cast of more than thirty. Even more important than the racial demographics of the cast, the opera consists of lyrics, musical scores, dance choreography, and semiotic devices that reveal the performance's true intent: to appropriate Avila's claim to land in the guise of honoring her defense of it. Renato Rosaldo (1989) has identified this type of appropriation as "imperialist nostalgia":

> Imperialist nostalgia occurs alongside a peculiar sense of mission, "the white man's burden," where civilized nations stand duty-bound to uplift so-called savage ones. In this ideologically constructed world of ongoing progressive change, putatively static savage societies become a stable reference point for defining (the felicitous progress of) civilized identity. "We" (who believe in progress) valorize innovation, and then yearn for more stable worlds, whether these reside in our own past, in other cultures, or in the conflation of the two. Such forms of longing thus appear closely related to secular notions of progress. When the so-called civilizing process destabilizes forms of life, the agents of change experience transformations of other cultures as if they were personal losses. (70)

Rosaldo extends the scope of false nostalgia to U.S. popular culture:

> Even politically progressive North American audiences have enjoyed the elegance of manners governing relations of dominance and subordination between the "races." Evidently, a mood of nostalgia makes racial domination appear innocent and pure. (68)

Written and staged exactly one hundred years after the United States took possession of California through warfare, and at a time when the hegemonic order was again on the verge of another racial transformation, *Modesta Avila: An American Folk Opera* resonates with *neo*-imperialist nostalgia. It purports to honor the Mexican rural population displaced by Whites even as its spectacular staging emerges as a latent lament for the impending loss of White land and power to the rising tide of racial minority migrants and immigrants.

From the opening act, the performance reveals itself to be informed by a feigned tolerance of racial and cultural difference. The spectacle begins with Mexican folkloric dance as well as American southern clogging and singing, giving the illusion of harmonic coexistence in nineteenth-century California. Indeed, the racial violence that has come to characterize the era is overaestheticized so it ultimately can be effaced. In the first act, for instance, conflict is introduced but amicably resolved through stylized

Figure 1.2. Poster for
*Modesta Avila: An American
Folk Opera*, by George G.
Siposs. Courtesy of Joy
Neugebauer, president,
Westminster Historical
Society.

Figure 1.3. Ticket order form for
*Modesta Avila: An American Folk
Opera*. Courtesy of Joy Neugebauer,
President, Westminster Historical
Society.

contests of male strength. After two White characters engage in a friendly bout of hand wrestling in the dance sequence, two more pairs of men enter center stage to engage in a pogo stick contest. In this performance, one pair was White and another included a White cowboy and the cast's only Mexican American actor, dressed as a *charro*, or Mexican cowboy. The contests are resolved in ten seconds, and the four men return to country line dancing in a scene reminiscent of Rodgers and Hammerstein's 1943 musical *Oklahoma*. As in that play, racial difference, and the attendant history of racial violence in the southwestern United States, is alluded to but immediately effaced. The succeeding choreography foregrounds the drama to come by presenting—though not allowing—the possibility of interracial romance between the Mexican *charro*/stick fighter and a blonde woman. But the otherwise flirtatious twirls, thrusts, and parries characteristic of Mexican folkloric dance routines are never consummated. As the couple separates, never again to perform Mexican folkloric dance, other characters and dance styles take over, with American southern clogging and Appalachian square dancing becoming the defining forms in the remainder of the opera.

The subtle but deliberate move of the opera from cultural pluralism to cultural chauvinism, however, had been foregrounded even before the singing and dancing began. Following the welcome by Westminster mayor Joy Neugebauer, the opera's producer, the audience was treated to a slide show that served as the opera's prelude. It featured several pastoral scenes with all-White subjects that marked the opera as a White claim to California: (1) White male farmer with a sickle, (2) young blond boy petting a horse, (3) assortment of regional birds, (4) White male rancher at work, (5) team of harnessed farm horses, (6) close-up of two farm horses, (7) family of White homesteaders in a wagon train, (8) dome of Mission San Juan Capistrano with the sign "San Juan Capistrano" in the foreground, (9) panorama of railroad tracks running into the horizon, (10) close-up of railroad tracks and, finally, (11) close-up of the opera poster that features Claudia St. James, the White brunette actress chosen to portray a sultry Modesta Avila. These photos served as an allegorical montage framing the meaning of the opera proper.

After these rhetorical devices located Whites at the center of the opera—and of the historical drama it seeks to redefine—the musical scores and lyrics appropriate Avila's claim to land in a more overt and definitive way. Similar to the faux cultural pluralism of the opening dance sequences, the opening chorus of male and female singers begins by foregrounding, and then effacing, the Mexican presence in nineteenth-century California. It begins:

> We're so happy . . . We are happy. *Cinco de Mayo*, let's celebrate. *Cinco de Mayo*. Let's celebrate.

The male chorus adds:

> Twenty-seven years ago, in 1862, two thousand Mexican soldiers won a battle against the French Army, the mighty French Army . . . and saved old Mexico. And set Mexico free.

Ironically, the opera begins with an homage to the anti-imperialist Mexican guerrilla campaign at the Battle of Puebla in 1862 that defeated the French Foreign Legion. The French troops were part of an effort to colonize Mexico and transform it into a French-controlled monarchy. But this apparent anti-imperialist paean is revealed to be a trite yet useful rhetorical device. After all, the song pays homage to the independence of "old" Mexico. The ensuing song, dance, and drama in this opera completely avoid mention of the U.S.-instigated imperialist war against Mexico several years earlier that had resulted in the colonization of one-half of Mexican national territory. Instead, Siposs pays homage to the modern land—upon which the "old Mexico" once extended—through pastoral allusions to the nationalist White yeoman mythology. This mythology is constituted in part by the trope of the White man's-errand-into-the-wilderness, which Rosaldo links to imperialist nostalgia (1989: 70). Pursuant to this appropriation, the male chorus's bilingual score effectively pacifies the Mexican insurgents with wine and song:

Come *amigos*, celebrate with us. Come *amigos*, celebrate with us. Let us eat and drink together. Let's have music. Let's have fun.

The population signified by the Spanish *amigos* initially is paired with, and absorbed by, the referent of the English "friends" when the full chorus adds:

We're California and we want a party . . . Let's have a party. Let's have a party . . . We love to dance.

The entire cast toasts. The occasion for the celebration no longer appears to be the Mexican anti-imperialist guerrillas celebrated in the opening song, but the White rural folk who toil in the fields on both sides of the railroad tracks that cross the length of the stage. The stage thus becomes a simulacrum of contemporary White imperialist desire for land and the restoration of their hegemonic status.

The invocation and appropriation of a Mexican claim to land becomes more overt as the chorus turns its attention to Modesta Avila herself. In the first act, Avila proclaims in a moving aria:

My mother owned all this land. It was granted to her lawfully . . . And she gave it to me before she died.

Yet the chorus, whose only Mexican American cast member is now barely visible upstage, sings:

This is *our* home . . . It takes care of *us* . . . The rain quenches *our* plants for *us*. This land, this land is *our* land. This is *our* home. *Our home.* (emphasis added)

The opera has progressively moved from celebrating Avila's claim to landownership, to supporting a claim on her land by the nineteenth-century White yeomen portrayed by twentieth-century local yokels. Modesta Avila's semi-epic struggle against the railroad behemoth is appropriated by the opera to serve as a metonym of White nineteenth-century rural folk's complaint against the encroachment of monopoly capital transforming the family-based yeoman agricultural economy. This point is reiterated in the second act as the full chorus subtly, but profoundly, continues to transform Modesta's lyric assertions. Avila sings:

> I don't want the train to trespass *my* land. (emphasis added)

But the chorus, which functions as an accompaniment in most operas, sings center stage:

> We don't want the train to trespass *our* land. (emphasis added)

From this point in the opera, the historical critique of the disruptive, but presumably productive, force of modernity and monopoly capital that the railroad represents becomes an Anglo-centric narrative. It both critiques and celebrates the hegemonic order through a nostalgic backwards glance toward the Mexican population that was, in its view, *necessarily* displaced. Hence, Modesta Avila becomes a metonym for Whites to politely justify conquest. Furthermore, she becomes the saintly Mexican woman who judiciously disappeared but is always present as a floating signifier for their use as needed.

This appropriative and incipiently imperialist discourse gains an even more pronounced resonance given that George Siposs, the opera's composer and librettist, was a White immigrant from Hungary.[13] The European immigration of which he was part, however, had by the 1980s proved insufficient to preserve White hegemony in this southern California region. The opera thus became a necessary venue for a symbolic performance of a claim to ownership by the European-descent cast and audience.

Walter Mignolo (2000) notes that in the wake of the relatively recent collapse of the center-periphery binary, colonial (and, I add, neocolonial) power has been decentralized, and subaltern identity, which he calls "colonial difference," diffused:

> The colonial difference is the space where coloniality of power is enacted. It
> is also the space where the restitution of subaltern knowledge is taking place

Figure 1.4. Opera still of Claudia St. James as Modesta
Avila. *The Orange County Register*, September 30,
1986. Courtesy of *The Orange County Register*.

and where border thinking is emerging. The colonial difference is the space
where *local* histories inventing and implementing global designs meet *local*
histories, the space in which global designs have to be adapted, adopted,
rejected, integrated, or ignored. (2000: ix, emphasis in original)

The grandiose billing of the two-day run of *Modesta Avila: An
American Folk Opera* as a "world premiere," even though it occurred in
a highly localized (if not altogether provincial) suburban community hall
(a former barn) that doubled as a museum (open only by appointment),
recalls Mignolo's adage that global imperialism, and its potential challenges, are experienced and performed on a local level. This low-budget
community opera may not have been a true world premiere, but it
definitely was a local performance of global political economy.

Underscoring this local performance of global designs, the opera's
neo-imperialist poetics nonetheless are innovative, complex, and quite

effective. For instance, the opera offers alternately cliché and ingenious uses of the otherwise dissonant sounds of modernity: Morse code, the train's blaring whistle, and excerpts from the "Star Spangled Banner," the U.S. national anthem. Throughout the opera, the country "hillbilly" music is interspersed with stylized Morse code flute notes that spell out "T-R-A-I-N" and mark transitions in the drama. The first use of this device interrupts the initial romantic interlude between Modesta and Bill in Act One, precluding further intimacy. The flutist's stylized code also introduces the evil foreman, who calls Bill to work by singing:

Come on. Let's go to the line. You are needed.

He later adds:

Come on there's no time now for this useless party. Come on, Bill. There is no time to waste on such a silly woman.

Here, the Morse code taps of "T-R-A-I-N" have an ominous resonance, but its repeated use is transformed into a more positive device as the train's horn itself is troped. Both these aural devices begin to sound as harbingers of the difficult yet *inevitable* progress narrative that the train represents. These sounds herald the future as if they were clarion calls announcing Manifest Destiny, the nineteenth-century doctrine that posited Whites as the rightful, divinely endowed civilizing heirs to the Western Hemisphere.[14] The coup de grace in the opera's creative neo-imperialist use of sound occurs when the orchestra plays "The Star Spangled Banner" in the first act. The score accompanies the foreman's lyric response to Avila's protestations that "we were born here; and we belong here; so what right do you have to cross in my fields?!" The foreman retorts:

You are a crazy woman. A law says the train goes through.

He continues by addressing both Bill and Modesta:

This woman is looking for trouble. Looking for trouble. Stopping the train. It's impossible to stop it. The train must go through and that is that.

As with the Morse code and train's horn, the anthem gains the force of law. It signals the new White hegemonic order and parallels the nineteenth-century Manifest Destiny discourse that posited this order as preordained. The anthem is played again in the third act to introduce the presiding judge in the dramatic staging of Avila's trial.

These three aural devices subsequently occur in unison to underscore the crescendo in the fourth act when Modesta dies. As this final act opens, Avila is coughing between her singing, and the Morse code is played on a flute as if it were a civilian form of "Taps," the song played at a soldier's funeral. After Avila cries out, "Don't let the railroad defeat me; don't let me die," the train's horn blares again during her death rattle, introducing Bill's closing line, proclaiming that "she died for her land." The audience already knew this would happen: the linkage of these neo-imperialist and nationalist aural devices underscores the inevitability, and necessity, of Modesta Avila's death. More importantly, this panoply of sounds—from the stylized flute notes to the obvious train horn to the even more recognizable U.S. national anthem—repackaged the otherwise elite opera form for popular consumption by an audience of White-flight suburbanites in 1980s California.

Finally, the progress narrative that informs the entire spectacle is reinforced through the operatic equivalent of cinematic excess: the redundant overemphasis of characterization and plot. In *Modesta Avila: An American Folk Opera*, this overemphasis is accomplished by troping miscegenation as incompatible with the new racial and economic order. As noted, the entire opera revolves around the ill-fated love affair between a handsome burly White railroad worker, Bill, and a sultry young Mexican American woman who dies fighting the railroad that enabled her to meet Bill in the first place. Their encounter at the end of the pastoral song and dance in the first act establishes the irresolvable dichotomy that renders their relationship as a preordained failed venture. After the train disrupts their embrace with its blaring horn, Modesta sings:

> The train, that awful train. . . . It so destroys the land and fills the colors of the sky with despair, despair, despair. . . . That's his job.

She moves closer to Bill and continues:

> But the train, that awful train, stands between us. . . . I'm worried about us. How can I have your love? How can I love you?

After Bill tries to reassure her that their love is true and eternal even though they effectively are married to different economic orders, Modesta shouts back:

Mine is the land. Yours is the railroad.

The tragic romance storyline is reinforced by the succeeding exchange:

MODESTA: Stay with me, Bill.
BILL: Modesta, I love you. I want to hold you every night but I must work.
. . . The railroad must not stand between us. But progress can't be stopped.
The train must run to San Diego.
MODESTA: But it's just a railroad. And it does not have a heart. And it has
no desire, no desire that I have for you.
BILL: People do count on me to lay the tracks to San Diego. It will bring a
better life. A better life. . . . The railroad is the job that I was trained to do.
The railroad paid me money. I must do my job before I can marry you. . . .
MODESTA: No. The railroad is not just your living. It is your life.

As this exchange predicts, the romance is never consummated.

The invention of Bill as a character in this historical story serves several
purposes. Haas has noted that Avila's real boyfriend was a Mexican
American who was fired by his employer for refusing to leave her (1995:
102). However, the opera's superimposition of Bill onto the historical
narrative not only drives the romance subplot, but also reinforces the
impossibility of the marriage between the semifeudal Mexican order
of family subsistence farming and the emergent technologically driven
monopoly capitalism that was imposed following the U.S. annexation of
half of Mexico in 1848. The consummation of this contrived romance
might signal the possibility of a syncretic future where both Mexican
American and White American populations might coexist in harmony. In
this opera, however, Modesta and Bill represent the quintessential "enemy
lovers" in the southwestern United States, and thus serve as metonyms
for a neo-imperialist, and fundamentally racist, discourse that relies on
the eugenicist belief in the incompatibility of different "races." They
cannot be allowed to sleep together—and they do not. The videotape of
the inaugural performance at the Westminster Historical Society Museum
ends with the White audience giving a standing ovation.

In this context, Bill and Modesta each represent incompatible historical and economic epistemes, and their characterization as ill-fated
lovers relies upon Avila's role as a classical tragic heroine. Within this
teleology, Avila's fall is predicated upon hamartia, a fatal flaw or mis-
judgment, which in the opera also appears to be pure hubris, or an excess
of pride. Similar to tragic heroines in classical Greek drama such as

Sophocles's *Antigone* (ca. 441 BC), Avila is headstrong and stubbornly determined to follow a higher law—love—than the one propelling the locomotive through her land. Worse, she fails to side with the forces of the future: monopoly capital and the rise of wage labor. She refuses to move aside to let the railroad pass, and therefore she must die. And she does. The opera's staging of her death is loaded with pathos. It is in this scene, set in San Quentin Prison, where all the opera's discursive and poetic strands converge, especially the trope of miscegenation. The audience knew from the start that this was an unlikely love affair, and, true to the neoclassical opera template as well as Modesta Avila's actual life and death, she dies in prison. Or rather, the prison, where she contracted a lethal illness, killed her. The opera, whose title promises to celebrate Modesta Avila's rebellious agency, ends by empowering the prison as a character in the opera proper and, in a broader context, as an agent of historical transformation. Even though audience members feel sadness at Avila's tragic death, they know that she must die for the story to retain its historical and discursive integrity as a White American progress narrative.

The time and place of the opera's staging were crucial to this performative discourse of White fear of racial minorities. Joy Neugebauer, a former Westminster mayor and the opera's producer at the time, was outspent, and outvoted by fewer than five hundred votes, in the 2003 Westminster City Council race by an Asian American opponent.[15] To the White residents, the threat that culminated in this electoral defeat was real, and so too was the need for the opera, which presents itself as pure neo-imperialist nostalgia.

"CHICANA FEMINIST FOREMOTHER":
MODESTA AVILA AS PARADIGMATIC PINTA

In opera, every prop is deliberate and meaningful. For the all-important death scene in the fourth act of *Modesta Avila: An American Folk Opera*, the main props are a bed, a small table upon which sits a jar of imaginary water, and a gray prison wall that bears a twelve-by-sixteen-inch framed pastel painting. Commissioned by the opera's director, Kent Johnson, the painting features the bust of a brown-haired, brown-eyed, and brown-skinned woman in a folkloric Mexican dress and a pink veil.[16] She is crowned with a halo.

Like all the opera's props—from the twelve-foot wooden locomotive, to the larger-than-life railroad tracks, to Modesta's modest clothesline—

the painting has a symbolically significant role. Whereas court transcripts from *The People of the State of California vs. Modesta Avila* depicted Avila as "malicious," "untrustworthy," "drunk," a "bad housekeeper," and a single woman with a bad or "darkened" reputation, this painting offers the second component of the virgin/whore dichotomy crucial to Avila's recuperation and appropriation by contemporary White Californians. Here she appears as a cherub-like angelic apparition. The image is framed in carved wood adorned with painted gold-borders, flowers at the top corners, and a cross that is centered above the entire image in the style of the ecclesiastical renditions of saints. The painting serves as a visual complement to the opening slide show by heralding and then confirming that Avila will soon be dead and will no longer disrupt the train or present a threat to the emergent White capitalism that the railroad helped to consolidate in the region. By the time of the

Figure 1.5. Painting from the set of *Modesta Avila: An American Folk Opera*. Artist unknown. Courtesy of Joy Neugebauer, president, Westminster Historical Society.

opera, Modesta Avila was safely dead and distant enough to be deified as a saint: the quintessential long-suffering, self-sacrificing, chaste mother figure. To emphasize the saliency of this virgin/whore dichotomy, the stage lights dim after Avila dies, and a spotlight illuminates the painting, whose halo seems to glow in the sepia filter. Like the drama, lyrics, and musical score, the lighting provides yet another theatrical device that is harnessed to enable the appropriative "celebration" of Modesta Avila's necessary martyrdom. The painting further confirms that the opera, like the trial, not only is a performance of neo-imperialist nostalgia, but a patriarchal permutation of it.

Nestor Garcia Canclini (1989) has argued that the salient meaning of modernist art and icons is disrupted and transformed in postmodernity through unique hybridizations and dissonant decontextualization. This slippage arises from "the breakup and mixing of the collections that used to organize cultural systems, the deterritorialization of symbolic processes, and the expansion of impure genres" (1989: 207). Similar to the floating signifiers that Garcia Canclini observes, the commodified decontextualizations of Modesta Avila as a regional icon are complex, ever-shifting, and, above all else, subject to a repeating pattern of appropriation and reappropriation. She is the necessary antithesis to ascendant modernity, and her postmodernist reincarnation places her meaning *sous rature*, or under erasure: under constant revision, it becomes a palimpsest, with the preceding versions still faintly visible. For instance, once reviled as a criminal in court and celebrated as a saint on stage, Avila recently has been included among thirty "women of courage" in Orange County history by the area YWCA and was the subject of a 1988 re-creation of her clothesline rebellion by Chicana actress Irma Camarena.[17] Even as various municipal Internet Web sites and reportage on Modesta Avila continue to resonate with the same neo-imperialist discourse that distinguishes the opera, she also has been reclaimed by Mexican Americans in a performance imbued with as much counterhegemonic potential as Avila's own acts. Indeed, whereas the actress who portrayed Avila in the opera is White, Irma Camarena, who portrayed Avila by stringing a real clothesline across the real tracks in the small southern California town of San Juan Capistrano just a few hundred yards from Avila's former home, is identified as Mexican American. The *Los Angeles Times* photograph of Camarena's reenactment shows White tourists in the background gazing with the same sense of fascination and bewilderment as a suburban, middle-class White audience out for a night at an opera. But this spectacle also pressures Garcia Canclini's adage that the decontextualized modernist icon loses meaning in the postmodernist re-territorialization. After all, the scene was recontextualized in virtually the same location where it originally took place. The artistic rendering of Avila's act was relocated not simply so its original meaning could be restored, but so it could continually be transformed through simultaneously overlapping and competing consumptions of it. Such re-creations of Modesta Avila's crime—a crime distinguished by its rejection of the commodification that was being introduced by monopoly capitalism—is itself commodified. This time, however, she was reclaimed by a descendant of the Mexican American population that Avila's rebellion indirectly sought to protect against the forces of modernism and capitalism.

The reification of Modesta Avila as a social bandit is underscored by the commodification of another iconographic depiction of her: the San Quentin Prison mug shot. In this photograph, Avila stares back from prison to invert the gaze yet again. As a Pinta, she has become not only a potentially counterhegemonic floating signifier, but a Bakhtinian chronotope: a figure whose significance is grounded in a specific time and place (Bakhtin 1981). Modesta Avila has served as a point of departure in Haas's contrapuntal historiography of California, but I argue that her San Quentin Prison mug shot enables a different type of spectatorship by contemporary Chicana/os. The composition itself invites this contemporary recognition scene. Similar to the opera painting discussed above, this close-up black-and-white photo shows Avila from the chest up. Her name and offense —"M. AVILA. FELONY"—are scratched in black capital letters across the top. Across the breast of Avila's prison-issued black button-down habit is etched her prison identification number "13793" in white relief.

This image, however, has a profoundly different resonance than the opera set painting. As required, Avila looked straight into the photographer's camera. Her reverse gaze, however, may not be as contained as the handwritten indictment might purport. Her dark brushy eyebrows are slightly furrowed, making her face appear humbled yet simultaneously defiant. Her apparently somber lips even appear to offer a slight smirk. She is accused, but may also be accusing, gazed upon but gazing back, possibly inviting a dialogue. This image has progressively grown in popularity among Chicanas because its ambiguity has the multiple-voiced force of a Chicana Mona Lisa: difficult to fix, and thus inviting a polyphony of interpretations.

This photograph of Modesta Avila—convicted felon number 13793—has been reclaimed by the noted author Elena Maria Viramontes, who has a copy hanging in her Cornell University office. A southern California native renowned for her collection of short stories, *The Moths and Other Stories* (1985), and the Chicana feminist bildungsroman *Under the Feet of Jesus* (1995), Viramontes thus confirms that Avila has been reified into a floating signifier. Her concerns as a writer and an activist have revolved around a simultaneous critique of patriarchy and a materialist explication of gender relations. Paula L. Moya (2002) has lucidly explicated how *Under the Feet of Jesus* maps the growth of its protagonist into a critical thinking agent of history. In one key scene set in rural southern California, less than a hundred miles from San Juan Capistrano, Viramontes's prepubescent character Estrella grabs a tire iron as a weapon to protest an unfair medical charge for a friend dying of pesticide poisoning. She tries to save her friend and, by extension, her community of farmworkers by resorting to violence. Whereas Avila used laundry, wagon axles, and loud speech, Estrella takes matters in her own hands through acts also gendered as female (e.g., the nurturing

Figure 1.6. Modesta Avila's San Quentin Prison mug shot. Courtesy of Helena Maria Viramontes.

mother figure), yet antithetical to conventional sexist gender norms (e.g., the threats of proto-revolutionary violence). Both these figures are bad-woman heroines in local performances of broader global power struggles against the primary apparatuses of industrialization, imperialism, and capitalism: the railroad and agribusiness.

In a presentation at the 1997 American Literature Association Conference in Baltimore, Maryland, on her planned historical novel, Viramontes proclaimed that "Modesta Avila is one of our Chicana foremothers. She had the conviction to lay her life on the line to fight the forces that sought to destroy her community" (n.p.). Viramontes's recuperation is significant because Avila had been characterized as "disorderly," with a darkened reputation, and as speaking and acting in ways deemed inappropriate, unreliable, and dangerous. Norma Alarcón (1989) has noted how Chicana feminists similarly have recuperated Malintzin, also known as Malinali and, the more derogatory term, La Malinche. Malintzin was the translator for the Spanish conquistador Hernán Cortés and the mother of their children. She is reviled among some ultra-nationalist Chicana/os as the quintessential "sellout" and cause of the cataclysmic Spanish conquest of Mesoamerica. Yet Alarcón reminds us that the historical Malintzin had been sold into servitude several times, first by her own family to avoid inheritance conflicts with a brother. Her usefulness to Cortés had been facilitated by an indigenous patriarchal exchange of women. In the process of being repeatedly sold, she acculturated to several native tribes and learned their languages, ultimately becoming Cortés's translator as well as his mistress and, later, his legal wife, before again being exchanged to one of Cortés's officers. Hence, Malintzin's use to Chicana feminists arises from her multilingual speech acts, even more so than her frequently ascribed role as the archetypal mother of the first mestizos. As a Chicana feminist, Viramontes's reclamation of Avila also resonates with the broader Chicana reclamations of Malintzin: both historical women were ostracized by contemporary Chicana/os for being too acculturated, relatively independent, publicly confident, outgoing, resilient, and, above all else, defiant. Viramontes's identification of Modesta Avila as a precursor, or "foremother," to Chicana feminists thereby extends discussions of Mexican American dispossession to the contemporary period. Modesta Avila, and especially her criminalized persona—Pinta #13793—is thus key to Chicana/o history, the history of Chicana/o criminality, and especially the reification of highly gendered discourses on criminality, all of which are reexamined in the next chapter.

CHAPTER 2

Chicana/o Archetypes
Jimmy Santiago Baca and the Pinto Picaresque

As noted in Chapter 1, Modesta Avila's short and tumultuous life dramatically illustrates the ephemeral yet enduring salience of paper as a trope of power and counterpower in the history of the southwestern United States. This trope, a veritable cliché in all literature, extends to contemporary Chicana/o prisoner writing. This was poignantly illustrated in May 2003 at the commencement ceremonies of the University of New Mexico. Among the graduates was Jimmy Santiago Baca, a fifty-two-year-old ex-Convict whose life has been traumatically disrupted and radically reconstructed through printed pieces of paper: from court orders committing him to an orphanage, to dollar bills he received as a drug dealer, to courtroom transcripts chronicling his crimes—and finally to the poetry chapbooks, short stories, and memoirs that enabled him to rearticulate a new persona as an artist. But Baca's Doctor of Philosophy diploma is more than simply another piece of paper: it is a touchstone in a turbulent life that has always been distinguished for defying the odds. Baca has transformed himself from an illiterate petty drug dealer into an internationally renowned author, has gained economic independence in the otherwise unprofitable genre of poetry, has cultivated a largely non-Latina/o audience by writing about a gritty Chicana/o underclass experience, and despite having learned to read and write at the late age of twenty-one, has had his personal papers purchased by Stanford University for permanent archiving in its distinguished authors collection.

Baca's literary recollections of past *movidas*, or the scams and criminal acts of his highly autobiographical poetic persona, the downtrodden plebian mestizo antihero, have led to his recognition as a writer-philosopher of post-Movimiento Aztlán. Rafael Pérez-Torres (1995) lauds Baca for the "complexity and nuance" of his poetry (121). Bill Moyers (1995) calls Baca a "leading voice" among contemporary American poets, and he is now regularly included in standard U.S. literature anthologies. This canonization of U.S. Latina/o authors, of course, is no longer as anomalous as it might have been a decade ago. But unlike the progress narratives informing working-class Latina/o authors and tales of anomie that animate middle- and upper-class Latina/o writers, Baca ironically has made a lucrative career of representing the travails of the Chicana/o lumpen, or dispossessed, especially prisoners.

Given the vast distances that Baca has traveled and challenges he has overcome, it is not surprising that movement—both lateral geographic travel as well as vertical moral and ideological growth—is a fundamental theme of his work. Baca's highly autobiographical writing thus invites comparisons with the picaresque: the medieval European genre about the quintessential underclass antihero, the *pícaro*, whose travels are punctuated by a string of misadventures. Originally written by Catholic monks to educate the illiterate masses about the presumed dangers of veering away from Church doctrine or of aspiring to upward class mobility, the picaresque tale is distinguished by the wayward protagonist's starvation, beatings, incarceration, exploitation, and other abuse. All these traumas result from the *pícaro*'s decision to leave home in search of greater opportunities. To further emphasize the antihero's de-territorialization, the protagonists of picaresque tales usually begin their tragic lives as orphans. The ensuing quest is often infused with scatological humor and, above all else, satirical depictions of institutions of power, especially the Catholic Church. Despite its satirical base, however, the genre presents an ideologically ambiguous discourse on displacement and redemption that begins and ends with the clergy.

Baca's multigenre corpus similarly features a Mexican American underclass antihero who animates the unique subcategory of modern picaresque literature that I call "the Pinta/o picaresque." As with the traditional picaresque, Baca's picaresque writings begin at home. He was born in Santa Fe in 1952 and grew up in the small rural town of Estancia, New Mexico. In *A Place to Stand: The Making of a Poet* (2001), Baca recalls that his mother, Cecilia, was from a Spanish-descent family whose members took pride in their light skin and looked down upon Indians and *mestizos*, or mixed-blood Mexicans and Mexican Americans. Because his mother was "fair-skinned, green-eyed, and black-haired," he writes, she was expected "to marry a well-off gringo with a big ranch" (10). Instead she fell in love with Damacio Baca, who was born to poor, racially mixed Indian and Mexican parents. (Baca's paternal great-grandmother was said to be of Apache heritage.) These contentious in-group racial dynamics, and his father's chronic alcoholism, presaged the collapse of his parents' marriage, which occurred when he was still a child. His mother abandoned Jimmy, his brother Mieyo, and sister Martina to marry a man with whom she had been having an extramarital affair—an overtly racist White American who would later murder her upon learning of her plans to divorce him. Baca's father, who had fallen deeper into alcohol dependency, was virtually absent from his children's lives, so Baca and his siblings were sent to live with their paternal grandparents in their hometown village.

The worst was yet to come for the young Jimmy and his siblings. Upon the death of Baca's paternal grandfather in 1959, he and his brother were sent to an orphanage in Albuquerque. Baca was seven years old. This was his first experience with institutionalization. It would not be his last. His orphanage ordeal—which is described in Dickensian detail throughout his corpus—was followed by a stint in a juvenile home, frequent sojourns in local jails, and aimless travels across the southwestern United States. Baca later became a petty drug dealer and, at age twenty-one, was convicted of drug possession and sentenced to five years in the Florence Penitentiary in Arizona, a maximum security institution where he served at least five years.

It was in prison that Baca evolved from a modern Mexican American *pícaro* into a prison intellectual and renowned Chicano poet. In *A Place to Stand* (2001), Baca recalls that he taught himself to write by phonetically sounding out words from a textbook he had stolen from a particularly abusive Mexican American jail employee. He recalls:

> Sitting on my cot, I smoked a cigarette, opened the big hardcover book, and leafed through it. . . . I set my cigarette down on the concrete floor and murmured the words, sounding out the letters deliberately to see if I could understand them. I had trouble. It seemed each letter was fighting me. Reading was frustrating because each letter slowed me down. While sounding them out, I had to remember what they meant when combined. It was a lot harder than I expected. As I struggled, time, jail noise, cells, and walls all vanished. (99)

He developed enough competence to compose letters and, eventually, poems. The difficulties arising from his limited literacy skills were compounded by the daily distractions of bloody fights among prisoners, an alleged contract on his life by the Mexican Mafia prison gang, regular guard brutality, and frequent trips to the isolation chamber. He also endured a brief stay in the prison's mental ward, during which he claims to have been forcefully medicated with powerful psychotropic drugs (*Working in the Dark*, 9).

But like Malcolm X and so many other prisoner authors before him, literature afforded Baca the opportunity to physically write himself out of prison. By Baca's own admission, his early poetry was naive and sentimental. These initial efforts at creative writing nonetheless were accomplished enough to be published in some of the nation's most renowned literary and political journals and magazines, including *The Greenfield Review*, *The Sun*, and *Mother Jones*. Baca published his first full-length poetry collection, *Immigrants in Our Own Land* (1979), after his release from prison. This collection received nationwide acclaim and was reprinted in 1990 with the addition of selected early poems. Baca also published chapbooks—*Swords of Darkness* (1981), *What's Happening* (1982), and *Poems Taken from My Yard* (1986)—all of which examine his prison experiences and post-prison struggles to reintegrate into society. His second full-length collection of poetry, *Martín & Meditations on the South Valley* (1987), a two-part lyrical and semi-epic poem that includes an introduction by Denise Levertov, received the American Book Award in 1988. Baca has since published several other poetry collections: *Black Mesa Poems* (1989), *Healing Earthquakes: A Love Story in Poems* (2001), *Set This Book on Fire!* (2001), *C-Train (Dream Boy's Story) and Thirteen Mexicans* (2002), and *Winter Poems Along the Rio Grande* (2004). Baca also has written two screenplays, one of which was made into the Hollywood prison film *Bound by Honor* (previously titled "Blood In/Blood Out" [1993]). He has complemented this poetic output with creative nonfiction, including a collection of essays and selected correspondence, *Working in the Dark: Reflections of a Poet of the Barrio* (1992), and the memoir cited above, *A Place to Stand: The Making of a Poet* (2001). He also has published a collection of short stories, appropriately titled *The Importance of a Piece of Paper* (2004). Baca has subsequently received numerous national and international awards, and has held the Wallace Stevens Endowed Chair for Creative Writing at Yale University.

But even as Baca's neo-picaresque travels and triumphs map his self-actualization as an artist, his eclectic deployment of multiple literary genres is rhetorically problematic and ideologically ambiguous. His neo-picaresque attempts to re-territorialize his highly autobiographical poetic persona—the tragic mestizo orphan-cum-prisoner-cum literary protégé—demand a closer scrutiny, which begins with genre analysis.

Marxist theorist Fredric Jameson (1981) has argued that all texts and genres demand a political interpretation. When properly historicized, he notes, a text will reflect the political economy of its respective milieu (17). Rosaura Sánchez offers such a historicized reading of nineteenth-century Mexican American testimonial writing (1995) and romance novels (Sánchez and Pita 1997), thereby enabling broader ideological critiques of Mexican American appropriations of canonical genres that lay claim to land and authority in both hegemonic and counterhegemonic ways. As noted in the introduction, such contrapuntal readings of mimesis as counterhegemonic praxis fail to allay questions about the potential limits of appropriation as poetic and political strategy. I submit that Baca's multigenre Pinto picaresque corpus offers unique insights into this problem.

In this chapter, I examine how Baca's writing renders the U.S. prison—and particularly the southwestern land expropriated from Mexico in the nineteenth century, and previously robbed from Native Americans centuries before—as complex and contested liminal zones. The picaresque master narrative enables Baca to historicize his own mixed-race birth, his subsequent abandonment and institutionalization, as well as his release and reintegration into society. But how might this genre's five-centuries-old teleology undermine Baca's ideological critique? Furthermore, how do Baca's tropes of place and space, which he uses to write himself out of prison and into the literary canon, rely upon problematically racialized and gendered archetypes that also inform neo-eugenicist discourses on Chicana/o criminality? Finally, how does Baca's gloss of contemporary permutations of the picaresque, such as testimonial narrative, introduce yet other tropes and archetypes that are central to Pinta/o discourse?

PÍCAROS, PRISON, AND PINTO PANTHEIST POETICS

As an author who became literate in prison, Baca has several precursors that distinguish his corpus from the standard minority progress tales. The most famous of these prison-educated authors, of course, is Malcolm X. Renowned for transcribing the entire dictionary, Malcolm X recast the old literary trope that linked writing with self-discovery by exploring the nation's atrocious history of race relations, namely slavery and its legacy of modern racism. By modeling the link between history, politics, and personal empowerment, *The Autobiography of Malcolm X* (1965) inspired legions of Black and other racial minority prisoners and nonprisoner authors. H. Bruce Franklin (1989) observes that prisoner writers are foundational to the evolution of American literature. He adds that many of the greatest American writers, such as Herman Melville, were shaped by their experiences with various forms of bondage, from slavery and indentured servitude to incarceration in jails and penitentiaries. Franklin situates the rise of this corpus in relation to "colonialism and large-scale mercantile capitalism in the sixteenth century," which, he adds, "have been developing as an integral part of the culture of capitalist society" (124). As the premiere capitalist nation, the United States has created a surplus population of disenfranchised and incarcerated *pícaros* whose underemployment is necessary to maximize profit. With the largest prisoner population in the world, the United States has also become the prime incubator of prisoner literature, a multigenre corpus that is larger than any other tradition and trend in the canon of American literature.

Michel Foucault (1979: 2002–2003) has observed that the panoptic architecture of the penitentiary is designed to place prisoners under the threat of constant surveillance so they censor their actions and thoughts. Yet for Baca and other prisoner authors, the prison also affords the time for materialist and metaphysical meditations on political economy and ontology. Instead of internalizing the panoptic gaze, many prisoners invert it: they co-opt the space and time to write alternative *sentences*, as it were, about crime, punishment, and overarching power relations. Baca, one of several Latina/o authors who appear in Franklin's three-hundred-entry bibliography, underscores his prisoner author genealogy in *Working in the Dark* (1992):

> I was born a poet one noon, gazing at weeds and creosoted grass at the base of a telephone pole outside my grilled cell window. The words I wrote then sailed me out of myself, and I was transported and metamorphosed into the images they made. . . . Writing bridged my divided life of prisoner and free man. (11)

Baca's writing is catalyzed in the act of gazing upon the signifiers of his imprisonment. The dissonant pairing of creosote and grass with bars and window panes foregrounds his material and metaphysical preoccupation with freedom. While Baca is renowned as a Chicana/o writer, in this scene he recognizes that he is, above all else, an author from prison and of prison. This realization is crucial to his overall poetic and, as I will show below, inevitably raises profound contradictions in his commodification as an author.

While this counterhegemonic appropriation of the prison is by no means the case for all prisoners, the proliferation of prison writers and the even larger number of nonliterary authors such as legal writ writers (also known as "jail-house lawyers"), and the corresponding volume of prisoner-authored texts and contestatory legal briefs, challenge Louis Althusser's (1971) notion of an all-encompassing ideology. Within this Repressive State Apparatus, the prisoner is always already on the verge of becoming the quintessential "bad subject": the self-consciously physical political threat to the hegemony that prisons both enable and represent. The recurrent wave of prison rebellions—especially those in the 1960s and 1970s that gave rise to prominent prisoner revolutionaries—in part lends testimony to this counterhegemonic potential. Franklin proposes a teleology of this transformation by proposing a "prisoner-as-victim-and-artist" dialectic:

> One conventional form for a convict's personal narrative was to begin by exploring his or her conversion to criminality, and then, by chronicling individual experience in crime and in prison, to arrive at some under-standing of both the self and the society that had shaped that self. (236)

The prison is the place where the *pícaro* becomes a prisoner, and the prisoner sometimes claims the power of his sentence to become a counterhegemonic Convict, as opposed to the more docile Inmate. They use their sentences to write a new narrative.

The literature through which this new subject is articulated is fundamentally defiant. Prisoner authors rarely offer protagonists who accept juridical guilt even as they unabashedly chronicle their crimes. Instead, they interrogate the circumstances and sources of their subaltern life in the free world, as well as their liminal and transformative experiences in prison. While much of prisoner literature has a visceral verité and violent quality to it—which creates part of its allure to prurient readers—virtually all of it is distinguished by its simultaneously materialist and metaphysical quality. Many prisoner authors are concerned with nothing less than a neo-Enlightenment model of human ontology.

This dual materialist and metaphysical poetic is evident in Baca's writing, especially his poetry, which is layered with gritty descriptions of prison horrors, pantheistic meditations on existence, and subtle critiques of legal discourse, settler colonialism, and contemporary racism. It is through these eclectic meditations that Baca's *pícaro* poetic persona eventually becomes a counterhegemonic Pinto philosopher. Baca's poem "The Sun on Those," which opens his 1979 inaugural collection, *Immigrants in Our Own Land* (1990: 1), foregrounds this lyrical transformation of Baca's poetic persona:

> The sun on those green palm tress, lining
> the entry road to prison. Stiff rows of husky-scaled bark,
> with a tuft of green looping blades on top, sword twirling
> in wind, always erect and disciplined, legallike. (lines 1–4)

Baca opens the poem by examining his loss of physical freedom and attendant loss of legal rights—his civic death—in relation to the lively free-flying trees, birds, and other flora and fauna that surround his penitentiary cell. The dissonance in the poem arises from the subsequent juxtaposition of images of pastoral tranquility and fertility with cellblock screams, bucketfuls of blood, "broken ribs, cutoff fingers / caught in the doors of cages," and "dead men thrown to the hoofed mud / like chewed corn husks" (lines 12–13, 14–15). His father, Baca recalls, used to plant trees to protect crops: "all that / he owned was those trees" (lines 25–26). The neo-picaresque poem ends with an epiphanic crescendo that foregrounds the younger Baca's emergent pantheistic sensibility:

> . . . I was not his only son. And when
> they captured me through the turn of my days, one was still
> free, greening more, spreading wide in wind, sheltering crows,
> and mourning our imprisonment, rejoicing our endurance, ever
> plunging its roots deeper into the face of progress and land-
> grabbers. Fences mean nothing to the trees.
> Walls and fences cannot take me away from who I am, and I
> know, as the tree knows, where I come from, who is my father. (lines 28–35)

For Baca, family is literally grounded in the earth; his brother is both a father's son as well as the symbolic and actual tree his father planted. This figural embedding of family in the land enables Baca to critique White settler colonialism (e.g., "land-grabbers") and defy them all at once (e.g., "rejoicing our endurance"). In this way, Baca explicates the depravity of imprisonment while figurally transcending it.

Baca's historicist and transcendentalist allusions also invoke the nationalist pantheism of foundational (Pan)American texts, such as Cuban José Martí's *Versos sencillos* (*Simple verses*, 1891), Walt Whitman's

Leaves of Grass (1892), and Chilean Pablo Neruda's *Canto general* (1950). For Baca, the land is both a metaphysical space and a concrete site upon which competing claims to nationhood are rehearsed. In the United States, the penitentiary is central to this process. It is a physical and political palimpsest—that is, a manifestation of state authority as well as a holding center for its antithesis. Penitentiaries and other related detention facilities have always served the racialized exercise of state power.[1] And Baca's poetic meditations have enabled him to realize that his family has been caught in this carceral:

> One day, looking up from my journal to stare absentmindedly at the cell wall, I experienced a revelation. In the wall—in the sand and mortar and stones and iron and trowel sweeps—were the life experiences and sweat of my people. It contained a mural of my people's toil, their aspirations, their pain and workmanship. I imagined my grandfather's hand smoothing out the concrete. I saw my Uncle Santiago stepping out of his truck, laughing, and I could hear him talking in his good-natured way to his friends.
>
> The iron that made the bars came from a mill in Silver City; the workers who had built the mill came from little villages on the plains. The dirt that mixed with the cement, before it was scooped up and trucked and delivered to make this wall, had been prairie soil where families camped and a woman had lain and gave birth to a child. (*A Place to Stand*, 2001: 238–239)

This lyrical pantheistic progression of previous labors on, and communions with, the land—all undertaken from prison—climaxes with his own recognition that the dust on his cell floor is also connected to the beloved earth of his hometown of Estancia a few hundred miles away. Grain by grain it is all the same sand and land. The prison thus not only represents the culmination of his previous de-territorialization but also has enabled him to lyrically explore his re-territorialization. The dirt upon which the facility is built, and the sandy dust that permeates the concrete and steel walls, is part of his patrimony as a mixed-blood Native American/Chicano prisoner. Baca underscores this neo-indigenist, pantheist sentiment when he recounts a response he gave to a Christian missionary who contacted him in prison:

> To me, God was nature, the mountains, streams, rocks, and trees, the sun and moon and stars. That was my God and always would be. (*A Place to Stand*, 2001: 188)

Baca's nationalist pantheist prison poetic is part of this personal and political recuperation. Furthermore, it sets the stage for a post-prison multigenre quest for a geographic place and social space of his own that, inevitably, situates his writing as part of the broader corpus of Pinta/o literature.

PRISONER AUTHORS, BAD-MAN HEROES, AND THE PINTO DILEMMA

The ever-growing corpus of Chicana/o prisoner writing has fueled productive critical debates about the counterhegemonic nature of Pinta/o literature (Villa 1996) and even whether a unique "Pinta/o poetic" actually exists (Candelaria 1986). Rafael Pérez-Torres (1995) notes:

> The prison within Chicano poetic expression comes to represent the embodiment of industrialization, control, and technological vacuity. It stands as the quintessential product of contemporary American society, with its dehumanizing processes, its violence, its rigidity, its sterile and murderous environment. As such, pinto poetry scrutinizes the underside of American power. (115)

Pérez-Torres adds that even as there may be common features to their writings, most contemporary Pinta/o writers—especially Baca—are too eclectic to confine within a single poetic tradition. Baca is unique, he argues, because his work "marks a significant shift in the form and function of Chicano pinto poetry" (121). This purported exceptionalism arises from Baca's fusion of the hypermasculinist bravado and tales of horror common to most prisoner writings with poignant meditative laments about human suffering that purportedly transcend the Chicana/o situation and race in general.

To a certain degree all these scholars are correct in their attempts to historicize Chicana/o Convict literature without overdetermining its form and content. But any claim that Chicana/o prisoner poetics transcend the prison poses the danger, however inadvertently, of decontextualizing the authors and texts from the material conditions in which they are produced. Even though Franklin and other scholars of American and Western prisoner literature have mapped a diverse gamut of prisoner signifying practices, they all confirm that the prison always serves as a necessary point of departure and ever-present frame of reference. Moreover, prison is constitutive of this literature. For male prisoners, the vernacular hypermasculine cultural context of the prison space is inextricable from the overbearing archetype of the masculinist bad-man-hero protagonist, for whom the penitentiary is both trauma and triumph. So even as Baca articulates a pantheist proto-nationalist discourse, his poetic is always grounded in the prison literature teleology outlined by Franklin. All of Baca's writings reveal that prison is central to his symbolic repertoire. Any exegesis that disarticulates Baca's poetic from the prison would be radically incomplete.

Such lacunas in Baca criticism arise in large part from a fixation on his ascetic lyricism. He is seen by many as the "good" Chicana/o prison poet largely because his work does not overly rely upon the gross scatological references that permeate much of male prisoner literature. Baca's writing also involves less overt vitriol against Whites than that of other Chicana/o prisoner authors, and therefore invites a wider audience. Baca's "crossover" appeal arises in large part from a recognizably "different" aesthetic vernacular lyricism. This is not to say, as fellow Pinto Ricardo Sánchez once did, that Baca "writes for Whites."[2]

Yet Baca's work does appear to pander to White stereotypes of the dangerously violent yet alluringly libidinal minority bad-man warrior hero. Baca's memoir *A Place to Stand* (2001), for instance, is replete with references to amorous encounters with women that feed into stereotypes of the Latin Lover. In *Working in the Dark* (1992), Baca even describes himself as "a teenage Chicano kid with balls so huge I was bowlegged at five, balls full of apocalypse emotion, aflame with love and bravado, grooving to the song 'Me and Mrs. Jones'" (108). This phallocentric thrust in his writing intersects with the broad corpus of male American prisoner writing, which is regularly critiqued for featuring highly masculinist protagonists who engage in graphic sexual escapades and gratuitous acts of violence.[3] While Baca does engage in candid critical explorations of his sexist socialization as a male, his poetic persona always emerges as a criminal yet seductive Latin lover. Furthermore, consistent with the trope in which the bad-man Convict-hero is figured as a literary genius, Baca sometimes overwrites prison horrors while simultaneously making the penitentiary appear as an Athenaeum-like writing workshop. Even though Baca's convoluted prose must be considered in the context of trauma literature, and perhaps even the literature of state terror—both of which involve dissonant descriptions that are as bizarre as the situations they represent are barbaric—Baca's aestheticized descriptions of prison seem calculated to appeal to a middle-class White readership:

they horrify, titillate, and please precisely because they meet these readers' Hollywood-bred expectations about prison and minority male prisoners.

Baca's corpus also involves several problematic translations. Even though he is bilingual, Baca's work is noticeably absent of the Caló and vernacular code-switching that distinguishes the work of other Pinta/o writers. Every use of Spanish in Baca's works is either translated literally or in context. Baca's tendency to translate for a monolingual English reader might be more inconsequential if he did not go so far as to translate his own first name, Santiago, into the English "Jimmy." His nickname, of course, could have less to do with audience and more with growing up in an Anglo-centric nation.

Baca's inability to adequately transform this reality is part of the problem. In a revealing January 2003 interview in *The Progressive*, Baca expresses profound ambivalence and angst over his problematic role as an underclass mixed-blood Chicano/Native American (ex)Convict literary star:

> I've got to say this. When I try to co-author something with society now, to do something about all these problems, somebody like the Lannan or the MacArthur Foundation will say, here's $500,000. It immediately, immediately screws you up. You're not supposed to give people a million dollars for what people do all over the world out of a sense of decency. You're not supposed to reward us for writing about how proud we are of being who we are. Don't fucking give us money anymore, because it's diluting the books, it's diluting the poetry, it's diluting our souls. It's making us a bunch of wimps: Oh, I know I'm going to write a really cool book about being a Chicano and about how bad life was to me, and it's going to win an international prize, and then Lannan or MacArthur is going to give me half a million dollars. That sickens me. I don't want to be rewarded for being special, because it takes away the edge from my effort, of going into the projects and working with people in a humble sort of way. Don't fucking give me money for this. (Stahura 2003: n.p.)

Yet Baca is one of the most financially successful authors and now regularly receives as much as $15,000 for a one-hour reading. As a writer whose claim to fame is measured by the distance he has traveled from illiteracy and marginality to literary stardom and canonicity, Baca is caught in a paradox: he is expected to keep marking his status as a "different" type of minority male ex-Convict through literary works that are nonetheless recognizable to a mainstream, primarily White audience whose expectations are shaped by at least two hundred years of bias.

The paternalistic commodification and reification of Baca as the palatable "convict genius" also is mapped onto other prisoner authors. In this regard, the literary market mimics the prison's ability to co-opt and contain its antithesis. The trope of writing one's self out of prison, as Joseph Bruchac notes in his seminal essay "Breaking Out with the Pen: Poetry in American Prisons" (1987), is wrought with profound contradictions even as it offers a potential means for prisoners' empowerment:

> Interestingly, it appears that the worst prison troublemakers often become
> the best writers. Further, after entering a workshop, they no longer cause
> trouble in the prison. (293)

In an illustration of the potential for the prison to reappropriate counter-hegemonic prisoner writing, Bruchac recalls overhearing the warden of San Quentin say, "Things are pretty tense down in C Block. Looks like we'd better get a poetry workshop going in there" (293). He notes that prison writing programs, and prisoner writing in general, can blunt collective political action even as they afford the possibility of early release for popular prisoner authors. This popularity, and the liberty and relative empowerment it enables, depends upon the exhibition of a unique intellect and skill that always must be featured in relation to the deprivation of the prison context in which it is cultivated. Baca, like all prisoner authors, is imprisoned, as it were, in the role of the *prisoner author*.

So while scholars have debated the existence of a Chicana/o prisoner aesthetic and poetic, they have failed to ask the even more important question about *how* it exists. Following Franklin's "victim-as-criminal-and artist" paradigm, I propose that all prisoner writing, including Pinta/o literature, is undergirded by a *prison-writing-prisoner* dialectic from which the author can never escape. In this new variation of the prisoner's dilemma, the prison will always be an overarching specter even when it is not mentioned in a text, and the writing itself always will be marked by the author's attempts to simultaneously claim and distance him- or herself from the prisoner identity. This is especially so in the highly commodified world of contemporary publishing, where vendors market an author's profile into a readily recognizable "product." Baca, like all (ex)prisoner authors, needs the prison as a reference to mark his literary fame even if his literary merit has taken him to vastly different places and spaces in his post-prison life.

MOTHERING, MOTHERFUCKERS, AND TRAGIC MESTIZOS

All picaresque tales involve movement across geographic place and social space, and for Baca's poetic persona, all past experiences and future possibilities are linked to land in a uniquely problematic way: women are at the nexus of the Pinto *pícaro*'s de-territorialization and desired re-territorialization. Despite Baca's self-censured diction, his neo-picaresque corpus is still embedded with the racialized and masculinist tropes that define much of Pinto discourse. In his two-part, semi-epic poem *Martín & Meditations on the South Valley* (1987), for instance, Baca introduces a thinly veiled autobiographical character, Martín, who presents a first-person account of his movement from trauma to redemption. The opening poem is set in the symbolically significant geographic locale of "Pinos Wells," a fictionalized subsistence ranch outside the New Mexico town of Estancia, Baca's beloved utopian birthplace:

> Blackened sheds rust
> in diablito barbs.
> In barn rafters cobwebs
> hang intricate as tablecloths
> grandma crocheted for parlors
> of wealthy Estancia ranchers.
> Now she spins silken spider eggs.
>
> My mind circles warm ashes of memories,
> the dark edged images of my history. (lines 14–22)

The land is now abandoned. All that remains are the narrator's nostalgic memories of stoic farmers who tilled fertile lands by day, and the restless teenagers who displayed their vitality by night. Martín's utopian past, we quickly learn, was replaced by a life of wandering from town to town, state to state, and institution to institution, which the author casts as an archetypal schism:

> Months after I headed West
> on I-40,

in my battered Karmen Ghia.
Desperate for a new start,
sundown in my face,
I spoke with Earth—
    I have been lost from you Mother Earth.
    No longer
    does your language of rain wear away my thoughts,
    nor your language of fresh morning air
    wear away my face,
    nor your language of roots and blossoms
    wear away my bones. (lines 143–155)

The trauma of his mother's abandonment, and her subsequent refusal to publicly acknowledge him as her son in front her new White husband, grounds this poem's otherwise cliché discussion of de-territorialization as a separation from "Mother Earth" ("I have been lost from you Mother Earth"). In *A Place to Stand*, Baca recounts how his mother once identified him to her husband as "a family friend." This de-territorialization is a real human drama and simultaneously an allegorical one. The poem ends with the pledge, "But when I return, I will become your child again" (line 156), thereby reiterating the quest motif central to all picaresque tales.

The quest is for a home, both real and metaphorical. But the narrator's reclamation of a home requires mothers to be present and absent simultaneously. He needs Mother Earth to link his quest to the land of his birth; he also uses this metaphor to usurp a human mother's unique ability to birth. This rhetorical invocation and displacement of the mother begins in the second part of the book, in which Baca's picaresque poetic persona Martín survives the orphanage and subsequent traumas of drug addiction and incarceration only to have his home—along with ten years' worth of poems—burn down. The balance of the tale involves an attempt to rebuild his house atop the ashes of the old one:

We started on the house.
At first there was the black mass
of garbage—
    loading burned rubbish
    en la truckita. (Part XXVII, lines 1–5)

The actual construction of the new building involves the felling of an ancient tree, an act that illuminates the painful realities of the life cycle and also recalls the pantheism in Baca's earlier poems. Martín understands this cycle through the labor of his hands, where he and a collective of other male outcasts rebuild atop the remnants of the old foundation, plank by plank, nail by nail. The narrator, who describes his new house as "my finest poem" (line 69), arrives at a unique epiphany in the next and final part:

> My house burned
> > and we re-built it.
> I felt hurt, yes . . .
> and grieved with the shovel of ashes,
> the ashes heaped on the truck,
> and drove it to the dump with a numb sense of duty
> I had to do,
> full of loss and grief, and joy
> that I was able to create
> > another house,
> > a child in its own image.
> I gave birth to a house.
> It came, cried from my hands, sweated from my body,
> ached from my gut and back. I was stripped down to the essential
> force in my life—create a better world, a better me,
> out of love. I became a child of the house,
> and it showed me
> the freedom of a new beginning. (Part XXVIII, lines 19–36,
> ellipses in original)

At this point, Baca's autobiographical poetic persona, Martín, refuses to accept his misfortune and subordination as natural consequences of his actions or as preordained by a divine power. Instead, he re-creates the past with his own hands in order to reshape his present and his future—all in the same place. Significantly, it is the narrator, as opposed to his biological mother or even Mother Earth, who "births" the new house (line 30). And, equally as significant, he is birthed by it (line 134). Women are entirely removed from the creative process.

This subtle yet deliberate effacement of women in *Martín & Meditations on the South Valley* is more pronounced in Baca's later poetry and prose, in which the eugenicist trope of the tragic mestizo occupies a central discursive space in his linkage of land and liberty. Baca understands that since the immigration of Europeans to the Americas, race relations in the southwestern United States have persisted in a state of chronic tension punctuated by atrocities committed by Whites against Native Americans and other non-White minorities. This theme of White racism has been a feature of Chicana/o literature since its inception in the mid-eighteenth century, which is not surprising since Chicana/os were constituted as a people as a direct result of the U.S. occupation of one-half of Mexico's national territory in a war that the United States provoked with this goal. By rehearsing the trope of a turbulently contested land, Baca aligns himself with Chicana/o literature's historical and political focus on racial conflict.

Unfortunately, like many Chicana/o cultural nationalist authors, Baca also invokes the figure of the tragic mestizo along with related misogynist analogues such as La Malinche.[4] He presents scenarios whereby racially mixed characters, as well as any who attempt to cross the racial divide through marriage or even friendship, are doomed to failure. This is the essence of the tragic mestizo trope. And for the most part, Baca blames women. By doing so, he engages the personal trauma of his particular family history, most notably his mother's abandonment of her dark-skinned children and her apparent attempt to "pass" as White by marrying a White male and moving to a White-majority suburb. Baca also seeks to evoke the historical trauma of European and then White American colonization in the lands of his indigenous ancestors, events that indelibly mark the Native American and Chicana/o experiences. The results are mixed in more ways than one.

Baca's overdetermined racial teleologies are simultaneously empowering and disempowering. In *A Place to Stand* (2001), for instance, he lays claim to place and social space in the title of the text and also in his discussion of his family home in Estancia, which roughly translates as a "room," "farm," "ranch," and, in some contexts, "place." As in the biblical Eden that serves as an allegorical reference to the traditional picaresque tale, Baca's link to this archetypal home is disrupted by a woman's "treachery." Baca's poetic persona begins his indictment by recalling how he first found refuge and reverie under his family's meager wood-frame shack:

I often bellied into the crawl space under our shack to be alone in my own world. I felt safe in this peaceful refuge. The air was moist and smelled like apples withering in a gunnysack in the cellar at my Uncle Max's ranch in Willard. A stray dog might be waiting when I entered. Happy to see me, he would roll on the cool earth, panting, his tail wagging, and lick my face.

> After playing with him, I'd lie on the dirt and close my eyes and float out of my skin into stories my grandfather, Pedro Baca, told me—about those of our people who rode horses across the night prairie on raiding parties, wearing cloth over their heads, as they burned outsiders' barns, cut fences, and poisoned wells, trying to expel the gringo intruders and recover the land stolen from our people. (7)

This refuge was traumatically interrupted one day as he witnessed, through a gap in the floorboard, his mother having an extramarital sexual affair with the White American man who would later marry and then murder her. In Baca's multitext exploration of this affair and subsequent interracial marriage, his mother is marked for having betrayed her family's rule against marrying a poor half-Indian Mexican, whom she later divorced. She also is condemned by her son, who recalls her other "betrayals." Even before she abandoned her children, Baca recounts how his mother would "point to White-skinned, blue-eyed children and say I should be like them" (2001: 14). This racial schism is further exemplified in Baca's memoir through his comparisons of the rural Mexican neighborhood of his birth to the largely White suburbs to which his mother fled with her new White husband. In *Martín & Meditations on the South Valley* and later writings, the barrio is described as utopian, whereas the White-majority suburbs are characterized as a "prison." This dichotomy of place and space is a touchstone in Baca's writing. His de-territorialization and resultant efforts at re-territorialization inevitably must go through and over women such as his mother, and also around and away from Whites—especially the White men who befriended but then raped his brother, and the White man who married then murdered his mother.

Baca's mapping of the racial binaries that structure the experience for America's indigenous-descent population—and all Americans for that matter—also emerges in the literary representations of his life on the road and in prison. Symptomatically, Baca's incarceration was facilitated by his drug-dealing partner, whom he describes in *A Place to Stand* as a "blond, blue eyed Kentucky countryboy" (72). This same White friend is revealed to have been a traitor even before his arrest and courtroom testimony against Baca, when Baca discovers that he had had an affair with Baca's Mexican American fiancée and subsequently became her new boyfriend. As before, the union of White males and Mexican American females presages tragedy. In this instance, it comes in the form of an FBI sting operation and subsequent arrest of the drug-dealing duo of Baca and his White "friend." To further accentuate the racial divide,

Baca recalls in *A Place to Stand* how he once performed a favor for his former partner by intervening to save another White prisoner from an assassination contract placed by the Mexican Mafia. As a result, Baca allegedly became the new target of the prison assassination plot. Instead of gratitude for this favor, Baca's White ex-partner gravitated towards the Aryan Nation prison gang in the racially stratified penitentiary. In a prison encounter, this man purportedly tells Baca:

> You're leaving soon, aren't you. I shot that FBI and saved your life and you're getting out while I've got a shitload of more years . . . I'm glad, because if you weren't I'd probably have to kill you. (252)

Despite Baca's repeated retort that the racial segregation and animosity that structures the social order of the U.S. penitentiary is "bullshit!" (252), he cannot dismiss the realities of discrimination and segregation in prison and out. In Baca's literary landscape, past racial injustices not only are reflected in the eclectic and beautiful colonial architecture that he notices throughout his travels in the southwestern United States, but also in the corresponding hostile neocolonial interpersonal relationships that permeate the entire region. This persistent dialectic between *mestizaje* and segregation compounds the historical tragedy that Baca reveals as the archetypal U.S. experience. For mixed-blood people like himself, life in this land is a living hell. Moreover, in his literary landscape, race is a historical reality and a barrier that, when crossed, ushers in profound tragedy.

As if he were trying to reconcile the mass appeal of his books with the static racial binary of his symbolic system, in recent interviews Baca has attempted to distance himself from what he calls his past "racial hatreds." But his proposed racial synthesis is overly nostalgic, far too convenient, and still contradictory. For instance, in charting his own development and understanding of the racial divides that still haunt the United States, Baca recalls in the conclusion to *A Place to Stand* how he once wandered into a Catholic church near his birthplace soon after his release from prison. He was surprised to find one entire side of the church occupied by Native Americans and the other side occupied by "regular" (non–Native American) parishioners. He realized that he had stumbled upon a special mass decreed by the Pope, in which the Catholic Church asked for forgiveness from the indigenous people for its brutal missionary and colonization activities over the past five hundred years. In a crescendo characteristic of the pantheistic tone in Baca's earlier writing, the narrator imagines himself at his own baptism, and begins to cry:

> And suddenly I began to forgive them for what they had done or had not
> done. I forgave myself for all my mistakes and for all I had done to hurt
> others. I forgave the world for how it had treated us. (264)

As he leaves the church, a soft rain begins to fall and the bells chime as
he thinks to himself that he is "truly free at last" (264), thereby invoking Martin Luther King's famous speech on racial tolerance. The still-
resonant history of the European and White American "conquests" of
Native America and the possibility of rapprochement between the two
groups in the southwestern United States ultimately merge in his mestizo
body. Yet the pews remained segregated.

Ironically, Baca proposes an ecclesiastical model of racial justice
even though his writing continues to revolve around racial and gender
binaries. Moreover, this climactic episode involves his "reconciliation" in
church with *the Church* in a scene that is characteristic of the medieval
picaresque, where the *pícaro* repents and appears to accept Catholic
dogma justifying social stratification. Whereas some medieval picaresque
tales, such as the anonymously authored *La vida de Lazarrillo de Tormes*
(1554), suggest an ideological critique of Church hypocrisy, Baca's closing
scene deliberately offers closure and accepts the legitimacy of the Church's
ability to resolve the conflicts it helped create.[5] Baca is thus caught in yet
another paradox: he successfully appropriates the picaresque genre as a
vehicle that accommodates his own personal traumas and triumphs to levy
historical materialist critique, with a special attention to race relations.
Yet his selection of a genre that, on the surface, appears appropriate,
degenerates into a reinforcement of the racial, gender, and class binaries
he apparently seeks to undermine.

TESTIMONIO AND THE PINTO INTELLECTUAL

Baca's problematic corpus can also be read as a contemporary gloss of
testimonio, or testimonial narrative, a multigenre literary mode that John
Beverley (1996) has identified as a modern counterhegemonic extension
of the picaresque tale. But there are profound differences between the
picaresque and the *testimonio*:

> The situation of the narrator in testimonio is one that must be representative
> of a social class or group; in the picaresque novel, by contrast, a collective
> social predicament such as unemployment and marginalization is
> experienced and narrated as a personal destiny.

> The "I" that speaks to us in the picaresque or first-person novel
> is in general precisely the mark of a difference or antagonism with the
> community, in the picaresque the *Ichform* . . . of the self-made man:
> hence the picaresque's cynicism about human nature, its rendering
> of lower-class types as comic, as opposed to the egalitarian reader-
> character relation implied by both the novel and testimonio. The
> narrator in testimonio, on the other hand, speaks for, or in the name
> of, a community or group, approximating in this way the symbolic
> function of the epic hero, without at the same time assuming his
> hierarchical and patriarchal status. (27)

Despite the limits of Baca's adaptation of the picaresque, it nonetheless enables him to synthesize a semi-collectivist literary persona and practice. He may malign some of his subaltern characters (especially women), but he consistently proclaims his allegiance with them.

Even as Baca reifies difference through the trope of the tragic mestizo, his corpus is undergirded by *testimonio*'s goal of developing circumscribed cross-class alliances.[6] This imperative is foregrounded in "I Am Sure of It" (1990: 10), one of Baca's earliest poems from prison. In this poem, Baca's autobiographical poetic persona is shaken from his cellblock solitude by a guard who calls out his prison identification number, "32581," and then leaves a letter between the bars:

> It's from a magazine I sent three poems to.
> On the envelope in bold black letters,
> it's rubber-stamped, FUNDS RECEIVED . . . AMOUNT $10.
> I open the letter and read the first paragraph.
> They usually don't pay for poems, they say,
> but wanted to send a little money in this case,
> to help me out. My poems were beautiful,
> and would be published soon. (lines 9–16)

The letter, money, and positive appraisal of his writing come as a shock to the novice poet:

> Holding this letter in my hand,
> standing in the middle of my cell,
> in my boxer shorts, it's now, times like this,
> rapt in my own unutterable surprise, I wonder about people. . . .
> (Lines 17–20)

This sense of wonder eventually leads to broader reflections on human ontology. The title foreshadows an epiphany, which Baca states in the staccato rhythm and passionate voice that defines much of his early verse: "This is life / even in prison, respecting each other, helping each other, / close or far away, it doesn't matter, I am sure of it" (lines 74–76).

Baca's corpus is more of a gloss of the testimonial narrative genre rather than real *testimonio* due to its insistence on plot closure at the end of *A Place to Stand*, and his subsequent move to short fiction in *The Importance of a Piece of Paper* (2004). But his multigenre, neo-picaresque corpus nonetheless assumes a testimonial-esque posture in this poem through his protagonist's meditation on solidarity across classes and other social groups. Baca recognizes the possibility of these alliances despite his persistent rendering of them as unavoidably tragic. The poem "I Am Sure of It" illustrates how Baca similarly engages in metacritical meditations on the role of writing and commodification, and, more importantly, how these market forces may enable coalition building across otherwise insurmountable boundaries, such as the walls of a maximum security prison or even more daunting obstacles such as race.

The commodification of Baca's work, and the attendant overdeter-mination of him as a "prisoner author," ultimately is empowering: he gets paroled, published, and paid in a lucrative post-prison writing career. But there is more. For Baca, writing—whether it be a divorce decree, commitment warrant, courtroom sentence, or death certificate—has always been invested with the hegemonic exercise of power, and his meticulous attempt to understand his social location has led him to finally understand that the written word can also work for the underclass. This is a cliché, yet it still remains a fundamental trope in prisoner, ethnic, feminist, and postcolonial literatures. Equally important, the metacritical testimonial text enables the subaltern author to address personal and political limitations, which Baca does in *Working in the Dark* as he begins to recognize his socialization as a misogynist (69–70).

Baca's reclamation of the written word thus introduces yet another important rhetorical device in *testimonio*: the troping of truth. As I have shown elsewhere (Olguín 2002), testimonial truth is complex: it refers both to factual information as well as to the Marxist notion of objective truth about the structural realities of political economy. In an illustration of *testimonio*'s filiation with the picaresque and the *Bildungsroman*, facts are not as important as the process of *concientización*, or political awakening. But in contrast to the picaresque and bildungsroman, which inevitably validate the status quo, *testimonio* seeks to map the political awakening of the subaltern-subject-in-struggle in order to educate, politicize, and motivate the reader to change "the system." Thus, a testimonial text can, at times, represent a historical event through embellishment. Like the African American slave narrative, the testimonial text does not necessarily intend to reveal all the factual details about a protagonist's flight and fight for freedom, which actually could undermine the efforts by exposing necessary secrets about insurgent solidarity networks. Instead, testimonial writing is at the service of a greater truth—objective and subjective truth about political economy and the attendant inequities in a capitalist society that illustrate the need for revolutionary change. *Testimonio* is concerned with rewriting—and thus righting—historical materialist wrongs.

Similarly, Baca's poetry and prose gesture towards a historicist and, at times, materialist rendering of his personal traumas. In *A Place to Stand*, Baca recalls how he discovered the unreliable yet cathartic value of memory and re-memorizing while in a prison isolation cell:

> The vivid reality of my reveries made these imaginary excursions so forceful it scared me. It became much more than idly remembering this or that. *I'd play a memory like a song, over and over, adding this or subtracting that, changing something in a scene or re-creating a certain episode and enhancing it with additional details.* Fearful I might be losing my sanity, sometimes when I came back to the present, I'd call out my name in the cell just to hear it or bang the steel door until my hands hurt. But, whatever was happening, I felt a wholesome fulfillment that delighted me, even in this dark pit. Memories structured my day and filled my cell. It was as if all the sorrow, fear, and regret I'd carried in my bones suddenly was swept away and my heart lifted itself into a realm of innocence before all sadness and tragedy happened. In my imagination I was safe and joyous again. The darkness of my cell glowed with the bright dawn light of Estancia. The walls of my cell slowly disintegrated into trees and a pond and village people coming out of their houses. *The ritual of re-creating my young life repeated itself every day after meals, almost without effort.* (139, emphasis added)

His writing reads as a retort, or an attempt to right the distortions and incomplete accounts offered in official "pieces of paper." Like other *testimonialistas*, Baca is concerned with rearticulating himself onto the past and re-articulating this past in order to intervene in the present.

Baca's attempt to revisit and rewrite/right old traumas, however, has become controversial because of his apparently selective and inconsistent rendition of facts. Ricardo Sánchez and Raúl Salinas have raised questions about the veracity of Baca's depictions of prison life. But as scholars and activists have observed about the infamous "Menchú controversy," this charge is, in part, overstated.[7] After all, the testimonial mode involves literary renditions of events elaborated, as needed, in an extra-textual effort to help remedy perceived social and political wrongs. Scholars of *testimonio* have noted that the testimonial text oftentimes claims the authority of an alternative courtroom testimony in which the facts are *re*-presented to be *represented* in a fuller context. Accordingly, Baca's multivolume accounts of his mother's death sometimes are recounted verbatim from text to text but also are *re*-presented through the strategic rearrangement of circumstances and interpretations of the significance of her death. In *A Place to Stand*, her death is identified as a murder by a racist White patriarch who shot her in the face, while in *Martín & Meditations of the South Valley* it is presented either as a "suicide" or the result of her "trying to be white" (75). Even though Baca's different accounts vacillate between a murder and a suicide, the fact remains that his mother died, and, equally as important, he represents her death as resulting from her violation of various cultural taboos, especially the ones forbidding "miscegenation" and women's independence from men.

The apparent discrepancies about his incarceration—sometimes he recalls serving five years, other times it is seven—do not necessarily reveal "lies," since Baca did serve a prison sentence. The number of years in prison is not as significant as what prison reveals about society and, more importantly, the role of prison in the transformation of the Inmate-cum-Convict's abjection and subsequent empowerment. This is not to say that there is no danger in the testimonial's alternative representation of facts. Baca's descriptions of past tumultuous relationships with some women raise the specter of spin doctoring. And he never completely disavows his previous use of tropes of female propriety to describe his mother, which ironically are the same ones that had been mapped onto Pintas such as Modesta Avila. But Baca neither celebrates nor condones his past criminal activities or attitudes. Rather, he attempts to situate them in the broader context of his familial and community contexts, especially the lingering legacy of European and American colonialism and attendant male privilege.

Another redeeming feature of Baca's writing may also arise from authorial intent. Baca's writing, like the writing of many *testimonialistas* and prisoner authors, is concerned with self-discovery and with his individual re-articulation onto a collective body politic. He illustrates how writing can involve a remaking of the self and the society in which this individual and the broader social group have been debased. Because of this didactic intent, the retelling of the experience is equally as important as the actual experience. In this overall literary-politico enterprise, the reconstruction of an individual's past becomes as essential as the construction of a community's future. Indeed, "giving testimony" becomes the condition for imagining that new future.

There is also a cathartic dimension to Baca's writing. In *A Place to Stand*, he recounts one of his many prison epiphanies:

> I was a witness, not a victim. I was a witness for those who for one reason or another would never have a place of their own, would never have the opportunity to make their lives stable enough because resources weren't available or because they just could not get it together. My job was to witness and record the "it" of their lives, to celebrate those who don't have a place in this world to stand and call home. For those people, my journals, poems, and writings are home. My pen and heart chronicle their hopes, doubts, regrets, loves, despairs, and dreams. I do this partly out of selfishness, because it helps to heal my own impermanence, my own despair. My role as witness is to give voice to the voiceless and hope to the hopeless, of which I am one. (244)

Similar to the medieval picaresque antihero's displacement by the Renaissance-era notion of the self-made Man of Letters, Baca's highly autobiographical persona also is redeemed and remade at each retelling. Like other *testimonialistas*, Baca's troping of truth thus enables him to reclaim the symbolic and material power associated with self-representation, and this has a transgressive resonance given that the bulk of his work revolves around an attempt to rehistoricize his picaresque-cum-prisoner persona.

Despite his complex, contradictory, and problematic symbolic system, Baca articulates a didactic, antiracist, anticolonialist, and immanently collectivist poetic persona: a Chicano prisoner, or Pinto, intellectual. Baca recalls that his own *concientización* as a Pinto intellectual was facilitated by an elder Chicano Convict, Chelo, whom he met in prison:

> He [Chelo] began teaching me Chicano slang, Mexican/Indian words originating from Mayans, Olmecs, Aztecs. When combined, these words

created our own distinct Chicano language, a language truer to expressing and describing my experience. In his early juvie days he had learned from older cons how to tattoo, and he'd done it for more than twenty years. His tattoos were like a walking library. He explained the significance of the turquoise Quetzal bird with expanding wings on his right shoulder, its feathers radiating red and blue rays in all direction. It was an Aztec sacred bird, its feathers more honored and valuable than gold or jewels. They were worn in priest headdresses and warrior shields. The jaguar, he said, lifting his arm to reveal a jaguar whose legs and head moved when Chelo flexed and unflexed his muscles, was a sacred animal. Holding class while we walked around the field, he shared with me the legends and folklore passed down to him from "pintos," Chicano prisoners. (223)

Through this recollection of a subaltern cadre of Pinto elders, Baca introduces an immanently collectivist Pinto permutation of Gramsci's "organic intellectual." Baca's meditations on political economy through oftentimes painful (though cathartic) meditations on his own personal depravity are crucial to this study on Pinta/o discourse because they enable a more honest assessment of an otherwise iconic figure—the Pinta/o—who has existed within two discursive poles: the pathological villain or victimized noble social bandit. But as noted, Baca's masculinist and misogynist metaphors, as well as his binary racial allegories, underscore the difficulty in ascribing an unqualified assessment of the Pinto intellectual's counterhegemonic status. In subsequent chapters, I further examine various models of Pinto and Pinta intellectuals through attention to the performative dimensions of their agency.

PART TWO

Embodied Discourses

CHAPTER 3

Declamatory Pinto Poetry

The Masculinist Poetics and Materialist Politics of Ricardo Sánchez's Poesía de Chingazos

> When in the course of human events, it becomes necessary for one people to dissolve the political bands which have connected them with another, and to assume among the powers of the earth, the separate and equal station to which the Laws of Nature and Nature's God entitle them, a decent respect to the opinions of mankind requires that they should declare the causes which impel them to the separation.
>
> —U.S. Declaration of Independence (1776)

> You have the right to remain silent. Anything you say can and will be used against you in a court of law . . .
>
> —"The Miranda Rights" (*Miranda vs. Arizona*, 1966)

> pues a la madre con la ley . . .
> i'm a city dude, ese,
> un pachuco del pasiente . . .
> i don't believe in god,
> society, nor pinches reglas . . .[1]
>
> —Ricardo Sánchez, "Otra vez" (1971)

THE PINTO DIALOGIC VOICE

In Ricardo Sánchez's poem "Otra vez" (Again), the author's autobiographical poetic persona, the Pinto poet, deploys various modes of resistance to his physical and psychological imprisonment. It is the "long hot summer" of 1967, and Sánchez finds himself in the Ramsey I Penitentiary Farm of the Texas Department of Corrections (TDC):

> otra vez, again
> and again and again,
> hated words
> of meskin, damn dirty meskin,

can't work, won't work,
won't give you nothin' to eat . . . (lines 1–6)

Sánchez's polyphonic soliloquy continues with the prisoner's subaltern voice of defiance claiming its space beside the jailer's:

pues a la madre con la ley,
but i won't pick
their goddamn goofyass cotton
[. . .]
for the judge he said
i sentence you, ricardo,
to do twelve years,
he didn't say a thing 'bout
rehabilitation through cotton picking. (9–11, 29–33)

In this dramatic dialogue with his internalized White jailer, a motif that first distinguished Sánchez's authorial voice in his foundational 1971 anthology of Chicano poetry, *Canto y grito mi liberación (. . . y lloro mis desmadrazgos . . .)—I Sing and Shout My Liberation (. . . and cry my motherfuckin' asswhippin's . . .)*—the author's autobiographical poetic persona has plucked out the quotation marks with the very same fingers he refuses to animate into picking his assigned row of cotton.[2] Ironically, the nameless jailer's bigotry and repression persist, and are even immortalized, through Sánchez's defiant words. In much the same way, the prisoner poet's psychological, spiritual, and even corporeal survival depends upon the concrete rebellion about which he writes. Sánchez's "liberation" thus lies in-between the objective reality of his imprisonment and the defiant poetry he writes from prison. *Liberación*—Sánchez's metonym for Chicano identity—is actualized by the sustained performance of a conflicted heteroglossia. For Sánchez, the Pinto is the quintessential heteroglot subject: as a self-consciously oppositional yet still incarcerated person, he personifies what some have theorized as Chicana/o ontology. Drawing from Mikhail Bakhtin (1981), Alfred Arteaga (1994) has proposed the Chicana/o as an "intercultural heteroglot" subject formed in the nexus of several coexisting dialogues and languages that include English, Spanish, and Caló. The Pinto, whose own discourse is violently embedded with its antithesis, illustrates this dialectical tension.

Despite the prison poet's claim to authorship and authority in the poem "Otra vez," the fact remains that Sánchez's Pinto poetic persona is still confined behind the electrified barbed-wire fences of the Ramsey I Penitentiary Farm. This prison facility is one of several rural prison plantations transposed atop the Mexican ranches expropriated by White settlers after the Texas-Mexican and U.S.-Mexico Wars from 1835–1836 and 1846–1848, respectively. The voices of White police investigators, prosecutors, judges, jailers, and even mercenaries and military historians are all inscribed in Sánchez's voice. These polyphonic imprints frame the oppositional potential of his verse: they prefigure the Pinto's mimetic prison epistemology and political praxis. In this poem and others the Pinto poet tropes his Chicano Convict body to propose sexual violence as power. His challenge to the ritualized emasculation proposed by the Texas Department of Corrections regimen of forced labor, starvation, and physical and psychological torture, which is represented in "Otra vez," is also ritualized through his vernacular shout, or *grito*, "pues a la madre con la ley" ("well fuck the law"), which underwrites a violently eroticized embodied poetics and politics. By articulating both his subordination and resistance in terms of *el desmadre*—a key element in the subtitle to his first collection of poetry—Sánchez invokes the misogynist Mexican and Chicana/o archetypal rape motif. This *desmadre*—roughly translated as "motherfuckin' asswhippin'"—refers to the violent epic subjugation of Mesoamerica by Spanish *conquistadores* in the sixteenth century. As noted in the preceding chapter, this epic conquest is troped through truncated misogynist figures of Mexican womanhood known as *las tres Marías,* or three Marias—La Malinche, La Llorona, and La Virgen de Guadalupe. Like Baca and other Chicana/o cultural nationalist authors from the 1960s and 1970s, Sánchez figures Mexican, Chicana/o, and his personal histories through the problematic notion of "fallen" women's sexuality. That is, Sánchez's model of Chicana/o identity is based upon a distinctly gendered Chicana/o body that is always marked by sexual violence; he seeks to invert the abusive exercise of power by figuratively and physically becoming the one "on top."

Beyond serving as a prototype of the misogynist and problematic Chicana/o cultural nationalist poetics of the era, however, Sánchez's masculinist corpus also is significant for privileging the status of the eroticized, racialized, and historically situated brown body in the performance of Chicana/o identity. Even as Sánchez's verse traffics in troubling sexist clichés, it gestures towards a historical materialist rupture from the even more essentialist conceptions of Chicana/o identity proposed by his contemporaries in the Chicana/o Movement, especially Alurista, the neo-indigenist poet renowned for inaugurating the syncretic

Chicana/o cultural nationalist ritual poetry known as *flor y canto* (flower and song).[3] Sánchez's articulation of a violently oppositional and performative *canto y grito*—song and shout—deliberately challenges the celebratory transcendental ethnopoetic model proposed in Alurista's foundational collection, *Floricanto en Aztlán* (Flower and song in Aztlán) (1971). Alurista's 100-poem collection serves Sánchez as a negative frame of reference for his own debut collection, published a few months later. Rather than Alurista's contrived poetic performances involving Gregorian-like chant, esoteric uses of Nahuatl vocabulary, and indigenous costumes through which the poet assumed the role of the shaman-priest-poet, Sánchez deployed his eroticized and criminalized Pachuco and Pinto body not just as metaphor or artifice, but as a violently lyricized poetic and political medium. His body became a weapon.

Ricardo Sánchez is one of the most denounced Chicano poets because of this masculinist symbolic system. He nonetheless is an icon in prisoner literature and continues to cast a long shadow in contemporary Chicana/o poetry due to his successful fusion of the vernacular with the canonical. His nuanced use of the body as metaphor and mechanism also serves as another touchstone in my mapping of Pinta/o poetics. Whereas Modesta Avila's persecution, subsequent counterhegemonic agency, and emergent iconic status are distinctly gendered as female, and Jimmy Santiago Baca's multigenre, neo-picaresque self-actualization narrative is articulated through and atop problematic archetypes of the treacherous woman and tragic mestizo, Sánchez's agency and identity are actualized by situating his corpus between these two poles: the subordinated (read feminized) and the conveniently liberated hybrid (read masculine). Ultimately, his poetic is reductive, misogynist, and homophobic. Yet it is consistent with broader male prisoner discourses on power and identity, and therefore demands closer scrutiny in any study of Pinta/o discourse.

Given the corrupt nature of all phallocentric models of power, can there be any potential political virtue in Sánchez's verse? I argue that the value of Sánchez's verse arises from its adumbration of what later will be codified in Chicana/o discourse as "embodied knowledge," or what Cherríe Moraga (1983) would later propose as a "theory in the flesh."[4] While the body, as a metaphor, always has figured prominently in Chicana/o verse, Sánchez is one of the first post-1960s Chicano poets to model Chicano identity as an oppositional consciousness grounded in bodily experience, knowledge, and the performance of power. His corpus—which spans from 1959 to his death in 1996—thus serves as a benchmark in the genealogy of Chicana/o embodied poetics that includes the mid-nineteenth-century epic heroic *corrido*, in which Chicano ballad-eers sang of heroic social bandits rebelling with their pistols in their hands; the early twentieth-century lyric verse of the Tejana revolutionist poet Sara Estela Ramirez, who celebrates the regenerative potential of the female body as well as militating on behalf of the anarchist tendency of the Mexican Revolution; and also more contemporary poets, such as Bernice Zamora, Alma Villanueva, Gloria Anzaldúa, Ana Castillo, Francisco Alarcón, and Sandra Cisneros.[5] With the exception of performance artists such as Guillermo Gómez-Peña and new poetry slammers such as Amalia Ortiz, whose scatological gestures form an integral part of their poetic performances, few Chicana/o poets so thoroughly integrate their corporeal selves into an embodied *performative* poetic as Ricardo Sánchez does in his declamatory, or *engagé*, format. Indeed, Sánchez can be described as one of the forerunners of the neo-Beat aesthetic of poetry slams. Sánchez's *Canto y grito* not only consists of lyrical soliloquies and populist refrains, erotic overtures and shouts, epic curses and threats of actual physical violence—it literally is composed and performed through them. Herein lies its uniqueness, or rather, its virtue—and, of course, its vice.

Sánchez's nimble use of code-switching and the eclectic Pachuco and related Pinto patois, Caló—along with the *engagé* deployment of his huge, powerful, and threatening physical presence—imbues his work with a complexity and importance that only recently has begun to be validated, even as it is still largely misunderstood and grossly undertheorized. The 2000 publication of *The Ricardo Sánchez Reader*, edited by Arnoldo Carlos Vento and Luís Leal, followed the purchase and permanent housing of Ricardo Sánchez's archives by Stanford University in 1992. These events mark the academic canonization of a Chicano poet who always has been a fixture in Chicana/o literature. Most discussions of Sánchez's complex corpus, however, reproduce misconceptions and misappraisals of him, his work, and his varied genealogies. Juan Bruce-Novoa's neo-formalist account in *Chicano Poetry: A Response to Chaos* (1982) not only overaestheticizes Sánchez's *ars poetica*, but individualizes and pathologizes it:

> Sánchez seeks to inscribe himself in the written language and tradition of the society he pictures as chaotic, hopeful that his voice will survive, though mindful of the futility of relying on others and the eventual destruction of the page itself. (158)

Bruce-Novoa further argues that for Sánchez, there is "no escape, just constant conflict," which suggests a nihilism that bespeaks the Pinto poet's active involvement in utopian social movements through militancy in organizations that range from the Brown Berets, a Chicana/o paramilitary organization, to La Resistencia, the immigrant organizing arm of the Maoist Revolutionary Communist Party. This pathologizing is reiterated in Miguel López's *Chicano Timespace: The Poetry and Politics of Ricardo Sánchez* (2001). López writes that for Sánchez, the "universal struggle for dignity and freedom . . . will become a tragic one as he becomes aware that it cannot be fully achieved" (6). Even Rafael Pérez-Torres misappraises Sánchez's work when he argues that some of Sánchez's poems are "grandiose" and "too melodramatic to be effective":

> At the same time, Sánchez's poetry, beyond the tediousness of its often bombastic style, is weakened by its overgeneralized view of Chicano life. The specificity and vibrancy of the different experiences his poetry seeks to evoke is lost in a tendency toward sweeping pronouncements about the overall conditions of humanity, illustrated by the dehumanizing experiences of the pinto. (1995: 117)

Ramón Saldívar (1990), José Limón (1992), Leticia Garza-Falcón (1998), and Louis Mendoza (2001) all have convincingly argued that Mexican American and Chicana/o writing is counterhegemonic because it explicates local events as the performance of global political economy. I submit that critics of Sánchez's work fail to recognize that his principal virtue as a poet and activist is his very tendency to globalize the significance of his particular—though not at all unique or individual—experiences as a Pinto. In contrast to Cordelia Candelaria's assertion that "it is a mistake to consider [Pinto poetry as] a distinct stylistic school identifiable by a unique poetics" (1986: 54), I propose that Sánchez's phallocentric Pinto poetry—his *Poesía de chingazos* (or, "Motherfuckin' asswhippin' poetics")—provides a coherent, though contradictory, model of an embodied ethnopoetics that is undoubtedly linked to, but also distinct from, other ethnopoetic practices in American, Chicana/o, and Latin American literatures.

Following Raúl Villa's linkage of Pinto poetry to the epic heroic *corrido*, which he argues is a "cultural taproot . . . providing models of social criticism, thematic strategies, and narrative or generic conventions that are adapted and transformed by socially critical pinto poets" (1996: 114), this chapter explicates how Ricardo Sánchez delves even further into the Chicana/o political unconscious. More importantly, Sánchez's poetry and related writings enable us to map the potential, and potential limits, that this rhetorical strategy entails for Pinto culture and agency. As I will show here and in the subsequent chapter, Pinto poetry is infused with a global significance articulated through highly localized Chicano barrio and prison signifying practices. These include the tattoo and graffiti art as well as the foul-mouthed, dozens-like diatribes known as *echando madres*—a form of cursing that literally translates as "spewing mothers"—which is based on the central trope of *el desmadre*, the epic rape.[6] Thus imprinted with Chicana/o history and vernacular culture, Ricardo Sánchez's ethnopoetics collapses the mythic into the material, the historical into the personal, the epistemological into the practical—all at the site of his own Chicano Convict body.

EL DESMADRAZGO: CHICANA/O HISTORY, GENEALOGY, AND POLITICAL CRITIQUE

In order to understand the nature and significance of Sánchez's problematic embodied ethnopoetics, one must consider the principal site from which, and through which, his verse was articulated: the prison archipelagos of violence. The poem "Otra vez" is exemplary. It was composed in the summer of 1967 while Sánchez was serving a twelve-year sentence in the Texas Department of Corrections for armed robbery, along with a concurrent one- to twenty-five-year sentence from which he had been paroled by the California Department of Corrections several years earlier.[7] Both penalties were being administered in the pre-reform (pre-1979) Texas prison system known to Chicana/o prisoners simply and succinctly as "la Tejana" (the Texan joint). In their study on the decades-long prison reform movement in Texas, *Texas Prisons: The Walls Came Tumbling Down* (1987), Steve J. Martin and Sheldon Ekland-Olson note that this prison system, the largest and one of the most profitable in the country at the time, was notorious for the frequent and unregulated use of physical violence by its guards—"attitude tune-ups" or "ass-whippings"—to humiliate, coerce, and very often kill prisoners (23–24). Michel Foucault (1979) has shown that throughout the history of the Western prison, such brutal penality was inextricably linked to political economy, specifically the upward transfer of wealth. Various case studies of convict-lease systems in U.S. penitentiaries reveal that even as the need for prisoner labor is always fluctuating and changing, the ritualistic emasculation endured by Sánchez frequently undergirded punishment-for-profit schemas.[8] Such forced labor was mandatory and virtually unavoidable due to the cruelly efficient design of the panoptic penitentiary. The goal of total containment through the all-seeing panopticon is a material reality in prison; it is also a fundamental goal of U.S. jurisprudence. The prison's function of collapsing the desired subject into the real economic imperatives in the form of the disciplined and re-formed model "Inmate"—a profit-producing medium—is predicated upon the juridical "sentence," the new narrative articulated in years. Contrary to "reform" discourses that, on occasion, emerge among penologists, the prisoner is not a potential bourgeois agent, but a threat to the bourgeoisie that must be contained or destroyed altogether. Violence, discursive and extra-discursive, is inscribed throughout this entire process of re-formation.

H. Bruce Franklin (1989) and others have shown that the brutal conditions of prison servitude may nonetheless facilitate the evolution of subversive practices. These include counterhegemonic Convict narratives. Confronted with brutal servitude and legislated silence that, ironically, is represented as a prisoner right in statutes such as the Miranda rights, cited as the second epigraph above, prisoners talk back. Franklin's teleological model of prisoner literature proposes a dialectical link between the legislated "right" to silence and prisoner resistance:

> The victims [of postbellum slavery] would have to be perceived as criminals, and they would thus be forced, for their very survival, to become artists of song and ballad and, later, of political autobiography, poetry, drama, and fiction. (101–102)

Franklin adds that these prisoner narratives sometimes evolve from simple meditations on criminality towards broader collectivist assessments of political economy (236).

This dialectical inversion of the panopticon is clearly illustrated by Ricardo Sánchez's imprisonment and publications. In "Míctla: A Chicano's Long Road Home" (1973b), one of Sánchez's many post-prison meditations on his imprisonment and his writing from prison, he recalls:

> I learned the bitterest of lessons: A CONVICT, especially a Chicano convict, IN TEXAS EXISTS ONLY TO WORK LIKE A BEAST. The cotton fields, the constant whippings, the mad sojourns to and from isolation, the pisser, and all the other manic forms of dehumanization now demanded that I go

deeper and deeper into the why of my existence. Each letter sent home was a labor of literary definition, definition of the topsy-turvy world that strove to obliterate convicts. Thoughts of publication ran through my mind, as if they were demons that demanded to be printed and distributed. (59)

Prison and poetry are linked in a dialectical relationship as Sánchez's rebellious acts of property theft—which he continually relives by writing and rewriting these episodes—problematize the two spheres of subordination: the extra-discursive space of the Ramsey I Penitentiary Farm, and the matrix of juridical texts buttressing the primacy of private property that makes such institutions inevitable. From the profit-producing cotton fields of the Texas Department of Corrections, Sánchez shouts out, "*Pues a la madre con la ley!*" and thus introduces the Pinto ethnopoetic practice that proposes multiple syntheses of prison, his prisoner experiences, and, most importantly, his Pinto identity.

Sánchez's recourse to the multilingual Pachuco argot—Caló—defined in large part by the scatological vocabulary of the street, is central to this ethnopoetic practice of remembering, resisting, and reconstructing. This linguistic repertoire enables him the latitude to improvise the neologism—*el desmadrazgo*—which is a crucial nodal point in the binary title of Sánchez's first edition of *Canto y grito mi liberación (. . . y lloro mis desmadrazgos . . .)*. This hybrid term is composed from his fusion of two vernacular Spanish terms fundamental to the Mexican and Chicana/o political unconscious—*el desmadre* and *el chingazo*. These root nouns, more commonly used in their verb forms—*desmadrar* and *chingar*—have colloquial meanings that roughly translate as "to beat" (or literally, "to separate an animal from its mother"), and "to fuck," respectively. The etymological definition of these Spanish vernacular terms emphasizes a misogynist sexual violence that Sánchez tropes as "motherfuckin' asswhippin'," retaining both literal and figural meanings. As noted in preceding chapters, this valence is historically and culturally grounded in Mexican and Chicana/o myth—specifically, the sense of consummate subordination associated with Malintzín, or La Malinche, the archetypal Mesoamerican mother whose "violation" by the "enemy" leads to the birth of the "mixed-race," or mestizo, peoples of the Americas.[9] She functions as the prototypical traitor in the three Marias archetype that includes La Llorona (the Weeping Woman), the prototypical victim condemned to lament her mixed-blood progeny, and La Virgen de Guadalupe, who emerged in the sixteenth century as a mestiza intercessor. Sánchez's rehearsal of this patriarchal paradigm is based upon Mexican

Nobel Laureate Octavio Paz's template in his (in)famous *The Labyrinth of Solitude* (1950). Paz proposes an etymology of *chingar*, the verb form of the noun *el chingazo*:

> The verb [*chingar*] denotes violence, an emergence from oneself to penetrate another by force. It also means to injure, to lacerate, to violate—bodies, souls, objects—and to destroy . . .
>
> The idea of breaking, of ripping open, appears in a great many of these expressions. The word has sexual connotations but it is not a synonym for the sexual act: one may *chingar* a woman without actually possessing her. And when it does allude to the sexual act, violation or deception gives it a particular shading. The man who commits it never does so with the consent of the *chingada*. *Chingar*, then, is to do violence to another. The verb is masculine, active, cruel: it stings, wounds, gashes, stains. And it provokes a bitter, resentful satisfaction.
>
> The person who suffers this action is passive, inert and open, in contrast to the active, aggressive and closed person who inflicts it. The *chingón* is the *macho*, the male; he rips open the *chingada*, the female, who is pure passivity, defenseless against the exterior world. The relationship between them is violent, and it is determined by the cynical power of the first and the impotence of the second. (76–77)

Sánchez invokes this highly problematic, extra-linguistic dimension of the Mexican and Chicana/o political unconscious by linking the collective memory of the earlier Spanish and subsequent Anglo-American conquests, or *desmadres*, to his own incarceration—his material and immediately experienced *chingazo*.

Sánchez's invocation of the trope of sexual violence is distinguished from other representations—especially Paz's—by the manner and degree to which Sánchez incorporates it into a performative embodied ethnopoetic practice that proposes to synthesize these traumas. Although Sánchez's masculinist signifying practices are grounded in the Mexican and Chicana/o political unconscious, they also are fundamentally linked to the regulating telos of the men's penitentiary—emasculation—and more immediately related to his pre-prison Pachuco ontology. His poetry gestures towards a post-prison utopia to be actualized through a masculinist performance of counterpower. In an undated prose piece in *Canto y grito mi liberación*, succinctly titled, "Desmadrazgo," Sánchez foregrounds his synthesis of his *desmadrazgo* by proposing a nostalgic

and somewhat embellished genealogy of the Pachuco, whom he claims
originated in the 1930s in his hometown barrio in El Paso, Texas:

> America was not willing—nor prepared—to receive the Chicano. And the
> Chicano not being too articulate, not yet being a politicized organizer, and
> not having avenues for meaningful confrontation, asserted his machismo in
> the garments of el bato loco (hipster): zootsuits, ducktailed haircut, khaki
> pants, french toed shoes, switchblade, chains, and caló (the language of the
> barrio). These formed his fighting and all around uniform.
>
> These were the first Chicanos in large numbers to become dedicated to
> fighting back, dedicated to promoting the community at all costs. These
> batos locos, with crosses tattooed on their hands, had a deep sense of
> respect and love for their families. (34–35)

Sánchez continues his construction of the lumpen Chicano male warrior
hero by proposing a rebellious Pachuco modus operandi:

> In his low-riding uniform, he cruised the streets—not asking, but demanding
> and taking what rightfully belonged to him. (35)

He concludes with a cultural nationalist paean to his barrio that also
names the object of his violent vernacular forms of resistance:

> In East El Chuco [east El Paso], there by the El Paso Coliseum was an old
> barrio—El Barrio Del Diablo [The Devil's Ward]. Here lived the batos from
> the X-9 gang. Batos sworn to protect the barrio from gringos. During my
> youth, I never saw gringos walk through the barrio. (35)

Sánchez's *pachuquismo* is defined by a cultural nationalist machismo
predicated on the legacy of invasion, violent dispossession, and most
importantly, subsequent acts of resistance and transgression (e.g.,
"[*Pachucos*] cruised the streets—not asking, but demanding and taking
. . .". This combative world vision permeates the barrio and manifests
itself both in its less organized internecine form of *chingazos* (e.g., the
fratricide evidenced in "street fighting" and "gang-banging"), to the
more "politically informed" use of violence, also troped as *chingazos*,
but directed against White-dominated institutions such as school systems,
police departments, and prisons. Modeling the dialectical relationship
between colonial and anticolonial violence that Fanon has explicated

(1982), Sánchez stresses that the robberies and assaults for which he ultimately served a total of nine years in prison all were committed against Whites, or business establishments owned by them.[10]

This combative cultural nationalist sensibility, and nascent socialist politics, is inflected through a scatological vocabulary that emerges in the hybrid interlingual Spanglish and Pachuco patois, Caló. This linguistic repertoire involves code-switching—various alterations of linguistic codes—as well as borrowing and substitution of words or phrases from another language. Cultural linguist Fernando Peñalosa (1980) notes:

> Chicano code switching can also be a verbal strategy for conveying social information, such as a sociopolitical identity marker or intimate relationship, for signaling social distance from a White role, and for implying that one's own interlocutor will not be offended by language mixture. (68)

Rafael Pérez-Torres adds:

> This type of linguistic interpenetration on the sociodiscursive stage forms a type of bilingualism (more precisely polyglossia) in which speakers use code-switching to establish numerous social relations . . . From a sociolinguistic perspective, this particular speech-act establishes or disrupts social roles, and aids or precludes the construction of community. (1995: 212–213)

Neologisms such as "el Desmadrazgo," vernacular phrases like "a la madre con la ley," as well as geo-cultural markers such as "el Chuco," "el Barrio del Diablo," and even epithets like "gringos," all underscore Sánchez's social location before prison and, above all else, his vexed relationship to the all-encompassing Althusserian model of Ideology as a result of his imprisonment: he is a "bad subject" who refuses to conform even though he is contained in the repressive state apparatus of prison.

The evolution of Sánchez's inchoate Pachuco praxis into a potentially empowering ethnopoetic practice is foregrounded in "Tiers/Tears" (*HS* 72–73), composed during his earlier period of imprisonment in Soledad State Penitentiary in Soledad, California, from 1959 to 1963. Prefaced as "Soledad, April 7, 1961," this poem maneuvers between lyric and elegy as the narrator recounts the emasculation of another Chicano prisoner who is laid out on the panoptic tiers of Soledad, which in Spanish, Sánchez's first, most intimate language, translates as "solitude." The piece opens with Sánchez's poetic persona, the elder Chicano Convict, stricken by the sight of another Chicano prisoner (perhaps also a representation of his alter ego) sobbing to himself after having been beaten—after having suffered a *chingazo*. The ensuing poem is written with a minimal use of punctuation, and composed in stanzas spatially arranged to invoke the image of tears trickling down the multileveled tiers of a penitentiary:

slow tears
trickling on the tiers,
his face hooted on
onto the hollows
of prison life;

        he tried vainly
        to escape,
        the beatings
        he received
        lashed/cut
        into hisemptysocketeyes
        and all his hurts
        ran together,

can one separate
one's life
into scattered fragments
of pain
and joy
and knowing?

        he tried vainly
        and then cried
        tears
        upon tears
        upon the steel
        prison tiers,

young hurting
chicanito,
he once shared
a cup of coffee,

told me his father
was también

        del chuco,
        and he wondered
        about a bordertown
        he'd heard about
        while growing up
        in los,

but los perros
lo golpearon
and he cried
upon that tier
and somehow felt
he'd lost
his manhood.[11]

In Soledad, the principal *chingazo* comes in the form of incarceration and the inability of the young *chicanito* to defy and strike back—to "demand" and to "take"—which, as previously noted in "Desmadrazgo," is central to the Pachuco raison d'être. The *chingazo* also takes the form of a very real beating by the White guards—"*los perros*" (the dogs)—which the young Chicano prisoner apparently was unable to fend off. This emasculated young Chicano, whose father is revealed in the fifth stanza to have been from the Edenic Pachuco place of origins, el Chuco (El Paso), therefore brings shame on his whole family and, subsequently, La Raza, his "Chicano People." He is a Chicano warrior who lost, and is thus perceived as the "passive one." The sharply enjambed lines that model the downward trickle of "tears / upon tears / upon the steel / prison tiers," underscore the image of a dehumanized and helpless, estranged, and impotent Chicano in captivity. The prisoner's tears for his lost manhood, flowing down the tiers, are unstoppable. The contracted phrase "hisemptysocketeyes" further associates life with death to underscore the prisoner's space in-between. Moreover, this graphic scene introduces Sánchez—the would-be participant-observer in a rebellion—as a permutation of La Llorona, as he is unable to do anything but cry at the loss of liberty/virility—his and another's. The global political economy of the *desmadrazgo* is experienced at the highly localized context of an imprisoned, lumpenproletarian Chicana/o body. Despite the sense of consummate subordination conveyed by "Tiers/Tears," however, the poem becomes an axis for the Pinto poet's performative synthesis of *el desmadre*. As foregrounded in the full title of the first edition of Sánchez's inaugural collection—*Canto y grito mi liberación (. . . y lloro mis desmadrazgos . . .)*—his *liberación*, or his identity as a Chicano, necessarily involves cries of anguish and defiant shout-songs. Here, Sánchez is a victim and witness of past *desmadrazgos* who exclaims that future *chingazos* will be directed outward, towards the enemy.

ECHANDO MADRES: A PINTO SENSIBILITY

Throughout his multivolume verse, Sánchez repeatedly pairs lamentations with compositions that proactively deploy the Pachuco signifying practice known as *echando madres*, or cursing. Literally translated as "eschewing . . . " or "throwing mothers," the practice of *echando madres* is akin to the African American vernacular signifying practice known as "the dozens." Both practices are attempts, albeit misogynist, to come to terms with historical rapes of Mexican and African foremothers that characterized Western imperialism in the Americas. The most aggressive participant—the one able to humiliate his interlocutor by casting the most humiliating aspersions on his mother or manhood—attains a position of honor, prestige, and relative power, while the defeated person assumes the role of a "passive" victim. He is figuratively "fucked" and reduced to the status of the raped woman.

This vernacular Pachuco and Pinto sensibility and practice is modeled in the poem, "and it . . ." (CG 39–40), dated as "*sin tiempo*" (timeless), which marks a crucial moment in Sánchez's consolidation of his Pinto poetic. In this loud, declamatory protest poem, Sánchez draws upon his previously articulated Pachuco episteme of liberty-as-phallocentric virility to deconstruct the U.S. Declaration of Independence, one of the founding documents of U.S. jurisprudence, the Pinto poet's arch-nemesis. The composition opens as a Pachuco mimic of the famous first lines, cited as the first epigraph above:

carnales,

cuando en el curso   del desafío y desmadre
it becomes imperative to pick up estoque and filero . . . (1–3)[12]

Although Sánchez's protests are similar to those levied by the Protestant colonists of 1776, here the vernacular *carnales* (blood brothers) addresses this new declaration to all Chicanos. It is a collective call to arms against Whites. The use of the Mesoamerican and barrio weapons such as *estoque* (club) and *filero* (switchblade)—figuratively associated with this segment of the lumpenproletariat—further contextualizes this *declaración* within the Chicana/o cultural nationalist struggles of the period. Unlike many Chicana/o poems of the era in which Caló presumably serves, according to Pérez-Torres, as a marker of multiple alienations (233), Sánchez's vernacular invocations in this composition instigate a new rupture while also serving as a claim to group membership with the Chicana/o community outside the walls. This Pachuco gloss of a White "revolutionary" document proposes the violent transformation of history through armed insurrection. Amid the turbulence of the "long hot summers" of the 1960s and 1970s, distinguished by prison revolts and related ethnic minority "power" movements, the utterance and the act converged. This performative text begins to approximate the engagé format that comes to distinguish Sánchez's signature poetic and political voice.

This counterhegemonic—and proposed extra-literary—engagement with U.S. jurisprudence and its historical and material legacy is informed by the political discourse of "internal colonialism," one theory that many Chicana/o activists and social scientists of the era used to interpret Chicana/o history since 1848. Though there are competing models for theorizing Chicana/o history, all recognize that Chicana/os—once a majority in their own land before the U.S. invasions in the mid-nineteenth century—have been subordinated and exploited through a variety of coercive mechanisms. These include intergroup rivalries such as racism, intragroup exploitations facilitated through class segmentation, and coercive institutions such as Eurocentric school curricula and prisons over which Chicana/os have little real control.[13] The cumulative effect is that Chicana/os, though legally declared equal citizens under the law, are in practice rendered second-class citizens, or worse.

Informed by these discourses, Sánchez's poem "and it . . ." not only critiques the repressive state apparatuses such as penitentiaries that buttress White capitalist hegemony, but even questions the very legitimacy of the "United States of America" itself. The succeeding lines, where the tempo, tone, and tension steadily rise in the Pinto poet's simultaneous indictment and expression of frustration, foreground the sentiment:

when, you bastards of the jive language,
it all becomes unbearable
to live duelo y pésame y desmadrazgo . . . (5–7)[14]

Still paralleling the rhetorical structure of the opening lines of the U.S. Declaration of Independence, this semantic fragment gains more and more force as it repeatedly demands a subordinate clause to complete the sentence and synthesize the sentiment: revolt is inevitable because the conditions for Chicana/os are so unbearable. Sánchez simultaneously proposes jurisprudence as the "jive language" of "bastards" (born of a different *chingada,* or the penetrated and "passive" one). In so doing, he discursively maps onto Whites the epic curse of *el desmadre* that for so long had been endured by mestizos in the Americas in its many forms and contemporary rearticulations: from 1521 to 1836, to 1848, to Sánchez's present reality as part of the disproportionately high percentage of Chicana/o prisoners. In this poem, "time" and the "sentence" are troped to illuminate cataclysmic events in Chicana/o history that the Pinto poet seeks to synthesize, linguistically and materially, through his writing and proposed fighting. Significantly, Sánchez' bitter critique of U.S. government hypocrisy ("old virginy lies" [line 15]) and oppression ("midst genocide and hatred" [line 18]) is issued from Sánchez's "central" position in the panoptic penitentiary.

This protest rises to a crescendo of potential violence and the longed-for virility that once again would affirm the Pachuco prisoner's "manliness"—his "freedom"—and also facilitate his people's *liberación* through the actualization of Aztlán, the Chicana/o homeland presently subsumed under the oppressive geopolitical nominative "southwestern United States." The suggestive declamations in the poem "and it . . ." propose a performance of the phallocentric model of "revolutionary" violence that would presumably enable these desired personal and historical transformations:

y mis huevos hinchados
bulging
con la angustia
    de mi alma desnuda . . .

i awaken
in the cauldron of reality,

hands stretching out
to garrote . . . (18–25, ellipses in original)[15]

As expected, Sánchez articulates his symbolic enactment of revolutionary violence through an orgasmic imagery: his bulging, swollen testicles ("mis huevos hinchados") are expanding with the rage and desire that his phallus ("garrote") will make manifest in the form of *chingazos*. Sánchez means to strike, beat, or otherwise do violence to his enemy in the ways Paz discusses in his etymology of the masculinist trope. Sánchez's fervor is intensified by the belief that more is at stake than his own individual liberty: he is fighting for his very existence as a Chicano; the survival of his symbolic family, la Raza; and the consolidation of his imagined nation, Aztlán.

Later his discourse will more consciously engage historical materialism as he seeks total *liberación*. In this instance, however, the Pinto poet reaches out helplessly to his "garrote" while the prison tower looms overhead, much bigger and stronger than his own phallic weapon. Hence, the poem is only provisionally successful. The profound silences forced by unorthodox spacing, harsh enjambments, and the repeated use of ellipses progress towards an anticlimactic exasperation:

chicanitos born only to die   swollen eyes
and bellies
            in the land of plenty   and it hurts,
    and it hurts
                    and . . . (43–45)

Sánchez's estranged autobiographical poetic persona can do nothing other than supply the missing term, "hurts," to the initially empowering but still incomplete title, "and it . . ." The poem, which began as a counterdiscursive act, eventually reads as a cry of impotence as the immanent revolutionary remains enclosed within the prison walls. Although he mocks the founding documents of the government that defines him as a criminal and permits his exploitation, and although he has some ephemeral success in writing his Pachuco subjectivity back into existence as a new construct—the defiant Pinto poet *echando madres*—Ricardo Sánchez is still in a prison of concrete and steel, and cannot escape. Yet.

Despite the anticlimactic closure, the poem nonetheless approximates the ethnopoetic practice that becomes the Pinto poet's hallmark: he cries, curses, and critiques even as he sings of an imminent redemption—all of which is articulated through his multifaceted discourse on the Chicano male body. It begins with cries. The emotional appeal posed by the pathetic image of the emaciated diminutive "chicanitos" toward the end of the poem "and it . . ." enables Sánchez to appropriate the Enlightenment discourse on the "universal rights of man" that purportedly underwrites the juridical texts the Pinto poet alternately derides and appropriates. As in the poem "Tiers/Tears" examined earlier, the image of La Llorona resurfaces. But the ellipses that follow the last word of the poem ("and . . .") indicate that the composition is incomplete, and the enunciated goal unfinished. This cliché foregrounds an epiphanic synthesis: there is a new narrative being formed, and, ironically but predictably, it will be crowned with the halo of a male-gendered version of La Virgen de Guadalupe: the Pinto. Through this poem and others to follow, Sánchez steadily merges mythic memory with the material; poetry becomes the means by which the Chicano prisoner/victim is performatively rearticulated as a transcendent Pinto intercessor: a Pinto Virgen. But unlike the apparently silent Virgen de Guadalupe icon, Sánchez's poems get louder, and the violent outbursts verbalized through the vernacular signifying practices of the barrio inevitably collapse the text into the body, and as such, begin to actualize Sánchez's *liberación*.

VERNACULAR INTERVENTIONS: RICARDO SÁNCHEZ'S *POESÍA DE CHINGAZOS*

As Sánchez's years behind bars continued, and as the various civil rights and racial minority power struggles being waged outside prison became more volatile, his poetry from prison began to reflect what Franklin (1989) and Barbara Harlow (1992) have identified as the ultimate synthesis in prisoner discourses: extra-discursive compositions that simultaneously propose structural critiques and material interventions. This is especially evident in the verse Sánchez composed or set during his incarceration in Texas from 1965 to 1969. During the later part of this period, Sánchez's increasingly more declamatory and engagé compositions begin to function as mnemonic devices used to guide his performance of the cultural nationalist model of difference—a simultaneous claim to sameness and community—that underwrites his proposed interventions into Chicana/o history. Tino Villanueva offers insight into the internal order of this engagé poetic in his examination of Chicana/o poetry from the 1960s and 1970s vis-à-vis various genres of "political" poetry in Europe and the Americas:

What most distinguishes engagé poetry from quotidian protest poetry is that in the former there is a direct participation of the poet. The poet is in direct contact in the protest, even attending politically-oriented meetings, writing protest letters, organizing street demonstrations, or even distributing fliers through the streets, joining picket lines in front of ominous sites from which injustice emanates, etc. That is to say that the poet lives the poetry and in composing his artistic work, incorporates an authentic experience with which he hopes to awaken other people towards the injustices, motivating them to act against those evil forces that corrode society. It involves, then, a total attitude: it is aural and belletrist . . . To be an engagé artist is to assume an attitude that the poet lives ethically and relives aesthetically with the objective of condemning reality and fighting to end injustice. He hopes with all this to change the status quo. (1975: 33)

Villanueva adds that both the poet and the engagé poem are infused with a wounded but combative spirit. The poetic cry/shout thus seeks to stir the reader/listener into joining the poet in struggle.

Although Villanueva does not discuss Sánchez's work, his theory of engagé poetry clearly applies to Sánchez's *Canto y grito*. As Sánchez's impending publication and release dates converge, his *llantos* (cries) are partially smothered by his *cantos* (songs) and *gritos* (shouts). Seemingly contradictory shouts of indignation and songs of affirmation together call for a reunion with La Raza beyond the walls. Towards the end of the mixed-genre, stream-of-consciousness poem appropriately titled "Stream . . ." (CG 73–83), he declaims, "GRINGOS MATENLOS . . ." (WHITEBOYS KILL THEM . . .), and further claims filiation to the Chicana/o cultural nationalist movement—El Movimiento—by descriptively proclaiming, "*grito ¡VIVA AZTLAN!*" (I shout LONG LIVE AZTLAN!). His compositions, which still bear the marks of textuality (e.g., "*I* shout . . ."), begin to cry out for the cultural nationalist reconstruction of Chicana/o identity ("VIVA AZTLAN!") through collective material actions in sites of power such as prisons, barrios, and the streets of "Amerika." Alongside his tears and cries, his *llantos*, Sánchez's engagé "shouts" of pain and potential, his *gritos*, function as another nodal point in his ritualized claim to community and agency. This relationship is underscored in poems such as "*Chingaderismo . . .*" (CG 113–114), where he pairs lyric lamentations with celebratory glosses of popular Movement songs (let me have a revolution, / Chicano power is my solution, lines 12–13), and belligerent shouts ("gringo te chingo / te chingo gringo" [whitey I fuck you / I fuck you whitey], lines 28–29).

In this way, the Pinto poet uses his voice as a misogynist weapon against White oppression.

Having thoroughly foregrounded *el desmadrazgo*, Sánchez continues to perform and synthesize the Pachuco and Pinto practice of *echando madres*. He directs his engagé *Canto y grito* poetics towards the actualization of an epiphanic, pseudo-revolutionary violence articulated through the body. Revising the individualistic *ars poetica* that informed his earliest prison writings, Sánchez's goal becomes to consolidate an ethnopoetic practice that transcends the merely counterhegemonic utterances of an individual prisoner. The poem "smile out the revolú . . ." (*CG* 139) is exemplary. This declamatory poem, dated "11/4/70" and appearing toward the very end of his inaugural collection, begins with the now familiar diatribe against White American capital and its beneficiaries: "chingue su madre the u.s.a. / burn, cabrones enraviados, / burn las calles de amerika / burn, burn, burn . . ." (fuck your mother the u.s.a. / burn, you diseased bastards, / burn the streets of amerika . . .," lines 4–7). He then pairs this invective with utopian *cantos* calling for a violently celebratory uprising by the Chicana/o community:

> escuchen el canto nuevo,
> sonrían la revolú
> que toquen tamboras fuertes,
> y quemen ya la nación . . .
>
> hoy broten
> Aztlán de nuevo
>
> hoy broten
> la orden social
>
> and burn out the old desmadre . . . (18–26)[16]

While Miguel López argues that Sánchez only advocated a "cultural revolution," I submit that poems such as "smile out the revolú . . ." are part of a broader political project that includes, and revolves around, armed revolutionary action. Indeed, in direct contrast to the pacifist *floricanto* festivals of the era inspired by Alurista's transcendentalist ethnopoetic celebration of *mestizaje*, Sánchez's declamations call for a direct violent confrontation against U.S. capitalist imperialism. Speaking to the lumpen Chicana/o masses, Sánchez's poem issues his call to action through plural imperatives such as "escuchen" (listen), "sonrían" (smile), "toquen" (beat), "quemen" (burn), and "broten" (give birth). Literally bringing his poetry to the people, Sánchez often performed his verse on street corners.[17]

Yet the possibility of revolutionary action is only partially articulated through the poem. The celebratory but nonetheless orthographically and semantically incomplete title, "smile out the revolú . . .," is constructed in an interlingual format that radically circumscribes its audience even as it demands that the reader/listener interpret, pronounce, and materialize the partially signified speech act. It demands action—*revolución*! Sánchez's poetry is thus part of a broader performance of counterpower. Indeed, throughout his life Sánchez frequently participated in mass demonstrations and militant organizations such as the Brown Berets, of which he was a member, and more mature revolutionary political parties like the Revolutionary Communist Party U.S.A., a Maoist organization that advocates world revolution, including, as needed and appropriate, armed insurrection. Anyone who suggests that Sánchez is merely a cultural ambassador has an incomplete understanding of his unique Pinto poetic, which is much more than simply poetry or art. This point was illustrated by the discovery of two loaded revolvers in Ricardo Sánchez's archives as they were being prepared for delivery to Stanford University for permanent housing.

Yves-Charles Granjeat (1986) offers an incisive assessment of this politically engaged and praxis-oriented ethnopoetics in "Ricardo Sánchez: The Poetics of Liberation":

> Writing, like shouting, is a means of summoning up essential life forces in the midst of a desperate struggle against death . . . Howls of pain are mixed with shouts of hate. The "grito" then develops into a threat and an indictment, a weapon hurled at the enemy, daring him to the fight . . . They [*gritos*] are also directed at the Chicano or other reader or listener, to sting, stab, jolt him out of his lethargy . . . and trigger him into action. (35–36)

The Pachuco, though imprisoned, challenges his juridical nemesis in the way he knows best—through *chingazos*. Ricardo Sánchez curses from his cell; he shouts his challenge through the pages of his verse; he sings "¡Viva La Raza!" and "¡Viva Aztlán!" Granjeat's assertion that Sánchez's poetry mimetically seeks to "provoke what it evokes" (36) in fact is borne out in this poem, which instigates for revolutionary rupture and a renewal that is at once linguistic and material. Even before the release of Sánchez's *Canto y grito mi liberación* in 1971, the Pinto poet's ethnopoetic practice had become a finely honed weapon or, at the very least, a means of fashioning one. From prison, he wielded it in the service of El Movimiento. In one poem, he even underscores his new-found lethal potential with a warning to the armed and mounted, tobacco-chewing, White American TDC prison guard: "you better kill me while you can . . ." ("Say, Tush-Hog Convict," *SP* 38).

Sánchez's call for violent extra-discursive rupture and renewal, however, is not completely revolutionary. It is misogynist to its core. His verse's complex polyphonic structure and vernacular (and cliché) engagement with Mexican and American history reveal Sánchez's *ars poetica* to be a *poesía de chingazos*. Although there is no adequate translation for this new ethnopoetic category, it is immediately apparent that the trope of *el desmadrazgo* underwriting it is in fact double-edged. As noted in the etymology of *el desmadre* and el *chingazo*, Sánchez both uses and is simultaneously wounded by his sharply honed, vernacular-signifying practice. Moreover, he is wounded at the very moment he strikes another. By articulating *liberación* in terms of violent sexual subordination, Sánchez preserves the memory of the trauma even as he challenges it. In so doing, he perpetuates the phallocentric paradigm that manifests itself in the misogynist myth of the three Marias, as well as in more concretely oppressive permutations such as penitentiaries, whose architecture also tropes sexual violence as power.[18] Sánchez offers a revealing explication of his maturing, but still problematic *ars poetica* in a 1980 interview with Juan Bruce-Novoa:

> Chicano literature is a political statement which derives its essence
> from socio-politico-economic realities vying with cultural and historical
> affirmations, and in so doing a language of engagement and confrontation
> takes form . . .
>   Words must be real, just as weapons are real—my writing, I strongly
> feel, must be a driving wedge and force, *una arma que se pueda usar para
> enfrentar lo social y crear mas que conciencia* [a weapon which can be used
> to confront the social and create more than consciousness]. (229–230, trans.
> Bruce-Novoa)

Like all metaphor, Sánchez's use of *una arma* is grounded in a concrete reality: he is in prison for having taken up a gun to "dispossess" a White

American in the southwestern United States, which to him is and always will be Aztlán. The phallic—and phallocentric—resonance becomes even more acute in the bilingual context of Sánchez's Chicana/o audience, where *una arma* takes on violently erotic connotations. Sánchez's *poesía de chingazos*—his "language of engagement and confrontation"—is still inscribed with the epistemology of *el desmadrazgo*. It is a *canto*, a *grito*, and a *llanto* all at once: a transgression and a trauma.

The two clauses that form the title of Sánchez's debut collection of verse are dialectically and inextricably adjoined. For the remainder of his life, they formed the parameters of his lyric theory in the flesh and, more importantly, his embodied poetics of engagement. The very title is troped and becomes a new ethnopoetic category in itself. Sánchez's *poesía de chingazos* involves not only the despair modeled in "Tiers/ Tears," but also the protest songs of a mature engagé poet whose corpus remains rich in lyricism even as it remains inscribed with a fundamental contradiction. While subsequent generations of Chicana/o poets, intellectuals, and activists must challenge this contradiction, Sánchez's historically informed, materially motivated vernacular intervention into U.S. colonialism cannot be dismissed. Rather, it anticipates and enables subsequent generations of Chicana/o revolutionary poetics.

What, then, is the virtue of an *ars poetica* that is articulated through the proposed violent subordination of other human beings? The significance, I argue, arises from the very contradiction: Sánchez's privileged use of the problematic signifying practices of the Chicana/o lumpenproletariat masses—that is, *echando madres*. By deploying this vernacular episteme as a master narrative, the Pinto poet models the counterhegemonic and extra-discursive potential of a Chicana/o ethnopoetic practice grounded in the emasculated body, even as he models its limits. This body is more than a metaphor for Sánchez. It is integral to the performance of a counterhegemonic identity where the enunciation and the actualization of dissent inevitably become reflexive and simultaneous acts. This performative function is alluded to in publisher Nicolás Kanellos's description of a Sánchez event, which was never just a "reading":

> Ricardo Sánchez, the minotaur poet. The bull in his stance, the throaty bellow of his voice as he reads, his unbridled energy, the looming threat of aggression, the violence of his past, and yes, the beauty and passivism of his thought today . . . all translate directly into poems of power and sensitivity, protest and love, impatience with the present, but confidence in the future.
> (1985: 7)

Sánchez merges the formal dimensions of his verse with his extra-discursive authorial intent by collapsing the text into his body through an engagé performance. It is pure spectacle.

In a related context, Patricia Liggins Hill (1982) has identified how Black Convict poet Etheridge Knight's "belly songs" gesture toward a visceral poetic that attempts to collapse the poet-audience divide by both invoking and performing rebellion. According to Hill, the "belly song" is a vernacular shout that is at once aesthetic and physical, spiritual and threatening. Similarly, what for Sánchez begins as a merely counterdiscursive gesture eventually becomes a lyric theory in the flesh, an embodied form of knowledge, and an extra-discursive practice—that is, an exercise of counterpower. It is a discourse on Chicana/o identity as an intercultural polyglot phenomenon, and a simultaneous performance of it. The historicized and racialized, eroticized and highly gendered Chicano body is not only the primary referent; it also underwrites the articulation of a counterhegemonic model of Chicana/o identity whose performance proposes an intervention into *el desmadrazgo* even as it reproduces it. Herein lies its virtue and vice.

Sánchez's tense, polyphonic poetry underscores the dialogic nature of Chicana/o literature and pushes the limits of this definition by inflecting his Chicana/o Convict body through his poetry and vice versa. While poetry is Sánchez's principal medium, the literariness of the "text" is almost coincidental. Ramón Saldívar has argued that Chicana/o narrative adduces the text as the performative space through which an ideology of difference simultaneously is expressed and produced (1990: 7–8). While Saldívar's claims may hold true for a small number of narrative texts, I argue that Sánchez's narrative and lyric verse—his *poesía de chingazos*—introduces an eroticized and politicized vocabulary of the Chicano body, and a corresponding extra-discursive method of using it. His engagé verse enables the performance of other dialectical models of difference directly engaged with Chicana/o history. And even though his violently eroticized, embodied ethnopoetics cannot account for nonaggressive, nonviolent, nonmasculinist, and nonheterosexual subjectivities, it unwittingly maps out a creative space for such rearticulations. He adumbrates, by necessitating, multiple rearticulations of Chicana/o identity and corresponding signifying practices grounded in the body for generations of Chicana/o writers to come. In the succeeding chapter, I examine how other Chicano Convicts have deployed this embodied knowledge in the continued articulation of a counterhegemonic, though complex and equally contradictory, Pinto intellectual.

CHAPTER 4

The Pinto Political Unconscious

Tattoos, Abjection, and Agency
in Raúl Salinas's Convict Body Altars

Neither slavery nor involuntary servitude, except as a punishment for
crime whereof the party shall have been duly convicted, shall exist within
the United States, or any place subject to their jurisdiction.

—Thirteenth Amendment, U.S. Constitution

Sometimes it is easier for people out in the freeworld to understand what
American prisons represent if they equate them to concentration camps,
where prisoners are systematically beaten, forced to work, and even killed.

—Raúl Salinas, #A-43203 (1996)

Arbeit Macht Frei (Work Brings Freedom)

—Sign on gate to Auschwitz

PAINTED, TAINTED, AND MARKED

In a 1993 episode of the popular reality crime series *COPS*, viewers are
brought along on a patrol of the racial minority South Sector of Fort
Worth, Texas.[1] Officer Benson, who is White, turns to face the camera
mounted in the back seat of his squad car and explains that he is en
route to join other officers at the "scene." They are to set up a perimeter
to corral the fleeing suspects of a recent burglary. We arrive in a matter
of seconds. After an abrupt stop, the cop and cameraman dismount
together to follow the lead from the police helicopter hovering overhead.
Suddenly, the television picture begins to shake erratically, giving the scene
the "real" feel promised in the promotional clips broadcast throughout
the week, assuring us of the show's veracity with claims such as "*COPS!*
Everything else is just fiction!" The chase is on. The tension builds as
the cameraman struggles to keep up with the cop, the picture bouncing
up and down and to the sides in the now familiar jolting motions that
allow us to participate in the hot pursuit of what the radio dispatcher has
described as two "Hispanic male suspects."

After an encounter between the White police officer and an ordinary house cat that the helicopter crew—armed with a military-issue infrared telescope—had mistaken for the two "suspected criminals," the excitement builds anew; the camera and the cop dart off after another specter. Despite the slippage in which humans are taken for animals and vice versa, the high-technology has forged a new alliance: the cop, through the hand-held camera, has enlisted us, the viewers, in the five-decades-old war on crime that has morphed into a domestic war on terror. When we finally catch up to the cop, he is standing beside an overturned children's wading pool with semiautomatic pistol drawn. Aiming directly into the center of the pool, out of which extend two sets of legs, the cop shoots his voice of authority: "I WANT TO SEE SOME HANDS, GODDAMMIT! NOW!" After no response, he violently kicks the pool over. The camera is there to record it all: the adult men are brown, their bodies adorned with hand-drawn greenish-black tattoos that the portable camera lights illuminate. As the men are being searched, handcuffed, and interrogated, the arresting officer pulls a gold medallion emblazoned with the image of Jesus Christ from one of the men's pockets. Holding this revered Christian icon directly in front of the portable camera lens, he sarcastically remarks: "That's terrible, burglarizing a house with Jesus in your pocket." After the close-up of the medallion, the camera shoots back to the brown and tattoo-marked skin, and then to the arresting officer—juxtaposing Christ, "criminal," and cop. Turning to his White colleague, Officer Benson gestures to his own forearm and right cheek as he presents his summary conviction: "Yeah, they got the tattoos on the arms, teardrops and all."[2] Nothing more needs to be said. The episode is over, and the overarching carceral narrative proceeds with the two other components of the public performance of power in the war on crime/war on terror: (1) the disarticulation ritual enacted through the trial, in which the "Hispanic male suspects" will be civically and ontologically excised from the polis as "convicted criminals"; and (2) the emasculation drama of the men's penitentiary, which ostensibly seeks to restore order though the physical containment and forced labor of these new "convicted criminals."[3]

Drawing upon Richard Johnson's (1987) post-structuralist cultural studies methodology, I view the arresting officer's cryptic signifying practices as a point of reference for examining how the adorned body of the collective and individual "Hispanic male suspect" is read and written upon by a variety of narrators: police officers, prosecutors, judges, prison administrators, guards, and, of course, prisoners. This marked body displays a network of signifiers that affirm the "suspected" or "convicted" criminal's personal identity while simultaneously confirming its bearer's abject status in society.[4] The chase/arrest scene described above represents the initial phase of what Michel Foucault identifies as a tripartite project of subordination, where police fill prisons so these institutions may in turn produce and reproduce the deviants and deviancy necessary in any hegemonic relation (1979: 282). Foucault maintains that the modern panoptic prison has replaced medieval public spectacles of torture and execution, but I submit that prime-time television shows like COPS highlight the ever-present threat of brutal state power, thereby demanding new attention to the body of the "convicted criminal." In the demographics of the contemporary U.S. prison system, this body is disproportionately dark skinned.[5] In the southwestern United States, this racially marked Chicana/o prisoner body illustrates that the panopticon is an instrument of neocolonial subjugation.

Rather than being a stable site where the "convicted criminal" is contained, however, the penitentiary becomes the staging ground for the dialectical battle over whether to preserve or to destabilize the war on crime/war on terror. The tattooed Convict(ed) body is the axis upon which this battle revolves. In this chapter, I examine how coordinated struggles to resist, transgress, and transform the containment proposed by the men's penitentiary pose significant, though still inconclusive, challenges to hegemony in the war on crime/war on terror. I draw upon the *placa*, or badge, episteme—the Chicana/o lumpenproletariat practice of ritually marking a space for the purpose of laying a symbolic, and even material, claim to it—to approximate a theory of the Pinto visual vernacular. I argue that a complex and coherent Pinto discourse is consolidated through the ritualized process of body tattooing in prison.

I use the Spanish term *tatuajes* rather than "tattoos" to underscore the culturally and historically nuanced nature of the Chicana/o permutation of this popular vernacular art form. For reasons as simple as skin pigmentation, and profound as Chicana/o Convict hegemony in the subaltern power structure of prisons throughout the southwestern United States, where *tatuajes* sometimes serve to distinguish "friends" from "foes," tattooing is more common among Chicana/o Convicts than any other prisoner group. The symbolic significance of Chicana/o Convict body tattoos therefore carries a political resonance different from, if not in direct opposition to, other prisoner-produced tattoos. Moreover, the *tatuaje*-marked Chicana/o Convict body becomes a site of individual and collective resistance to regimes of control; thus, my related neologism, *tatuteando*, to underscore the distinct liminal, transgressive, and transformative ritual.

This tattooed brown body symbolically and materially challenges the overt and indirect forms of domination—peonage, proletarianization, and mass incarceration of Chicana/os from 1848 to the present—which Ramón Saldívar maintains are the distinguishing feature of Chicana/o narrative (1990: 24). This oppositional posture is made manifest by *tatuajes*, which carry symbolic and material immediacy impossible to achieve through strictly "literary" forms of writing. So whereas the oppositional quality of the *corrido* can degenerate into "canonized" Chicana/o *belles lettres*, *tatuajes* remain inscribed in the brown bodies of the lumpen and proletarian segments of the Chicana/o body politic and continue to resonate with a material force not readily apparent in, for example, Chicana/o autobiography, autobiographical fiction, *testimonio,* or contemporary Chicana/o poetry. *Tatuajes* underscore the vernacular dimension of Chicana/o *difference*. But several questions emerge. What is the relationship of this differential consciousness to Ideology?[6] How does the highly eroticized Pinto body relate to archetypes associated with, or deployed by, Pinta/os discussed thus far? What are the strengths and limits of this permutation of the Pinto political unconscious? And how does this Pinto visual vernacular introduce a new discourse on counterpower?

CUERPOS PINTAOS: CHICANA/O CONVICT BODY TATTOOS

Rather than accept a Foucauldian dislocation of power and the attendant notion of a totally contained and disempowered subject/object, I extend R. Theodore Davidson's (1974) discussion of prisoner nomenclature to propose that a certain cadre of prisoners empower themselves precisely through their classification and commodification as "convicted criminals" by developing a collectivist epistemology based upon their resistance to bondage and censorship. It is moot but not insignificant to recall that "convicted criminals," as a category or "class" of people, are governed by the statutes outlined in the Thirteenth Amendment of the U.S. Constitution: the purported "abolition" amendment that still explicitly allows for "involuntary servitude" in cases where a person has been "duly convicted." They are further classified as "property of the state," which is underscored by their new numerical identities.

Many scholars have itemized the ways that these "convicted criminals" are legally coerced into prison occupations ranging from textile and agriculture production, food and custodial services, and even "plant maintenance" through jobs such as that of the infamous "dog boys": Texas Department of Corrections prisoners selected to mimic escape in order to be hunted down by prison bloodhounds and mounted guards as a training exercise for the killer dogs and entertainment for the guards and their guests.[7] This last occupation is paradigmatic of the dialectical nature of the exercise of power in prison: it illustrates how the very model of order imagined by the penitentiary is potentially subverted precisely as it is enacted, since sometimes the "dog boys" never returned from work! Separate from concrete acts of sabotage, the counterhegemonic dimension of prisoner labor is underscored by the subaltern economy that evolves out of, but functions in direct opposition to, the penal project of subordination enacted in the men's penitentiary through various forms of ritualized emasculation. As an illicit complement to prison-supplied amenities, prisoners produce and distribute supplemental, and thus contraband, goods and services to prisoner (and sometimes guard) consumers that range from informal legal assistance, letter writing, artwork, specialty foods, liquor, other drugs, and sex. Beyond serving as producers and consumers in company town–like prisons, prisoners further commodify the Convict(ed) body in their subaltern economy through sub-industries, including prostitution. Since the order of this illicit system of trade operates along a "code of honor" enforced by death, the profit-producing body of "convicted criminals" emerges as a vernacular form of currency; its value has a lethal and powerful resonance as it is redeployed to pay for a new transgressive narrative scripted by prisoners who defiantly identify themselves as oppositional "Convicts" instead of the more docile "Inmates." These prisoner reappropriations of the Convict(ed) body as a commodity and profit-producing medium become rituals of identity (trans)formation that directly contest the proto-fascist war on crime/war on terror that U.S. penitentiaries are perpetuating.

The inherently transgressive Convict economy, through which "criminality" is elaborated and refined into a vernacular epistemology and theory of praxis, gains a unique cultural and historical significance as Chicana/o Convicts excel in the prison sub-industry revolving around the production and consumption of *tatuajes*, the group-specific tattoos that are illegal, difficult to obtain, and thus highly valued in prison. This transgressive vernacular *écriture*—both the tattooing process and product—facilitates the constant re-elaboration and transformation of the already marked body of the Chicana/o Convict, as well as of the collective

Chicana/o Convict body involved in the complex production process. This *writing* ritual has a liminal resonance: in direct opposition to prison officials who (mis)classify body tattooing as an illegal form of "self-mutilation" and subsequently penalize it as they do all forms of "destruction of state property," these prisoners reappropriate the juridical narrative of abjection mapped onto their encaged brown bodies by "deforming" them and thus transforming their significance. They simultaneously preserve and rearticulate their abjection onto the freeworld subjectivities for which they had previously been incarcerated (recall the above chase/arrest spectacle in which tattoos legitimated a summary conviction). These and other criminal(ized) activities linked to the subaltern prisoner economy enable all the prisoners involved in the transgressive processes to reclaim and re-connote the category of "convicted criminal." They become "Convicts"—the defiant and fundamentally subversive subjects who resist the containment proposed by the juridical term "model Inmate," the more passive "go-along-to-get-along" prisoner. For Chicano Convicts, already painted, tainted, and marked by the color of their skin, their distinct form of body tattooing, *tatuteando*, enables their rearticulation as *Convictos* or, more precisely, Pintos.[8]

As noted in the introduction, the self-referential use of the term "Pinta/o" by Chicana/o Convicts also marks a specific moment in their process of *concientización*, or political awakening. This "naming" forms the nexus of their thoroughly vernacular and inherently collective and oppositional theory of praxis. Calling oneself a Pinto is itself a transgressive act of self-affirmation precisely because this utterance alludes to signifying practices that not only proclaim difference but model abjection as defiant, ennobling, and above all, enlightening. The practice of *tatuteando* is one such transgressive bodily act that calls attention to the Pinto body and the symbolic and material challenges it represents. Franklin (1989) provides a useful framework for examining *tatuteando* as a transformative writing ritual in his observation that African American and other Convict writers progressively gain knowledge and symbolic power by using personal narratives to explore their "conversion to criminality, and then, by chronicling individual experience in crime and in prison, to arrive at some understanding of both self and the society that shaped that self" (236).[9] But unlike the ideologically unstable category of "prisoner narratives," the practice of *tatuteando* and the resulting *tatuajes*—both criminal(ized) forms of "writing"—enable epistemological transformations that necessarily involve a nonindividualist theory of knowledge and praxis. This distinction arises from their illegality. Unlike other commodity exchanges in the subaltern prisoner economy, where written records of transactions cannot be kept for security reasons, and in contrast to prisoner (literary) writing in general, which cannot be expressly outlawed due to "First Amendment rights," prison-made "illegal" tattoos openly and defiantly record and give testimony to continued transgressions, especially among Pintos: like the mark of their skin color, the India-ink-colored marks *under* their skin are permanent.[10]

The abject significance, and transgressive value, that *tatuajes* assume as a vernacular form of writing is introduced in the preproduction phase as Pintos actively transgress laws to procure the raw materials to produce their art: ink, needles, "flashes" (copy sheets), and stencils. "Crime" is essential to this ritual. As confirmation that all Convicts and prisons are pitted against one another in a never-ending battle to control material and symbolic (narrative) resources (and thus monopolize the resource of authorship), the same signs posted throughout many American penitentiaries and jails prohibiting "illegal forms of self-mutilation" also explicitly warn that such practices (or even the mere possession of related paraphernalia) "will be treated as attempts to escape."[11] Accordingly, an entire macro-system of punishment to complement the overall penitentiary project of control and subordination is erected with the sole aim of stemming the production of prison tattoos and counteracting the threat that they—as verifiable "crimes-in-progress"—pose to the panoptic narrative order of the penitentiary. Thus, even before *tatuajes* are fabricated, the paraphernalia used to produce them become sites of struggle in the overall battle to contain the Convict(ed) bodies of Chicana/o prisoners, or the *cuerpo pintao* (painted corpus).

The term *cuerpo pintao* is my syntactical and orthographic vernacular neologism formed from the Chicano colloquial version of the standard Spanish past participle *pintado* (painted). Although it is not used by Pintos, it represents my attempt to underscore the difficulties that arise from academic disarticulations of Pinto discourse resulting from classifying it as "prisoner narratives" or "folk art." Since the body is central to the elaboration of the Pinto, and the body of writing that comprises Pinto discourse in general, such a term is indispensable in recognizing the ambiguity of form that distinguishes this vernacular *corpus*: it is painted, tainted, and marked in multiple ways.

In an interview with Louis Mendoza, Pinto poet and activist Raúl Salinas notes:

For some prisoners, tattooing becomes a means of survival; they are artists who ply their trade, who work at it in order to get items such as cigarettes, toothpaste, and other things, by exchanging tattoo work.

And of course, in every prison I've been in, *tattoos, and the paraphernalia and other materials used to produce them, are considered contraband*. To get a tattoo put on in prison, you're going to have to do it in a clandestine manner. You have to do it underground. So that it itself is part of the whole underground social and economic system that prisoners operate. (Mendoza 1993a, emphasis added)

For Pintos who are recognized in prison, and out, for their prolific and stylistically unique tattoo work, the threat of punishment (or rather more punishment) underscores the abject value of *tatuteando* as a criminal(ized) practice, and *tatuajes* as a criminal(ized) commodity.[12] Salinas adds:

It's a matter of degree. If they catch you actually tattooing the guy, and you're busted with the needle, the ink, and everything, it's a month in solitary.

Deterrence? No. Of course not. No one ever thinks about stopping just because they went to the hole [solitary confinement], or somebody else went to the hole. That's part of your daily existence—taking a risk.

As is the case with the daily consumption of other contraband goods and services, extra punishment and persecution are also acceptable "business risks" precisely because they are directly related to the symbolically and materially enhanced Convict standard of living in prison not accessible to Inmates. The Chicana/o practice of *tatuteando* through which *tatuajes*, like extended "sentences" or supplemental penalties, become badges of honor and status symbols, effectively recasts the epistemological status of "crime" and "punishment" by unmasking the hegemonic and inhumane function of jurisprudence. *Tatuajes* represent a victory—a testament to the survival of the human spirit—that begins with a "crime."

The *modus operandi* for procuring the raw materials used to produce *tatuajes* adds to the transgressive value that *tatuajes* later assume as commodities, and that *cuerpos pintaos* take on as cultural capital. Drawing from Pierre Bordieu's (1985, 1990) notions of "cultural capital" and the "market of symbolic goods," I underscore that *tatuajes* mark "different," or rather vernacular, and stratified forms of "literacy" and "capital." For instance, the ability to "read" *tatuajes*—unique to the lumpen segment of the Chicana/o community—enables various economic and political interactions, both symbolic and material. Moreover, the ingenious and subversive methods that Pintos employ to procure raw materials essential to their vernacular "writing" rituals are strategic victories that illuminate the contours and significance of *writing* resistance from prison perhaps even more than does the folk figure of the prisoner author.[13]

When Convicts cannot obtain the preferred indelible ink pigment (also known as "India ink"), they fabricate it illegally by adapting materials readily available within the penitentiary. One process involves burning plastic spoons, newspapers, toilet paper, or even official legal correspondence to generate carbon that is subsequently collected on the walls of a legal-size sheet of paper rolled into a cylinder; the residue is then scraped off and blended into an alchemous mixture of shampoo (for consistency), water—and a little spit for good luck! The needles used to pierce and pigment the skin are fabricated from staples removed from religious pamphlets (generously distributed by prison administrators) or other prison-approved documents and subsequently scraped on the prison's concrete floors or walls until sharpened to a fine point. The improvised needle is then attached to a pencil or popsicle stick (available from the prison canteen) with thread taken from the Convict's prison-issued uniform to serve as a reservoir for the pigment.[14] The practice of appropriating prison resources to fashion criminal(ized) materials for the production of criminal(ized) commodities—marked Convict bodies—becomes even more threatening to the monopoly on symbolic and material resources signified by the panoptic guard tower. This threat is underscored by the frequency with which guards and other prison functionaries are co-opted into smuggling the necessary ink and other tools that Convicts later use to "mutilate" the model Inmate.[15] The co-optation of guards into this preproduction phase thus undergirds the Pintos' challenge to their individual and collective "emasculation" and effacement as speaking subjects. The panopticon is inverted through the production of the tattooed Pinto body.

POINTMEN AND THE DIVISION OF LABOR:
TATUAJES AS CULTURAL CAPITAL

In addition to the subversive methods used to procure raw materials for *tatuaje* production, Pintos deploy the collective Chicano Convict body (along with other non-Chicano Convicts) in the production process to further subvert the panoptic apparatus designed to survey and contain their collective criminality. The act of tattooing becomes a collectivist ritual of social production in the continued transformation of Convict subjects. Despite their individual motives for participating in the tattoo production process, they must work together as a group, a Convict corpus. Clinton Sanders has noted that the social organization of tattoo production in freeworld tattoo parlors involves an interactive and stratified division of labor involving the tattooist, tattooee, apprentice, and audience members, all of whom collectively enable an ephemeral oppositional collective of "symbolic physical devian[ts]" (1989: 2–3). In prison, this affinity group takes on more deliberate collective and transgressive overtones because both the practice and the products not only are viewed as "deviant" but are expressly classified as "illegal."

In the dialectical battle between the penitentiary guard tower and the prisoners who defiantly identify themselves as Convicts and Pintos, the Chicano tattoo artist, or *tatuísta*, is *not* a central figure, as might be expected.[16] In prison, two equally important figures are the tattooee, who functions as a "living canvas," and the "point man," sometimes referred to as the "jigger man" by Convicts. This prisoner (always a Convict, not an Inmate) is a trusted confidant who serves as a lookout. The very nature of the point man's "job"—standing guard against detection—involves the inversion of the panoptic penitentiary even more profoundly than the subversion resulting from the struggle to procure raw materials. The point man is charged with exploiting the tension that exists between the two complementary but competing knowledge/power systems structuring the U.S. carceral system: the one revolving around visibility, and the one dependent upon concealment. His goal is to uncover the prison unit's weak points and the moments of panoptic slippage (e.g., the hidden crevices in the physical plant or gaps in the surveillance regimen, such as weekends, when most guards are off-duty). Pintos and other Convicts can then appropriate these weak points in the production of their own counterhegemonic narrative. Because the cultural practice of *tatuteando* must remain clandestine during the crucial early stage in production, when it is most vulnerable to disruption by prison authorities, the point man is strategically deployed to survey the production process and any potential threat. If the process and participants are discovered before the *tatuaje* wounds have a chance to "heal" and thus cover up evidence of the "crime-in-progress," everyone found to be involved is subjected to extra punishment that often includes being placed in isolation, where each *re*-convicted prisoner becomes the object of even more (judicial) surveillance. Such an interruption makes any future work on the disrupted tattoo more difficult. If the point man is successful, though, the *tatuaje* will permanently record the prison's "failure" and persist as a prominent and permanent mark of defiance because there is no way to eliminate the visible criminality the mark will later represent as a finished product. No legal privilege permits prison authorities to remove it; after all, bodily mutilation is illegal in prison!

Moreover, the challenges posed by the guard tower's overarching gaze often necessitate the cooperation of several point men. The job of countersurveillance thus gets diffused throughout the broader Convict body. This simple act of transgression—covering for each other— sometimes transcends the strong racial stratification among prisoners (unofficially sanctioned by prison administrations and reinforced by in-group stereotypes and competition for scarce resources). It enables the development of an even more overtly politicized oppositional con- sciousness. All Convicts become potential point men, thereby posing an almost insurmountable obstacle to the penitentiary system of surveillance and containment. Amado "Mayo" Pardo, a Pinto formerly incarcerated in the Texas Department of Corrections and forced to labor on its rural plantations, recalls:

> The thing we had to be careful of was when we worked in the field. . . .
> When we came in they made us undress, so we had to hide the tattoos that were in progress. If they saw one they flagged you down for punishment.
> But we all covered for each other pretty well. (Mendoza 1993b)

The reliance upon a point man, or men, to produce *tatuajes*—born out of the cruel forms of bondage and heightened conditions of censorship that distinguish the U.S. carceral apparatus—marks the form and content of this vernacular *writing* ritual: the production and consumption of *tatuajes* is a collective enterprise from the start.

Herein lies the symbolic use-value of *tatuajes* in prison: they represent cultural capital that all can share—even those without tattoos. Of this nascent political consciousness that arises in the production phase of this transgressive bodily, and socially symbolic *écriture*, Salinas reiterates:

> Well clearly it's an act of defiance. First of all, it's illegal—"How dare you break our rules!" It's made criminal. But to defy rules is to recognize that you are engaged in a psychological battle with the prison authorities, the guards. Similar to the intellectual's declaration that "you can jail my body but you can't jail my mind," the act of tattooing oneself, or soliciting an

artist to tattoo you, is an act of defiance that declares: "You can jail my body, but you can't control it; you can put me in solitary as punishment, but you can't take my tattoos away from me." So it is an affront; it's a threat to the very notion of confinement, of detention. The designs that are created in these conditions, under insurmountable odds, threaten the whole system of incarceration because it shows ultimately that there are still ways to retain one's dignity. (Mendoza 1993a)

Rather than simply modeling the exotic difference of the "other," *tatuajes* instead offer to expose the dialectical forces at work in the articulation of difference, even as these texts produce a counterhegemonic ideology of difference beyond the literary forms Saldívar identified (1990: 7–8). The Convict body in general—and especially the brown, *tatuaje*-marked *text* of the Chicana/o Convict body—makes manifest their challenge to the underlying subtexts: the peonage and proletarianization of the racially marked Chicana/o people since 1848 and the concurrent commodification of the "convicted" brown body. Transgression, as articulated through vernacular writing rituals such as *tatuteando*, thus becomes the ontological basis of the new counterhegemonic Chicana/o subject.

Aside from the nascent group consciousness that permeates this "writing" ritual, where the capital gains for each participant in the criminal(ized) production of *tatuajes* are difficult to quantify, point men, almost always involved in the process out of personal friendship and allegiance to the project of transgression that *tatuajes* illuminate, are also "paid." According to Salinas, point men, like the *tatuísta*, are rewarded with various forms of barter, "be it with wine, food or cigarettes" (Mendoza 1993a). Payment may even come in the form of a *tatuaje* for the point man himself, thus reproducing the need for more concealment and more point men to effect this subversion ad infinitum. The already over-determined criminal—the Convict—is reified. The convicted and *tatuaje*-marked bodies of Pintos, though still commodified in the licit prison economy as well as in the illicit Convict economy and its *tatuaje* sub-industry, ultimately becomes a value-added product that buttresses a *different* narrative order.

THE SEMIOTICS OF THE *PLACA*: RAÚL SALINAS AND THE TROPE OF THE PINTO VICTIM/SAVIOR

For Pintos, the act of marking, painting, and further tainting their already Convict(ed) bodies resonates beyond the prison walls in ways other than merely distinguishing them as objects of suspicion or targets for arrest. Aside from the transgressive value of the *tatuteando* process, *tatuajes* have a distinct use-value as finished products grounded in the culturally distinct style and often cryptic iconography of the "writings" themselves. Their relative value to various segments of the Chicana/o community can be gauged more precisely when *tatuajes* are "read" within the episteme of *la placa*: a badge, tag, or other distinguishing sign. A *placa* can come in a variety of visual and oral forms, including the stylized graffiti signature commonly known as a "tag," hand signals, or a spoken "nickname." It is used to mark or claim a space as one's own.[17] So aside from serving as "traveling art shows" facilitated by prison-ordered transfers and/ or reconvictions of (ex)Convicts, for some "convicted criminals" these tattooed bodies link Pintos to the broader Chicana/o community by invoking the barrio *rasquachismo* aesthetic:

> Rasquachismo is a vernacular system of taste that is intuitive and sincere,
> not thought out and self-conscious. It is a way of putting yourself together
> or creating an environment replete with color, texture, and pattern;
> a rampant decorative sense whose basic axiom might be "too much
> is not enough." Rasquachismo draws its essence within the world
> of the tattered, shattered, and broken: *lo remendado* (stitched together).
> (Ybarra-Frausto 1991: 156)

Tomás Ybarra-Frausto adds that *rasquachismo* "assumes a vantage point from the bottom up" and, moreover, "through such strategies of appropriation, reversal, and inversion, Chicana/o youth cultures [who deploy this aesthetic] negate dominant models and values, [that is], rasquachismo feigns complicity with dominant discourses while skillfully decentering and transforming them" (1991: 160). I argue that within this cultural milieu, Pintos, through their *tatuajes*, lay claim to the free world by proclaiming their racialized barrio identities, albeit in truncated and highly stylized forms, as *cuerpos pintaos*.

Raúl Salinas's own *tatuajes*—which precede, inform, and indelibly mark his succeeding body of work of published poetry and corresponding activist interventions—illustrate the complex space Pintos, and their *cuerpos pintaos*, occupy in the Chicana/o community and beyond. Margo De Mello (1993) has argued that "the Convict body is itself counterhegemonic in that it incorporates both the system (prison) and the challenge (tattoos): through bold markings on the face, hands, neck and arms, it represents a willful defiance of the Man" (13). Following De

Mello, as well as Barbara Harlow's (1992) premise that any reading of prisoner writing as counterhegemonic must invariably link the text and its prison context, I propose that Salinas's *tatuajes*, which consciously and unconsciously syncretize both the system of oppression (such as the raw materials taken from the prison) and the transgressive challenge to it (the resulting tattoos), provide an important access point to a complex and coherent discourse produced by Chicana/o Convicts from the late nineteenth century to the present.

Placas, in the form of *tatuajes*, become floating signifiers that remain grounded in the material and subjective conditions of their production and consumption. Salinas's symbolic system is recognizable to his primarily Chicana/o audience precisely because he is synthesizing common signifying practices in his use of familiar scripts and styles, as well as icons and archetypes used among Chicana/os in prisons and barrios throughout the contested space of the southwestern United States. Salinas's sign system, like that of other Pintos across time and space, is steeped in the Chicana/o political unconscious. His Pinto political unconscious involves constant synthesis as various symbols and icons are troped and embedded with meta-discourses arising from newer markings—other *placas*—that are both visually and metrically rendered. This materialist and historicist linkage is often glossed over by critics who limit their analysis to Salinas's poetry. Just as Salinas's Pachuco, Pinto, and political activist personas are inextricably linked, I argue that his distinct and varied forms of "writing" are inseparable from, and constantly interacting with, one another and thus must be read as a whole. Salinas's *tatuajes*—which span the years from 1951, when he first marked his body with his *placa* in the form of a *tatuaje* that affirmed his barrio allegiance, to 2008, the year of his death, as he continued to mark and distinguish himself through his various vernacular formats—emerge as fundamental keys to the multigenre symbolic system of his entire corpus.

The consolidation of Salinas's vernacular symbolic system is fore-grounded in his semiepic, semiautobiographical poem "A Trip Through the Mind Jail," which first appeared in May 1970 in the cultural nationalist prisoner newspaper *Aztlán de Leavenworth*, published by Chicano Convicts in Leavenworth Federal Penitentiary in Kansas. This poem, a foundational work in Chicana/o letters, is Salinas's "signature piece," his verse *placa*, as it were.[18] The poem literally facilitated his release from prison by attracting the attention of a cadre of activist literary critics who successfully campaigned for his release based on arguments that Salinas had received an unusually harsh sentence (he was purportedly

Figure 4.1. First issue of *Aztlán de Leavenworth* (May 5, 1970). Courtesy of Green Library Special Collections, Stanford University.

Figure 4.2. Original publication of "A Trip Through the Mind Jail," by Raúl Salinas. *Aztlán de Leavenworth*, May 5, 1970. Courtesy of Green Library Special Collections, Stanford University.

sentenced to five years for the possession of five dollars' worth of marijuana) and, more importantly, had become a writer of world-class caliber who exhibited profound political values and personal ethics.[19] The poem thus became an important site of struggle and articulation for Salinas's revolutionary utopian project, which necessarily involves his brown body and written corpus as well as the entire Chicana/o body politic.

Through the use of various *placa* formats—from poetry to graffiti to *tatuajes*—all of which are interwoven into a tapestry of vernacular verse that converges around La Loma (The Hill), the name of Salinas's east Austin barrio, the Pinto poet is able to reclaim the free world—that is, his barrio. He paradoxically *rewrites* himself into the embodiment of his barrio's underdevelopment (e.g., "LA LOMA / Neighborhood of my youth . . . / you live on, captive, in the lonely / cellblocks of my mind," [lines 1–2, 5–6]). This process of critique and rearticulation reaches a crescendo as the opening strophe, "La Loma," is troped through its use in other parts of his corpus. The tenth stanza, a multigenre segment composed of free verse, stylized Chicana/o graffiti, and hand-drawn symbols of Salinas's barrio *placas*, serves as the nexus around which La Loma will be transformed into both a nostalgic representation of the free world—any place outside the penitentiary—and also a manifestation of the effects of the U.S. carceral system—that is, colonization and the related local effects of underdevelopment.

Even as Salinas celebrates the barrio ("Fiestas for any occasion / holidays holy days happy days / 'round and 'round the promenade / eating snowcones—raspas—& tamales . . .," [38–41]), he morosely recalls it as a "Neighborhood of endless hills / muddied streets—all chuckhole lined—that never drank of asphalt" (7–9); "Neighborhood of dilapidated community hall" (19); and "Neighborhood that never saw a schoolbus" (60). Through Salinas's verse, La Loma becomes an ambiguously endearing place of unrealized dreams, ambitions, hopes, and material needs as well as this Pachuco/Pinto's ontological homespace, the terrain upon which he will battle various forms of containment through his *placas*. Ironically, but powerfully, La Loma becomes both a product of U.S. hegemony and the site of counterhegemonic signifying practices.

Salinas proclaims the allegorical dimension of his writing in the text proper at the end of the tenth stanza, where he says, "the art form of our slums / more meaningful & significant / than Egypt's finest hieroglyphics" (108–111). The virtue of this bold, almost chauvinistic claim, reminiscent of the cultural nationalist essentialism that prevailed in the era, is borne out in other *placas* that distinguish Salinas's symbolic system. When read

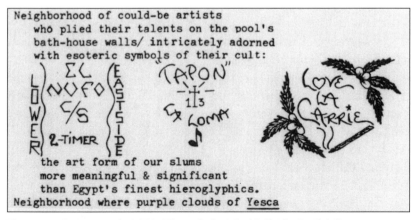

Figure 4.3. Stanza 10 of "A Trip Through the Mind Jail," by Raúl Salinas. Courtesy of Raúl Salinas.

as complementary signifying practices, they reveal that this mixed-genre stanza is in fact embedded with truth: the *placas* that mark the poem as Chicana/o art also mark Salinas as a Pachuco, a Pinto, and a Chicano artist whose corpus informs the consolidation of the male permutation of a protorevolutionary Pinta/o discourse.

Contrary to Juan Bruce-Novoa's contention that the Pachuco graffiti art adorning the pages of Salinas's poetry (and body) is so "esoteric" that it exhibits how "Pachucos limit (read 'contain') themselves" (1982: 43), I propose that the metaphoric iconography of Salinas's *tatuajes* and other *placas* historicize his corpus by grounding it in the lived experiences and corresponding Chicana/o political unconscious. Salinas's *tatuajes* are central to what David Ericson identifies as a dialogic aesthetic directly linked to public discourse:

> [Salinas] pushes the ideal of literary heteroglossia as far as a single author can by working with several languages (and dialects within languages) and a variety of textual forms, including with the poems, drawings, tattoos, graffiti, oral legend, song, and prose letters. (1989: 8–9)

The significance of Salinas's conscious and unconscious assault on disciplinary (and disciplining) genres and forms resides in the manners and degree to which he is able to deploy his multigenre format to participate in the process of self-discovery, self-awareness, and rearticulation with the historically marginalized Chicana/o community of east Austin from which he had been excised through his imprisonment. The teleological model of *concientización*, or political awakening (which Franklin identifies in his study of primarily African American prisoner narratives, and that I link to Pinto intellectuals Jimmy Santiago Baca and Ricardo Sánchez in preceding chapters), is also at work in Salinas's multimedia text. Except in Salinas's case, it is thoroughly oppositional. Salinas ultimately challenges the containment proposed by the page and the prison, the text and the tower, and, in a broader context, the overall carceral apparatus. "A Trip Through the Mind Jail," then, serves as a blueprint, a prescriptive methodology, that enables us to access his complex corpus in which his *tatuajes* and other *placa* formats are central.

The relation between this poem and Salinas's other forms of "writing," his *tatuajes*, revolves around the center-most symbol of the Pachuco glyph that marks the tenth stanza. Salinas locates his Pachuco persona—symbolized by the graffiti script of his barrio nickname, Tapón—in the text by locating this *placa* atop the Pachuco cross and the stylized graffiti script "La Loma," which is further personalized by a musical note invoking his virtuosity as a prison saxophonist. This "La Loma" depiction is similar to the *tatuaje* on Salinas's left hand in the symbolically significant space between the index finger and thumb, where Pachucos usually tattoo a cross.[20]

Salinas deploys these personally nuanced marks of distinction to locate his individual Pachuco and Pinto subjectivities in his text, while simultaneously locating his text into a broader context of subordination that encompasses many other barrios beyond La Loma, as is underscored by the barrio roll call that closes the poem:

> i respect your having been:
> my Loma of Austin
> my Rose Hill of Los Angeles
> my West Side of San Anto

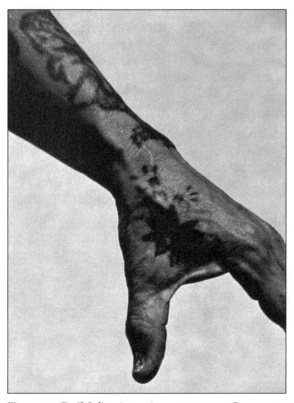

Figure 4.4. Raúl Salinas's *crucita* tattoo, 1993. Courtesy of Raúl Salinas and photographer Cristina Ibarra.

my Quinto of Houston
my Jackson of San Jo
my Segundo of El Paso
my Barelas of Alburque
my Westside of Denver
Flats, Los Marcos, Maravilla, Calle Guadalupe,
Magnolia, Buena Vista, Mateo, La Séis, Chíquis,
El Sur, and all Chicano neighborhoods that
now existed and once existed;
    somewhere . . . , someone remembers . . . . . (lines 153–166)

These *placas* enable him to represent internal colonization, and subsequent challenges to it, through the barrio metonym of under-development: the asocial, lumpenproletarian Pachuco, petty property thief, drug dealer, Convict, and eminent socialist—Raúl Salinas, aka El Tapón de La Loma. Unlike other cultural workers of the Chicano Movement such as Alurista and Ricardo Sánchez, who disseminated neoromantic portraits of the Pachuco as a defiant male warrior hero, Salinas presents a more problematic portrait of Pachucos imprisoned by drug addiction and held captive by a phallocentric notion of empowerment that leads to various forms of individual and collective self-destruction, including fratricide. For example, two stanzas below the aforementioned Pachuco glyphs, Salinas recalls how "Lalo shotgunned / Pete Evans to death because of / an unintentional stare" (119–121) and also relates how "El Güero drunkenly stabbed Julio / arguing over who'd drive home" (126–127). Here, phallic objects such as a shotgun and a knife illustrate how subordination is a collective experience that Pachucos (and male Chicanos in general) inadvertently facilitate. Rather than serving as a self-denigrating diatribe against Pachucos, as Bruce-Novoa (1982) would have us believe, Salinas is reconstructing "La Loma," the prototype of the underdeveloped barrio, as a subaltern space where the legacy of colonialism continues to manifest itself, as Fanon (1982) observed, through tragic, seemingly senseless but ultimately significant episodes of internecine violence. Ericson adds that "Salinas knows that illegal modes of street survival are not ahistorical problems of individual psychopathology, but rather a result of the material conditions by which Chicanos are victimized in the segregated barrios" (1989: 35). Raúl Salinas—an elder Pachuco permanently marked by La Loma, imprisoned for having participated in the subaltern economy of the illicit drug trade, and a newly politicized Convict repeatedly subjected to supplemental punishment for his efforts to organize prisoners during

the turbulent 1960s era of prison rebellions—becomes the personification
of containment, subordination, victimization, and more—all of which is
further elaborated in the *tatuajes* he bears.[21]

Salinas's discourse gains even more counterhegemonic significance
as he further elaborates a collectivist theory and praxis that not only
includes Convicts and Pintos, but also incorporates his community
beyond the walls of the prison. The *tatuaje* of Cristo (Jesus Christ) that
Salinas bears on his back is a central icon in his symbolic system and is
fundamental to his articulation of his model of Pinto discourse onto the
Chicana/o community.

Salinas's *tatuaje* of Cristo was produced in 1964 by *tatuísta* Paulo
"Chino" Montes of Corpus Christi, Texas (along with a cadre of other
transgressing Pintos) while Salinas was incarcerated in the Walls Unit

Figure 4.5. Raúl Salinas's tattoo of Cristo, 1993. Courtesy
of Raúl Salinas and photographer Cristina Ibarra.

of the Texas Department of Corrections.[22] Alan Govenar (1988) cites Lawrence Honrada, a Chicano Convict from east Los Angeles, who also bears a Cristo on his back, to contextualize this symbol:

> In prison, I could understand better what Christ must have gone through as victim and prisoner. The tattoo represented the quest for freedom that everyone in the joint must feel. (1988: 211)

This icon further problematizes the juridical category of "criminal" by linking Convicts to Jesus Christ, the prototypical victim; even more, it makes accessible the sanctity that Saint Dismas, the petty property thief executed with Jesus Christ, achieves as he becomes for Catholics the patron saint of all prisoners. Every Chicana/o Catholic knows this story; the sight of Christ on the body of a Chicano Convict unconsciously evokes the linkage even as this very *tatuaje* marks the object/subject as the "ex-con" who some people, like the police officers in the *COPS* episode, suggest should be feared.

Thus, Salinas's *tatuaje* of Cristo represents a synthesis of a common signifying practice grounded in the prisons and barrios, and therefore has much broader implications. Its greatest significance revolves around the universality that such an icon makes accessible to "La Loma," inscribed into Salinas's hand, his poem, and elsewhere. Despite Salinas's disavowal of Catholic ideology, this symbol of Cristo, part of his secular Pachuco and Pinto repertoire of *tatuajes*, distinctly identifies him as a prototypical Christ-like victim; its material basis lies in his natal experiences in his east Austin barrio of La Loma, which has been systemically underdeveloped into a prison of America's racially marked lumpen-proletariat. Salinas's reappropriation of the Christ motif becomes a discursive maneuver crucial to the evolution of Pinto discourses that propose a victim/vanguard role for Chicano Convicts. This link is underscored by the distinct resemblance of Salinas's Cristo to his own face. Ethan Hoffman and John McCoy note that this resemblance is a common feature of the prisoner visual vernacular, since the tattooist faces the challenge of elaborating the likeness of a never before seen figure such as Jesus Christ upon the very real and constantly visible Convict's body, whose own likeness stands presently and prominently before the artist. From this specific and personal vantage, Salinas's discourse begins to move towards a moral universalism by laying claim to the allegorical value encoded into this and other Christian archetypes.

This visual link to his community's political unconscious is further grounded through the *tatuaje* of La Virgen de Guadalupe that Salinas bears upon his chest.

Even more definitively than the Cristo icon, La Virgen, central to the Mexican and Chicana/o Catholic pantheon, imbues Salinas's multigenre discourse with the collective and counterhegemonic value embedded in the very process of *tatuaje* production in prison discussed earlier. This *tatuaje* remained a "work-in-progress" throughout Salinas's life, and La Virgen's halo was never fully inked-in before he died in 2008. While Salinas noted that the incomplete status of this *tatuaje* was a direct result of the difficulties involved in the production process discussed above, he also relished the opportunity for further collective action by inviting others to contribute to the development of this *tatuaje* and its significance. Borrowing a term coined by San Antonio photographer and

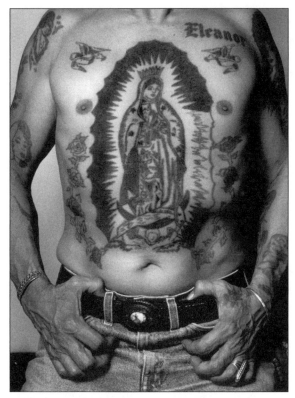

Figure 4.6. Raúl Salinas's tattoo of La Virgen de Guadalupe. Courtesy of Raúl Salinas and photographer Al Rendón.

painter Mary Jessie Garza, Salinas stated that "la Virgen is part of my body altar," emphasizing that an altar is a communal space where people converge to meditate, pray, and hope.[23]

Viewed as such, La Virgen de Guadalupe, the patron saint of Mexican and Chicana/o Catholics, links Salinas's *cuerpo pintao* not only to the collective memory of colonization and exploitation, but also to the redemption and salvation this mestiza demigoddess simultaneously represents. Salinas's Virgen is distinguished from other depictions of Virgin Mary by her clasped hands, as opposed to the open ones common in some representations in Europe and Latin America. The image's monochromatic color scheme, which in reality has a significant two-tone quality that features "Chicano brown" against "India ink black," as well as other accoutrements such as a full-body halo, two hovering birds (instead of angels), and one angel below the mestiza savior, again invokes the popular Mexican and Chicana/o myth of *las tres* Marías. Some scholars propose that La Virgen's sixteenth-century appearance consolidated the *mestizaje*/conquest by legitimating Catholicism (and colonialism) for the indigenous population while simultaneously offering a brown-skinned Virgin as a recognizable symbol of redemption: she would be the intercessor between the subordinated indigenous masses and her son, Jesus Christ, their purported savior. Despite these misogynist aspects of the myth structure, La Virgen, as represented in her full-haloed glory upon Salinas's chest, serves to synthesize the victim motif presented throughout the rest of his corpus. As the number of years that Salinas spent behind bars grew, his multimedia narrative of subordination, presented in part through "A Trip Through the Mind Jail" as well as through the poem's and the poet's corresponding *placas*, gains another dimension: the legacy of victimization encoded into the figure of Christ is complemented by Jesus Christ's mother as represented in Salinas's Pinto permutation of the Virgin Mary. As such, Salinas's *cuerpo pintao* assumes the role of the prototypical victim/savior, a mythologized subject position he simultaneously embraces and rearticulates into his historical materialist agenda. Even as these *placas* mark him in the eyes of all as a Pinto, a "convicted criminal," they record and give testimony to the fact that Salinas is a survivor of unspeakable horrors that included forced servitude, public beatings and humiliating body cavity searches, prolonged sensory deprivation in specially designed "control units" such as the Marion Federal Penitentiary that literally "houses" prisoners in underground cells, and involuntary subjection to psychiatric drugs designed to incapacitate him.[24] He is painted, tainted, and marked—and in the eyes of some, so much more noble because of this.

These *tatuajes*, keys to Salinas's interactive symbolic system, further "rewrite" the value of his Convict(ed) body by imbuing his other *tatuajes* with even more layered significance, chief among them his Texas Department of Corrections (TDC) prisoner identification number, A-43203, which he had tattooed on his inner left calf. This India ink–colored number was etched into Salinas's skin just above the caricature of a "Texas Convict" bearing a field hoe of the type issued to TDC prisoners, all of whom are forced to labor for a minimum period of time on the state-owned plantations that were tilled by African American slaves until the mid-nineteenth century. It is a mark that Salinas "voluntarily" placed upon his own body while being shuttled from unit to unit in the

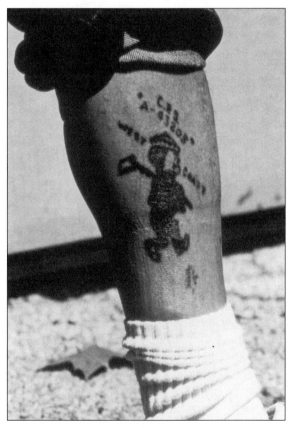

Figure 4.7. Raúl Salinas's "Convict" tattoo. Courtesy of Raúl Salinas and photographer Cristina Ibarra.

vast Texas prison system, and which he subsequently revised during a prison stint in California by adding the letters "CPS," the Convict abbreviation for "California Prison System," which challenges the sanitized representation of penitentiaries by such official euphemisms as "California Department of Corrections." He also added the "West Coast" heading, transforming the heretofore immanent critique of the earlier icons by explicitly historicizing his corpus with direct and concrete references to the contested lands of the "southwestern United States," a geopolitical space that came into being only after the U.S. imperialist incursions into, and subsequent occupation of, almost one-half of Mexican national territory at the twilight of African American slavery. This *tatuaje* suggests linkage among Pintos from La Tejana (the Texas Joint) and those from Califas (California), as both systems have converged upon Raúl Salinas's *cuerpo pintao*.

Salinas makes other links as well. This *tatuaje* of Salinas's TDC prisoner ID number ultimately represents a Pinto reappropriation of the collective Convict body above and beyond the Chicano body politic: the cruelties encountered in any given penitentiary unit become a secondary concern as the ultimate object/subject of his critique is the overall U.S. carceral apparatus. Salinas resists his containment and exploitation by rolling up his pants to expose it! So, when he states, "I have many numbers. Many!" —referring at once to his various local, state, and federal prison identification numbers, as well as to the CIA and FBI surveillance files, which also catalog his criminal(ized) post-prison activist work—Salinas is in fact deploying his marks of abjection to signify the transgressive posture of his Pinto and activist subjectivities and also link his defiance to the collective *cuerpo pintao*, as well as to other communities in struggle. Like other marks inscribed into and onto his body, these numbers are abject marks of distinction.

In direct contrast to the role that indelible ink markings have played in recent history—such as in Nazi Germany, where similar tattooed numbers facilitated the identification, exploitation, and subsequent extermination of over six million Jews and other people in concentration camps throughout Europe—this number models a counterhegemonic challenge to this very commodification, consumption, and extermination. This *tatuaje*, then, in the context of the others examined above, represents the "bonds" of "bondage" unique to the Pinto experience. And it signifies much more. The counterhegemonic potential of this painted, tainted, and marked body is further enhanced by the fact that this *tatuaje* became slightly withered, faded, and blurred as Salinas aged and matured politically; the image of the Convict forced to labor on prison plantations subsequently invited new readings—the field hoe, once a tool of exploitation, seemed raised in the air as if it were an improvised weapon pointing toward the free world. Cumulatively "read," Salinas's overall *cuerpo pintao* models the difference that dialectically challenges the binary paradigm of power that necessitates a Texas Department of Corrections, a California Prison System, or even an Auschwitz, whose gateway sign—*Arbeit Macht Frei* (Work Brings Freedom)—appears as the third epigraph above.

THE SACRED AND THE PROFANE: PINTO DISCOURSE
AND THE POLITICAL UNCONSCIOUS

These same *placas* that mark Salinas for persecution also enabled him to literally *write* himself out of prison and, ultimately, facilitate his rearticulation as a Pinto intellectual. The consolidation of this politicized Chicano Convict intersects with, but diverges from, various other reformulations of Antonio Gramsci's (1971) paradigmatic vanguard figure. These include Franz Fanon's (1982) "native intellectual," who fights selfish bourgeois tendencies in an attempt to readapt colonial training to new nationalist ends; Renato Rosaldo's (1989) "native ethnographer" and Henry Louis Gates's (1988) "vernacular interpreter," both of whom are engaged in a project of translating their cultures (not unlike Homi Bhabha's "mimic man") even as they seek to challenge the normative codes of their respective disciplines; and also Gloria Anzaldúa's (1987) "mestiza," who is most enabled as a subject and most effective as an agent of change when guided by the latent power of "*mestiza* consciousness." Drawing from this genealogy, I locate Salinas's Pinto intellectual at the center of the emergent cadre that José David Saldívar identifies as the "School of Calibán":

> The phrase suggests a group of engaged writers, scholars, and professors
> of literature who work under a common political influence, a group whose
> different (imagined) national communities and symbologies are linked by
> their derivation from a common and explosive reading of Shakespeare's last
> (pastoral and tragicomic) play, *The Tempest*. The phrase also emblematizes
> not just the group's shared subaltern subject positions, but the "schooling"
> that their enrollment in such an institution provides. (1991: 123)

As Salinas shows, Pinto intellectuals deploy their prison-enhanced oppositional consciousness—a sensibility linked to the political unconscious of the Chicana/o community through signifying practices such as *tatuteando*—in the service of the subordinated populations located in barrios, prisons, and other sites of struggle throughout the southwestern United States and the world at large. From this "central" position in the margins, Salinas deploys the Chicana/o vernacular episteme of the *placa* to articulate a relatively empowered oppositional subject engaged in diverse populist struggles, undergirding prisoners' rights campaigns (including efforts to free U.S. political prisoners such as Leonard Peltier and Mumia Abu Jamal), the struggle for Puerto Rican independence, volunteer work with the Venceremos Brigade in solidarity with the Cuban Revolution, militancy on behalf of the American Indian Movement, youth counseling with the Barrios Unidos Coalition to End Barrio Warfare, and grass-roots organizing with El Comité en Solidaridad con el Pueblo de Chiapas y México (Committee in Solidarity with the People of Chiapas and Mexico).[25]

Figure 4.8. Raúl Salinas at Vieques, Puerto Rico. Courtesy of Raúl Salinas and photographer Alan Pogue.

Salinas's use of the episteme of the *placa* to mark himself as a paradigmatic Chicano—an imprisoned yet defiant subject—links him materially and symbolically to his community, his people, La Raza, and other peoples in struggle throughout the world.[26] Without these familiar marks of distinction, not only would he be an outsider, but he would not have the knowledge and conviction that make him such a successful organizer and an organic intellectual.

Nevertheless, his model of empowerment, scripted on and through his tattoo-marked brown body, is painted, tainted, and marked by the patriarchal milieu of the barrio. The sexist subtext is intensified by the hyper-masculinist context of tattoo production in prison.[27] For instance, the image of La Virgen adorning his chest was framed by images of several other women: some of them bare-chested, others present only as disembodied heads or stylized names in the Old English script favored by Pintos.

Ironically, Salinas's claim to, and of, a space as a speaking subject—the hypermasculinist Pinto—is articulated through images of women.

Figure 4.9. Raúl Salinas's tattoos of La Virgen and other women. Courtesy of Raúl Salinas and photographer Cristina Ibarra.

This paradox demands a nuanced "reading" of Salinas's *tatuajes* that takes into account not only the material conditions of production, but also specific generational and Chicana/o cultural contexts. Such an approach to Salinas's symbolic system simultaneously illuminates the counterhegemonic dimensions of his signifying practices while also enabling a critical assessment of very common features of Pinto discourse in general—namely, the presence of naked women on the Convict(ed) body.

At one level, Salinas (along with other Pintos involved in the transgressive bodily act of *tatuteando*) symbolically and publicly proclaims that he still has human needs, passions, desires, and because of these, human rights. This claim to humanity is underscored in an interview with Louis G. Mendoza:

> MENDOZA: Why do people choose to have women reproduced on their body in prison?
> SALINAS: Well, without trying to put a Freudian spin on it, I would say that what is represented in those pictures is what is missing in their world. Certainly it's true in the case of shots of women and family.
> MENDOZA: It's interesting that those are two different kinds; sexual and familial, the profane and the sacred.
> SALINAS: Well yeah, but it's still portraying a loss, that which is not there.
> MENDOZA: Do you think that's a mixing of two different worlds, that it's contradictory to have those two together?
> SALINAS: Well if I have a portrait of my wife on one arm and a picture of a naked woman on the other, it can seem contradictory, but to me it's an expression of loving women and missing them. I suppose it can seem like an infidelity to say "I love my wife so much I have her symbolically placed on my arm," when there's a portrait of another woman on my other arm. I don't know. I do know, that because of the whole consciousness raising that has happened in society in the last twenty years, about women and how we relate to others . . . that we must be very careful about not reproducing systems and relations of oppression. I know that in the same way that there are political symbols I would wear now, there are also symbols which I would not wear. I would not have something sexually explicit on me.[28]
> (Mendoza 1993a)

Here, Salinas illustrates how Pinto discourse is inscribed in the binary phallocentric paradigm of emasculation that underwrites the penal apparatus it ostensibly seeks to challenge. But as he notes, the tattoos occasion further syntheses and consciousness-raising opportunities when confronted with newer generations of organic intellectuals influenced by feminist, queer, Marxist, and postcolonial theorists. This paradigm shift enables the recognition that these very problematic *tatuajes* demand the continued development of the transgressive collectivist epistemology arising from the preproduction and production process of *tatuteando*— one moving towards a more truly collective praxis that is at once personal and political.

New opportunities for political education and action also arise from the multiple commodifications of his corpus, including the sale and reinstitutionalization of his manuscripts, personal papers, photographs, and miscellaneous paraphernalia to Stanford University for a five-figure sum. As part of the dialectical negotiation of power that has distinguished Salinas's prison and post-prison counterhegemonic agency, this exchange of Salinas's vernacular *écriture* subsidized his community store, appropriately called Resistencia Books, throughout his life and even after his death. Hence, his process of transformation did not end with his release from prison; it has merely arrived at another synthesis in his continued and sustained work toward resolving contradictions.

Tatuteando inevitably illuminates the collective condition of post-1848 Chicana/os, whose colonial status after the U.S.-Mexico War that resulted in their absorption into the "United States" is more sharply defined by their disproportionate incarceration rates and, even more, by the very process of incarceration itself. By further painting, tainting, and marking the criminal(ized) brown body of the "Hispanic male suspect," Pintos like Salinas call even more attention to themselves; sometimes inadvertently, and at other times consciously, they expose the distinctly racialized and inherently classist nature of the hegemonic notions of "criminality" and "normalcy" that inform the war on crime and its contemporary analog, the war on terror. But the greatest significance lies in the multiple challenges this "illegal" *writing* ritual poses to the narrative order of the all-important and centrally located penitentiary. Even before the *tatuajes* themselves are completed, the practice of tattooing in prison models a collective mode of empowerment by facilitating—even demanding—a collectivist epistemology necessitated by the prison regimen of bondage and censorship in which tattoo production, tattoos, and their bearers are all (further) criminalized. The resulting icons—grounded in these objective conditions while also linked to the shared political unconscious of the predominantly Catholic Chicana/o community—symbolically articulate these individual experiences of colonization and imprisonment to the more general practice of penology worldwide. Eventually, these socially symbolic markings facilitate a universal moral—and always political—objection to systematic human degradation. For Chicana/os caught up in the carceral web of the war on crime/war on terror, *tatuajes* enable their rearticulation as oppositional subjects with human needs, desires, rights, and, above all, counterhegemonic agency as Pinto intellectuals.

PART THREE

Crime and Commodification

CHAPTER 5

Hollywood *Placas*

Semiotics, Spectatorship, and Ideology
in American Me

RE-VIEWING THE CRIME SPECTACLE

Outside of Chicago, behind the castle-like prison walls of the shuttered Joliet Correctional Center, temporarily reopened and renamed Fox River State Penitentiary for the 2005 Fox Television serial *Prison Break*, Michael Scofield gazes upon the full-body tattoo he designed for himself. He is not appraising the artistry or regretting the marks. Rather, he is *reading* his tattoo. A structural engineer by training, Scofield meticulously designed the tattoo before being sent to prison for armed robbery. It literally holds the key to freedom: beneath the gothic scripts, goblins, and other apparently meaningless marks lay the complete blueprints of the penitentiary, which he helped his architectural firm design prior to his imprisonment. In what can only be described as the quintessential Hollywood prison fantasy show, the 2005 premier of *Prison Break* presents a protagonist, Scofield, who deliberately commits an armed robbery so he can be sent to prison and bust out his brother, Lincoln (think "Honest Abe"), who sits on death row after being framed by fascist shadow government forces for killing the U.S. president's brother. Armed with India ink and a multiracial team of scheming prisoners with various motives, Scofield succeeds in breaking into, then out of, the penitentiary at the end of the first season, only to be ruthlessly hunted in subsequent seasons by an FBI agent who learns piecemeal how to read photos of Scofield's tattoo design. In a performance of the dangerously hegemonic hermeneutic that accompanies counterhegemonic tattoo writing (discussed in the previous chapter) the FBI slowly reconstructs Scofield's meticulously laid out plan for escape. The chase is on . . . again. But in contrast to Raúl Salinas's counterhegemonic tattoos, Scofield and his brother eventually join forces with the FBI to thwart the real enemy, who in the era of the war on terror can be none other than "domestic terrorists" and "rogue" law enforcement agents. Thanks to a tattoo, the carceral apparatus is preserved!

152 | Crime and Commodification

Even before Hollywood executives symbolically reopened the 158-year-old Joliet Correctional Center, the mass commodification and consumption of the once-outlawed art of tattooing had taken many forms. This reification includes highly publicized tattoos on Hollywood actresses and even a reality TV show, *Miami Ink*, which features the daily designs and travails of a multiracial cast of skin artists in a Latino-owned tattoo shop in South Beach, Florida. Yet the racial and class crossover of this once ostracized vernacular art form does not efface the difference that such marks denote in a racially stratified society. On the contrary, the prison and barrio tattoos discussed in the previous chapter retain their abject status precisely because of their crude, homemade, and culturally specific styles and, above all else, the brown bodies that bear them. Even as tattooed White supremacist prisoners are similarly stigmatized outside prison for their marked bodies, the bearers remain White in a racist society and thus enjoy the White privilege that affords relatively more opportunities to function in, if not reintegrate into, the polis. This is what Scofield represents. In fact, his tattoos ironically contain Celtic mythic iconography common in White supremacist prisoner tattoos (and never present in those of Chicana/o or Black prisoners). That the entire drama revolves around a tattooed White protagonist using his marks to gain access to and then break out of prison illustrates the hegemonic function of his vernacular pièce de résistance. *Prison Break*, the latest incarnation of the old cops-and-robbers show, reveals that prison tattoos, and tattoos of prison, continue to be imbued with a highly racialized use-value.

Gangster-style tattoos—which usually involve Old English script proclamations of neighborhood allegiance, cryptic in-group codes, and culturally resonant images such as religious icons—have served as indispensable accoutrements for characters in vérité prison and gang films since the 1980s. In his 1992 barrio and prison gang saga, *American Me,* Edward James Olmos elevated the Chicano tattoo to a virtual protagonist deserving its own close-up shots. Similar to Salinas's *placas* and Scofield's White prison gothic designs, tattoos in *American Me* function as a key semiotic device: tattoos equal liberation. But liberation means something completely different in all three iterations. In Salinas's barrio and Pinto *placas*, the vernacular markings become politico-economic critique, buttressing a de-colonial imaginary and enabling *concientización* toward the consolidation of a third world revolutionary subject: the nascent Chicano communist Pinto activist-intellectual.[1] In *Prison Break*, on the other hand, Scofield's tattoos serve to reintegrate him into the White capitalist society that had rewarded him with a riverside penthouse apartment in downtown Chicago prior to the crime against his brother that led to his own imprisonment. I submit that tattoos in *American Me* have a complex semiotic function between these two poles that can only be understood by first locating the film within its appropriate cinematic genres and historical material contexts.

As noted by Rosalinda Fregoso (1993), the story in *American Me* is loosely derived from Beatrice Griffith's 1948 anthropological profiles in a book of the same title, as well as from an unrelated prison gang screenplay by Floyd Mutrux and Desmond Nakano.[2] The plot of *American Me* traces the rise and fall of a Mexican American barrio boy, Santana, whose tragic fate is overdetermined by the rape of his mother by a U.S. sailor during the infamous 1942–1943 zoot suit riots, resulting in his "bastardized" birth. In a culmination of the stereotypical tragic *mestizo* trope involving a Freudian love-hate relationship with his Mexican stepfather—who still impotently seethes at the "Anglo blood" running through his stepson's veins—the young Santana is sent to juvenile detention after a botched burglary.[3] While there, he in turn is raped, murders his rapist, and then eventually founds the Mexican Mafia to provide protection for "his people" after being sent to Folsom Prison for the "honor killing." The Mexican Mafia grows and extends its drug and extortion empire throughout the California prison system and the state's major cities through the use of chilling brutality, including internecine murder. The film focuses on the cyclical nature of such violence, with special attention to various initiation rites, which always involve the real or figural drawing of blood. Throughout the film, several rapes are committed and more than twenty people killed, including a pathos-laden gang-banging in the final scene that serves to underscore Olmos's stated intent: to graphically illustrate, and thus help end, the tragic and nihilistic nature of fratricidal gang warfare and its brutal impact on the Chicana/o community.

The film's visceral depiction of rape and murder, however, has led many members of the Mexican American bourgeoisie and intelligentsia to critique Olmos for focusing on the violent underside of barrio life. Such critics include Pinto Raúl Salinas, who rebukes the film for "glorifying violence and gang life." He argues that "*American Me* is just another 'gangxploitation' film that exploits a community tragedy to make a buck."[4] In an unpublished review, Ricardo Sánchez also criticizes the film, not only for its gratuitously graphic scenes of violence, but for its emphasis on the use of sexual violence among men in prison to exercise relative power. Sánchez claims that Santana's rape in juvenile detention never would have resulted in the victim's rise to the role of Chicano prison gang leader.[5] While Sánchez's criticism is bound by a binary homophobic logic, such criticism also is grounded in the strict social order of male prisons. These depictions have had lethal consequences: three former Mexican Mafia associates who served as consultants for the film were assassinated in gang-style ambushes, purportedly for revealing in-group insights and, worse, because the film depicts the über-masculine Pinto as being effeminized through anal rape.[6]

While there may be some basis to both trajectories of critique, I argue that the Brechtian dénouement, sensationalist depictions, and visceral cinematic techniques undergird a complex *anti*-gangxploitation teleology. In response to critics, Olmos (1993) has stated that he made this film out of a personal commitment to help end the epidemic of barrio gang warfare and, to a lesser degree, as an antidote to the meaningless glorification of underclass violence that proliferates in Hollywood and network television, where he makes a comfortable living. *American Me*, he argues, is a deliberate attempt to break from the gratuitously violent gangxploitation genre, for which Walter Hill's 1979 *Warriors* and Dennis Hopper's 1988 *Colors* serve as some of the most egregious examples.

While gangxploitation, and what I am calling "anti-gangxploitation," has many antecedents—Westerns, "greaser" films, "social problem" films, Black-produced "race films," Hollywood Mafia films, cops-and-robbers shows, modern action films, and even cross-racial buddy films—most scholars concur that the foundational genre of counterhegemonic racial minority filmmaking is "Blaxploitation." The term is a double entendre that simultaneously alludes to purportedly affirming portrayals of Blackness in Black-produced films that emerged from the Black Arts Movement of the 1960s and 1970s as well as their antithesis: Black exploitation by Whites. Renowned for their Black vernacular styles and settings, Blaxploitation films reject the stereotypical depictions of African Americans that date back to the birth of modern cinematography with D. W. Griffith's 1915 paean to the Ku Klux Klan, *Birth of a Nation*.[7] Films like Melvin Van Peeble's *Sweet Sweetback's Baadasssss Song* (1971), Jack Hill's *Foxy Brown* (1974), and Gordon Parks's *Shaft* (1971) initially were produced, directed, or written by Blacks and always featured an underclass Black hero (usually a petty criminal-cum-social bandit or revolutionary) who fights against evil forces that threaten the Black community. This common plotline inevitably leads to the true villain: White dope dealers, corrupt White cops, or evil White politicians who manipulate Black crooks to help them exploit and subordinate their own community. Like the poetry and other art forms of the Black Arts Movement, these films were used to levy political analysis, including incisive in-group critiques.

Blaxploitation eventually was absorbed by Hollywood studios, which perverted the genre into a new permutation of the old cops-and-robbers and Mafia films: the action-packed, violent, and libidinal gang sagas that came to be known as gangxploitation. Gangxploitation films proliferated to the point where even decidedly anti-gangxploitation films such as John Singleton's *Boyz-N-the Hood* (1991) and Albert and Allen Hughes's *Menace II Society* (1993) have been eclipsed by the Hollywood fetish for the presumed minority predisposition to pathological conduct. This subversion of the potentially oppositional anti-gangxploitation genre—such as Robert Collins's *Walk Proud* (1979) and Michael Pressman's *Boulevard Nights* (1979)—also arises from contemporary Chicana/o- and Mexican-produced gangxploitation films such as Cesar Alejandro's *Down for the Barrio* (1996) and several dozen similar low-budget films that continue to be made for the DVD market.

This proliferation of gangxploitation films has been accompanied by predictable critiques from scholars of Chicana/o films, as well as a more pregnant dissensus regarding the relationship between ideology and various crime literature and film genres. Chicana/o film scholars such as Christine List (1996), Charles Ramírez Berg (1990), and Gary Keller (1994) suggest that modern Chicana/o gang films and the attendant Chicana/o gang characters are merely contemporary permutations of the racist Hollywood "greaser" or *bandido* films of the 1920s and 1930s, and the subsequent "social problem" film genre from the 1940s to 1980s. List notes:

> Still driven by animalistic cravings, the gang member is particularly savage and brutal. Like the bandido, his nature dooms him to come to a tragic end. Reminiscent of the border region of the western, the urban settings for these gang films are mapped as sites where lawlessness and violence prevail. (1996: 33)[8]

While this formula certainly does exist, scholarship on general market gang films and literature is bifurcated on the issue of film as an Ideological State Apparatus, Louis Althusser's (1971) term for the cultural processes by which hegemonic power relations are discursively reinforced. These critical debates are summarized by Stephen Brauer (2001). He notes that one argument, of which Nicole Rafter (2000) is the most lucid proponent, posits that crime film genres offer only a modicum of political critique because the usual happy ending and inevitable defeat of evil (usually "rogue" cops or sadistic gangsters) ultimately restore the exploitative status quo. This genre, Rafter argues, inadvertently serves as a metaphor for power: Ideology is preserved precisely because it was threatened. On the other hand, critics such as Jonathan Munby (1999) suggest that government censorship and bourgeois critiques of these films versus their popular appeal and mass consumption reveals that crime cinema may actually enable critique among its underclass spectators: "As most gangster films demonstrate, they are less about reinforcing ideals of capitalist success than about the rules and prejudices that bar specific groups from access to power."[9]

Erin A. Smith (2000) attempts to mediate between these two critical poles by taking into account the complex cultural economy of such films, specifically the varied and complex forms of consumption. Brauer (2001) notes that Smith

> asks us as critics to navigate in the more ambiguous spaces of the narrative's
> social function so that we can not only chart out the reification of the
> status quo or the subversive potential of the narrative but so that we can
> also investigate the social processes through which the text embodies
> issues of masculinity and femininity, consumption and individuality, and
> spectatorship and surveillance. (544)

But none of these critics fully examines the status of race in these films and among their audiences.

In their dialogue with Laura Mulvey's (1975) explications of scopohilia, feminist, postcolonial, and critical race studies film theorists have long argued that spectatorship is highly variable across time and place, race and class, gender and geography, and therefore it is impossible to ascribe a master narrative to any given text. In his study of Black male spectatorship of *The Birth of a Nation*, Manthia Diawara (1993) challenges the notion of a passive subaltern spectator by proposing a "resisting spectator" who, depending on the scene, setting, and plot, may identify with a character even if this spectator rejects the legitimacy of the story. Cultural theorist bell hooks (1995) extends minority spectator agency by noting how African Americans perform a subversive and defiant "oppositional gaze" to critique Hollywood representations of Blackness by daring to look, and simultaneously refusing to look, at the film spectacle in the ways that White Hollywood producers and directors prescribed. However, hooks, Stuart Hall (1989), Rey Chow

(1995), Fatimah Tobing Rony (1996), and Fregoso (1993) all variously argue that subaltern spectatorship involves a dialectical process in which the abject (usually racialized) spectator simultaneously acts upon, is acted upon, and has his or her "racialized" identity overdetermined by the film text.

If Chicana/o spectatorship is as varied as Black, Asian American, and other postcolonial audiences, and if the film text can be reclaimed by the resisting spectator, might *American Me* also be re-viewed outside the current binary appraisals of its depiction of masculinist barrio warrior heroes/villains? Can *American Me* accommodate class-segmented Chicana/o spectators and still retain Olmos's purported attempts to subvert gangxploitation? That is, can the film act upon, and be acted upon by, its multiple Chicana/o audiences in productively problematic ways as anti-gangxploitation? I believe so, and submit that tattoos are the key to unlocking the film's complex poetics and engagé cinematography: through a vernacular rehearsal of the Lacanian *placa* recognition scenes discussed in the preceding chapter on Salinas's resistant body altars, *American Me* posits a Chicana/o subject who is oppositional *and* hegemonic in ways that further complicate Pinta/o discourses on power, identity, and ideology.

RECLAIMING THE GAZE: THE VERNACULAR SEMIOTICS OF *AMERICAN ME*

Fregoso (1993) provides a counterpoint to the negative reviews of *American Me* and corresponding criticisms of Olmos. Rather than glorifying violence or perpetuating negative stereotypes of Chicana/os, Fregoso argues that the film is notable for its "shrewdly oblique refusal to romanticize the defiance of the masculine heroic figure (*cholo, bato loco*), as was done in the *Pachuco* character that Olmos himself had played in *Zoot Suit*" (1993: 123).[10] Fregoso acknowledges that the graphic violence depicted in this prison gang saga was designed as an intervention into the lethal crisis of internecine violence eviscerating working- and underclass Chicana/o neighborhoods, or to use Edward James Olmos's more problematic characterizations, the "cancer" in our barrios. She adds that the film is relatively successful at delivering its viscerally shocking get-out-of-gangs message in part because of its deliberate mimesis of Convict gestures, walk and speech rhythms, and other "cultural codes" immediately recognizable to the film's targeted audience: primarily the Chicana/o lumpenproletariat. Fregoso aptly concludes her assessment of *American*

Me by arguing that in order to fully appreciate the significance and intent of this film, as well as others made by Chicana/os, "one has to be literate in certain cultural codes" that undergird Chicana/o cinematography in general (129). Unfortunately, except for her identification of the film's Malinche subtext and a passing suggestion that the rhymed elliptic tone of the Chicano Convict letters that frame the film function to signal the plot's "authenticity," Fregoso fails to explicate the cinematic, semiotic, and other cultural codes she maintains are crucial to understanding the film's purportedly anti-ideological function.

Extending Fregoso's apt but underdeveloped and undertheorized allusions to the culturally nuanced cinematic techniques at work in *American Me*, I propose to explicate the film's complex troping of color. I submit that in addition to the frequent close-ups of brown bodies, both diegetic and nondiegetic sounds are fundamental elements in the immanent theory of Brown-ness deployed by the film to reach its targeted Chicana/o audience. From the very beginning of the film, the heavily accented speech and vernacular Chicana/o Spanish, or Caló, words such as *ese* (you), *vato* (dude), and especially *carnal* (blood brother), though relatively foreign to Hollywood feature films, are immediately familiar to Chicana/o spectators. On the surface, this vernacular vocabulary apparently invites a self-indulgent gaze by this audience by signaling the film as another feature on the lumpen via the crime, gangxploitation, and prison genres.

Tattoos similarly locate the film in terms of genre and also mark its claim to "authenticity" and "authority." This is where the cinematography gets complicated. At one level, the tattoos challenge the pathologizing of the minority underclass male by Hollywood gangxploitation films by repelling bourgeois Mexican American spectators who have neither an understanding of nor an affiliation with Chicana/o barrio culture. The tattoos also serve as a critique of White spectators who benefit from barrio archipelagos of poverty and who secretly relish in gangxploitation the confirmation of their bias, even though convinced of their feigned empathy. More importantly, the tattoos will invite "homeboy" or underclass minority spectators by affirming, however problematically, their barrio-rooted agency. It signals to them that the film is "legitimate" and that their conditioned resistant spectatorship to Hollywood representations of them is not necessary for this film. This cinematic "throwing of signs," a claim to barrio legitimacy, ultimately enables a visceral didactic message about the ills of gangbanging.

This anti-gangbanging message—which I show below will involve a partial self-erasure for its intended audience—would immediately be rejected by this audience if Olmos did not tread lightly. He had to subtly foreground his argument that gangs themselves involve an even more profound and permanent self-erasure than his critique of them. In the very first scene of the film, tattoos metonymically proclaim the film's own claim of being *del barrio*, or of the barrio, through a montage that cuts from Santana's tattooed body in a cell in Folsom Prison, to his stepfather's

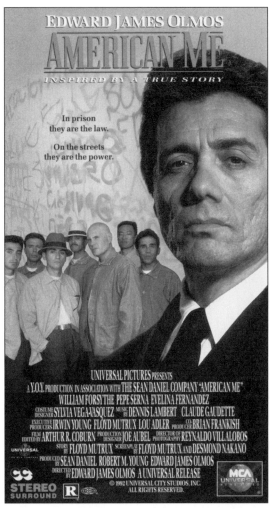

Figure 5.1. VHS box cover for *American Me* (1992), by Edward James Olmos. Courtesy of Universal Pictures.

tattoo session in a downtown tattoo parlor, a 1940s Los Angeles trolley car taking Santana's mother to join her future husband at the downtown parlor, and a close-up of a cross tattoo on Santana's stepfather decades later as he gazes upon the past from an east Los Angeles barrio tenement. Tattoos thus underwrite *American Me*'s claims to be both *from* and *of* the barrio. This distinction is crucial, as one's "authority," and especially one's presumed "authenticity," in the subaltern context of the east Los Angeles gang culture depicted here is in part determined by whether or not the subject in question has been initiated, often violently, *into* the barrio. While discourses on "authenticity" are always suspect, markers of membership in a subculture or community, though varied, nonetheless are recognizable to those members (even as they sometimes are essentialized into stereotypes or dismissed as "too essentialist" by outsiders). Just as a nondescript business suit and tie are necessary accoutrements of high finance culture, so, too, are certain *placas*, or tags, necessary for inclusion among specific communities located outside the centers of economic power. This claim to being *del barrio* is crucial to Olmos's proposed intervention into the epidemic of barrio fratricide. As a film text explicitly produced to draw in spectators weaned on popular crime and gangster films, *American Me* necessarily must engage the exoticist gaze that previously had identified the source of this violence as the inherent pathology of dark-skinned males. Olmos does this, quite vividly, by invoking the very features of the gangxploitation genre he seeks to undermine, constructing the film as a series of violent clashes: no less than four rapes and twenty murders. Significantly, and deliberately, all of them are presaged by Chicano tattoo rituals.

Once established, these barrio verbal, bodily, and tattoo recognition scenes enable Olmos to deconstruct the defining plot device of gangxploitation: violence. The opening montage introduces the operative discursive device: a semiotic confirmation that tattoo rituals are linked to violence and eventually death. Moreover, tattoos not only introduce the tragic episodes of violence that befall the Chicana/o protagonists, but the tattoo-violence nexus also serves to recast the plot of the traditional Hollywood gang violence scene. Violence, in *American Me*, is initially proposed as the result of White, rather than racial minority, pathology. As noted, the opening scene depicts the notorious Los Angeles zoot suit riots of 1942–1943, in which marauding gangs of off-duty White U.S. servicemen attacked, beat, violently stripped, and even raped Filipino, Black, and Chicano zoot suiters and Pachucos for flamboyantly taunting their difference at a time of national crisis and austerity. This racial scapegoating, of course, was not anomalous, since the U.S. government actively sought to promote a unified front in the war effort through the xenophobic demonization of Japanese and anyone else that the government associated with enemy nations. Immediately after getting a tattoo proclaiming his love for his girlfriend, Pedro, Santana's future stepfather, is caught in the maelstrom of White G.I. rioting: he is carried over his attackers' shoulders with his newly tattooed arms spread out, Christ-like, then savagely beaten and stripped by White U.S. servicemen and police officers while his girlfriend, Esperanza, Santana's future mother, is gang raped by a group of smirking and cheering White sailors.

Notwithstanding Olmos's overbearing, cliché invocation of the misogynist Malinche myth, this film nonetheless evokes Luis Valdez's 1981 film *Zoot Suit* in an attempt to recast this episode of White-Chicana/o conflict as the "White U.S. servicemen's riots" instead of the "zoot suit riots," the term that Hearst newspapers used.[11] Olmos's cinematic representation of this violent episode in U.S. history effectively challenges the very construction of the Chicana/o as a predatory gang member and inherently violent menace to society by suggesting a more historically situated cultural and political conflict manifesting itself as a race war. *American Me*, which has been critiqued inaccurately as the quintessential gangxploitation film, actually begins by undoing its apparent filiation with one of Hollywood's most racist genres through perspective shots that enable us to recast the gaze at the cultural, historical, and material arenas in which Chicana/os are figured and treated as one of America's abject populations. In this scene, and in every other episode to follow, tattoos signify a claim to place, ontological space, and even power, however relative, while also presaging their loss. This is the nexus in the epistemology of race undergirding *American Me* (which is subsequently complicated beyond this binary, as I will show below). However staged this plot device may be, tattoos presage tragedy, and therein lies the didactic opportunities to reach its targeted spectators—homeboys—with its didactic get-out-of-gangs message.

The anti-gang objective of the film requires a deconstruction of barrio spatial ontology. Raúl Villa (2000) has lucidly illustrated how a Chicana/o "barrio-logos"—or Chicana/o-centric elaboration of physical places—enables the actualization of empowered counterhegemonic subjectivities. Mary Pat Brady (2002) further explores the symbiotic relationship between statutory and cultural regulations of space and Chicana subversions of these norms through symbolic literary renovations of specific places that otherwise would render them subordinate. I argue that Olmos takes Villa's barrio-logos practice to its logical conclusion in ways similar to Brady's assessments of Latina authors through his own symbolic deconstruction of the barrio space. For instance, just twelve minutes into the film, we are presented with a tattoo initiation ritual that surreptitiously and significantly occurs in a mausoleum. Using the young Santana and his two barrio homeboys—J.D., a White boy born and raised as a Chicano in Santana's barrio, La Primera, and Mundo, an abbreviation of Edmundo that also means "world"—Olmos foregrounds his theory of race, power, and survival by gesturing towards a materialist analysis of the barrio as place. As Mundo receives the small indelible ink barrio tattoo of a cross with three extending rays between the thumb and index finger (which virtually everyone in the film bears), Santana rehearses a somewhat overwritten, but useful didactic discourse on barrio spatial ontology:

> We got our own clica [gang], homes, a strong clica. Finally getting into our own. You know, gaining respect.

In-between pin pricks, he adds:

> La Primera [The First Street Gang] lives through us, ese. It gives to us.
> It is us.

Lest the audience miss the materialist explication of homeboy tribal and spiritual affinities to land that they do not legally own but that was part of their historical legacy, J.D. adds:

> Our clica, our barrio, our families, that's all we got, ese.

This tattoo ritual, which immediately follows shots of the tenement dwellings of these lumpenproletariat protagonists, literally grounds the characters in their politico-economic context. Thus contrary to Fregoso's claim that the film fails to offer a materialist analysis, this scene, and others to follow, clearly show that *American Me*, marked as being about and of the barrio, is in fact framed within an incisive politico-economic critique. The profound innovation of Olmos's cinematography arises from his deconstruction of this claim to allegiance with La Primera: he initially signals this allegiance as a defiant claim of subaltern identity, but subsequent scenes illustrate how this barrio tribalism actually overdetermines homeboy marginalization and worse—annihilation. This irony is again foregrounded when Santana welcomes the newly tattooed Mundo into the barrio by saying, "Welcome to the clica, carnal," to which Mundo responds, "Por vida, carnal, por vida" (For life, brother, for life). This self-affirming barrio initiation rite functions to collapse race into place and subaltern space, but as I show below, this recognition scene is represented with the express purpose of deconstructing itself.

THE SELF-REFLEXIVE GAZE: *PLACAS, CARNALISMO, Y CONCIENTIZACIÓN*

Pursuant to his intended anti-gang and anti-gangxploitation message, Olmos uses these and other *placa* recognition scenes to revise the vernacular codes that undergird gangbanging, from vernacular tattoo initiation rituals to related membership rituals of violence. He seeks to enable a critical in-group gaze. Whereas Luis Valdez proposed the rebirth of a masculinist Mesoamerican warrior hero from the ashes of emasculation in *Zoot Suit* (1981), which Fregoso proposes as a precursor to *American Me*, I submit that Olmos uses tattoos to question the male warrior hero model of identity and agency. After all, Olmos's film is about the rise *and* fall of a barrio warrior hero. Having gained his targeted audience's attention by the barrio marks that link the three principal male characters in the film, Olmos graphically and convincingly exposes the perverted sense of *carnalismo* in *la vida loca*, or "the crazy life." The *placas* that bind, he will show, also divide and destroy. As in the opening scene in which Santana's mother is raped by White sailors after his father receives a tattoo signaling his allegiance to her, tattoos also presage violent tragedy for the adolescent boys of La Primera. For instance, in the scene immediately following the mausoleum initiation ritual, Santana's *clica* defiantly transgresses a rival gang's turf to prove their masculinity, thereby setting off a chain of events that results in J.D. having his leg shot off, the incarceration of all three gang members for burglary, and Santana's rape by a White prisoner while in juvenile detention. In another rehearsal of the Malinche myth and related honor plays in which blood must be spilled in order to restore male honor and patriarchal order, Olmos portrays Santana as the Chicano avenger: Santana promptly pierces and thus murders his rapist with the same shank, or prison-made knife, used to hold him at bay as he was being raped. As a result, he gets an extended sentence that will ensure his transfer to an adult prison, which enables him to rise to a position of leadership in the juvenile prison. Santana soon reunites with his old friend from La Primera, J.D., who joins the new pan-barrio *clica* Santana has established in prison for self-protection.

This reunion enables Olmos to begin his deconstruction of *carnalismo* by first disarticulating it from place, then race. When J.D. says he thinks he recognizes someone from an enemy barrio, Santana says, "Chale" [Fuck that], there ain't no barrios in here." On the surface, Santana is reiterating the fact that group affiliations are defined by race regardless of a person's freeworld barrio allegiances. But within a few seconds of this speech Santana also responds to a young Chicano's admonition for letting J.D. join their new pan-barrio Chicano *clica* because "he ain't Mexican." With his arm around J.D., Santana responds, "This right here is my best crime partner. Sabes que, es mi hermano" (You know what, he's my brother). This scene is important to Olmos's deconstruction of gang *carnalismo* because it disarticulates Brown-ness from the pathology ascribed to it by the Hollywood gangxploitation formula and thus directs more attention to pathology as an aspect of male culture in general. The plot still takes place in a Chicana/o lumpen and prisoner context, but it is transformed in a way that enables this twisted model of manhood to be further deconstructed. This critique of *carnalismo* involves a cinematic exploration of several sets of biological and barrio brothers: Puppet and Little Puppet, Santana and J.D., Santana and his younger brother Paulito, and finally, Paulito and another young barrio preadolescent gang-banger initiate. Already having cinematically birthed these barrio brotherhoods through the aforementioned tattoo rituals, every one of these pairings is didactically actualized—and simultaneously destroyed—through murder, including literal fratricide.

The axis around which race, tattoos, and violence conclusively come to signify something other than marks of filiation and brotherhood (or the purportedly predetermined tragedy ascribed to *mestizaje* that Gutiérrez-Jones [1995] and Fregoso [1993] discuss) occurs midway through the film in another tattooing scene in the yard of the old Folsom Prison. Little Puppet, who has been picking a tattoo into fellow *mafioso* Pieface's bare brown torso as the latter lifts weights, is asked to move aside by an Asian American member of the gang who demands to finish the job. He does so by plunging the improvised tattoo stick and needle into Pieface's gut where the tattooed woman's pubis was to have been drawn. Significantly, their *carnal* was murdered for refusing to murder the Chicano leader of a rival gang, Nuestra Familia (Our Family), because Pieface simply could not bring himself to kill a man he had identified as "my crime partner," with whom he had shared "many a cooker," small bottle-cap vats of heroin heated into liquid so it can be injected. Their exchange of *chiva* (heroin) and blood, the main commodity and currency in this subaltern economic context, had made them *carnales*—literal blood brothers. And Pieface died because of his loyalty at the hands of his other blood brothers.

This tattoo/murder scene synthesizes previous tattoo recognition scenes into an in-group and potentially self-critical gaze at gang *carnalismo*. Exploiting the simultaneously homoerotic, homosocial, and incipiently homophobic context of the tattoo rituals discussed in the preceding chapter, Olmos inverts the masculinist discourse on power that drives this story on "brotherhood." He shows that the model of *carnalismo* undergirding *la vida loca* is in fact neither brotherly nor manly. Like Esperanza and Santana before him, Pieface is violently penetrated by the same type of tattoo implement that had marked his allegiance to the barrio *familia* as a "man." Moreover, he is killed by it. In a problematic but very recognizable masculinist trope, the scene closes with a close-up of the tattooed females on Pieface's penetrated and thus emasculated body. The targeted spectators, already captivated by "realistic" tattoo rituals that earlier had functioned as recognition and initiation scenes, are now forced to confront, and it is hoped, act upon the dissonance caused by this ritual in its new configuration. That is, tattoos, as *placas*, are becoming recognizable for the self-erasure they presage. What makes this otherwise cliché message—gangs kill others and their own—is the visceral resonance of such scenes, which are accompanied by reflex motions from the tattooees, who sometimes jerk from the pain of the pin pricks, as well as similar reflex repulsions in the audience from the "swooshing" and "slushing" sound effects that accompany the deeper pricks: the stabbings and phallic thrusts of rape. This is what makes the film much more than a simple sermon one might hear from a "gang squad" police officer or member of the clergy.

From this point, tattoos gain a symbolic significance different from their function in the first half of the film: they now signify violent betrayal of the Chicana/o community that they earlier had served to historicize and consolidate. This shifting signification is catalyzed in the viscerally disturbing and much-discussed dual rape scene. Like the penetrations of the opening prison and tattoo parlor rape scenes, and similarly foreboding penetrations of needles filled with heroin or India ink, this violent montage scene alternately is set in Folsom Prison and in La Primera. After having juxtaposed the palatial wealth of the Italian

American Mafia drug importer—marked as White in the barrio—with the cramped Chicana/o barrio homes of his consumers, the dual rape scene enables a perverse visual pleasure (at seeing the son of this White drug scion emasculated and impaled in the anus with a double-edged, stainless steel "arrowhead" knife after being gang raped by the Mexican Mafia). It simultaneously exposes this model of power as corrupt, given that this rape and murder are paired with Santana's forced sodomizing of Julie, his soon-to-be ex-girlfriend. The Mexican Mafia that Santana heads, after all, kills the Italian American *mafioso* prisoner in order to replace his family as the distributor of heroin in the Chicana/o community. Thus any potential "pleasure" that the subaltern Chicana/o subject may gain by viewing this scene—a literal "sticking it to the man"—is undone by pairing it with the rape of a Chicana. This rape, a very real event, can also be read as a metonym within Olmos's masculinist symbolic system: it is the rape of the Chicana/o community by Chicana/os who peddle drugs in their own barrio.

Olmos has suggested that the dual rape scene, as disturbing and disgusting as it is, was designed to "scare straight" (no pun intended) its targeted audience.[12] One can argue that the scene is still highly problematic since the graphic details—camera close-ups of body parts and more "swooshing" sounds—do not necessarily efface, but perhaps enable, male spectator visual pleasure. Frederick Aldama (2002) provides a compelling reading of the trope of penetration in the film. He argues that this is one of the semiotic codes that infuse *American Me* with a subversive resonance in the face of the standard Hollywood gangxploitation film:

> Santana's struggle, finally, is about how he breaks free of age-old binaries— colonizer vs. colonized, bully vs. sissy, male vs. female, *activo* vs. *pasivo*, buggerer vs. *maricón*, hole maker and holed one—that continue to inform and control from within the Chicano/mestizo subject today. (80)

Aldama further argues that Olmos queers the hyper-masculinist barrio and prison cultural milieu by presenting Santana as a contemporary barrio Chicana/o permutation of a transgendered Zuni *berdache* spiritual leader:

> Not only does Santana represent an alternative, nonbiologically produced savior narrative that dialogues with and subverts Judeo-Christian religious paradigms, but his coming into his role as a storyteller who leaves behind the concrete artifact of his written story/testimony for future generations

positions Santana within a long line of asexual, bisexual, and homosexual spiritual figures traditionally responsible for holding together communities before and during the conquest. (90)

Kathleen Newman proposes a similar reading by proposing that Santana shape-shifts from male to female so "that gender and sexuality are denied as appropriate criteria for the exclusion of anyone from the neutral status of citizenship and the nation as an ensemble is affirmed" (1996: 104). These provocative readings, however plausible, nonetheless rely on graphically violent impalings far removed from any romance or empowering claims to gender or sexuality outside a heterosexual and homophobic context. The trope of penetration appears more likely to reinforce the masculinist order of the film's cultural milieu by trafficking in, rather than undermining, the outdated fucked/fucker binary discussed in previous chapters.

Notwithstanding the problematic depiction of anal penetration (figured as sexual subordination) as the worst thing that can happen to a male—a depiction that has provoked Chicana as well as Chicana/o Queer resistant spectatorship—this scene responds to the cultural context of its targeted gangbanger audience, which, as noted, is decidedly masculinist, misogynist, and homophobic, yet also profoundly homosocial and perhaps even homoerotic. Queer men are not readily accepted in Chicana/o barrio lumpen communities and often are the targets of homophobic violence that includes rape. Olmos knows this and uses it to buttress his get-out-of-gangs message. Unfortunately, this is one of the semiotic codes to which this community immediately responds, and by the time this dual rape scene is presented, rape is troped as a paradigm of power alternately used by Whites to subordinate Chicana/os, as well as real sexual violence by Chicanos to lay claim to authority within racialized and gendered hierarchies. Within this disgusting logic, this rape scene is a viscerally effective way to expose the corrupt form of *carnalismo* and related model of Chicano identity within *la vida loca*. *Carnalismo*, emasculation, murder, and the loss of masculinity are all intertwined. Join a gang, the film deliberately suggests, and you will figuratively and literally get fucked.

Now that the film has gotten the attention of its targeted audience, Olmos introduces the most important plot device in *American Me*: the conversion or barrio disarticulation scene. As in *Boyz-N-the Hood* and *Menace II Society*, murders are preceded by a climactic opportunity to refuse participation in the impending tragic crime.[13] This telos is first introduced in a Folsom Prison scene involving Puppet and his younger brother, Little Puppet. In a twisted model of brotherly love, Big Puppet volunteers to commit a murder that has been assigned to his little brother. Little Puppet, on the other hand, is scared but feels he must carry out the murder. After all, he has directly witnessed what befalls those who refuse to carry out a Mexican Mafia hit. This becomes the worst decision of his life. During the attack, he is wounded in the palm. Once renowned as the "best tattoo artist in East L.A.," his drawing hand is now mangled, leaving him incapable of making art. In a drunken fit of regret during his post-prison barrio wedding reception, he publicly rebukes the Mexican Mafia and also becomes indirectly responsible for getting Santana thrown back in jail. Little Puppet mistakenly took Santana's tuxedo jacket, leaving Santana to take his, which contained a packet of heroin. A police patrol found it on Santana as they searched him after seeing the tell-tale signs of criminality: his tattoos. This sequence of events inevitably marks Little Puppet for murder. The hit is assigned to his older brother, Big Puppet, who now must confront the ultimate prisoner's dilemma: if he does not murder his biological brother, his "brothers" in the Mexican Mafia will put a hit on his entire biological family. This murder is overlain with a series of climactic murders in which tattoos again serve as a staging device for Olmos's steadily deepening message of get-out-of-gangs-or-get-betrayed-buttfucked-murdered-and-cursed-by-God.

The multiple murder montage scene interweaves and brings closure to the discourse on personal choice through cinematic redundancy. Tattoos not only are central to the film but have now shifted to the role of antagonist. This troping begins with Santana in his Folsom cell again, reminiscing about the series of events and decisions that led him there. His meditation on the past is framed by a voiceover of the younger Santana, J.D., and Mundo in the mausoleum (e.g., "Welcome to the clica, carnal" and "Por vida, ese, por vida"). The film takes this last response by the younger Mundo to its logical conclusion. The older Mundo, now the head of the Mexican Mafia hit squad sent to kill Santana for having "shown weakness" in his call to transform the Mexican Mafia into a Chicano version of the Black Panthers, stops by the cell of the Asian American member who carried out Pieface's murder. Mundo invites him to join the hit squad, asking, "Coming out, ese?" to which his non-Chicano *carnal* responds, "No, I'm staying in." Mundo is a bit surprised at this decision and asks, "You sure you know what you're doing, ese?" The response, "Simón" (Yeah), will seal the rebel's fate: he'll be marked for death. But

Olmos never shows this murder, even though he graphically depicts the thuds, slashes, slushing, and gurgles of Santana's murder. When viewed alongside the other decisions made by characters in the montage, the Asian American Convict's refusal to participate in yet another fratricidal killing will leave the viewer with the slim hope that he may survive and perhaps reconstruct a life outside the fatal *carnalismo* that defines the subculture of which he once was an integral part.

The climax in the scene occurs with several pairings and disartic-ulations. First, Little Puppet is killed by his own brother. The fratricide occurs immediately after Little Puppet shows his big brother the pictures of their mother at Little Puppet's wedding party. As Little Puppet is being strangled by his older brother in an epic replay of the Cain and Abel allegory—underscored by Big Puppet's cry to the sky "Goddamn me! Goddamn me!"—Santana's own little brother, Paulito, rehearses the barrio version of the overall story. Another cross-cut shows Paulito picking the tattoo of a barrio *crucita* upon the hand of a preadolescent initiate as he recites the vernacular liturgy: "La Primera lives, ese. It lives through us. It is us." Another *clica* member dutifully adds: "Simón, ese, it's all we got." Paulito completes the ceremony: "It's all we ever had." Puppet dies in the next cross-cut. Then the camera cuts again to the scene in La Primera. Pedro, Santana's father, calls out to his younger son Paulito to come inside the house. But Paulito decides not to listen, leaving the father to impotently gaze at his own *crucita* tattoo while he stands in the symbolically significant threshold of a door. The camera then cuts again to Santana being repeatedly stabbed and thrown off the prison tier by the Mexican Mafia *carnal*, Mundo, whom he had initiated in the mausoleum. The final cut in this scene features the new initiate being given a gun as the next generation of La Primera gangbangers drives through a rival barrio. When the young boy, in a haze of aerosol huffing asks, "Which one, ese?," Paulito concludes the discourse on gang membership-as-self erasure: "Don't matter." After a nihilistic "Fuck it, homeys, La Primera lives!" the boy fires to kill. His existence, the existence of La Primera, requires that someone die; if he does not make the decision to get out, he eventually will die, too. While a virtual cottage industry of resistance discourses have been erected around the barrio bad-man warrior hero, Olmos graphically and, he believes, conclusively, reiterates that this form of subaltern identity and agency inevitably leads to one's own and the community's annihilation. Fregoso aptly states that the film serves as a critique of the "masculine heroic figure" (1993: 123), and I add that the way in which it does so—through a viscerally violent contrapuntal deployment of the epistemology of the *placa*—is what gives the film its potential counterhegemonic use-value.

CONCLUSION: *AMERICAN ME* AS ASSIMILATION NARRATIVE

In a review of *American Me*, Ricardo Sánchez dubs Olmos "Edward James Almost" because he believes the film fails in its representation and critique of Pinto and barrio masculinity.[14] Pinto life, Sánchez always maintained, involves more mundane daily routines than the spectacular episodes of violence fetishized in Hollywood films. While I defer to Sánchez about the accuracy of Olmos's representation of prison sexual politics, I disagree with his suggestion that Olmos's film is "useless." I do believe, however, that Olmos is only partially—or "almost"—successful in his appeal to barrio youth with his simplistic reduction of *la vida loca* as a matter of personal choice. As Joan Moore (1978, 1991), Martín Sánchez-Jankowski (1991), and James Diego Vigil (1988) have noted, there are many reasons for joining gangs, most of which are *not* pathological. Few scholars, activists, and gang counselors will claim that the "decision" of whether or not to join a gang is an easy choice, or even a real choice free of extenuating circumstances such as peer pressure, material necessity, and cultural influences. Olmos recognizes these contingencies by having his characters repeat the historical materialist mantra "It's all we got, ese" and "It's all we've ever had." Nonetheless, Fregoso and other scholars have expressed frustration at the film's purported inability to provide an extended critique of the root causes of gang membership. Even granting that a two-hour feature film cannot be expected to provide a comprehensive analysis, I contend that the film should be critiqued for the ideological closure it proposes.

I have argued that the value of the film lies in its subversion of potential homeboy resistance to watching a film that decries their very identity. Yet the film also asserts that identity in ways bourgeois Mexican American and "liberal" White critics have denounced. Regarding this contradiction, Rob Canfield confirms:

> While it may be true that Olmos ends in re-representing violent images
> for Chicano youths that might be misinterpreted and misinternalized,
> we realize that the alternative would perhaps be misrepresentation of an
> otherwise "true story" (as Olmos re-emphasizes in the final frame). If one

is to actualize a revolution of the popular image, one must first perform a recognition of that image. Only then will the sites of struggle become arenas of awareness, and only through this awareness, as Bhabha might conclude, is real revolution and artistic revelation possible. (1994: 67)

But herein lie the greatest ironies and outright contradictions of the film. Having exposed *la vida loca* as an overdetermined fratricidal tragedy—a literal dead end—Olmos proposes the only alternative as being another form of self-erasure: assimilation into the White mainstream through upward mobility into the Mexican American middle class. While Canfield's observation that the tattooed cross between thumb and finger—the mark of *carnalismo* or blood brotherhood—transforms its bearers into mimetic perpetrators of violence similar to that of the White servicemen rioters and rapists of Santana's mother (63), he is incorrect to suggest that Julie's covering of her own cross at the end of the film will prepare her for the "real revolution: her enrollment in university courses" (66–67). Julie's act of erasure and reinstitutionalization in a university cannot be understood without first examining how it is foregrounded. The recipe for change she will represent is foregrounded by the Asian American *mafioso* who chose to stay in his "prison cell" rather than participate in another fratricide, specifically Santana's murder. Santana also is instructive on this point: after committing or ordering numerous murders, he finally recognizes that the gang he established was part of the very problem—individual and community disempowerment—that he initially sought to address.

It is only after Santana's archetypal betrayal and murder by his *carnales* that Julie's trajectory emerges as an alternative. Through her, Olmos ultimately re-inscribes the plot of *American Me* within another genre unintentionally signaled by the very title, which proclaims, ironically at first, but deliberately by the end of the film: "I am an American," indeed, *the* prototypical American. The film thus shifts into a conventional American assimilation narrative, which involves the always-incomplete racial minority subject's affiliation with the White bourgeois mainstream. Again, the operative cultural trope in the construction of this message is the barrio tattoo, which in its final synthesis is fundamentally ideological: *Placas* are the marks one must never get or, once gotten, must cover up and erase forever—or at least try.

This barrio *sous rature* is performed by Julie in the last five minutes of the film, in which she is inadvertently recast as a modern permutation of Malinche—*la vendida* (the sellout)—but in ways very different than those Fregoso proposes:

> In his final despair, Santana acknowledges a new possibility in the Chicana who shows him to love, who tries to teach him to dance. But like his repentance, his recognition comes too late. Too late for us and too late for her. Who is this new subject, this Chicana whom Edward James Olmos claims is the heroine of *American Me*, the hope in our barrios? His story ends before hers can begin. In the final close-up shot of a cross tattooed on Julie's hand resides her untold story. (133)

Julie's apparently minor role, however, becomes foundational in the final synthesis of the (erased) tattoo. However disappointing it may be, Julie—Santana's lover-cum-rape victim—is recast as the prototypical outcast-savior—La Malinche reborn as Malintzin—through the erasure of her tattoo. This is her full story within the ideological order of the film. When Julie dabs the tattoo with makeup base prior to leaving for night school, she thereby covers up her ties to her barrio identity in favor of the mainstream literacy and legitimacy—a university education—that presumably will lead to other opportunities in her new out-of-the-barrio life. While Julie goes off to join the managerial class (she earlier had mentioned her goal of opening a business), her erstwhile homeboys continue gangbanging. Part of Julie's assimilation is underscored by her refusal to allow her son to join the other young boy who was just initiated in the barrio, instead sending him "inside" the house, away from the barrio street. The cinematic effect of this tattoo erasure, reinstitutionalization, and rehousing is, quite simply, a reductive multimedia "stay-in-school" slogan.

While there is always the possibility that Julie will take Chicana/o studies courses and become an activist—which might lead her to recover her partially hidden indelible tattoo for a truly revolutionary cultural agenda—she is more likely to become the new conservative "Hispanic," or member of the Mexican American bourgeoisie, a subject position possible in this film's semantic order only through her partial self-effacement. Elizabeth Coonrod Martínez (1995) has argued that the central tension in *American Me* is between collective and individual identity, in which "brutality and violence committed against members of an opposing group . . . eventually affects and destroys the original group, and in the process, the individual" (17). What I am arguing is that by presenting Julie's rejection of her barrio identity, Olmos in effect establishes a new binary—a Chicana/o *Up from Slavery* self-help, pick-yourself-up-by-your-*calcos* discourse.[15] Even if he has succeeded at co-opting a partially resistant subaltern spectatorship, or establishing a spectatorship of resistance in his target audience, this audience is left with little more than a pipe dream: the American dream of individual upward mobility, which invariably excludes increasing numbers of Black and Brown lumpenproletarians in underdeveloped, inner-city U.S. neighborhoods. It is just not realistic, especially without any reference to the necessary social and economic support apparatus that would make the get-out-of-gangs mantra viable.[16]

So how does Olmos's cinematic discourse on identity and empowerment relate to Pinto discourse? As noted, it deploys Pinto signifying practices such as *placas*, but it also diverges significantly from Pinto self-representations. Some Chicano prisoners, such as Baca, present exoticized versions of the Pinto bad-man hero, while others, such as Sánchez and Salinas, articulate the Pinto as über-revolutionary. Olmos's film about Pintos enacts their self-erasure. Brett Levinson (1996) locates *American Me* within the nihilistic social psychology of Octavio Paz's 1950 *Labyrinth of Solitude*, which is notorious for proposing the Pachuco as the flamboyant antithesis of "true" Mexican-ness. While Levinson overburdens his reading of Santana as the postmodern actualization of the Mexican's and Mexican American's purported role as the personification of the discursive limit—the quintessential liminal subject who is never actualized as whole—he nonetheless provides a productive linkage between Chicano masculinity, homosocial desire, and self-erasure. In Olmos's cinematic vision of Chicana/o empowerment, Pinto identity remains pathological and must disappear if the broader Chicana/o community is to survive. After all, Pintos are necessarily defined by incarceration, which is more likely to lead to an intensification of nonrevolutionary criminality than a revolutionary form of it.

Ultimately, Olmos's alternative discourse—a veritable call for assimilation predicated upon the erasure of vernacular knowledge, for which the tattoo serves as a metonym—rejects the revolutionary potential of Pinto consciousness that Louis Mendoza (2006), Alán Gómez (2006a, 2006b), Dylan Rodriguez (2006), and I have shown to be quite viable and very real. Despite my critiques of Avila's mimetic commodity fetish, Baca's replicating binaries, and Sánchez's and Salinas's misogynist signifying practices, I underscore how these Pinta/os pose significant challenges, albeit inchoate, to their neocolonial realities as members of a community peonized and subjugated by the U.S. invasion and occupation of over half of Mexico's national territory since 1848. These challenges are not merely counterhegemonic, but in some cases revolutionary.

By contrast, Olmos's film proposes a hegemonic notion of the American "me" that inevitably undermines its gang-intervention message. Contrary to Rob Canfield's suggestion that *American Me* revolutionizes popular stereotypical images of Chicana/os (such as the gangster) by transforming them into, or replacing them with, more autonomous and empowering models of identity and agency, I suggest that Olmos's film ironically, but not surprisingly, proposes that the optimized Chicana/o subject can be achieved only through self-effacement—that is, individual, cultural, and historical erasure. It is pure Ideology, the cinematic equivalent of an ontological drive-by shooting.

This is not to say that Olmos's film is irredeemable. On the contrary, it could very well be the single most important and cinematically innovative Chicana/o-made film to date. After *American Me*, no one will ever look at the Chicana/o tattoo in the same way. By the time the young gang initiate pulls the trigger on a twilight street filled with children, elders, families, and other Pendleton-clad barrio boys, the spectators who may themselves have "put in work," as the practice of gangbanging is euphemistically called, are meant to become viscerally disturbed by the colors and images on the screen and on their own hands and bodies. However, I submit that the film's inability to intervene on the scale Olmos intends, rests in part on the film's demand that the resistant minority spectator ultimately efface her- or himself. The film presents no viable socioeconomic alternative other than cultural genocide.

Having viewed the film with a younger brother in Houston, Texas, as well as with young lumpenproletariat Chicana/os and other Latina/os in California and New York youth detention facilities who are similarly marked, I know for a fact that the film's cultural codes have an impact upon the spectators. Even as these young prisoners and probationers consume the gangster aura and marketing that surrounds films like *Menace II Society* and *American Me*, they are visually moved and even disturbed, if not scared, by the verité depictions of Olmos's film. Their reactions are not provoked by the cinematic violence, but what accompanies it. But the "stay out of gangs and go back to school" message promoted in Ramón Menéndez's 1988 feature film, *Stand and Deliver*, in which Olmos plays the role of a school teacher who rather naively pontificates that "you've got to want to succeed in order to succeed," is much less accessible to this target audience. Material circumstances for these youths—encaged by the underdevelopment resulting from White capitalist seizure of Mexican land in the nineteenth century and continuing exploitation of Mexican and Chicana/o labor ever since—are so dismal that it is facile, if not cruel, to spout mottos such as "you've got to want to succeed in order to succeed," which Olmos frequently repeats at his screenings. Although a few young Chicana/os are certainly able to get out of *la vida loca*, others intuitively know that they are not the primary source of the "cancer in our barrios." They refuse to accept primary blame for their community's underdevelopment, criminalization, and mass incarceration. Rather than assimilate, these resistant subjects refuse to renounce their identity, which is constructed in and through their working-class and lumpenproletarian barrios, where their families live. It's all they've got. Herein lies the paradox of Olmos's cinematic intervention into the gangxploitation genre and *la vida loca*, which it ultimately rejects: it uses Pinto culture to complicate (if not outright efface) Pinto counterhegemonic discourses on identity and agency that, as I have shown, have the potential to produce a truly collectivist revolutionary consciousness.

Given this profound limit in Olmos's use of Pinto semiotics—particularly tattoos and other verbal *placas*—to levy a critique of Pintos themselves, several questions emerge. Could he have intervened into *la vida loca* without recourse to a self-defeating discourse of self-erasure? More importantly, why did Olmos need to resort to the misogynist master narrative of La Malinche? Various Chicana/o authors, artists, and scholars have proposed incisive interrogations of *la vida loca* without overlaying their texts with such an overbearing and overdetermined archetype. These include, but are not limited to, Yxta Maya Murray's novel about gang girls, *Locas* (1997); Allison Anders's feature film on *cholas*, *Mi Vida Loca* (1993); and Marie Keta Miranda's participant-observer study, *Homegirls in the Public Sphere* (2003). Juanita Díaz-Cotto's recent study, *Chicana Lives and Criminal Justice: Voices from El Barrio* (2006), which blends sociological analysis with Pinta *testimonios*, is exemplary for giving voice to Pinta visions of themselves outside the reproduction of stereotypes. I further show in Chapter 7 that Pinta poet Judy Lucero has proposed alternatives to Olmos's failed attempt to negotiate commodified archetypes such as the pathological gangbanger, the tragic mestizo Pinto, and the upwardly mobile Mexican American bourgeois subject. The complex commodifications of Pinta/os is the subject of the succeeding chapters.

CHAPTER 6

The Pinto as Palimpsest

Fred Gómez Carrasco and the South Texas Culture Wars

PINTOS, FAMILY PORTRAITS, AND COLLECTIVE MEMORIES OF THE U.S.-MEXICO WAR

I first heard "El corrido de Alfredo Carrasco" in 1974, when I was nine years old, in my maternal grandfather's cantina. The working-class bar, called Sananí's Place, was on the corner of 74th and Harrisburg Streets in Magnolia, the southeast Houston barrio where I was born and raised. This *corrido* is more commonly known as "La muerte de Alfredo Carrasco" (The death of Fred Carrasco, Variant B),[1] whose subject was better known by his Americanized name, Fred Gómez Carrasco: the infamous San Antonio–based Mexican Mafia baron who ran a ruthless heroin cartel in south Texas for several decades. Carrasco eventually was arrested in a dramatic police dragnet at the Tejas Motel in south San Antonio, imprisoned, and ultimately killed on August 3, 1974, during an even more dramatic escape attempt from the Walls Unit of the Texas Department of Corrections in Huntsville. His death concluded an eleven-day armed takeover of the prison library that made front-page news throughout the country. Having perpetrated the longest prison takeover in U.S. history, Carrasco, like his Pinta/o precursors, was immediately reified into a palimpsest and floating signifier in competing Chicana/o and White narratives of nation and identity in south Texas.

Although I did not realize it then, the cantina and the *corrido* were profoundly significant to my family. Sananí's Place, named after a cousin from the agricultural town of Poteet, Texas, remains the only legitimate business venture any family member has ever attempted. Even though our family cantina failed as a business, it offered an ephemeral yet symbolically significant performance of economic independence by my maternal grandfather, who never quite made it to the proletariat, much less the bourgeoisie. Because of this subaltern legacy, the *corrido* about Carrasco had an even greater resonance for our family.

At the time of the debut of "La muerte de Alfredo Carrasco" in 1974, one of my uncles had been serving a decades' long sentence in the Texas

Department of Corrections for engaging in a quintessentially capitalist enterprise: the illicit drug trade—specifically, traffic in heroin. Before my grandfather ever ventured into the world of "legitimate" capitalism, his son had been earning money as a member of a loosely knit cartel that eventually evolved into the Mexican Mafia in Texas, the organization that Carrasco is credited with consolidating. Our links to the Mexican Mafia created intense anxiety, especially since we had seen the televised coverage of the bloody massacre in which Carrasco, one of his two confederates, and two of their hostages were shot dead in a hail of bullets fired by a phalanx of prison officers, FBI agents, and the ever-present Texas Rangers. Despite our fears, and our hatred of the heavy toll heroin was taking on our family and other families in our barrio, we nonetheless were mesmerized by the *corrido*. As the song played on the old Victrola jukebox, my grandfather and his patrons—primarily my parents and other relatives—continued talking in hushed tones. We played the song over and over until we had memorized the details of the event as if it were a family story recounted from generation to generation. In a sense, it was.

In previous chapters I showed how competing claims to the southwestern United States converged at the Pinta and Pinto body, and I maintain that this historical struggle extends to the present in ongoing efforts to narrativize, and thus claim ownership of, Fred Gómez Carrasco. In this chapter, I map the complex signifying practices that undergird these competing commodifications and consumptions of Carrasco, paying particular attention to the contested model of the bad-man hero to further historicize Chicana/o criminality and Pinta/o culture. My examination of Carrasco as a volatile floating signifier is informed by critical assessments of the conflictive relationship between Chicana/o literary arts, mainstream media, and legal discourse.[2] Following Stuart Hall's exposé of the racial subtexts of British media accounts of crime (1978, 1980, 1981, 1989), I explicate how mainstream accounts, or encodings, of Carrasco are readily consumed, or interpretively decoded, by many White Americans in relation to long-standing racist stereotypes about Mexican *desperados*. On the other hand, Mexican American versions vacillate between similar accounts of this stereotype, as well as overly romantic yet nonetheless oppositional decodings of Carrasco as a defiant social bandit and eminent revolutionary. Carl Gutiérrez-Jones has noted that Chicana/o artists complement their critiques of the objectivist claims of hegemonic institutions and disciplinary discourses such as jurisprudence by introducing alternative dialogic interpretive frameworks (1995: 6–7). I would add that by simultaneously incorporating and challenging official and semiofficial accounts of Carrasco as a *desperado*, Chicana/o artists and activists, including other Pintos, enable a critique of Carrasco's violent model of agency while also historicizing the material conditions that make this type of outlaw hero inevitable.

WITH HIS PISTOL IN HIS HAND: THE HISTORICIST POETICS AND MASCULINIST ORDER OF THE CARRASCO *CORRIDOS*

As scholars of the epic heroic *corrido* have noted, this octosyllabic acoustic ballad form recounts the individual experience of its protagonist and the broader collective memory of subordination, resistance, and complicated claims to counterpower. Américo Paredes (1958) has shown that this *corrido* subgenre arose in the crucible of the Texas-Mexican and U.S.-Mexico wars in the mid-nineteenth century as a counterpoint to the ascendant White capitalist hegemony in the region that became the southwestern United States. It is distinguished for celebrating the martial exploits of ill-fated yet perennially defiant Mexican and Mexican American male warrior heroes who fight against bigoted White tyranny and encroaching capitalism. Extending Paredes's archaeology of this performative vernacular ballad form, contemporary cultural critics such as José Limón (1992), Teresa McKenna (1997), and Ramón Saldívar (1990) have proposed the epic heroic *corrido* as an oppositional master narrative for Chicana/o literature and culture, even as they recognize this subgenre's masculinist conceits.

Seen as more ideologically coherent, the epic heroic *corrido* is sometimes juxtaposed against the more recent *narco-corrido* subgenre, which presents a more ambiguous hero: the violent *narco-traficante*, or drug dealer. While the *narco-corrido* has come under increasing scrutiny for its masculinist symbolic system, it is important to recognize that this subgenre, like the epic heroic *corrido*, is an autochthonous form of discourse through which Chicana/os both figuratively and performatively struggle against perceived injustices. Despite the fact that *narco-corrido* protagonists such as Carrasco often are killed by representatives of the hegemonic order, the communal singing of these songs also involves a popular counterhegemonic recuperation of criminalized Chicana/o subjects. Indeed, even if *corrido* protagonists usually fail to develop their provincial social banditry into broader revolutionary agency, these ballads nonetheless model what Gutiérrez-Jones identifies as Chicana/o counterhegemonic signifying practices that propose radical ruptures in the objectivist claims of legal discourse and dominant historiographies.

As Paredes (1995) and María Herrera-Sobek (1990) note in their respective taxonomies of *corridos*, the *narco-corrido* subgenre usually involves a lower-class male protagonist who rises to the top of the gangster underworld through cunning, daring, and sheer brutality. Not unlike the male protagonist in the epic heroic *corrido*, the *narco-traficante* typically is renowned for repeatedly outwitting law enforcement authorities, and, as such, he symbolically threatens the status quo. However, even though the bad-man hero of the *narco-corrido* sometimes rises to the role of a populist folk hero for demonstrating his superiority over his White antagonists, he usually is condemned to living life on the run and, ultimately, meeting an untimely and violent death. Herrera-Sobek (1999) has identified this fate as a crucial element of the "moral code" undergirding the *narco-corrido*, which she claims serves to indict its protagonist, who, after all, is a drug dealer. Despite the unsavory character of the *narco-corrido* protagonist, this *corrido* subgenre is underwritten by a complex, though problematic, code of ethics and class politics that are tantamount to an underclass form of chivalry. The violent protagonist is not necessarily fighting on behalf of his people, as did epic heroic *corrido* protagonists like Jacinto Treviño and Juan Cortina, but the *narco-traficante* is still bound by similar patriarchal role expectations that situate him between a social bandit and a blood-thirsty gangster. (Female *narco-traficantes*, such as the one recounted in "Camelia la Tejana," appear in this genre less frequently.) These governing edicts are similar to those that undergird the epic heroic *corrido* and include a paternalistic "respect" for women and the civilian population not directly involved in the drug trade, as well as unflinching bravery even when faced with certain death.

These masculinist ethics imbue the *narco-traficante* with the aura, though not necessarily the substance, of a social bandit, which Eric Hobsbawm (1965, 1969) and Antonio Gramsci (1971) identify as a common folk figure arising from desperate conditions of oppression. This counterhegemonic aura surrounds the first of the four known variants of the Carrasco *corridos*, titled simply enough, "El corrido de Alfredo Carrasco" (The ballad of Fred Carrasco," Variant A), which was written and composed in 1973 by San Antonio native Daniel Garcez and Salomé Gutierrez.[3] True to its roots in the epic heroic and *narco-corrido* subgenres, this ballad critiques Carrasco's legendary brutality even as it celebrates him as a hero who resists emasculation both in and out of prison. It describes Carrasco, who survived four bullet wounds during his capture at the Tejas Motel, as being as virile as "a mountain lion /

because he is the captain / of the Mexican Mafia" ("un león de montaña / porque es el capitán / de la mafia mexicana," lines 6–8).

A forerunner to the later hit single "El gato negro," by Rubén Ramos and the Texas Revolution, which recounts the exploits of a *narcotraficante* who repeatedly escapes from the most notorious prisons in Texas, this first variant of the four Carrasco *corridos* recounts the hero's previous escape from a prison in Guadalajara, Mexico. Moreover, it emphasizes Carrasco's enduring threat even after his capture by recalling the unusually high number of guards assigned to prevent another Carrasco escape, and it concludes on a prophetic note:

Ya me despido cantando
y esta historia no termina
la ley vigila a Carrasco
como cabeza cosida.

[Singing my farewell to you all
But this story is not over
The law keeps watch on Carrasco
Like a head ready to explode.] (lines 29–32)

Even though the final stanza praises the San Antonio lawmen for "using all their intelligence / in order to have him captured" ("pusieron su

Figure 6.1. Photograph of wounded Fred Gómez Carrasco. Courtesy of the *San Antonio Express-News*.

inteligencia / para poderlo agarrar," lines 35–36), the preceding stanzas transform Carrasco's legendary animalistic brutality into predatory virility through the symbols of a majestic mountain lion and a loosely sewn head always ready to explode.[4] The apparent hegemonic closure signaled by Carrasco's capture is always under threat, which is a signature feature of the epic heroic *corrido*. Even if Carrasco is not figured as a revolutionary, he nonetheless is reconfigured as a resilient and salient counterpower who cannot easily be contained.

The counterhegemonic potential of the Carrasco *corridos* also arises from the format of the *narco-corrido* and epic heroic *corrido* subgenres: the celebratory public performance of Carrasco's criminality through *corridos* is itself a socially symbolic act of resistance and transgression by the broader Mexican and Mexican American communities. As Teresa McKenna (1991) notes in her examination of a *corrido* about a Pinto in 1970s New Mexico, the public performance of *corridos* continues to function as a form of oral history and alternative historiography, similar to its original uses in the early nineteenth century. Following McKenna as well as Stuart Hall (1978, 1980, 1981), who has proposed that the production of news has been commodified as a product and reified as a site of ideological interpellation, I submit that the Carrasco *corridos* composed after his death similarly function as alternatives to the official history promulgated by law enforcement agencies and mainstream media outlets, all of which have sought to claim ownership over the "meaning" of Fred Gómez Carrasco's violent claim to power.

The postmortem Carrasco *corrido* I heard in my youth in the family cantina, for instance, was spontaneously composed by Salomé Gutierrez and originally recorded by his conjunto group Los Socios on the night of Carrasco's death. Even before an investigation could be mounted— Carrasco's bloody, bullet-riddled body was still lying on the ground while the song was being recorded—the Mexican American community knew, a priori, that this killing of one of their own at the hands of the Texas Rangers would be "justified" like so many others before. Indeed, this *corrido* resonated as a challenge to law enforcement and mainstream media claims that Carrasco and his confederate, Rodolfo Dominguez, committed suicide with self-inflicted gunshot wounds to their heads. The song begins:

El sábado trés de agosto
el año setenta y cuatro,
en la prisión del estado,

mataron a Fred Carrasco.
Lo acribillaron a tiros
en companía de otros cuatro.

[On Saturday, August the third,
the year nineteen seventy-four,
in the state penitentiary
they killed Fred (Gómez) Carrasco.
They filled him full of bullet holes
in the company of four more.] (lines 1–4)

In the *corrido* reportage of Carrasco's death, there is no doubt that Carrasco, Dominguez, and their hostages were "killed" by gunfire from law enforcement officials.[5] The *corrido* reports that they all "died in the shootout" ("murieron en la refriega," line 40). This alternative is underscored by the *corrido*'s reference to the prison-made bulletproof iron helmets that the Chicano Convicts were wearing at the time of their deaths. The popular view in the Chicana/o community is that Carrasco and Dominguez were wounded in the torso and were still alive when Texas Rangers removed their bulletproof helmets to fire a coup de grace into each Chicano Convict's head.

Figure 6.2. Improvised armor and weapons used by Fred Gómez Carrasco. Reprinted from *Fred Carrasco: The Heroin Merchant* (1974). Courtesy of Wilson McKinney and Heidelberg Press.

The counterhegemonic potential of this *corrido* counter-reportage is indirectly underscored by the defensive tone of a *San Antonio News* front-page story on August 6, 1974. "Carrasco Corrido Stretches Truth," by Wilson McKinney, ran immediately after the *corrido*'s debut on the popular Spanish-language radio station KEDA. In an illustration of popular consumption of Carrasco as an ambiguous though nonetheless defiant rebel, within a week of the shooting, Salomé Gutierrez pressed the unusually high number of 5,000 single records for sale, which sold out in less than a month. In contrast, Daniel Garcez's two versions (Variant A, "El corrido de Alfredo Carrasco," or "El corrido del Tejas Motel," and Variant C, "El corrido de Alfredo Gómez Carrasco") take judgmental tones towards Carrasco, include praise for police officers and prison guards, and also repeat the official story that Carrasco committed suicide. As a result, Variants A and C initially were rejected by local San Antonio radio stations for fear of a public backlash. *San Antonio Express-News* journalist Wilson McKinney demonstrated the ideological nature of the battle between the *corridos* and the mainstream media when he noted that Daniel Garcez "made no apologies for his song [and] San Antonio's newspaper, radio and television reporters made no apologies for their accounts of Carrasco's capture, either" (1975: 210).

In this war, the contestatory potential of the Carrasco *corridos* arises from their martial vocabulary. The racialized representation of violence, fundamental to the epic heroic *corrido* subgenre, and the direct challenge to state authority, definitive of the *narco-corrido* subgenre, both inform the Carrasco *corridos*.[6] The ballads' figurative linkage of racial conflict, outlaw sensibility, and masculinist performances of power to the broader legacy of war and armed resistance between Whites and Mexican Americans in the southwestern United States is illustrated in the two postmortem Carrasco *corrido*s: the aforementioned "El corrido de Alfredo Carrasco" (or "La muerte de Alfredo Carrasco," Variant B) by Salomé Gutierrez, and "El trágico fin de Carrasco" (The tragic end of Carrasco, Variant D), written by José E. Morante and recorded by his conjunto group El Repertorio Norteño Internacional. Similar to its epic-heroic precursors, in which a hero defiantly and resiliently confronts a numerically superior enemy force, these Carrasco *corridos* focus on their (anti)hero's armed confrontation with a phalanx of law enforcement officers that included armored personnel carriers, U.S. Army helicopters, and surveillance planes. The conflict's military overtones were underscored by Carrasco's request for six bulletproof vests, three bulletproof helmets, three two-way radios, and three M-16 automatic assault rifles with five magazines and three hundred rounds of extra ammunition. Even a nearby army unit was placed on alert with orders to be prepared to deploy within twenty-four hours, with later orders to deploy within an hour. In a modern portrayal of the horse chases of the late nineteenth- and early twentieth-century epic heroic *corridos*, such as "The Ballad of Gregorio Cortez," Gutierrez's "El corrido de Alfredo Carrasco" (or "La muerte de Alfredo Carrasco," Variant B), celebrates Carrasco as a modern-day mounted warrior who, like the U.S. Army, has replaced the horse with an armored personnel carrier.

Similarly, the Morante Variant D version, "El trágico fin de Carrasco," pays particular attention to Carrasco's infamous "Trojan horse," which he used to exit the prison library (lines 37–44). Built out of portable chalkboards taped together and surrounded by a symbolically significant layer of bulletproof law books, Carrasco and his confederates adorned the entire apparatus with Mexican flags torn out of prison library books. Their bodies were pulled from it and laid out on display like killed prey or nineteenth-century Mexican "bandits."

This martial and incipiently cultural nationalist symbolic system, which in the epic heroic *corrido* functions to transform its underclass protagonist as a metonym for the continued resistance of a militarily defeated population, similarly resonates with a broader social and political significance in the Carrasco *corridos*. The epic heroic and *narco-corrido* subgenres converge in their portrayal of Carrasco as a bad-man,

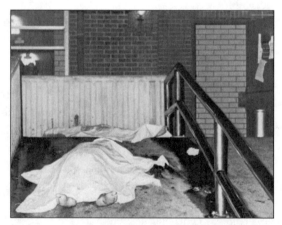

Figure 6.3. The dead bodies of Fred Gómez Carrasco and Rodolfo Dominguez. Reprinted from *Fred Carrasco: The Heroin Merchant* (1974). Courtesy of Wilson McKinney and Heidelberg Press.

or Pinto, warrior hero and quasi-social bandit. This cultural nationalist resonance is underscored by the oft-reported fact that Carrasco named his son after the famed Mexican Revolutionary leader Emiliano Zapata.

The fundamental trope undergirding the postmortem Carrasco *corridos*, however, is death. In a posteriori genres such as the epic heroic and *narco-corrido* subgenres, the ending always is predetermined. In these postmortem Carrasco *corridos*, the manner of Carrasco's death becomes the nucleus and most important aspect of the historicist poetics of this hypermasculinist lyric form. Confronted with certain death, like his epic heroic counterparts, Carrasco is celebrated for fearless defiance of his historic enemy and, more importantly, for his martyrdom. The Gutierrez version, "La muerte de Alfredo Carrasco," Variant B, proclaims:

> Quería enseñarles que hombre
> que miedo no les tenía.
> [. . .]
> Bajó por las escaleras
> sabiendo que lo esperarían
> armados hasta los dientes
> montones de policías.
>
> [He wanted to show as a man
> he had no fear of them at all.
> [. . .]
> He went down the stairs
> knowing they all awaited him
> armed to the teeth
> a multitude of policemen. (lines 11–12, 33–36)

Even though his fate was sealed by the technological and numerical superiority of his enemy, Carrasco is celebrated for putting up a fight of heroic proportions.

The oppositional potential of this masculinist martial vocabulary is synthesized in its most extreme form in Variant B by the introduction of phallic references:

> Prisión de Huntsville mentada
> guardianes y policías
> aunque quisiera negarlo
> no olvidarán el mal rato

que les daría ese gallito
llamado Gómez Carrasco.

[Cursed Huntsville penitentiary
police guards and policemen too
although they try to deny it
they'll never forget the bad time
given by that little rooster
whose name was Gómez Carrasco.] (lines 43–48)

The figurative transformation of Carrasco into a cultural icon—the epic heroic Pinto martyr—is consolidated through the image of the *gallito*, a diminutive term of endearment for "rooster" or "fighting cock." The *gallo*, used in the illicit recreational diversion of cock fighting very popular among Mexican Americans, is an animal that inevitably dies in battle. Its violent death is assured because each adversary the champion *gallo* kills in battle will be replaced by ever more competitors until the champion *gallo* himself is killed. Within this martial economy, the cock's style of fighting—and dying—becomes the primary criterion through which it gains value. Like the *gallo*, Carrasco becomes a celebrated Pinto icon precisely through his fearless and heroic fight to the death, which, as the *corrido* notes, will never be forgotten. By invoking this masculinist symbol, this Carrasco *corrido* figuratively transforms death as martyrdom through the trope of sexual violence. However, this recentering of the male body through the figure of the phallic "fighting cock" ultimately is invested in a highly problematic binary logic—the "fucked" verses the "fucker"—that I identified in other Pinto signifying practices in previous chapters.

These troubling masculinist signifying practices, in which the hero is celebrated for his martial prowess and martyrdom, nonetheless are the very features that ground the Carrasco *corridos* within Mexican American culture and history. This trope of death-as-martyrdom forms the nucleus of Variant D, Morantes's "El trágico fin de Alfredo Gómez Carrasco," which was written and published as a broadside shortly after Carrasco's death. Radically different from Gutierrez's version (Variant B), the second part of Morantes's *corrido* repeats the official story that Carrasco and Dominguez committed suicide with shots to the head and even appears to pass judgment against them through a biblical reference: "he who lives by way of the sword / will also die by the same way" ("el que vive en la violencia / entre ella misma se muere," lines 83–84).

Yet, whereas this *corrido* appears to denigrate Carrasco and Dominguez through references to them as "cowards," a closer reading reveals that the main critique of these Chicano Convicts, which revolves around the allegation that they committed suicide, nevertheless gains a more complex meaning when considered within Herrera-Sobek's and Paredes's topology of the *corrido*. As Herrera-Sobek notes, suicide represents a cowardly way out of conflict, one that the true "manly" hero of this genre is not permitted: he must stand and fight with his pistol in his hand. The apparent critique of "cowardly suicide" thus may be heard by some as an indirect call for armed rebellion, and even martyrdom. After all, it invokes the popular collective memory of the many Pyrrhic victories Chicana/os have had in their historical confrontations with White law enforcement officers such as the Texas Rangers, the nineteenth-century vanguard of the White capitalist order in the southwestern United States. Even if the composer did not intend this reading, he has little control of how an audience will consume and decode the ballad, especially in the racially polarized context of 1970s south Texas. Here, violent death goes hand in hand with Chicana/o history, and Carrasco would be deemed a coward if he had refused to follow the course of the many Chicana/o folk heroes who came before him. Rather than being dissonant with the other Carrasco *corridos* that proclaim Carrasco as a defiant martyr, Variant D is "tragic" only if Carrasco failed to meet his destiny: death in battle against the Texas Rangers and their racist ilk.

The dialogic vocabulary of Variant D also links it to the more overtly oppositional poetics of Gutierrez's version (Variant B), which alleges that Carrasco and Dominguez were assassinated. Aside from implicitly expecting, and perhaps even demanding, Carrasco's martyrdom, Morante's "El trágico fin de Alfredo Gómez Carrasco" also pairs its cultural nationalist symbols with explicit references to the Texas Rangers as "*los rinches,*" which rhymes with *pinches* (bastards), the epithet popularized by epic heroic *corridos* of the nineteenth and early twentieth century. The counterhegemonic valence of this diachronic reference resonates even more when one considers that the Texas Rangers also were part of the virtual army of law enforcement officers stalking Carrasco as late as 1974. As noted, they are the ones rumored to have assassinated Carrasco as he lay wounded on the ground. The Texas Rangers thereby become a unifying transhistorical trope that imbues an otherwise judgmental *corrido* with a counterhegemonic valence.

Carrasco's symbolic value within the economy of the Carrasco *corridos* is dependent not so much on his life or death, but the manner in which he lived and died. His life as a ruthlessly successful subaltern capitalist and his death during his defiant confrontation with the Texas Rangers and other law enforcement officials both imbue his agency with the aura of a social bandit, although not an anticapitalist revolutionary. After all, aside from his profiteering, Carrasco enrolled his daughter in an elite, East Coast private prep school. One might even argue that Carrasco's most profound challenge to the triumphant White-dominated capitalist order in which Mexican Americans were consigned to the margins is most salient *after* his death and subsequent canonization through the *corrido* form. While the *corridos* figure Fred Gómez Carrasco as a metonym for a Chicana/o critique of capitalist political economy, the reliance on the bad-man hero motif not only rests upon masculinist conceits, but also lends itself to appropriation by Whites as "confirmation" of Chicano pathology and inherent criminality. These competing narrativizations of Carrasco have also played out in another popular media format: the true crime genre.

TRUE CRIME, CHICANOS, AND COMMODIFICATION IN SOUTH TEXAS

As Fredric Jameson (1991) and other Marxist cultural critics have noted, one of the most salient powers of late capitalism is its ability to appropriate and even commodify its antithesis. This certainly is true of Carrasco, whose uniquely efficient ability to make money by distributing booklike stacks of heroin in the illicit economy of the drug trade was eventually commodified in the legitimate economy in the form of actual books stacked in respectable literary emporiums throughout his native San Antonio. Less than five miles from the Alamo, in the exclusive White-majority, inner-city municipality of Alamo Heights, former *San Antonio Express-News* journalist Wilson McKinney's 1975 book-length investigative account of Carrasco's rise and fall, *Fred Gómez Carrasco: The Heroin Merchant*, currently sells for $75 plus tax. According to Cece Cheever, owner of Cheever's Bookstore, which does a lucrative business hawking this hard-to-find tome to its primarily upper-class White clientele, this book is a hot collector's item.[7] Extrapolating from Richard Johnson's discussion of the complex processes of production and consumption, I submit that while Carrasco is transformed into a social bandit, or a palimpsestic Pinto icon, through the popular *corrido* form, he simultaneously is reified as a floating signifier in White claims to the southwestern United States. He becomes for racist Whites a Mexican pariah who legitimates the continued segregation of San Antonio and, more broadly, the draconian police state that anticipated the rise of the prison-industrial complex and the war on crime/war on terrorism.

Carrasco's commodification and consumption as the "heroin merchant" and a lower-class Mexican American pariah are undergirded by the voluminous reportage that continues to appear in national and local daily newspapers. Alongside recent stories in the *New York Times*, the *San Antonio Express-News* continues to reference Carrasco in its annual retrospectives under headlines such as "Crimes of the Century," in which Carrasco is paired with the quintessential, though unwitting, Mexican American social bandit Gregorio Cortez, about whom several epic heroic *corridos* have been written.[8] The *San Antonio Express-News*—which is both renowned and denounced for having provided the most extensive news coverage of the hunt for, capture, and trial of Cortez in the early 1900s—also is credited by McKinney with having its reporters conduct as many "stakeouts" as the police in the hunt for Carrasco in the 1970s. Carrasco's reification and commodification as a lower-class Mexican pariah is further actualized by McKinney's descriptions of Carrasco as a *desperado* and modern-day Mexican *bandido* in a region whose citizens are weaned—and polarized—on ballads and other tales of social banditry involving Mexicans, Whites, and, of course, the racist and blood-thirsty Texas Rangers.

Based in large part on the investigative reports he wrote as the lead journalist for the *San Antonio Express-News* special series—which ran under the conspicuous header *¡Carrasco!*—McKinney's book dismisses the populist social bandit angle, focusing instead on exploring the organized crime, or Mafia, storyline. Capitalizing on the popularity of the 1971 hit film *The French Connection*, which opened during Carrasco's rise to power, McKinney also invokes the *narco*-film and true crime genres in order to push "The Mexican Connection" angle. Like Cortez, Carrasco conveniently became the object of a nationwide campaign by local, state, and national law enforcement agencies—led by the Texas Rangers—to reassert the "rule of law." The racialization of the story through McKinney's unnecessary use of the inverted exclamation mark as a header to his investigative reports, which is a Spanish-language convention, and his subsequent introduction of other racialized cues in his book that further darken Carrasco, inevitably implicates the broader Mexican and Mexican American population in the Southwest.

These racialist signifying practices are foregrounded by other sensationalist headlines that accentuate the perceived threat that the

"Carrasco gang" posed to the local, and even global, population. These include early reports such as "Officers Claim Carrasco 'Territory' Worldwide." The mainstream print media even paired Cold War "red baiting" with a romantic Latin lover subtext with headlines such as "'Liberty or Death,' Cries Carrasco," "Carrasco: 'Prepare for War!'" "Carrasco Has Bombs—Vows to Use Them," "Carrasco Wants to Go To Cuba," "Troops Put on Alert," and "Carrasco Love Letter: 'My Dearest, I Now Bid you Farewell.'" After Carrasco's death, the *San Antonio Express-News* (which is owned by the Hearst Corporation, infamous for pioneering the yellow journalism that helped instigate the zoot suit riots discussed in Chapter 5), wrote an extended epitaph under even more vitriolic headlines, including "An Atheist with an Ego," "Death Comes to El Señor," and "World Better Carrasco Dead." At the height of the Cold War, these stories effectively demonized Carrasco not only as an overly libidinal Mexican *bandido* similar to the figure in the infamous Hollywood "greaser" films of the 1930s and 1940s, but also as a communist and atheist.[9] For south Texas Whites during the 1970s, Fred Gómez Carrasco became a metonym for all things evil. As reported in a *San Antonio News* article on July 29, 1974, during the height of the Carrasco prison breakout attempt, the 49th Division of the Texas National Guard was put on alert and ordered to be ready to deploy for service at the Huntsville Penitentiary on an hour's notice. Their enemy: three Mexicans.

Alongside Carrasco's reification by the White residents of Alamo Heights is his appropriation by the San Antonio Mexican American bourgeoisie in their problematic claim to inclusion in the polis. They further complicate the racial significance of Carrasco's Pyrrhic claim to power by accentuating class conflict in a racially segmented capitalist society. Capitalizing on the media's heightened attention on Carrasco, San Antonio's famed Democratic representative Henry B. Gonzalez warned against glamorizing him in an August 10, 1974, editorial in the *San Antonio Express*. Gonzalez quotes directly from one of Carrasco's personal letters:

> I did not take a straight career because I saw the injustice of the system. I could have chosen to be a doctor or a lawyer, but I would have been part of the system. The truth is I didn't have the heart that Henry B. Gonzalez has. (1)

Apparently oblivious to Carrasco's critique of the U.S. apartheid system that Gonzalez enables as a token Mexican American elected official, the "gentleman from Texas" (as Gonzales was dubbed by his congressional colleagues), gratuitously adds:

> I will continue to endeavor to do everything one single isolated congressman can do to root out this evil, if not from the state, if not from the country, certainly from the 20th District of the state of Texas. (1)

Already renowned as a virulently outspoken opponent of Mexican American civil rights organizations such as La Raza Unida Party and the Brown Berets, and even more famous for having punched a man who accused him of being a Communist, Gonzalez found a new negative reference point against whom he could obfuscate the historical and class conflicts underwriting Mexican American history in his own bid for power. His strategy worked: Gonzalez was reelected with an overwhelming majority, including a large percentage of the White vote.[10]

These racialist, exoticist, sensationalist, and ultimately capitalist signifying practices underwrite hegemonic representations of the "true story" of Carrasco's bloody and fatal claim to power as little more than the desperate acts of a pathological killer or modern *desperado*. These hegemonic accounts include *The Carrasco Tragedy: Eleven Days of Terror in the Huntsville Prison* (1975), written by the prison librarian Aline House, who was held hostage by Carrasco and, like McKinney, claimed prison warden Jim Estelle "should be commended rather than condemned for resolving the situation without greater loss of life" (n.p.). Warden Jim Estelle also produced a graphic photo documentary, *A Forgotten Time Remembered* (n.d.), in which he judiciously documents his handling of the prison breakout attempt "to set the record straight" (n.p.).[11] Together, these texts provide a complementary frame to *The Heroin Merchant*, which uncritically cites from the same official law enforcement sources. The ideological function of McKinney's book is unmasked in the foreword written by Ernest J. Marquardt Sr., the assistant regional director in Texas of the Drug Enforcement Agency. Marquardt introduces the ideological trajectory of McKinney's text by emphatically stating,

> neither the slums, the ghetto nor the barrio can be attributed as primary reasons for Carrasco's development into a heroin trafficker [because] such environmental influences were also present in the thousands of honest, successful Americans of Mexican or other minority extraction [*sic*] who have not become criminals. (xi)

In *The Heroin Merchant*, which prominently bears Carrasco's stylized gold-leaf signature above a syringe being squeezed by a skeletal hand, brown skin converges with the subaltern commodity known as *la carga blanca* (the white cargo) for consumption by a White audience primed by decades of yellow journalist accounts of the "Mexican menace."

The hysteria surrounding Carrasco was made all the more "real" by the fact that Mexican Americans comprise over 50 percent of the population in the highly segregated city of San Antonio.[12] Not only did Carrasco become a staple story that helped fuel the success of the newly consolidated *San Antonio Express-News* (thereby increasing the paper's profit margin), but this "Mexican boy from the barrio," to cite McKinney's problematic term of endearment, also sold many books.[13] Indeed, Carrasco became a veritable cottage industry in and of himself.

This reification of Carrasco demonstrates the cruel truism that capitalism is powerful and dynamic enough to legitimately profit from a subaltern capitalist whose claim to fame is his illegitimacy. However, as Marxist and postcolonial theorists have emphasized, subaltern communities actively complicate this process of exchange in a variety of

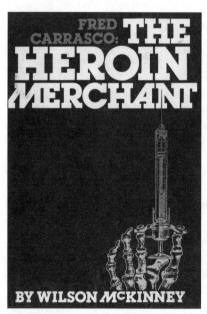

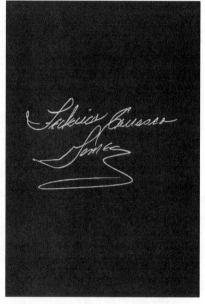

Figure 6.4. Book jacket for *Fred Carrasco: The Heroin Merchant*, by Wilson McKinney. Courtesy of Wilson McKinney and Heidelberg Press.

Figure 6.5. Book cover for *Fred Carrasco: The Heroin Merchant*, by Wilson McKinney. Courtesy of Wilson McKinney and Heidelberg Press.

ways. My own family history bears this out through our consumption of Carrasco as a surrogate family advocate. Rather than dehistoricizing Carrasco, as many White consumers in Alamo Heights have done, I submit that Chicana/o reclamations of this south Texas (anti)hero in part illuminate the historical and material significance of Chicana/o criminality and related incarceration rates. In contrast to the White reification of Carrasco-as-book, some Chicana/os have defiantly reclaimed Carrasco through the very book that fetishizes his identity as a kitschy stereotype, the drug-dealing villain who, in part, fueled an even larger economy: the prison-industrial complex.

One of the most compelling of these Chicana/o reclamations was played out over the very commodification of Carrasco through McKinney's book. According to Raúl Salinas, who also served time in the Walls Unit of the Texas Department of Corrections, soon after the publication of *The Heroin Merchant*, a truck carrying a shipment of these books was hijacked by a group of Pintos. They later redistributed the books free of charge throughout the barrios and cantinas of south Texas. Curiously, Salinas sold *The Heroin Merchant* for about $15 from his small, wood-frame storefront, Resistencia Books, located deep in the south Austin barrio. Resistencia Books' stock includes so many boxes, they have yet to sell out, even after Salinas's death. Although Salinas always refused to say where he got the books, he noted, with a wide-toothed grin, "This is what you call *rasquache* literary criticism," referring to the art of improvisation practiced by Mexicans and Chicanos of limited economic means. "Carrasco," he added, "may have been a ruthless gangster, but he was *our* gangster."[14]

At the most basic level, this armed and potentially lethal reclamation, accompanied by the socially significant bargain-basement barrio price of the book, illustrates the racialized and class-based dimensions of the ongoing battle to consume and control the narrative of Fred Gómez Carrasco. While Whites pay excessive amounts of money to consume the image of a racialized male menace to society, or modern *bandido*, this macabre and somewhat narcissistic Pinto reappropriation of Carrasco as a counterhegemonic outlaw figure has a metonymical resonance. The radically different use-value mapped onto Carrasco by Chicana/os in the barrios of south Texas illustrates that they continue figuratively—and even physically—to resist the hegemony of White capital and the attendant commodification and containment of the Mexican American population in the Southwest. The rising incarceration rates for minorities imbue this culture war with an even greater sense of urgency. The historical resonance of this reification and commodification is unmistakable: more than 160 years after the battle of the Alamo, Whites and Chicana/os still are fighting to define and control the meaning of a south San Antonio motel named "Tejas" and a prison chillingly dubbed the "Walls." At stake is the very historical definition of the "southwestern United States/Mexican northeast" as either the "United States of America" or "Aztlán."

POETIC LICENSE: FRED GÓMEZ CARRASCO AS PINTO REVOLUTIONARY

Following Salinas's reclamation and redistribution of *The Heroin Merchant*, the late Pinto poet Ricardo Sánchez added to the subaltern resonance of Carrasco's violent claim to power. A longtime resident of San Antonio, Sánchez was the proprietor of a community bookstore, Paperbacks, Etc., in San Antonio's primarily Mexican American Westside barrio, from which he similarly peddled a curiously large stock of *The Heroin Merchant* at a discount price. Beyond his own reappropriation of this book, Sánchez resisted the ahistorical reification of Carrasco-as-book, instead memorializing him as a Pinto icon for his defiance of the Texas Rangers, whom historian Rodolfo Acuña (2004) has dubbed "professional Mexican killers" for their infamous brutality against the Mexican American civilian population of south Texas. In "Cabalgado como bestia" (Corralled like a beast), an undated mixed-genre verse *testimonio* composed shortly after Carrasco's prison rebellion, Sánchez describes Carrasco as "ese carnal tan netamente chingón" ("that brother who was totally badass"), and notes how other Convicts wanted to "horrendously mimic" him "in order to recoup some sanity" (lines 61–63). Sánchez, the Pinto poet, further lionizes Carrasco for embodying the ethos of the Pachuco warrior hero:

> carrasco did his number,
> pride/love
> flowed within my veins,
> i understood his wrath
> as furious bullets cut him down,
> i writhed within from wanting
> for him to turn the tide,
> and as he held his stand
> for much more than a week,

i joyfully did laugh
to hear that he'd demanded
a pair of stacey adams
and good suits from the streets,
he made us realize
that he would die in freedom
and not in pinto shoes
nor wearing prison whites,
murió como él vivió,
    su cantogrito laughing
at social cobardías . . . (lines 123–142)[15]

Sánchez references the fact that even as Carrasco was surrounded by a virtual army of "good ole boys" with badges, he requested designer clothes worth more than $600, including a pair of shiny patent leather shoes known by their brand name "Stacey Adams," a favorite of the lumpenproletariat Pachuco also known as the zoot suiter. Indeed, throughout his eleven-day standoff with law enforcement officers from the FBI, the Texas Department of Corrections, and the Texas Rangers, Carrasco was purported never to have made an appearance without his suit jacket, which added to his growing mystique as "El Señor," or the Mexican Don.

I submit that while the local media further racialized Carrasco's flamboyance through references to the infamous 1943 zoot suit riots in Los Angeles, Sánchez's celebration of Carrasco's sense of style resituates Carrasco in the subaltern class context that virtually overdetermined his outcast and outlaw subjectivity. The Pachuco has been criminalized as a menace to society (Rosaldo 1989; Mazón 1984), pathologized as a cultural aberration (Paz 1950), and infantilized as a victim in the zoot suit riots. Yet Franz Fanon's (1982) social psychology of colonized subjects enables us to read the Pachuco's concern with style as an attempt by a subordinated outcast subject to overcompensate for a lack of economic and political power through the excessive performance of images of wealth and rebellion. Sánchez's invocation of the Pachuco zoot suiter, who is never complete without the patent leather shoes favored by Carrasco, thus becomes a symbolic performance of a utopian cultural nationalist desire for self-determination. Sánchez's troping of Carrasco's dress as resistance not only gains a racialized significance, but also an oppositional class significance. Revealingly, "style" in the vernacular context of Pachucos, often is referred to as "class."

Sánchez's celebration of Carrasco as a Pachuco also enables the Pinto poet to resituate the gentleman gangster—not only geographically, but politically. In "Tinieblas Pintas Quebradas," his mixed-genre introduction to the 1976 special issue of the Chicana/o cultural nationalist journal *De Colores* dedicated to "Los Pintos de América," Sánchez links Carrasco's violent claim to power not only to his own struggles in prisons in California and Texas, but also to the other prison struggles of the 1970s, which has come to be known as the era of U.S. prison rebellions:

> whipped, abused
> in the texas
> department of deformation's
> cotton fields,
> or mind controlled
> in califa's
> menticidal therapeautical communities,
> caught in attica by wanton fire power,
> inflamed by anger
> un fred gómez carrasco
> fought
> un pinche estado
> to an eleven day standstill. (1976b: 7–8)[16]

Himself a former Pachuco from the quintessential Pachuco town of El Paso, Texas (renowned as "El Chuco," or "Pachuco City"), Sánchez identifies with Carrasco in a significant passage from his Pinto corpus that enables him to globalize Carrasco's significance. By linking Carrasco's Pachuco and Pinto subjectivities, Sánchez more definitively approximates Hobsbawm's model of the "social bandit." He further articulates Carrasco onto broader subaltern struggles. This expansion is performed in the same text through Sánchez's pairing of Carrasco with other famous Convicts, including Socrates, Jesus, Gandhi, George Jackson, and Malcolm X (1976b: 7–8). Although Sánchez takes considerable poetic license in his references to this historical gallery of Convict heroes, his association of Convicts from Carrasco to Christ nonetheless functions as a poetic extension of what José David Saldívar (1991) has dubbed the "School of Calibán." Indeed, Sánchez extends and repopulates Saldívar's primarily literary cadre to include subaltern subjects renowned for their highly publicized contestatory writings as well as their nonliterary forms of agency—including the hijacking of trucks carrying commodities destined for the capitalist marketplace.

Similar to the reconstruction of his own past, Sánchez reconfigures Carrasco's criminality, and criminality in general, as legitimate subaltern political and economic agency. For Sánchez, as for Fanon, crime in a colonial context can be revolutionary. As discussed in previous chapters, Sánchez's model of revolutionary agency necessarily involves transgression and even outright sabotage, theft, and armed insurrection. Carrasco is thus an ideal subject for Sánchez, who also merged his outlaw and literary efforts with direct action through his membership in the Brown Berets, the Chicana/o cultural nationalist organization loosely modeled on the Black Panthers and the American Indian Movement. According to David Montejano, who conducted extensive field research as an honorary member of the San Antonio chapter of the Brown Berets, Carrasco was seen by some members as a potential catalyst that could spark the "Chicano revolution."[17] During Carrasco's ill-fated prison breakout attempt, for instance, several members of the San Antonio chapter proposed to converge on Huntsville in an armed rear-guard action designed to help their newfound hero escape from bondage.

Ironically, the Brown Berets attempted to resituate this subaltern capitalist Carrasco—who, as noted, had enrolled his daughter in a prestigious East Coast prep school—within the working-class south Texas barrio that he no longer claimed except as a market for his addictive and lethal commerce. Although an armed revolutionary insurrection never materialized, Carrasco's figurative reclamation by working-class Chicana/os like Brown Beret Ricardo Sánchez succeeded in hijacking Carrasco anew. Indeed, Sánchez converts Carrasco into a palimpsestic icon—the Pinto revolutionary—by imbuing his violent claim to power with a transhistorical and global resonance, while still grounding this episode in south Texas: birthplace of the Texas-Mexican and U.S.-Mexico wars. This battle to control and consume the narrative of Fred Gómez Carrasco as a metonym for race and nation has become a spectacle of almost epic proportions that has played out in yet other cultural forms.

SCENES OF THE CRIME: STAGING CARRASCO AS SPECTACLE AND FARCE IN CHICANA/O THEATER AND HOLLYWOOD FILM

Despite the fact that the popular Chicana/o insurrection hoped for by the Brown Berets never materialized, Gregorio Barrios's agitprop *Acto*

¡Carrasco! raised the stakes in the battle to control the meaning of Fred Gómez Carrasco through a socially symbolic and physically threatening staging.[18] Written in 1974, shortly after Carrasco's death, the play was performed by El Teatro Estudiantil Chicano de Cristal at the Festival Floricanto in Austin, Texas, in March 1975 at the foot of the Texas state capitol building—the quintessential symbol of state authority. According to Barrios (2004), he designed his *Acto* to counter McKinney's racialization of Carrasco as a signifier of abjection. Barrios sought to deploy Carrasco as a medium to politicize and mobilize the Chicana/o community during the activities that later came to be known as the Chicano Movement, or El Movimiento. His use of nonprofessional actors—a cast of high school students from Crystal City, Texas, considered by some to be the birthplace of the Chicano Movement—followed the tradition of the *Acto* established by Luis Valdez and Teatro Campesino (Farmworker Theater), who pioneered the use of agitprop theater with workers and amateur actors as part of union efforts to politicize and mobilize semiliterate farmworkers.[19]

Figure 6.6. Woodcut advertising for *¡Carrasco!* by Gregorio Barrios. Courtesy of Gregorio Barrios.

TEATRO ESTUDIANTIL CHICANO
de CRISTAL en

¡CARRASCO!

Following the *Acto* tradition in which performers humorously yet incisively engage a current social issue relevant to Chicana/o empowerment, *¡Carrasco!* satirizes Governor Dolph Briscoe for his role in the alleged cover-up of the Carrasco assassination by the Texas Rangers, the Texas Department of Corrections, and the FBI. At key moments in the play, actors shout in unison: "¡¿Qué pasó!? ¡¿Qué pasó!? ¡¿Qué pasó?! ¡¿Qué!? ¡¿Qué pasó con Carrasco?!" Dressed as human *cucarachas* (cockroaches), they then seize Governor Dolph Briscoe and Lady Bird Johnson (dubbed Miss Lady Bug in the play). After capturing the representatives of the "official story," the Cucarachas, a term often used to denigrate Chicana/os, but also reconfigured as a signifier of subaltern resilience by authors such as Oscar Z. Acosta (1973), proceed to rewrite the significance of this tumultuous event from the bottom up—or from a roach's eye view. This symbolic reenactment of Carrasco's hostage-taking drama figuratively raises the stakes as the cast seizes both the governor of Texas and the wife of the U.S. president! Given the militancy at the time of Chicano Movement activities, which included everything from armed confronta-tions to the airplane hijacking by Ricardo Chávez-Ortiz discussed in the introduction to this study, the play gained a material resonance that could never be mistaken by any of the authorities in Austin, including the Secret Service, which is charged with protecting the president and his family, as well as the Texas Rangers, which are based in Austin.

Even more dramatically, the cast proceeded to reenact the final day of the prison breakout attempt in slow motion, thus placing the action in broader relief to allow the audience to scrutinize all that had been obfuscated by the bureaucratic legalese and apologist media justifications of Carrasco's assassination. In this episode, Barrios rewrites the *desperado* trope of White accounts by emphasizing the "gentlemanly" aspect of the male warrior hero invoked by other Chicana/o representations of Carrasco. He specifically alludes to Carrasco's chivalrous treatment of women. Carrasco is renowned for his kind treatment of his former hostages, and he even wrote librarian Aline House a lyrical shaped-verse "get well" card after releasing her before the shootout. In the play, Carrasco and Dominguez are shown using their own bodies as shields to protect Julia Stanley and Elizabeth Beseda, the hostages they are alleged to have murdered. As a response to the media blackout of the final moments of the siege, and to Texas Ranger claims that they lost the video of the prison shootout in which Carrasco was killed, Barrios ends this scene with Texas Ranger officers firing the coups de grace at Carrasco and his confederate Dominguez as they lay wounded. Carrasco's death, represented as martyrdom yet again, is now staged for all the public to see and, true to the *Acto* ethos, to respond with actions.

This invocation of pathos as a call to action is performed by none other than the character of Rosa Carrasco, to whom the play is dedicated and who was still on the lam as it was produced. In a cameo appearance, Rosa appears as a defiant *soldadera*-like matriarch who pledges her love for Carrasco in a politically charged Spanish-language soliloquy in which she proclaims:

> I do not claim to be perfect.
> Neither was my husband. . . .
> [But] he never had the opportunity
> to be honest. The law
> in Texas doesn't give a damn
> about Chicanos. . . .
> Fred tried to show everyone
> the situation of thousands, yes,
> thousands of Chicanos in the prisons.
> He did what some only dream
> of doing.
> He lifted the spirit of the brothers
> in prison. (35, translation mine)

Although Barrios's ventriloquized rehearsal of political and economic critique through Rosa Carrasco does not completely mediate the masculinist imprints in popular reclamations of the gangster hero, the setting of this soliloquy, and the attribution of this materialist critique to Carrasco's wife, gains an emotional force that no other cultural form had been able to accomplish. She is the wife who not only grieves for her slain husband, but the mother who demands justice for her symbolic children: the Chicana/o people. In this context, the play ends with an indictment directed at the White hostages. Characteristic of the cultural nationalist rhetoric of the period, one of the *cucarachas* proclaims:

> Maybe you still don't realize it, but Carrasco represented our mistreatment and anger in your system. But let me tell you something. The day is near when we will destroy the gringo system, and all it represents. (37)

The curtain closes with the B-side of the Garcez recording of Gutierrez's postmortem *corrido* (Variant B), a Tex-Mex polka that sets a festive, celebratory tone and is accompanied by *gritos* of rebellion and celebration by the cast, who immediately break into a fast-paced *norteña* dance.

The counterhegemonic resonance of this staging notwithstanding, Barrios's celebration of Carrasco as a chivalrous social bandit also lent itself to a series of somewhat farcical adaptations through film, thus bringing full circle the complex process Richard Johnson (1987) identifies as the "circuits of culture." Even before Barrios was staging his dramatic *Acto*, and thereby performing an intensified challenge to White capitalist hegemony, both Mexican and Hollywood film producers had been negotiating with Carrasco and his lawyer about the possibility of making a movie based on his life. In an even more bizarre complication of Carrasco's commodification as a modern day *bandido*, Carrasco himself was reported to have been negotiating the rights to his life story during his eleven-day siege from the very prison library in which he was ensconced. After his death, producer Rogelio Agrasanchez, head of International Center Producers, along with Universal Studios in Hollywood, pursued possible film titles that included "¡*Viva Carrasco!*," "The Longest Siege," and "The Mexican Connection," the first alluding to the Mexican revolution film ¡*Viva Zapata!* and the last to the blockbuster film about the underground heroin trade on the East Coast, *The French Connection*. At least one script is known to have been written, with the role of Carrasco set to be played by Charles Bronson. Yet another version was proposed by the famed Tex-Mex singer Freddy Fender, himself a former prisoner and notorious womanizer. Bringing the commodification of Carrasco to yet another level of ahistorical absurdity, Fender enthusiastically pursued the romance angle between Carrasco and his wife Rosa, which was to feature the sultry Rita Moreno as his costar! In one report, Rosa Carrasco even offered to serve as a consultant on the film.

Neither of these films was ever produced, but several Carrasco-esque films were made over the next three decades following his death. The *narco-traficante* film genre, like its *narco-corrido* counterpart, is a staple in Mexican cinema, and several films have included recognizable fragments of the Carrasco story, especially his prison breakout from Guadalajara. One gloss of the Carrasco saga, in which his wife Rosa takes center stage, also migrated into a version of the Camelia la Tejana film series, which was inspired by the famous "Camelia la Tejana" *corrido* about a drug-dealing, pistol-packing matriarch. The attention to Rosa

Carrasco after her husband's death serves as confirmation that Carrasco had passed into the pantheon of *rasquache* popular icons simultaneous with his canonization as a counterhegemonic model of Chicana/o identity. All things Carrasco had become potential profit-producing mediums, and much more.

LAYERING THE PALIMPSEST: THE CARRASCO CULTURE WARS CONTINUE

These convoluted commodifications and consumptions reveal that Carrasco had become a veritable palimpsest of the Southwest: decades and even centuries of racial, gender, national, and international conflicts were mapped onto the hyperlocal space of a south Texas Pinto. The Chicana/o community's appraisal of Carrasco perhaps is best summed up in an August 2, 1974, editorial in the *Chicano Times*, a now defunct San Antonio Chicana/o community newspaper that ran extensive coverage of the Huntsville prison breakout attempt and related stories. In a rehearsal of the aforementioned readings of Carrasco as a social bandit, Armandina Salazar, the paper's lead investigative journalist, wrote:

> Carrasco may be a criminal but he has exhibited other traits which men have admired in men for centuries. These include intelligence, daring, courage, and chivalry. (1974a: 2)

After raising the possibility that Carrasco was assassinated because he "knew too much" about misconduct, including drug dealing, by San Antonio Police Department officers as well as other Texas officials—a common perception among Chicana/os—Salazar continues:

> The American people have made folk heroes out of such people as Davy Crockett, James Bowie, Jesse James and Billy the Kid. (1974a: 2)

Therefore, she prophetically adds:

> it is probable that Federico Gomez Carrasco will join Juan Cortina, Joaquin Murrieta, and Gregorio Cortez in the pantheon of Mexican American folk heroes. (1974a: 2)

The transformation of Carrasco into a populist icon arose in part from his rebellion against the brutally racist regime of the Texas Rangers and the apartheid White capitalist hegemony they buttressed at the time. Mario Compean, a prominent south Texas activist and former gubernatorial candidate of La Raza Unida Party, recalls that he was greeted with enthusiastic applause and *gritos* in an unidentified barrio cantina in Houston after ending a political speech with the shout of "¡Viva Fred Gómez Carrasco!"[20] Moreover, immediately after Carrasco's death, the *Chicano Times* ran several cover stories featuring headlines such as "Reflections on Chicano Folkheroes and Carrasco" and "Federico Gómez Carrasco—Hero or a Criminal?" These editions also feature vitriolic editorials suggesting that Carrasco was murdered to keep from exposing the Texas law enforcement officials' involvement in the drug trade. The covers stories were illustrated with photos of the dapper Carrasco as a Pachuco with slicked back hair, as well as a photo of Carrasco's unmarked grave alongside a painting of the famed social bandit Joaquin Murrieta, renowned as a Chicano avenger who carried out counterattacks against racist Whites in late nineteenth-century California.

This Chicana/o community reclamation of Carrasco in print media took yet another turn as Gregorio Barrios (author of the aforementioned

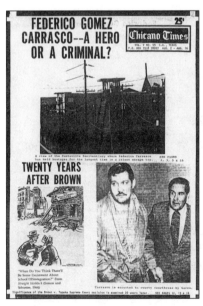

Figure 6.7. Front page of *Chicano Times* 5: 49 (August 2–16, 1974). Courtesy of the Texas History Room, San Antonio Public Library.

Figure 6.8. Front page of *Chicano Times* 5: 50 (August 16–30, 1974). Courtesy of the Texas History Room, San Antonio Public Library.

play *¡Carrasco!*) published a retrospective on the Carrasco affair after assuming the role of book editor for the *San Antonio Express-News* in 2001 (Barrios 2001b). In direct contrast to the yellow journalism legacy of his employer, Barrios used the pages of this newspaper to recenter Carrasco in the cultural and political imagination of the Chicana/o community. His article was titled "The Outlaw King: The sound and fury of Fred Gomez Carrasco," and was written to set the record straight by challenging White attempts to use Carrasco as a metonym for minority pathology in south Texas.

In a continuation of the Carrasco culture wars, several books continued to be published by White "Carrasco survivors"—some of whom were nowhere near the prison library—three decades after the prison breakout attempt. These include Ronald W. Robinson's *Prison Hostage: The Siege of the Walls Prison in Huntsville* (1997), William T. Harper's *Eleven Days in Hell: The 1974 Carrasco Prison Siege in Huntsville, Texas* (2004), David Clinton Owens's and Virginia Stem Owens's *Living Next Door to the Death House* (2003), and Carlton Stowers's and Carroll Pickett's *Within These Walls: Memoirs of a Death House Chaplain* (2002).

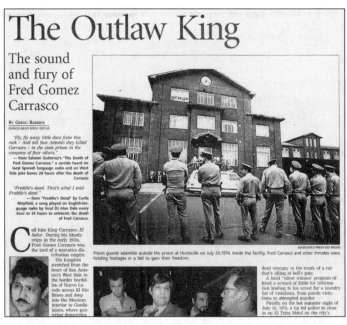

Figure 6.9. Retrospective on Fred Gómez Carrasco by Gregg (Gregorio) Barrios, *San Antonio Express-News*, July 22, 2001. Courtesy of the *San Antonio Express-News*.

Carrasco is also included in Frank Richard Prassel's *The Great American Outlaw: A Legacy of Fact and Fiction* (1996).

Barrios challenges these sensationalist attempts to profit on Carrasco's death and legacy by including a companion sidebar to his *San Antonio Express-News* story consisting of a verbatim excerpt of the Carrasco diary that was smuggled out of his legal file before it could be destroyed by authorities (Barrios 2001a). In the face of yet other mainstream White attempts to reimprison the Carrasco legend within the blood-thirsty *bandido* or diabolical genius paradigms, Barrios plans a full-length play of what he calls the "rebellion." The new play—also to be titled

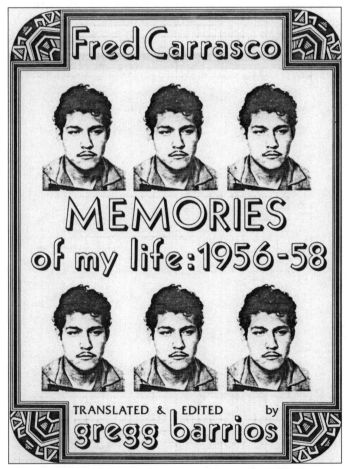

Figure 6.10. Cover design for Fred Gómez Carrasco's diary. Courtesy of Gregorio Barrios.

206 | Crime and Commodification

¡Carrasco!—is to deploy, as part of the set, Brechtian blow-ups of front-page headlines and sensationalist book jackets—including his own!

In a cruel postscript to all these attempts to judge Carrasco and his confederates, Ignacio Cuevas, the only surviving prisoner in the Carrasco escape party, was executed May 23, 1991, after having become a cause célébre in the Chicana/o community. One of the main organizers of the campaign to get a new trial for Cuevas was led by Alvaro Hernández Luna, the recently reimprisoned leader of the National Movement for La Raza, discussed in the introduction. In an ironic twist of events that illustrates the intersecting histories of crime and counterhegemonic Pinto agency, Hernández Luna is now the new cause célébre in grassroots campaigns to free Chicana/o political prisoners. These attempts to represent and resolve the tension between the Chicana/o canonization of the Pinto as a counterhegemonic cultural nationalist icon vis-à-vis the White capitalist reifications of him as a floating signifier in their own imperialist claims to the southwestern United States, anticipate the Hollywood and anti-Hollywood battles over the substance of the gangxploitation genre of the 1970s and 1980s discussed in the preceding chapter. But there are other voices and visions that avoid, and deliberately challenge, the phallocentric paradigm undergirding Pinto discourse as heretofore presented, which is the subject of the next chapter.

PART FOUR

Storming the Tower

CHAPTER 7

Judy Lucero's Gynocritical Prison Poetics and Materialist Chicana Politics

So much work remains to be done around prisons in general—pending revolutionary change, we have to raise the demand that prisons in their present form be abolished. As an inevitable by-product of a male-oriented society and consequently still male-oriented movement—which women are however increasingly contesting—sufficient attention has not been devoted to women in prison.

—Angela Davis (1971)

The work of mestiza consciousness is to break down the subject-object duality that keeps her a prisoner and to show in the flesh and through the images in her work how duality is transcended. The answer to the problem between the white race and the colored, between males and females, lies in healing the split that originates in the very foundation of our lives, our culture, our languages, our thoughts. A massive uprooting of dualistic thinking in the individual and collective consciousness is the beginning of a long struggle, but one that could, in our best hopes, bring us to the end of rape, of violence, of war.

—Gloria Anzaldúa (1987)

PRISONS, POWER, AND CHICANA POETRY

While journalistic exposés and independent research studies decry the profound racial disparities of the male prison population—including the oft-cited statistic that one in four Black men between the ages of eighteen and twenty-four will be caught in the criminal justice web of prison, jail, probation, or parole at least once in their lives—the U.S. Department of Justice reports that the disparities in incarceration rates are even more pronounced for women. A 1994 study by the U.S. Department of Justice, *Women in Prison*, notes that although women made up only 6.3 percent of the U.S. population under correctional supervision, their rate of incarceration was growing almost twice as fast as the incarceration rate for men (1995: 5–6). By 2009, the incarceration rate for women prisoners was set to double again.[1] José Luís Morín confirms that the racial disparities in male incarceration rates are also seen among women: he notes that in eight states "Latina women are incarcerated at rates that are between four and seven times higher than those of white women" (2005: 70). In her research on Chicana and other women prisoners in California, Yvette Flores-Ortiz (1995a, 1995b) suggests that the disparity in incarceration rates for women is in part attributable to the claim frequently made by women prisoners: that they were incarcerated for crimes that were coerced, or even committed, by their male partners, for whom they "took the fall" under the mistaken belief that a woman would get a more lenient sentence.[2] Surveys conducted by the U.S. Department of Justice also reveal that prior to their own imprisonment most of these women prisoners had been victims of child abuse, sexual assault, domestic violence, or coerced drug abuse involving older men; in other words, crimes committed against them by men presaged these women's incarceration (1994: 6). Even more troubling, Dowling and Atwood (1998) have estimated that as many as one in sixteen women are pregnant upon entering prison, while the U.S. Department of Justice adds that over 78 percent of the roughly one million women under correctional supervision in jail, prison, probation, or parole are mothers (1994: 6–7).

Judy A. Lucero was one of them. Renowned for frequently having gone into debt to lend money to her friends, thus earning the endearing prison epithet "soft touch," Lucero also exhibits other characteristics of women prisoners in the United States. According to José Armas, editor of the Chicana/o cultural nationalist journal *De Colores*, Lucero was a lumpenproletariat Chicana introduced to drugs at the age of eleven; a victim of domestic violence that caused her to miscarry twice; a drug user addicted first to heroin, then to the "cure," methadone; a mother forcibly separated from her daughter after her convictions and incarceration; and, finally, a woman who died in prison of a brain hemorrhage, the cumulative effect of a lifetime of beatings (1973: 71). Lucero fits the composite profile of the Pinta that Díaz-Cotto features in her study *Chicana Lives and Criminal Justice: Voices from El Barrio* (2006). But like many other prisoners, she was not simply or solely a victim. As noted in my preceding discussions of Pinta and Pinto agency, prisoners often participate in alternative commodifications and reclamations of their criminalized subjectivities.[3] However, unlike the hypermasculinist poetics and homosocial politics of Pinto signifying practices—which merge both sacred and profane images of women, thus keeping intact the phallic resonance of the panoptic penitentiary guard tower they otherwise seek to subvert—Chicana prisoner literature is invested in a uniquely different poetic and political project.[4]

Michel Foucault has lucidly explicated the power dynamics of panopticism (1979), yet feminist scholars aptly have critiqued his "degendering of the disciplined body" (Howe 1994, Deveaux 1996), critical race studies scholars have challenged his deracinated prisoner body (Davis 2005), and cultural studies scholars have challenged his undertheorized model of power that effaces prisoner capacity for resistance (Harlow 1992). Barbara Harlow (1992), for instance, has surveyed the link between embodied forms of protest and the development of a "resistance literature" by women prisoners in the colonial and postcolonial worlds, and Juanita Díaz-Cotto (1996) has observed how women prisoner reconstructions of "family" kinship networks pose complex challenges to the highly gendered forms of containment that women experience in prison.

Following these scholars, I submit that Judy Lucero's three collections of autobiographical prison verse, published posthumously from 1973 to 1980, collectively seek to reappropriate the multiple abject subjectivities that figure her as a "fallen woman." She challenges the phallocentric paradigm that sought to "rehouse" her in prison, which Angela Davis proposes as the quintessential site of patriarchal authority and White male privilege in the first epigraph above (1971). Lucero's signifying practices fluctuate between an essentialist yet symbolically empowering model of identity reminiscent of gynocritical theories of identity contemporaneous with her imprisonment in the 1970s and 1980s, and an exploration of structuralist models of subjectivity grounded in the economic base.[5] Through her syncretic gynocritical and materialist poems from prison, Lucero was able to recuperate her status as a daughter, a mother of a daughter, and, ultimately, a historically situated Chicana. Her embodied poetics not only challenge the phallocentric paradigm of prison but the equally masculinist Pinto contestatory discourses. As a Pinta intellectual, she also used the women's penitentiary as both a metaphorical and a real point of departure to propose a celebratory yet materially grounded model of an insurgent subaltern Chicana identity, thereby adumbrating subsequent generations of Chicana feminist artists, theorists, and activists.

OF DEITIES AND DEVILS

Lucero's gynocritical dismantling of the Foucauldian guard tower is foregrounded in her first collection of poetry, published in the 1973 winter issue of *De Colores*.[6] This challenge necessarily begins with an interrogation of the legal and ontological effacement her incarceration simultaneously represented and reproduced. Like many prisoner writers, Lucero underscored this erasure by signing her poems with her assigned prison identification number "21918" rather than her real name. But in direct defiance to the patriarchal power imprinted throughout her life experiences—for which the penitentiary guard tower is a metonym— her poetry contests the effacing prison regimen that objectified her as a number and separated her from her daughter. Indeed, she proclaims herself and her daughter as inseparable, ennobled, and manifestly divine precisely because of her incarceration. She eventually recast herself as a Convict Mother Goddess—the über Pinta—in ways unburdened by the phallocentric conceits undergirding Pinto uses of related Virgen archetypes, as illustrated in Chapters 3 and 4.

In order for Lucero to effect the beatification of her poetic persona, Prisoner #21918, into Pinta #21918, however, she had to first rhetorically establish the divine space. Her poem "Face of Fear" (1973: 72), which opens her first collection, reads as a symbolic enactment of this utopian desire. In this poem, Prisoner #21918 introduces the Judeo-Christian God of her youth while simultaneously displacing it by an even more powerful deity: the penitentiary. This displacement, which allows for a more important dislocation to come, is facilitated through a rhymed, free-verse gloss of a Psalm-like prayer that establishes the divine space of authority through religious symbol and form:

> Stay with me . . . God . . . The night is dark.
> The night is cold; My little spark of
> courage dies. The night is long.
> Be with me, God, and make me strong. (lines 1–4, ellipses in original)

By assuming the voice of a young girl in prayer, Prisoner #21918 models the total subordination that her truncated signature represents. On the surface, Prisoner #21918 appears to be the passive subordinate of the panoptic tower, which she later describes as the "God of Strength and Gentleness," a description that resonates with Foucault's description of the cruelly efficient panopticon that she will later undermine. For the moment, however, the deceptively innocent tone of her childlike plea takes on a pathetic resonance as her desperation becomes the somber, resigned whimper of a faithful Christian who has "fought the good fight" but lost. The poem continues in various past tenses:

> I knew what we were fighting for.
> Some peace for the kids, Our brothers'
> freedom, A kinder world, A cleansing mind. (5–7)

The fight is apparently over and everything seems lost: the kids' future, and hers; a sibling's freedom, and everyone's; a world without violence that she has never known; an ontological resolution free from the confusion arising from her drug addictions. As the dramatic dialogue progresses, it devolves from a prayer into an ominous premonition, with "the haggard Face of Fear" staring her down just a few lines below, heralding Lucero's inevitable and humiliating death in prison as an anonymous number. This impending death was preceded by that of Modesta Avila and countless nameless women deprived of the opportunity to speak back.

But Lucero did resist. Faced with the ever-present specter of death in prison, Lucero was able to symbolically recast the significance of her legally sanctioned bondage and exploitation by resituating it within the Christian redemption myth. Amid the apparent vortex of existential despair expressed in the first lines of "Face of Fear," Prisoner #21918 foregrounds a subversive blasphemy against her old Judeo-Christian God that clears the divine space of authority for the new deities to come. Midway through this one-stanza poem, she writes:

> I'm but the one my mother bore
> A simple person and nothing, nothing more.
> But . . . God of Strength and Gentleness,
> Be pleased to make me nothing less . . . (7–11, ellipses in original)

In a feigned humility that serves as the nucleus of her later beatification as a Mother Goddess, Prisoner #21918 asks little more than what her mother—not the God—gave her: life. However, before Lucero is able to invoke this liberating matriarchal bond to facilitate her lyrical metamorphosis from Prisoner #21918 into the Christ-like daughter of a mother and then the prototypical Mother God(dess) herself, Lucero must first accentuate her immediate material bondage and suffering. Thus, at this moment in her antilyrical passion play, her eventual claim to matriarchal authority and divinity initially functions as a prayer-like plea for the courage and strength to endure her day-to-day execution as an anonymous number. This strophe forms the axis around which the old Judeo-Christian deity is displaced by the new one—the penitentiary—the secular God of the lumpenproletariat. In this preliminary dislocation, facilitated through prayer, the "God of Strength and Gentleness" assumes a dual significance. First, the trope refers to the "God of Light" of Judeo-Christian myth (e.g., "Stay with me . . . God . . . The night is dark"). Then, as this being is shown to be impotent, and perhaps even malevolent for not intervening to end her ordeal, a new deity emerges to occupy the center. Prisoner #21918's prayer, initially offered to a celestial "God of Strength and Gentleness," is intercepted by the panoptic penitentiary god through its phallic palisade priest—the all-seeing guard tower—which claims the symbolic power of an erect phallus. This morbid scenario, foregrounded in the very title of the poem, "Face of Fear," is underscored in the final four lines, which propose the consummate subordination of the prisoner who tries to speak from beneath the frightening and disempowering gaze of the tower:

Help me, O God, when Death is near, to
Mock the haggard Face of Fear.
Then when I fall, my soul may Triumph in the
Dust . . . . . (12–15, ellipsis in original)

The composition, which begins as an homage to a Christian God with assumed powers, ends as a pathetic paean to a real penitentiary god, whose power over life and death, and the prisoner's space in-between, is confirmed by the captive soul's abortive flight after its eventual release from the soon-to-be dead body of a female Inmate, which can only "Triumph" in the "Dust." At this moment in Lucero's antilyric representations of her experiences as Prisoner #21918, only death offers an escape from the penetrating gaze of the concrete, steel, and barbed-wire penitentiary god.

DESCENT INTO THE ABYSS

Perhaps anticipating her prison death, Lucero was able to reclaim her subaltern subjectivity by successfully inscribing her own personal experience of incarceration within the descent motif of Christian myth as well as within materialist critiques of the political economy of the prison. She thus begins to claim her new identity as a Convict. For instance, in the succeeding untitled poem that begins "Heartache's story here is told," Prisoner #21918 represents herself as a martyr condemned to a daily death in a "Dark and Silent and Cold" prison tomb. This four-stanza composition, which dramatically ends with a single strophe description of Prisoner #21918 as "This shell that once was a Woman," ultimately serves to link Lucero's metaphysical meditations on her imprisonment to a burgeoning materialist explication of the inner workings of this secular god in other poems. Similar to the appropriative paradigm of other ethnic minority prisoner writers, whom H. Bruce Franklin notes are "forced, for their very survival, to become artists" in order to reconfigure the penitentiary as a site for counterhegemonic knowledge and agency (1989: 101–102), Lucero performatively underscores her multiple forms of alienation in order to indict and ultimately appropriate the prison regime of truth that is obfuscated by sanitized nomenclature (e.g., "U.S. Department of Justice" and "Department of Corrections").

Still glossing the morbid nursery rhyme scheme of her previous poems, the rhythm of the poem "Jail-Life Walk" (1973: 77) also mimics the sounds of a complex factory machine efficiently and malevolently producing its product. The poem opens:

Walk in the day . . . Walk in the night
Count off the time . . . One to Ten
Then you'll be free . . . Free again.
(lines 1–3, ellipses in original)

The silent, ordered shuffle of prisoners walking from dinner back to their cell, from work detail to their cell, and from recreation back to their cell again, conjures up the image of an almost surreal purgatory where one's sentence is silence, and the key to survival is passive conformity. By complying with the litany of dehumanizing penitentiary routines, for which the trope "walk" serves as a metonym, Prisoner #21918 seeks the momentary catharsis that conformity offers (e.g., "Walk . . . / Then you'll be free . . . Free again"). But here, "freedom" refers more to the protection from the punishment meted out to nonconformists rather than to an actual release from prison, which Lucero achieves only through death. Moreover, the "freedom" encoded in the juridical vernacular "to walk" (as in to be released from bondage regardless of a conviction) is not only parodied, but identified as absolutely inaccessible for this Chicana prisoner. In fact, the "peace" that Prisoner #21918's compliance "earns" her actually serves to animate the power of the penitentiary, which constantly informs the prisoner that she must be silent, that she must conform, walk in line, one, two, three. . . .

In this figurative illustration of the alienating and domesticating function of the penitentiary, Prisoner #21918's internalized jailer speaks to her with more force as the panoptic gaze of the guard tower is complemented by delineated rules stenciled on signs strategically placed throughout the penitentiary's labyrinthine corridors. This ideological function of the women's prison, Adrian Howe (1994) and Juanita Díaz-Cotto (1996: 277) observe, is further actualized by socially symbolic prison rituals such as the use of color-coded uniforms (usually white, pink, or red), rigidly enforced speech codes that prohibit "unladylike" words (cursing), and a domesticating regimen of forced prison labor in jobs such as sewing, laundry, cooking, and cleaning. Within this patriarchal network of rules and routines designed to rehouse the "fallen woman" prisoner, prison itself becomes part of Lucero's poetry as she writes:

> Walk til you see . . . . . See the sign
> Look at the sign . . . . . Walk in Line! (lines 5–6, ellipses in original)

They are everywhere. Furthermore, these signs, which assume the function of an additional set of "eyes," cue the penitentiary god's disciples—Inmates—to replicate, and thus increment, its malevolent production of numbered beings. As Davidson has noted, prisoners who conform to these subordinate roles earn the epithet "Inmate," the official prison administration term for prisoners, while those who resist assume the vernacular accolade "Convict," which signals their defiant refusal to passively or complicitously accept subordination (1974: 45–50). Within this tension, "Jail-Life Walk" continues:

> Then walk in hate
> Walk without the world
> Walk in fear . . .
> See the anger
> In their eye
> Just walking by . . . (lines 7–12, ellipses in original)

Explicating firsthand the mechanics of panopticism, Lucero shows how the penitentiary factory becomes a paradigm of efficiency, with the

Inmates themselves participating as principal agents in both the destruction of their civic subjectivities and the production of their abject identities. As previously noted, this efficient interpellation of contained subjects is imbricated with the profit motive legitimated in Article 13, Section 1, of the U.S. Constitution, the purported Abolition Amendment of 1869 that permits legal servitude "as a punishment for crime whereof the party shall have been duly convicted." Lucero's poetry from prison accordingly illustrates that she and the other prisoners are legal slaves of the state. They are compelled to walk, work, and produce profit, thus facilitating their transformation into Inmates and their resultant estrangement from their freeworld subjectivities.

However, Lucero's performative explication of the symbolic and political economy of imprisonment, in which prisoners are reduced to acting like animalistic predators who prey on and discipline each other, inevitably exposes the slippage in the prison's discursive constitution. In the last stanza of "Jail-Life Walk," for example, she exposes the inaccessibility of the juridical trope "freedom," which proposes "rehabilitation through time served." She writes:

The only thing free
is your mind
Free to count
As U walk in Line. (lines 13–16)

Marta E. Sánchez aptly underscores the significance of this paradox when she notes:

the poem . . . demonstrates that her fight to assert freedom is inseparably
bound to her material condition. Her mind is free to mark the count of
the jail walk. With each count her "free" mind acknowledges her physical
imprisonment. The dialectic of the poem is knowing that her freedom lies in
knowing she is not free. (1978: 69)

Ironically, by representing her alienation in prison, Prisoner #21918 recognizes her status as a "fallen," or rather Convict(ed), Woman. She is fundamental to the maintenance of the penitentiary order and the profit-driven prison industrial complex that requires her exclusion from the polis. Her existence is both intolerable and necessary, and she now knows this.

CONVICT MOTHER GODDESS

While Lucero's alter ego, Prisoner #21918, is forced to facilitate her own alienation by "walking," Lucero's deliberate and damning representation of her status as a Convict(ed) Woman ultimately enables her to appropriate another penological trope: the sentence. In so doing, she rewrites the defeatist paradigm Foucault (1979) articulates when he proposes that counterpower is always already co-opted by the hegemonic order, especially in prison. Having first displaced the Christian God who has betrayed her, and then disrupting the vacuous moral allegory of "reform" promulgated by the apocryphal penitentiary god, Lucero's metaphysical and materialist signifying practices climax together in other poems such as "A Little Girl's Prayer" (1973: 73) and "Christmas Sacrifice" (1973: 78). Lucero extends the family/kinship network that Juanita Díaz-Cotto has observed in other women's prisons in the United States, "in which Latina (and non-Latina) prisoners supported one another [by adopting] the roles of husband, wife, mother, father, sister, brother, etc." (1996: 298). Indeed, these poems, which appear as the second and penultimate compositions in Lucero's first collection of poetry, can be read as complementary compositions in her gynocritical and materialist recuperation, reconstruction, and celebration of her subaltern subjectivity as a Convict, a mother, and, above all else, a Convict Mother Goddess— the ultimate matriarch.

In sharp contrast to the subservient, infantilized persona that Lucero assumes in earlier compositions, such as Prisoner #21918 in "Face of Fear," Convict #21918 assumes the role of omniscient narrator in order to complete the Christian allegory of descent invoked earlier by pairing it with the related resurrection topos. In "A Little Girl's Prayer," for instance, Lucero introduces her distinct fairy tale with the standard expository phrase, "That night in a Prison far away . . ." (line 10). However, her appropriation of a cultural form that traditionally functions to prevent the emergence of the "fallen woman" (or to rehouse her after she "falls") involves a profound transformation of the fairy tale. In Lucero's version, the Convict narrator recounts how a daughter's prayer—"Please God, send my Mommy home on Christmas day . . ." (line 4)—is ultimately paired with the mother's simultaneous entreaty in the last two stanzas of the poem—"Please God . . . watch over my Little Girl . . ." (line 14). These corresponding appeals form a new "bond" that transcends the "bondage" imposed by the walls of the women's penitentiary. Lucero, the narrator, is thus able to link mother and child despite the tower's penetrating and prohibitive gaze. She herself assumes the archetypal role of storyteller, a role that Trinh T. Minh-ha (1989) locates within a strategically essentialist model of matriarchy that is transhistorical and central to human history despite a millennia of attempts by men to suppress it. In telling this fairy tale from and about her prison hell, Lucero, through Inmate-cum-Convict #21918, lays claim to the authorial space that previously had been occupied by the masculinist gods charged with rehousing and deconstructing her into a profit-producing Inmate. Modeling what Mary Pat Brady (2002) identifies as an insurgent Chicana spatial poetics, the narrative in "A Little Girl's Prayer" finally dislocates the apocryphal gods foregrounded in "Face of Fear"—the Judeo-Christian deity and the secular god of the lumpenproletariat, the penitentiary—both of whom have usurped a cultural feminist model of "Woman's space."

In the complementary poem "Christmas Sacrifice," Convict #21918 more conclusively encloses the phallic palisades of the penitentiary guard tower, her real-world nemesis. What began as a subliminal form of blasphemy and empowerment in earlier poems such as "Face of Fear" (e.g., "I'm but the one my mother bore . . . / Be pleased to make me nothing less") becomes a deliberate and spiritually empowering affirmation of herself as a woman, a mother, and a storyteller: that is, a creator and the Creator. Lucero foregrounds this metamorphosis of her alter ego by writing, "only time I guess will tell / if it was all worth this time in HELL" (lines 11–12). She then concludes this apocalyptic strophe with the climactic tragedy that lifts her from the phoenix's ashes, catapulting her—and her daughter—into the heights of divinity:

> But even tho I can't help remember
> That God's son died to make things better, and
> So also I know, that I must pay
> No, sacrifice my Christmas day—my daughter's gone. (lines 17–20)

The prayer motif, coupled with the Christmas setting where Christians celebrate their messiah's birth, here serves to catalyze the ultimate synthesis of her abject subjectivities and experiences. The Christian legend of God's holy child Jesus, who descended into the abyss to rise again more ennobled, is paired with the experiences of the Convict(ed) Mother, Judy Lucero, and her only surviving daughter, a de facto prison orphan. In this secular scenario, Convict #21918, who had previously assumed the nobility of Christ through her own descent and penance in "Jail-Life Walk," is now canonized through the sacrifice, albeit an unwilling one, of her own daughter. In the process, Lucero's absent daughter assumes the role of the holy offspring given up for the salvation of all. In this epiphanic crescendo of role reversals, Convict #21918 transforms herself into the archetypal Mother Goddess/Mother of Goddess—a Convict Virgin of Guadalupe—and her daughter becomes the new archetypal victim/savior—a female Christ.[7] Lucero thus symbolically transforms the lower case "i" presented in the first stanza of "Christmas Sacrifice" (e.g., "I sometimes ask myself, 'just who am i?'"), into the deified upper case "I" that appears towards the end of this poem and in others to follow.

TOWARDS A MATRIARCHAL PANTHEISM

Whereas Lucero's first collection of poetry focuses on the battle for control of the penal space of authority—alternately occupied by God, prison, and finally by the Convict Mother and Daughter Goddesses—her second collection of poetry, "Ocho poemas de amor y desesperación" (Eight poems of love and desperation), published in the 1976 special issue of *De Colores* dedicated to "Los Pintos de América," is distinguished by a pantheistic lexicon far removed from the harsh concrete reality of the women's penitentiary. Lucero's vocabulary now invokes trees, leaves, rivers, wind, sky, and the seasons of the year. In so doing, she emphasizes the epic dimensions of Convict #21918's epistemological and material battle to deconstruct the "fallen woman" paradigm that has led to her multiple abjections: since the spectacle could be occurring anywhere, it potentially is everywhere.

Anticipating by almost a decade similarly syncretic gynocritical and materialist feminist discourses by Alma Villanueva (1977), Lorna Dee Cervantes (1981), and Gloria Anzaldúa (1987), Lucero's nuanced gendering of this ambiguously situated geopoetic space enables a matriarchal pantheism that dissolves the imprisoning binary paradigm promulgated by Patriarchy/Prison. She thus recenters the status of women on earth as Convict #21918 previously had done in the heavens. For instance, in "Ocho poemas de amor," Lucero's earlier theme of estrangement is reconfigured in terms of Convict #21918's relationship to Mother Earth. Human Rights Watch has denounced the legacy of abuse in women's prisons, in which male guards often "provided unobtainable goods and services to the [women] prisoners in exchange for various forms of sexual intercourse or sexual touching" (1995: 168). Even before these abuses were exposed, Lucero symbolically challenged the commodification of women prisoners by redeploying the female body through a verse that now more overtly emphasizes the cyclical, regenerative qualities of nature's and women's life cycles.

Echoing her previous modus operandi, Part I of this eight-part poem opens with the dichotomy she will later dissolve:

> If I could conquer the wind
> I'd send my love on a breeze. But
> The devil sends a black night—
> My heart drops like Autumn leaves. (lines 1–4)

The conditional clause of the opening strophe ("If I could conquer the wind") underscores the idea that Lucero, as Convict #21918, is still estranged from her "species being," which in this case is embodied by her absent lover—perhaps her daughter, another woman, maybe a man, or something else altogether. At this moment, we cannot know for sure with whom or with what she desires communion because Convict #21918's yearning is thwarted by "the devil," who has now replaced (or unmasked) the penitentiary god. Like her efforts to rearticulate herself with "U," the freeworld reader in another desperate poem titled "I Speak in an Illusion," this attempted reunion is thwarted by her nemesis: the penitentiary's "black night." Invoking both the desperation and fatalism of earlier poems such as "Face of Fear," which is also set in a "dark," "cold," and long "night" from which death seems to be her only form of escape (e.g., "Then when I fall, my soul may Triumph in the / Dust . . . . ."), Convict #21918 again anticipates her eventual release from, and triumph over, her imprisonment only in terms of death. This part of the poem, for instance, ends with the image of autumn, when trees lose their foliage in preparation for winter (e.g., "My heart drops like Autumn leaves").

As in her first collection, however, Lucero's existentialist despair has a liminal and transformative resonance. In "Ocho poemas de amor y desesperación," the transformative potential of Lucero's verse revolves around her new meteorological symbolic system. By invoking the syntax of the Romantic tradition in which nature sometimes assumes anthropomorphic traits, and humanity and its creations pantheistic qualities, Lucero foregrounds her next synthesis of the celestial Convict Mother (of) God(dess) adumbrated in her first installment. In Part II of this poem, the Convict Mother (of) Goddess becomes the terrestrial goddess, Mother Earth, upon whose back the devilish patriarchal prison illegitimately perches:

If you will give your strength to me
We'll conquer all these things.
We'll ride the wind, walk hand in hand
Forever, like in Spring. (lines 1–4)

The image of autumn's colorful dead, which must lay fallow for an entire season—winter/prison—before the brittle ashes of fallen leaves can renew the immortal spring/freedom, underwrites a new allegory. Still imprisoned, Convict #21918 offers a collectivist resolution to the conditional clause ("If you will give your strength to me / We'll conquer all these things"). That is, through the "strength" of collective acts of resistance and transgression called for here and in previously discussed poems such as "Christmas Sacrifice," Convict #21918 confirms that the devil and his powerful wind can be conquered and transformed into the type of fertile liminal moment foregrounded by autumn, in which death enables life, and the end introduces a new beginning.

The relocation of the phoenix motif (initially presented in her first installment of poetry in terms of the Judeo-Christian resurrection myth) onto this meteorological space thus facilitates her most important synthesis yet. She proposes that the process of subordination and resistance, which many male Convict writers often represent as violently dialectical, is ultimately a cyclical phenomenon that can be understood in terms of Mother Nature and the female body: winter is always followed by spring; bleeding by (re)birth. Moreover, Lucero suggests that her own resistance to the women's penitentiary and other Repressive and Ideological State Apparatuses that threaten everyone's freedom must be a cooperative and collective process: with our help, Convict #21918's prison hell will soon end, and with her help, so will ours.

Lucero's previous explications of bondage and alienation, as well as her desperate though confident struggle to rearticulate (with our help) Inmate #21918 into Convict #21918—Woman, Mother (of) Goddess, and, ultimately, Mother Earth—is further consummated through the more overtly female-centered signifying practices that distinguish subsequent parts of "Ocho poemas de amor y desesperación." She relocates her symbolic challenges to Patriarchy/Prison onto a more palpable and real terrestrial battleground.

Part IV, for example, begins with a "mountain" performing the oppression previously attributed to the phallic penitentiary guard tower, which foregrounds yet another synthesis of Lucero's counterhegemonic subjectivity. Still glossing the nursery rhyme-scheme introduced earlier, she writes:

> Down in the deep dark valley
> The river runs muddy and dry
> The river's in love with the mountain
> But the mountain loves only the sky
>
> The river *she* weeps so sadly
> Because *she* feels so alone
> *She* begs the mountain to love *her*
> But it sits like a throne (57, lines 1–8, emphasis added)

As illustrated in Lucero's previous explications of the women's penitentiary, the phallic guard tower and its effaced and dehumanized subordinate observee, the Inmate, are now more overtly gendered: the former is now a "mountain" that protrudes into the sky unhindered, immaculate "like a big pretty throne," while the latter is represented by the symbol of the "river," whose potentially powerful and regenerative flow is rendered into a trickling, muddy weeping. The mountain's wanton penetrations into the heavens have resulted in a disharmony between it and the "river," which occupies the subordinate/prisoner space in the "deep dark valley" *below*. The *river*—like Inmate #21918, whose alienation in earlier poems is underscored by the succeeding litany "Who am i?"—is virtually dried up, dead.

Despite its morbid tone, however, this allegorical linkage of the prisoner with a distinctly gendered geopolitical space, battlefield earth, enables Convict #21918 to expand the celestial Mother (of) Goddess model of identity presented in her first collection by linking the Mother (of) Goddess to a terrestrial matriarch able to synthesize the binary oppositions that initially necessitated Lucero's utopian construction. The prisoner-cum-river's transformation into Mother Earth is consolidated in the third and fourth strophes of Part IV, where Lucero rhetorically asks:

> Who am I? Who am I?
> Still it sits like a big pretty throne
> The tears that I shed for the river
>
> The flowers just grow and grow (lines 9–12)

Similar to Minh-ha's linkage of lyric storytelling with matriarchal creative capacity, Convict #21918's poetry from prison also claims a regenerative power. Her verses, which heretofore have resonated with a sense of profound desperation ("These tears that I shed for the river"), now flow with a menstrual regularity that creates life ("the flowers just grow and grow").

As the poem progresses, the morbid tone that distinguishes Lucero's corpus climaxes in an apocalyptic but pantheistic orgy of creation, a birthing ritual that simultaneously serves as a metacritical explication of her *ars poetica* as an *ars política*:

> Someday, the mountain will crumble
> And the sky will shed tears
> So the mountain will reach the river
> And the bondage they feel will show
>
> Who am I? Who am I?
>
> *And their bondage will show I know.* (lines 13–20, emphasis added)

The deified Convict's tears fall from their celestial perch, engulfing everything on earth in a nurturing moisture. The once imposing mountain is washed away into the now powerful flow of the river, enabling an ontological resolution to the recurrent existential inquiry, "Who am I?" Precisely because of her tears—and her poems from prison—Lucero, through Convict #21918, confirms her regenerative potential as the Convict Mother (of) Goddess, who is also Mother Earth, the giver and guardian of all life. Thus, in "Ocho poemas," Lucero affirms—as if she were speaking from a position of power and authority—that as surely as she writes today, women's apocalyptic confrontations with patriarchy/prison/devil/death will be followed by a revolutionary rebirth in which old structures and paradigms will give way to new ones adumbrated by women's embodied knowledge and agency. This last symbolic synthesis of her identity as the celestial Mother (of) Goddess and the terrestrial Mother Earth brings Lucero even closer to the Chicana/o community from which she has been disarticulated and separated by a violently unjust juridical system and its extralegal counterparts. She merges her gynocritical poetics with a materialist preoccupation that revolves around land, which is not solely a metaphor, but the very object of the struggle.

REWRITING AND RECLAIMING AZTLÁN

In the eighth and final part of "Ocho poemas de amor y desesperación," Lucero introduces the figure of "un bohemio" alone in a barrio cantina. A modern permutation of the *pícaro* (discussed in Chapter 2), this *bohemio* is drinking and wallowing in his sadness after having been "betrayed" by an unnamed "lover," from whom he is now estranged. Despite the specificity of the *bohemio*'s individual circumstances, this scene nonetheless introduces Lucero's final and most significant spatial relocations. Through her cross-gendered invocation of both the theme and form of the *corrido*, the popular Mexican and Chicana/o folk ballad form that one often hears in the quintessentially male setting of a cantina, Lucero resituates her gynocritical discourse onto the traditionally phallocentric space of the barrio, the heart of Aztlán, the Chicana/o cultural nationalist homeland.[8] More precisely, Lucero figuratively revises and reclaims Aztlán by radically transforming the masculinist ethos of violence that undergirds the traditional epic heroic *corrido* discussed in the preceding chapter.

In contrast to the violent social bandit or bad-man hero wielding his phallic "pistol in his hand," and celebrated by male *corridistas* and their Chicano cultural nationalist protégés, Lucero presents a hero "ya sin fe" (with no more faith) who, significantly, has resolved to passively drink away his sorrows. Lucero's hero—whose own story of suffering and loss resonates with Lucero's preceding verse treatment of her tragic life—refuses to strike back and instead claims the symbolic moral high ground associated with his status as an aggrieved underdog. Whereas Raúl Homero Villa (1996) has identified the epic heroic *corrido* as the master narrative for an oppositional Pinto poetry, I submit that in this poem, Lucero rejects the simple inversions of the violent binary paradigm of power modeled by the *corrido* and, by extension, the derivative cultural nationalist poetic of Pinto poets, which is replete with masculinist imagery and graphic threats of sexualized violence. Having been victimized by the violent masculinist exercise of power that informs the *corrido*, Lucero intervenes. Her performative transformation of the epic heroic *corrido* occurs in the second stanza of the poem, in which the third-person narrative is interrupted by the protagonist himself. The passage, complete with the orthographic and syntax errors that mark the subaltern status of the poet and the working-class Chicana/o cultural context of the setting, reads:

Moso, sirvame la copa rota
Sirveme que me destrosar
Esta fievre de obsessión
Moso, sirvame la copa rota

Quiero sangrar gota y gota . . .

[Bartender, serve me the broken glass
Serve me so it destroys for me
This fever of obsession
Bartender, serve me the broken glass

I want to bleed drop by drop . . .] (lines 32–36)[9]

Rather than simply signaling the closure of the ballad, as this third-person narrative interruption sometimes does in the traditional *corrido*, Lucero's self-reflexive protagonist's intervention is open-ended. Instead of having her hero rise up in violent acts of retribution as in the epic ballad she invokes, Lucero's *bohemio* languishes on his imprisoning bar stool, lamenting and, significantly, embracing his *desgracia*, or misfortune.

Lucero's tragic tale of the downtrodden *bohemio* thus becomes far more than simply a tragic love song. It also functions as a heuristic device that extends the gynocritical allegory of the collapsing mountain in Part IV of "Ocho poemas." Here, Lucero is modeling the nonbinary exercise of power she calls for from her freeworld readers, to whom (and ultimately of whom) she sings. This poem also is a tale about telling tales; that is, a metacritical *ars poetica* that proposes Lucero's didactic fairy tales from hell as interventions in and of themselves. As in Part VI of "Ocho poemas," in which the narrator pledges to her never-identified lover to "write for you the story of our love / . . . with the blood red ink / of the Heart . . .," the *bohemio*'s conscious decision to drink from the broken glass, which he knows will tear his mouth into a bloody faucet, serves as the leitmotif of Lucero's entire corpus. Fully aware of the horror and trauma she will revisit, Lucero, through Convict #21918, explicates in intimate detail the penitentiary that has ripped her into a "shell that once was a Woman." Like the suffering *bohemio* in her poem, Lucero embraces, cultivates, and ultimately appropriates her abject status in prison (and her life before) in the hope of transforming her complex social location into a symbolic and materially liberating liminal space, which she proposes to rewrite with her regenerative woman-centered cultural nationalist verse.

To this end, Lucero's gynocritical and materialist imperatives converge with the populist poetics of the *corrido* in her last known poem, "Humilidad" (*sic*), published posthumously in 1980, seven years after her heart and brain literally exploded into her powerful "blood-red ink."[10] In this poem, written in the same vernacular style and lexicon as Part VIII of "Ocho poemas," Lucero more conclusively locates her lyric appropriations in the cultural nationalist terrain of Aztlán by specifically addressing her poem to the culturally specific referent "*mi RAZA*," which roughly translates as "my PEOPLE" even as it still resonates with the false cognate "my RACE." Loosely modeling the octosyllabic quatrains of the *corrido* form, she writes:

A mi RAZA aquí les cuento
Y los quero dejar saber
Como pobres seremos para siempre
Y sin nadie que los platique porqué.

[To my PEOPLE I tell you here and now
And I want to let you know
poor we are and always will be
And with no one to explain to you why.] (lines 1–4)

Although the octosyllabic meter and "a-b-c-b" rhyme scheme of the standard form of the *corrido* is not consistently preserved, the form of the "people's song" as sung by a bard-as-witness (and sometimes participant) is immediately invoked from this first stanza, which functions like the *corrido*'s declamatory invocation. The references to poverty and anomie facilitate yet another figurative displacement in which Lucero's new protagonist, "*mi RAZA*," implicitly is inscribed with several of her previous picaresque heroes: a Chicana mother forcibly separated from her daughter, a dried-up river, and even "*un bohemio borracho*." More importantly, the possessive pronoun *mi* (my) here serves to rearticulate Convict #21918 back onto her "Raza." Her concurrent use of the third-person plural (*nosotros*) conjugations of the verbs "to be" (e.g., "seremos" [we will be]) and "to suffer" (e.g., "hemos sufrido" [we have suffered]) further collapses the space between her own suffering and her people's collective subordination. "We have suffered," she implies, "together." In direct contrast to the humility suggested by the title of this poem, Lucero claims the proud and even audacious license foregrounded in her very first composition, "Face of Fear," in which she proclaims to be "nothing less" than "the one my mother bore." Lucero omnisciently proposes her *historia* as the *historia* of La Raza, and vice versa. Nothing more; nothing less. Her bold linkage and diachronic invocation of a cultural form that apparently arose as a popular performance of resistance to White colonial subjugation and the attendant capitalist mass-scale exploitation that ensued after the end of the U.S.-Mexico War in 1848 enables Lucero to historicize her incarceration as a continuation of her people's colonial subordination. By merging her embodied poetics with the broader Chicana/o body politic, she articulates the type of women-centered "resistance literature" that Barbara Harlow links to other modes of gendered resistance such as "no-wash" protests (1992: 82), in which women prisoners in Northern Ireland refused to wash their menstrual fluid, urine, and excrement in an attempt to repel the abusive male guards with their collective body odor. Lucero, in a figurative but no less visceral way, recenters her body in Aztlán through her Chicana feminist nationalist poetics.

As the new epic bard of an Aztlán she had previously reconfigured in terms of an innovative matriarchal pantheism in "Ocho poemas de amor," Lucero models a new insurgent subaltern Chicana Convict subjectivity. By claiming the separate but central role as bard-as-witness/participant, Lucero rejects a simplistic and submissive Marianist model of womanhood in favor of a newly empowered speaking subject, Malintzin, whom Norma Alarcón (1990) has proposed as a foundational multilingual archetype for Chicana feminism. Unlike Pintos such as Ricardo Sánchez, Lucero's poetic thus avoids replicating the masculinist paradigm of prison. Her new Chicana "translator" takes the form of a Pinta, a racially conscious, politicized Chicana prisoner who functions as a Chicana permutation of the counterhegemonic subject enunciated by the vernacular prison moniker "Convict," discussed above. She is an organic Pinta intellectual. And it is from the depths of her prison hell that she comes closest to her people; it is also from here that she and they together are able to reclaim Aztlán.

In her last published poem, Lucero's Convict Mother (of) Goddess thus returns to earth, not so much as the Mesoamerican savior, Quetzalcoatl, but as a deified Malintzin who is translating a new story of liberation.[11] For instance, in the last stanza of "Humilidad," Lucero further undermines the feigned humility alluded to in the title by offering a prophetic utopian resolution of her own and her people's collective suffering:

Los errores que pasan por la Vida
Todo esto algún día va cambiar

Tengan Fe mis Hermanos, no se fijen,
Por eso estos Versos se los quero Dedicar!!!

[The defeats that occur in Life
All of this will one day change
Have Faith my Brothers, don't worry
This is why these Verses I Dedicate to you!!!] (lines 17–20)[12]

As in the traditional *corrido* she glosses, Lucero's closing stanza emphasizes the continuation of the struggle it recounts (e.g., "All of this will
one day change / Have Faith my Brothers. . ."). The *bohemio* "ya sin fe"
introduced in her previous collection, along with his symbolic siblings,
La Raza, are now implored by the Pinta poet to stand firm in their convictions that they are not merely the downtrodden poor, but the defiant
underdogs who are destined to transform their defeats into a far-ranging
liberation—provided, of course, they refuse to simply invert a binary
model of power. Anticipating Gloria Anzaldúa by more than a decade,
Lucero thereby proclaims the birth of a new mestiza heroine invested
with the nonbinary epistemology that distinguishes the gynocritical and
materialist *mestiza* consciousness described in *Borderlands/La Frontera:
The New Mestiza* (1987), excerpted as the second epigraph above.
Lucero's contestatory verse thus no longer languishes in despair or
simply heralds death, but instead proclaims an ontological resolution
and communion with her "RAZA," which, significantly, is written in
all capital letters as if it were a shout. She further models this utopian
desire by signing her last poem from prison with her full name—Judy A.
Lucero. She has discarded her prison-issued number.

With her final signature, Lucero's poems from prison synthesize her
sentence and institutional erasure. She canonizes herself. Even though she
dies in prison—a fact that can never be glossed over by celebratory readings
of her verse—Lucero foregrounds the "resistance and affirmation" topos
crucial to paradigms of Chicana/o culture, art, and identity. Indeed, her
very institutionalization, along with her critical challenge to her erasure,
canonizes her within the genealogy of modern Chicana feminist poets.
Like the Chicana poets of the 1980s and 1990s Latina Renaissance that
she anticipates, Judy A. Lucero reclaimed not only the right to name and
rename herself, but also the power to name and rename her world as a
Chicana.

Lucero's lyrical deconstruction of the phallocentric paradigm undergirding the penitentiary, as well as proposed Pinto challenges to it, calls

attention to the power of literature to imagine new material realities. However, the fact that her nemesis—the prison guard tower—remains standing demands further scrutiny of the limits of the literary arts in prison. That is, Lucero enables scrutiny of the U.S. Carceral while also inviting prisoners, prisoner rights activists, and educators to join her in prison to propose new theories of praxis. This "prison work" is the subject of the next chapter.

CHAPTER 8

Writing Resistance?
Academic Institutions, Ideology, and "Prison Work"

> For those of us who are *visiting*—and this, indeed, is the greatest privilege—
> our status is in our faces, our movements, our bowels. We know, and we
> cling to this as we might to our children, that *we shall walk out of here,*
> *tonight, at a certain hour.*
>
> —Kenneth McClane (*Walls*, 1991)

LIVE AT FOLSOM PRISON

The gothic gray granite stones of the original Folsom Prison were mor-
tared in place from 1878 to 1880 by prisoners forced to work under
threats of violence. The buildings were designed to look like medieval
fortresses, their roofs and guard towers crowned with staggered stone
bulwarks originally designed to protect archers. California Department
of Corrections snipers now occupy the space and made a point of being
visible as we approached. But we were headed past them, towards the
"new" Folsom Prison, the one built in 1986 by the State of California at
the start of the largest prison construction boom in U.S. history. We were
entering Folsom to teach a creative writing seminar. The new prison,
subsequently renamed the California State Prison at Sacramento, was
to be a "model prison." The first thing we noticed was the architectural
contrast to the old Folsom: a minimalist exterior and immaculate, sterile
interior corridors lined with six-foot-tall lockers placed at ten-foot
intervals. Except for the fact that these lockers are used to cage prisoners
at the discretion of guards, this model prison can easily be mistaken for
one of the millions of nondescript high schools designed to impart the
nation's values to a never-ending stream of young adults.

We had come to Folsom to teach something else—or so we thought.
At the invitation of Francisco Dominguez, a photographer and poet
from northern California, Raúl Salinas and I had joined Dominguez's
weekly poetry workshop in the spring of 1993 as part of the California
Department of Corrections Arts-in-Corrections Program. Salinas had
been visiting Stanford University to inaugurate the housing of his personal

archives in the Cecil Green Library Special Collections. As a Stanford graduate student and member of the team that facilitated the university's acquisition of Salinas's papers, I used the opportunity to organize a Bay Area reading tour. The plan for the Folsom gig was to have Salinas present a featured reading for prisoner workshop participants, followed by a short open mike session and group discussion. I went simply as an observer to learn about prison education from two esteemed "Xicanindio" elders and experienced prison educators.[1]

It could never have been that simple.

The first problem arose from the fact that Salinas and I have criminal records: Salinas for drug-related felonies in his youth, and me for misdemeanors. Despite California Department of Corrections prohibitions against allowing anyone with a record to enter prison except as a prisoner, the Folsom education liaison, a gregarious White male, allowed us to enter as his guests. Tensions had been rising and would eventually explode into a full-scale riot one year after our visit, so this special allowance would later make me question my belief that we "had gotten one over on the Man." Our "clearance" to enter the prison would later resonate with Joseph Bruchac's (1987) observation that prison creative writing workshops sometimes had a hegemonic role.

Another problem was dress. Salinas's identity since leaving prison in 1972 revolved around his ex-con "urban Indian" style—blue jeans, turquoise and silver jewelry talismans, and a braided pony tail—signaling him as a warrior and married man. But in California prisons, denim is standard issue for prisoners, and everyone else is prohibited from wearing blue jeans. The prison education attaché bluntly stated, "We don't want you to be mistaken for prisoners and get shot by a guard in the event of an incident." This distinction of *us* and *them* caused Salinas a considerable amount of angst since his identity as a Chicano, Native American, poet, and revolutionary was inextricable from his transformative twelve years in prison, including Soledad State Penitentiary, less than three hundred miles south of Folsom. A cheap pair of jogging pants from the nearby Wal-Mart, built shortly after the new Folsom, helped solve the dress code requirements; however, we could no longer efface the more substantive issue of our freeworld identities and status. We were entering the prison by choice and could leave of our own volition as "free" men—provided we did not break any laws while inside, the chief one being the introduction of "contraband."

The writing workshop was "successful" and went without incident, as they always did. Much of the time was devoted to workshopping several prisoner poems, with the discussion focusing on the mechanics of poetry and complex cultural poetics. The interplay between Salinas and the other prisoner poets was electrifying and defiant. Salinas even read his poem "News from San Quentin," dedicated to Black revolutionary George Jackson (1990, 1994), who was assassinated by San Quentin Prison guards on August 21, 1971, just 150 miles away from Folsom. Salinas's voice steadily rose as he reached the crescendo of Convict solidarity:

Those few
who have been touched
by
MADNESS
in silent darkness pray
to the spirit of Ho Chi Minh
and grow impatient/intolerant
of the oppressed . . .
those who wish to stay that way.
There's no turning back for us.[2]

I listened silently from my chair in the corner, enthralled by the passion, grassroots pedagogical method, and revolutionary poetics and politics, when all of a sudden a Pinto turned to me and asked: "What are you doing here?"

After the long silence that reflected my shock, all I could say was that I was a student, here to learn, and thanked them for letting me observe the workshop. I knew better than to tell them I was there because I could not afford a flight home to visit an uncle incarcerated at the time in the Texas Department of Corrections, or to speak about my father's own incarcerations and his judicially sanctioned exile from home, other Convict uncles, my own brutalization at the hands of the Houston Police, and my overwhelming desire for revenge. In prison, this is everyone's story.

I received my Ph.D. shortly after the Folsom workshop, but the question posed by a Pinto followed me to my first academic job in the English Department at Cornell University. I had been told by the interview committee that my dissertation on Pinta/o poetry (upon which this book is based) was so "good" that I was offered the job immediately after my interview. But what did this mean? How could I capitalize a career, salary, benefits, and even more social status by writing about human beings, prisoners, whose existence was defined in terms of their deliberately diminished material and social status? What exactly is the nature of what academics and activists call "prison work?" Why was I really doing it? Was it for the self-aggrandizing sense of empowerment that a former White male writing instructor mentioned he felt each time he left prison after his writing workshop? Was my prisoner "solidarity" work really resistance or, in reality, simple co-optation? Worse, was I a participant in a new type of exploitation whereby academics build careers by writing about the unfathomable misery of prisoners? Was I an opportunistic anthropologist who had staked a claim on a new "lost tribe" in order to make a name for myself among academic aesthetes?

These and related questions culminated in a 1996 prison education course that I used to explore exactly what it means to do "prison work" as an academic and activist. This course, "Writing Resistance: U.S. Minority and Third World Prisoner Writing," was a Ph.D. seminar that attracted a multiracial group of twelve students, most from the working class. Our charge was to explore the lingering question we all felt in a variety of different ways: "What are *we* doing *here*?"—"here" being the Ivy League and also the youth detention facilities and maximum-security prisons where we began offering our workshops. Even if no single course could ever bridge the proverbial town-gown divide, we would try to recognize, learn about, and intervene into our complex location within these social divisions through our readings and our prison service learning projects.

I should have known from my experience at Folsom that it could never be so simple.

In the balance of this chapter, I offer a candid examination of select prison literature and culture programs in the United States and Canada to assess my own course and the student-led prison education projects it inspired. I do so with the awareness that these projects were offered and undertaken for course credit in the Ivy League institution whose own clock tower was constructed of the same hewn shale stone as the one capping Auburn Prison less than a hundred miles away.[3]

"PRISON WORK" AND IDEOLOGY—OR, WHY IT MATTERS THAT SHAKESPEARE WAS NEVER BEHIND BARS

Joseph Bruchac's observations about the inevitable hegemonic appropriation of proposed counterhegemonic prison writing workshops illustrates the interrelated disciplining role of prisons, asylums, schools, and the military identified by Michel Foucault (1979). Raymond Jones and Peter d'Errico add:

> the learning available to prisoners has tended to be in the service of the
> panoptic regime of discipline, surveillance, and control. Learning was
> tolerated within the prisons only to the extent that it participated in
> the reformative project that emerged from the birth of the prison. . . . It
> was and continues to be learning termed "correctional," bespeaking its
> compatibility with the "unmaking" of human beings, denial or limitation
> of human potential, and ease with participation in the historic failure of the
> prison's reformative project. (1994: 15)

This overdetermined failure to "reform" prisoners notwithstanding, scholarship on the effectiveness of prison education confirms one self-evident outcome of the myriad educational programs available in jails and penitentiaries: recidivism rates are substantially lower for prisoners who have participated in educational and vocational programs due to prisoners' increased marketable skills as well as critical-thinking and problem-solving capacities.[4]

Other studies, however, raise questions about the racial- and class-based nature of the establishment, exercise, and appraisal of prison educational programs. Howard Davidson (1997) recalls how prison has always been the site of ideological conflicts between prison reformers and punitive politicians and prison administrators. Patricia Case and David Fasenfest (2004) add that prison educational programs fail to overcome another binary division: racism in the freeworld job market. They note that unlike White prisoners, Black prisoners see college education as impractical for a post-prison job market. Many college courses are designed for white-collar jobs that, increasingly, require background checks that "weed out" convicted felons. The irony is that advanced training becomes accessible to the racial minority and overall lumpen class segments only in prison, whose context subsequently makes these jobs inaccessible.

So what constitutes success in a prison education program? And how are we to gauge the goals in relation to Ideological and Repressive State Apparatuses such as the penitentiary?

Regardless of whether or not prison educators acknowledge it, their methodological approach ultimately overdetermines the potential, and limits, of their proposed intervention into the disciplining regimes of prison. In the humanities and, more precisely, in basic literacy, literature, and creative writing workshops, the tension between hegemonic and proposed counterhegemonic prison education programming is performed in terms of canonicity. The acclaimed "Shakespeare Behind Bars" project at Framingham Women's Prison, which evolved from a standard introductory literature course first offered by Jean Trounstine, a former English teacher, in 1987, illustrates the potentially hegemonic role of prisoner education projects, especially those based on a Eurocentric literary canon. Trounstine's memoir, *Shakespeare Behind Bars: The Power of Drama in a Women's Prison* (2001), serves as a touchstone in assessing the nature of prison work. Despite the fact that her prisoner students consisted primarily of minority and working-class women, Trounstine's syllabus consisted of several plays by Shakespeare as well as ancient Greek and colonial and modern White American texts. In discussing her reasons for choosing a canonical text for the prisoner drama workshop's first play, Trounstine notes:

> I first focused on Shakespeare's *The Merchant of Venice*, filled with conflicts about love and law and peopled with fascinating characters I hoped would engage the prisoners and their audience. I believed that if my students tackled Shakespeare, a writer they thought was beyond reach, they would also be learning to take on what was most difficult in life. (2001: 1)

From this canonical permutation of the pop-social psychology axiom that posits "what doesn't kill you makes you stronger," Trounstine's resultant syllabus, with all its presuppositions about culture, ultimately overdetermines the hegemonic containment of the project—and the continued ideological containment of her prisoner students.

Her rationale for using canonical texts is itself shaped by a profound bias for she reifies her prisoner students as tragic Shakespearean archetypes:

> Instead of frightening me they seemed lost, with tragic lives—lives like those of Shakespeare's characters, complete with flaws, comic mishaps, and ironic endings.
>
> I began to understand that female prisoners are not "damaged goods," and to recognize that most of these women had toughed it out in a society that favors others—by gender, class, or race. They are Desdemonas suffering because of jealous men, Lady Macbeths carving the power of their spouses,

Portias disguised as men in order to get ahead, and Shylocks, who, being
betrayed, take the law into their own hands. (2)

Furthermore, despite her very different racial background as a middle-
class White woman and former hippie, she overstates her affinity with
the prisoners. Even after learning that many women prisoners were
convicted as accomplices to male-instigated crimes, for murdering abusive
male partners, or for engaging in economically and physically coerced
prostitution, Trounstine adds:

> There's something about a woman who dares to get in trouble that has
> always been close to my heart. As a sixties rebel, I lived in a commune, had
> unsafe sex, and moved in with someone I'd known for only twenty-four
> hours. (5)

Instructor identification with prisoner students is one of the most important—and perhaps even necessary—elements motivating prison educators,
and Trounstine should be lauded for her years of community education
projects with drug addicts, runaways, and "at-risk" youth. Yet she too
conveniently effaces the profound experiential differences between herself
and her prisoner students. Her memoir reveals this identification to be a
personal quest for self-actualization when she writes: "I felt a chemistry,
a link between their lives and mine, a connection partly due to gender
and partly due to yearning" (3).

This simultaneous differentiation and leveling does not necessarily
imply that Trounstine's value-laden selection of Shakespeare and
other White male authors could not yield productive and symbolically
empowering opportunities for the prisoner students. The Bard, after all,
was from the provincial working class in early modern England, and
his plays are populated with ruffians, *pícaros*, and ordinary Elizabethan
archetypes who serve both as stock characters and well-rounded subjects
of history. Correspondingly, many of Shakespeare's elites function as
antagonists. Shakespeare's insights, which came from his working-class
origins as well as his nouveau riche status later in life, have offered many
opportunities for creative restagings of his plays across time and place.
Following a student's complaint that "Shakespeare is a white man's
theater," Trounstine replies, "Not if we do it" (45). She then facilitates
the multiracial production of *Rapshrew*, a hip-hop adaptation of
Shakespeare's *The Taming of the Shrew*, a play about duplicitous and

misogynist courtship. To her credit, Trounstine successfully passed the reins of the classroom to Bertie, a previously uncooperative prisoner incarcerated for killing an abusive husband:

> She's the one who's gathered the Shrews, our rap group, turning them into dancers, while I coach them on diction. Their torsos bumping and grinding, arms swinging and heads wagging, they belt out, "Rollin', rollin', roll with the Shrews now, everybody sing!" (71)

The prisoners were ecstatic at being able to offer entertainment for a multigenerational audience of family and friends. The play allowed them to transform the otherwise humiliating and demoralizing family prison visit regimen into something fun and personally validating. That the play facilitated positive self-esteem for cast members is underscored by Trounstine, who cites Bertie's entry in her class journal: "I know now I am somebody" (72).

While the *Rapshrew* refrain of "I'm a shrew, I'm a shrew, she's a shrew, I'm a shrew" may not successfully undermine the otherwise ideologically closed nature of the original text, which ends with the containment of the resistant woman through the institution of marriage, other Shakespeare plays performed by the group afford a burgeoning metacritical consciousness of subaltern identity. In their viewing, and later staging, of *The Merchant of Venice*, for instance, prisoners engaged in a debate about whether or not Shylock, the play's Jewish character who is vilified for demanding justice after multiple betrayals by the Christian community, deserves a second chance for his acts of retribution. When Rose, another prisoner, uses Method acting to inhabit her own Shylock, the entire class is moved to tears. Trounstine describes the climactic soliloquy:

> She stands, clutching her script, walking to the center of the cleared space, and gestures with her free hand, the crippled, one, cutting through air. She's forceful now, crying out as though she is accusing us all, "If you prick us, do we not bleed? If you tickle us, do we not laugh? If you poison us, do we not die? And if you wrong us, shall we not revenge?" She walks over to her seat, lowering herself into it, and says softly, "The villainy you teach me I will execute, and it shall go hard but I will better the instruction." (113)

In an illustration of this profound cross-class, cross-racial, and cross-gender self-recognition, Rose later asks Trounstine, "Does it really hurt like this, for actors, onstage? (113).

Other adaptations of canonical texts apparently were too successful for some prisoners, creating profound dissonance. When they staged Nathaniel Hawthorne's 1850 canonical American novel, *The Scarlet Letter*, as a play about a prisoner with AIDS, one prisoner refused to play the part of Hester, the patriarchally marked "fallen" woman, for fear of the stigma she might assume if other prisoners believed she really was HIV-positive. Ultimately, and perhaps inevitably, the canon becomes an overbearing ideological presence. After a cast member who had been accused by a prison administrator of brewing contraband alcohol was found not guilty, the cast shouted for joy because one of their own had escaped extra punishment. Yet Trounstine recalls being startled:

> And then Kit cackles in this eerie way that fills the room, a laugh much louder and longer than anyone else's laugh in Program Room 2 that evening, a wicked-witch laugh right out of *The Wizard of Oz*, and one that I later hear in my dreams, a laugh that forms the foundation of her portrayal of a Puritan woman in our production of Nathaniel Hawthorne's *The Scarlet Letter*. Kit haunts me in that play, grinning toothlessly up at Hester Prynne, waving her script in the air, crying out gleefully, "Show us the mark of your shame! Shame! Shame!" (80)

Trounstine's seamless merging of Kit's joyous laughter as a member of the group of prisoners rooting for each other with a villainous, haunting theatrical howl is both a function of Method acting and of Trounstine's persistence in mapping the canon—replete with its racist and misogynist poetics—onto her underclass students. After all, the wicked witches in L. Frank Baum's 1939 *The Wizard of Oz* are deemed antagonists because they disrupt the symbolic quest of a young White woman, Dorothy, for a home of her own.

The significant racial and class differences between teacher and student also have an ideological effect. In an inverse performance of Homi Bhabha's (2007) subversive colonial mimic, Bertie, originally from the former British colony of Jamaica, and whose pidgin English simultaneously disrupts yet remembers multiple levels of colonial subjugation, beams to a reporter, "I'm Jamaican . . . and this play is giving me self-confidence to speak better. I'm learning English, American-style" (120). Earlier, Rhonda, another cast member, had noted, "A lot of people are afraid of Shakespeare. . . . But I've always liked the King's English" (118). Trounstine allows these comments to stand as success stories. The drama workshop, after all, is categorized within the prison education system as an English course, which is part of the legacy of English departments that emerged, according to Gauri Viswanathan, to buttress imperialism in India and to control the working class in England:

> As late as the 1860s, the "literary curriculum" in British educational establishments remained polarized around classical studies for the upper classes and religious studies for the lower. As for what is now known as the subject of English literature, the British educational system had no firm place for it until the last quarter of the nineteenth century, when the challenge posed by the middle classes to the existing structure resulted in the creation of alternative institutions devoted to "modern" studies. (1995: 434)

Shakespeare might never have been behind bars, but students throughout the world were placed behind the bars of colonialism and class hierarchies precisely by the study of Shakespeare and other British authors.

For all her good intentions, and even a slight expansion of the canon through the use of Maya Angelou's *I Know Why the Caged Bird Sings*, Trounstine's privileging of Shakespeare as paradigmatic resulted in some troubling effacements of the prisoners' own writing:

> Now we're reading Shakespeare's sonnets, and in their journals, the women are writing whatever they feel like writing, responses to the readings or to prison life. We often make poetry from their material, shaping what I call their "stuff" into poems. (140)

The rigid poetic form of the Shakespearian sonnet is given the status of a master genre, while the vernacular writings by prisoners of differing literacies is consigned to the amorphous antithetical status of "stuff."

In an illustration of the inherent limits of canonical prison education projects such as "Shakespeare Behind Bars"—an admittedly innovative program that involved creative stagings—all the plays at the Framingham Women's Prison were performed in front of the "dungeon," a set of nineteenth-century cells that were never removed but simply—yet incompletely—covered over by the palimpsestic prison stage of the present. Unconsciously echoing Bruchac, Trounstine recalls overhearing one workshop participant problematizing the cathartic benefits of the theater workshop when she notes, "This play is controlling me better than all the tricks the Department of Corrections has ever had up its sleeve" (152). While Trounstine judiciously recalls this comment, this brief mention is the closest she comes to problematizing her own prison work.

Even if the author of *Shakespeare Behind Bars* had not begun her final acknowledgments by thanking her literary agent, this book would still fall within the self-aggrandizing memoir subgenre that can only be described as the exoticist account of a freeworld sojourner who achieved self-actualization through contact with prisoner abjection. Norman Mailer's championing of Jack Henry Abbott stands as a warning to overzealous cross-class and cross-institutional overidentifications: just six weeks after Abbott's release from prison, and one day before the release of Mailer's *New York Times* laudatory book review of Abbott's *In the Belly of the Beast* (1981), Mailer's protégé murdered a waiter over a perceived slight.

Trounstine's memoir ends with an epilogue that satiates the "yearning" she foregrounds in the preface. In addition to her self-congratulatory tone, she even thanks the prison guards, thus distinguishing her memoir from counterhegemonic prisoner writing, which never recognizes guards as anything but coercive and brutal cogs in the prison machine. The hegemonic role of canonical projects such as Trounstine's is confirmed when she concludes her memoir with recommendations for prison staff and other educators on how to use theater for anger management exercises. She fails to recognize how her method might be used to control and subjugate prisoners. She closes by advocating that less money be allocated for building new prisons and more be devoted to prison programming. Presumably this would include more Shakespeare workshops.

Trounstine's canonical paradigm, which certainly predates her, eventually replicated itself in an even more acclaimed version of "Shakespeare Behind Bars" in the Luther Luckett Correctional Complex, a men's penitentiary in Kentucky. The workshop participants consisted of a multiracial cast, primarily Blacks, who staged a version of Shakespeare's 1610 tragicomedy, *The Tempest*. The documentary film chronicling the program received much critical acclaim. A recurrent trope in this reportage involves the affirmation that prisoners can also be human and creative regardless of what they have done—as if the reporters were surprised at the very thought of a prisoner's humanity.[5] One review of the documentary, however, notes that the play's transformative role in the prisoners' lives is much more complicated than educators might have imagined:

> We'd all like to believe that art is a lot more powerful than it is, but during rehearsals, two inmates who swear that Shakespeare has shown them the light are instead cast off to the Hole for breaking prison rules. An inmate in a previous production was granted parole but asked to stay for two more months because he had never finished anything in his life before. He did the play with pride. He was released. Then he committed suicide. (Smith 2006: n.p.)

That question I first heard at Folsom Prison, it seems, can be lethal when left unanswered.

TOWARDS A FREIRIAN PRISON PEDAGOGY

If the "Shakespeare Behind Bars" workshops represent the ideologically closed nature of Eurocentric prison education workshops, Freirian-inspired projects seek to privilege the prisoners' lived realities. James B. Waldram, a medical anthropologist, explores the successes and limits of one such initiative in *Way of the Pipe: Aboriginal Spirituality and Symbolic Healing in Canadian Prisons* (1997). In collaboration with Canadian Aboriginal (also known as First Nation) prisoners in five Canadian prisons in the 1990s, he chronicles the movement to reintroduce traditional healing practices—sometimes called the "Red Road" or "Way of the Pipe"—for imprisoned Aboriginal men.

In contrast to Trounstine, Waldram neither reifies the institutional divide between the privileged academic and prisoners, nor does he irresponsibly efface it. But he does reject the strictures of his own discipline, anthropology, which continues to demand a detached scientific vocabulary and faux-objective gaze of the "detached" scientist. Instead, Waldram sought to produce a book that would be accessible to a wide audience. His goal was to illustrate, with due constraints, the successes of, and need for, expanded alternative cultural programming for Aboriginal prisoners in Canada and elsewhere. The therapy model he deployed was not designed to have prisoners acquiesce to their imprisoned condition, but to reintegrate them into their Native culture.

Significantly, Waldram refused to appropriate these prisoners' experiences for his own self-aggrandizement, as Trounstine did. Instead he decided to release much of the control of his manuscript, fully realizing that it might actually hurt his academic standing since the manuscript is the quintessential commodity upon which pay raises, promotions, and professional stature is based:

I issued several basic promises to those who participated in the study as a way of ensuring accountability. Where possible, transcripts of interviews were returned to Elders and inmates. All Elders and Native liaison personnel were given the absolute right of control over their interviews, and interview transcripts were provided to them for additions or deletions. Where possible, draft copies of the manuscript were returned to the Elders for their perusal. In many instances, Elders returned their copies with valuable suggestions and criticism, and I gave serious consideration to their ideas when preparing the final manuscript. (xiii–xiv)

Waldram used his research monies to purchase Native studies books for detention facilities where he conducted his research, and he donated all of his book royalties to the Native Brotherhood at the Regional Psychiatric Centre in Saskatoon, Saskatchewan, for use as they deemed appropriate. Departing still further from the "objective" posture mandated by the discipline of anthropology—one that has a colonialist legacy for Aboriginal peoples in Canada and throughout the world—Waldram also respected all requests for anonymity and the excision of information that might be used to punish prisoners. This inversion of the hierarchies of scholar-informant, and teacher-student, did not go unnoticed. As Waldram claims, prison administrators and guards tried to sabotage this cross-class and cross-racial collaboration, including the deliberate botching of meetings in which Waldram and Aboriginal prisoners were scheduled at two different locations at the same time.

Most significant is the project's refusal to accept a teleological model or a celebratory tone. Waldram's research project chronicles the introduction of a way of life as a process of recuperation by Aboriginal peoples who have been colonized and marginalized precisely by the systematic denial of their cultural practices and Native identities. The irony remains that these cultural activities occurred in prisons; these prisons, like other Western institutions introduced by European settler colonialism, served to contain these Aboriginal men for transgressing against laws that are part of a society whose very foundation was predicated upon their demise as a people. Of this unresolved (counter)hegemonic institutional paradox, Waldram writes:

Coming on the heels of the Aboriginal Justice Inquiry of Manitoba, whose recommendations were quickly consigned to the dustbin, I found myself walking into an environment in which "research" was a dirty, exploitative concept. Particularly difficult was my attempt to explain my understanding of how policy change ensues and how my role as a researcher is largely marginal to this process, since I did not work for the correctional system. But, as a research and university professor, what I lacked in inside clout, I perhaps made up in my role as a "scientist" who could "objectively" research and "tell it like it is." Some inmates clearly saw me as an advocate, a few as a typist ("we'll tell you what to say, and you put it down"), and thankfully only a few as part of the correctional establishment. (xii)

Waldram emphasizes that his collaborative research likely would not lead to immediate, or perhaps any, institutional changes, even though his goal was to enable them. Nonetheless, his intervention was designed to disrupt the carceral apparatus and educational institutions—including his own—as governing paradigms of order.

Similarly motivated, Rena Fraden's *Imagining Medea: Rhodessa Jones and the Theater for Incarcerated Women* (2001), focuses on a multiyear theater project for women incarcerated in the San Francisco County Jail system. The Medea Project represents a mediation between the canonical and Freirian paradigms: it uses a canonical text—Euripides' ancient Greek tragedy *Medea,* about a betrayed woman who kills her children in an act of revenge against her husband—but with radical revisions that remove it far from a classicist, Eurocentric, or masculinist context. Founded and directed by Black playwright and performer Rhodessa Jones, who claims inspiration from the women's prison theater project at Framingham Prison, the Medea Project uses the myth of Medea as a touchstone for contemporary women, mostly racial minority, to explore their own marginalization and exploitation in a racist and classist society. One staged skit in the repertoire theater has a contemporary Medea uttering a vernacular soliloquy that includes the following indictment of famous U.S. patriarchs:

> Motherfucking bastard! . . . You Clarence Thomas, David Duke, Wilt Chamberlain, William Kennedy Smith . . . looking ass nigger! Son of a bitch motherfucker, I hope your dick falls off! (57)

This redirection of Medea's rage away from helpless children towards a list of rapists, pornographers, and philanderers proposes a radical revision of the original text.

An even more provocative dimension to this project is Jones's insistence that the theater troupe perform both outside and inside the jail to force a dialogue, however contentious, between imprisoned and freeworld women and their families. On this blurring of lines, Jones stresses:

> Word came out that one critic has said, "We've seen *The Medea Project.* Why see it again?" Well, the reason is, this is the voice of the people here, of women, and women are mad as hell. It's lawless out there. We ask the question why more and more women are going to jail; what's happening to our children. . . . This is theater for the twenty-first century. The evening news doesn't get it; it talks about African American men. But we want to take a global look, at all of it. . . . If you think jail doesn't have anything to do with you, someday, just wait, a ten-year-old will be pointing an Uzi in your face. Just as we've seen AIDS touch us all, so will this violence. (2)

Unlike Trounstine, Fraden prefaces her institutional approaches to analyzing Jones's project by calling attention to her own privileged subject position as a middle-class White woman college professor. Nevertheless, this personal and political epiphany came only after Jones challenged Fraden for expressing surprise that a Rhodessa Jones, a Black woman, was a professional theatrical director. Jones also rebuked Fraden for her initial approach to the "subject" as a detached scholar. She repeatedly told her project participants that "no one can sit on the sidelines" (xvi), and Fraden finally realized that this also applied to her. Yet drawing upon her interviews with Jones and prisoner participants, Fraden adds a sobering acknowledgment about the Medea Project that illustrates the limits even of Freirian-inspired prison education programming:

> Theater may have saved Rhodessa Jones's life, but it might not be enough for these women. Some of the incarcerated women who performed in the first play were empowered but not yet freed. The questions still lay before them: what it meant to be Medea, to become Medea, to kill Medea. Who else might they become as they represented their lives as drama? (66)

With institutions such as prisons and universities so interrelated, and even complicit, in the production of gender, racial, class, and other hierarchies, could there really be a happy ending to such otherwise provocative prison education projects? After all, it is one thing to recognize these hierarchies, and another to dismantle them. In their diachronic overview of prison education paradigms and programs in Europe and the United States from eighteenth-century religious paradigms to the Arts-in-Corrections program I observed in California in the early 1990s, Jones and d'Errico observe one constant in the continuously evolving nature of prison education: "higher education seeks to transform the social status of prisoners in ways that fundamentally contradict the degraded and delinquent status that prisons reinforce" (1994: 16). They conclude that either the educational program fails in its mission, or the prison does.

THE FAILING SUCCESSES AND SUCCESSFUL FAILURES OF THE CORNELL PRISON EDUCATION PROJECT

The Cornell Prison Education Project consisted of five student-led, prison-based workshops that lasted six to eight weeks and were undertaken as part of the course requirements for a graduate seminar I taught in the English Department at Cornell University, "Writing Resistance: Minority and Third World Prisoner Discourses." The course was designed to survey prisoner literature as part of broader interrogations of culture, politics, and power in the Western world, and included a candid, performative interrogation of the problematic nature of nonprisoner solidarity work with specific prisoners and various prisoner-led struggles.

Unlike other graduate English seminars, this one incorporated a model of "fieldwork" that I prefer to call "engaged research." Invoking the Gramscian model of the organic intellectual who deploys institutional training and privilege in solidarity with members of a marginalized community in struggle, we drew upon the Service-Learning paradigm. Service-Learning is a well-established educational philosophy and practice in U.S. universities that seeks to enhance and politicize the educational experiences of students through community service projects. The first iteration of Service-Learning in the United States followed the 1862 Morrill Act, which established land grant institutions whose mission involved extension services to local communities, especially farmers. The model came to fruition as a Freirian initiative in 1979 with the establishment of the National Center for Service-Learning, which identified three fundamental principles:

> those being served control the services provided; those being served become better able to serve and be served by their own actions; those who serve also are learners and have significant control over what is expected to be learned.[6]

In 1985, a National Campus Compact was formed by the presidents of Brown, Georgetown, and Stanford universities and soon grew to include universities from every state, including Cornell, which houses the well-funded Cornell Public Service Center.[7] This institutional legacy immediately raised important questions about the oppositional claims undergirding our approach to prison work, especially given that even a land-grant institution such as Cornell University was heavily invested in training not only the managerial class but the multinational capitalist elite. Cornell is, after all, an Ivy League university.

Further illustrating the complexity of our proposed counterhegemonic activities was the demographic range of the students in the course, which included a relative of high-profile attorney Johnny Cochran, as well as Jonathan Jackson Jr., the son of slain Jonathan Jackson and nephew of assassinated Black revolutionary George Jackson, whose work we were reading in the class. (Jackson Jr. withdrew from the course after two class sessions because, he said, "it hit too close to home.")[8] The final course roll consisted of twelve students: six female, six male, three Black, five Latina/o, two Native American, two White, and one openly gay, with several of the students being mixed-blood or interracial.[9] Four other Cornell students, all White (two male and two female), were not enrolled in the course but joined one Service-Learning team, bringing the total number of students involved in the initiative to sixteen, plus one staff liaison from the Cornell Public Service Center (a political exile from Chile).

We were not able to apply the first principle of Service-Learning—the right of communities being served to determine the services they need and want—due to the prisoners' lack of authority over curriculum. Nonetheless, our minority-majority class enabled limited insights on the politics and practices of incarceration based on extended family legacies. Most students had relatives who had been in prison or currently were in prison. We drew upon these relationships to develop our curricula, fully aware that we were still privileged outsiders.

During the first month of coursework and discussion, affinity groups evolved based on identity politics, ideological dispositions, or area interests which facilitated the formation of teams around variously themed projects that "seemed" to be "needed." The projects were:

1. Seminar on Manhood and Responsibility at the Louis Gossett, Jr., Residential Center (for adolescent men)
2. Young Women's Literature Seminar at the Lansing Residential Center (for adolescent women)
3. Young Women's Creative Writing Workshop at the Lansing Residential Center (for adolescent women)

4. Native American Resource Workshop at the Auburn State Prison (for men)
5. Latino Expressive Arts Workshop at the Cayuga Correctional Facility (for men)

We developed a syllabus for each proposed project with the goal of making our pilot project feasible within a semester time frame, but still flexible enough to continue beyond the graduate seminar. (In addition, there were two projects not based on prisons in the area: one was part of a dissertation on spatial studies in southern California that examined the role of prisons as part of the U.S. colonization of the Southwest; the other was a guide to Web-based resources for prisoner education and activism.) After collectively drafting budgets, we prepared a general funding proposal to solicit cosponsorship from various academic units, including the Latino Studies Program, the English Department, Cornell Public Service Center, College of Arts and Humanities, and the Cornell University Bookstore. Every request was met, and our total budget was $6,740 (plus in-kind support such as reduced costs for 315 books) for five prison education projects serving ninety-five prisoners.

These projects were significant to me as an educator for many reasons. The least important was that they enabled the course participants to resolve a literary crux debated by theorists for ages that posits literature's function as either to teach or to entertain—but not both. This binary was revealed to have no currency in Freirian-inspired cultural studies. For us, there was a humanist impulse in introducing prisoners to culturally relevant and, yes, entertaining books, yet this impulse did not necessarily contradict a materialist desire to participate in various institutional subversions. Simultaneously, these Service-Learning projects were valuable precisely because they not only "complemented" the primary and secondary readings, but enabled us to explore a different way of doing graduate study. English and literature departments already had been transformed by cultural studies paradigms for at least a quarter century, and our plan was to continue extending the paradigmatic boundaries by doing research that involved more than simply pulling a book from the shelf. We would "read" the prison itself.

The biggest challenge was getting into the prisons without being contained as a result of the negotiations we deployed to gain entry. Each team divided tasks internally, with at least one member assigned to conduct research on institutional contacts at the targeted youth detention facility or penitentiary. We used the workshop sessions at the end of our weekly course seminar to role-play our pitches to prison administrators. Because our plan was to break *into* prison through Service-Learning projects, we were forced to deploy the same institutional "reformation" discourses that serve to pathologize prisoners. Our projects thus were pitched as therapy, self-help, remedial skills training, and individual catharsis, all of which would "complement" the institutional mission of prisoner reformation. The rationale undergirding the need for each of these projects would be focused on the prisoners and the conduct identified by the courts as legitimating their incarceration.

My team's encounter with an administrator at the Gossett detention facility, however, immediately illustrated the inherent limits to this mimetic approach. For different reasons, she had asked a question similar to the one posed by a Folsom prisoner, "Why are you here?" Although I had been reluctant to discuss my own family imprisonment legacy with prisoners at Folsom, my discussion of a "wayward youth" and "commitment to helping other people's brothers like someone once helped me," satisfied the White female prison administrator to whom we pitched a "self-help" workshop titled "Manhood and Responsibility." But any thoughts that our academic permutation of a Trojan horse would succeed in subverting hegemonic institutions from within was immediately debunked by her instructions to our team. As she escorted us out of the electronically controlled front door, she noted that the New York State Division of Criminal Justice sign urging anyone to report any instance of abuse or wrongdoing by correctional staff was indeed "important," but all reports should be made to her office instead.

The administrator repeated this usurpation of authority in a variety of ways with an extended discussion that left no doubt that approval of our project would be contingent on the hypercontainment, and perhaps concealment, of any guard or administrator misconduct. She was foregrounding the possibility of prisoner abuse while simultaneously circumscribing any extra-institutional prisoner advocacy from a regulatory agency—even the very New York State Division of Criminal Justice that had built the prison and purportedly retained jurisdiction over it. She had no fear of our project because, after all, it would be occurring in a detention center that she proclaimed to be an autonomous disciplinary apparatus. In fact, she wanted us there.

This co-optation of our planned countersurveillance of the prison regime presented itself even more acutely in one of the two Lansing-based projects. In their collectively written research paper, the team of two Chicanas and two Black women exposed the disciplinary function of personal aesthetics by identifying how Lansing hairstyle restrictions contributed to the piecemeal, genocidal self-imaging of the young women prisoners. Most of them were Black and Latina (with many of the Latinas also identifying, or being identified, as Black), yet Lansing policies prohibited "Afro" hairstyles while simultaneously promoting straightened or "conked" hair. Even though the forcible straightening of naturally kinky hair requires burning or treatments with chemicals, both prohibited in prison, the institutional privileging of this Eurocentric aesthetic functioned as a salient ontological and epistemological disciplining practice. Hair became the site where the prison became both a Repressive State Apparatus and an Ideological State Apparatus. When coupled with the different color-coded uniforms, highly gendered vocational training, a tiered benefit system that rewarded subservience, and attendant prohibitions against speaking about any aspect of their pre-prison lives—including families, friends, or experiences—the Black female body became the de facto site of containment.

One team member's report on the restraints used on female prisoners provided further illustration of the inherent limits of prison education projects, which have also been observed by Jones and d'Errico (1994). The media profile on our course and related projects by Jill Goetz (1997) in the *Cornell Chronicle*, a monthly newspaper sent to students, staff, and alumni, noted:

> Cherene Sherrard, a graduate student of English, found it especially difficult to watch teen-age girls marching in unison and being restrained at the Lansing women's center. But she and her classmates said such experiences were more than offset by the rewards of reaching the incarcerated men and women with whom they worked. (1)

The reference to the use of restraint led to an immediate written complaint by Lansing staff, who denied using any "force" during the time frame of the workshop. All penal institutions keep a log of "violent incidents" and "forcible restraint use," which usually are followed by in-house "investigations" of the prisoners and staff involved to determine whether the actions were warranted. The "restraints" Sherrard referred to, however, were not merely shackles, lockstep marching, and enforced silences—these were real and publicly acknowledged—but also locks of forcibly straightened Black hair, and all that these strands implied.

The team's observations, theorizations, and, above all, public report-age linking all these forms of restraint inevitably broke the multi-institutional bond that posited Cornell and the local juvenile detention centers as united in their "educational" missions. Indeed, although two of the five Service-Learning projects continued well beyond the graduate seminar that spawned them—one eventually leading to the marriage between a workshop facilitator and an Auburn prisoner, and another continuing for another four years with an expansion to a second youth detention facility[10]—the two Lansing projects were not extended. By bearing witness to disciplinary regimes—a resistance in itself—this Lansing team succeeded precisely because it failed to be silently complicit in neocolonial practices. But the successful resistance reportage also represents a failure because future scholar activists were prevented from "breaking into" Lansing.

By way of a postscript to the Lansing team's intervention, a September 25, 2006, *New York Times* story by Lisa W. Foderaro opens:

> Lansing and Tryon. They are among the most secure facilities in New York State for girls who have crossed the law—remote state-run institutions located far from New York City, where most of their inmates are from. And to the girls who are sent there, the facilities are notorious.

One prisoner is quoted in the next paragraph as saying, "They restrain you for no reason." The story cites a 134-page report by Human Rights Watch that notes how the girls at these two centers "are being abused and neglected—violently restrained for minor infractions, subjected to sexual harassment and assault, cut off from families, and provided little meaningful rehabilitation."

MANHOOD AND IRRESPONSIBILITY: HETEROSEXUAL NORMATIVITY AND THE CARCERAL APPARATUS

While the Lansing Young Women's Literature Seminar illustrated the inherent limits of institutionally sanctioned "resistance" to institutional containment, the Gossett Manhood and Responsibility Workshop, which was run by me and two male students, revealed other contradictions in the exercise of power—our own.

This project had been pitched as a candid, self-help group encounter session that would explore some of the pathological dimensions of male

Figure 8.1. The author (*left*) with volunteers at the Louis Gossett Residential Center for Boys. Courtesy of the *Cornell Chronicle*.

identity that may have contributed to these young men's incarceration. This was particularly important given that the Gossett facility housed young men under eighteen who had been convicted of felony theft and violent crimes, including sexual assault. We entered the prison with the rather self-righteous idea of introducing some "tough love" through literary exposés of male privilege.

Even though we were prohibited from showing our chosen film, *American Me,* in its entirety, we still included texts such as Luis Rodriguez's gang *testimonio, Always Running* (1994), and Piri Thomas's foundational 1967 underclass urban memoir, *Down These Mean Streets* (1997). The Rodriguez text led to surprisingly candid discussions about the epistemology of violent initiation rights, especially violence-as-membership and violence-as-revenge. After we were corrected by prisoners about the different initiation rites in East Coast gangs such as the Latin Kings, whose members were heavily represented at Gossett, we placed more emphasis on Thomas's gritty tale about his coming-of-age in "El Barrio," or Spanish Harlem, in Manhattan. The text was grossly outdated, but it was nonetheless set in the same neighborhood where many of Gossett's prisoners were born and raised, and therefore was enticing to many of them.

This shift in texts, however, only served to illuminate our complicity in heterosexual normativity within—and without—the carceral apparatus. Having been briefed by a Gossett staff member about a recent incident in which a young male prisoner had been threatened with rape by a group of older prisoners, we were informed that we could not include texts or films that involved overt violence, and definitely not any with graphic scenes of sexual violence. References to nudity and allusions to sex also were forbidden. The word "censorship" was used repeatedly without the least concern that the concept is verboten in the academy under the vainglorious principle of "academic freedom." Because of the prison context and the fact that the prisoners were all minors, we would be required to have all questionable materials approved beforehand, and to have a prison guard on duty at all workshop sessions.

These restrictions notwithstanding, we had some provocative discussion sessions, but even more problematic silences. Though not overtly planned, we failed to discuss the homosocial male-on-male sex scene in *Down These Mean Streets,* even though it occupies a prominent role in the first part of the text. The scene involves a group of Thomas's adolescent friends visiting the apartment of transvestites in search of free marijuana as well as oral and anal sex—and ultimately ends in a gay bashing. Part of our unspoken unease and attendant silence, I believe, arose from the subtle yet clearly mocking attitude some students expressed towards one of our team members, an openly gay Black man. Was this more than a missed opportunity to utilize a teachable moment? Of course it was. Indeed, it was a homophobic cop-out in which we too readily acquiesced to unspoken, but clearly foregrounded, institutional censorship of all things sexual, as well as the homophobic male culture of U.S. prisons.

This silence about homosexuality and homophobia—like the masculinist sexual violence in *American Me,* the film we were prohibited from showing in its entirety—became part of our own institutional complicity in the regimes of power and privilege that we had proposed to challenge by going into prison in the first place. Of such failures, Jones and d'Errico offer yet more incisive observations:

> The principal question that those who conduct prison higher education programs must ask themselves is where, in conforming to or contesting one or another dictate of a prison administration, the program is likely to compromise fatally its own goals and objectives. And this is a question that must not be asked only once, but constantly. (1994: 13)

We certainly asked this question, but less often and much more selectively than Jones and d'Errico demand. In contrast to the exposé that led to the termination of Cornell workshops at Lansing, we failed to challenge the heterosexual normativity of the male prison in our Manhood and Responsibility Workshop. The project was subsequently invited back in various incarnations and iterations for the next four years.

If the Manhood and Responsibility Workshop at Gossett had any success at all, it arose from team member Tim Mitchell's expert introduction of Augusto Boal's "Theater of the Oppressed" paradigm. Based upon the "pedagogy of the oppressed" of his fellow Marxist educator and activist Paulo Freire, Boal's "theater of the oppressed," which he outlines in a 1974 book of the same title, was first developed in Brazil in the 1960s and 1970s as a populist organizing tool to confront a fascist dictatorship and encourage the development of an egalitarian socialist society. The premise of "theater of the oppressed," according to Boal, is that life imitates art, and therefore the ideological role of the arts, especially canonical theatrical genres such as tragedy, romance, and epic, can be readapted to facilitate collective interventions into oppressive situations through role-playing exercises designed to culti-vate critical consciousness. "Theater is a weapon," Boal argues, "a very efficient weapon" (1979: ix).

Pursuant to the development of new theatrical forms to facilitate political consciousness raising experiences, Boal draws from various schools of theater, especially Brechtian-inspired forum theater that creates dissonance while simultaneously offering opportunities for introspection and intervention. More than being merely artistic endeavors, "theater of the oppressed" exercises serve as a site for ideological role-playing and related critique pursuant to revolutionary transformations of society—one localized sphere of conflict at a time. This is achieved, in part, through breaking down the wall between audience and stage so that everyone becomes a "spectactor." The goal is to change passive spectators into "subjects, into actors, transformers of the dramatic action." Boal emphasizes that the "spectactor" "assumes the protagonic role, changes the dramatic action, tries out solutions, discusses plans for changes—in short, trains himself for real action" (122). In order for "spectactors" to produce critical understandings of their material, or objective, realities, however, they must be honest, even when it is painful and renders the participants vulnerable. Thus, the method's many exercises always include a post-performance discussion session. "Theater of the oppressed" also calls on all participants to avoid or identify "magic," or easy, answers that may not have real-world applications.

During the pilot project at Gossett, we used several types of exercises, including "image theater," specifically "image of the word" exercises, which are collective, improvisational body-sculpting events. In this exercise, one or more persons stand at the center of a circle formed by the rest of the group, and group members repeatedly change the frozen motions of the central figure or figures pursuant to the word at play. It is a sort of sculpting with a human being as the clay. The idea is to repeatedly "model"—and thus perform and transform—the word or concept so that the succeeding group discussion can explicate the political and social significance of our individual and group embodied meditations on it. This type of exercise is particularly useful in social settings such as a prison, where prisoners' limited reading and writing skills—or rather, different literacies—impede "normal" classroom learning from the start. In discussing an "image of the word" exercise from a subsequent Gossett workshop after our pilot project, Mitchell notes in his doctoral dissertation:

> It isn't stretching the term "alienation effect" too much to claim that the young men were performing and witnessing their own alienation through the violent images they created. Though Brecht uses these terms to describe techniques and practices that break a theater audience of the habits of empathy and realism in order to awaken critical distance, Boal relies upon such Brechtian techniques to break participants, "spect-actors," of perceptual habits that prevent critical perspective. (2005: 7)

In one such "image of the word" exercise that I helped facilitate, we asked a student to rise and give a form for "power," then subsequently asked another person to amend that image, followed by another, then another, until the "stage" included an ensemble of "spectactors." The body sculptures began with a raised fist, then moved to a gun, mock fighting, a series of handshakes that introduced vernacular culture and a dose of humor, then back to a multiplicity of fists raised in the air interspersed with joined hands. As per "theater of the oppressed" methods, we then sat back down in a circle to collectively explicate the different images and everyone's role in the transformation of our performance of "power." The question of "magic" answers was chief among our topics, as we noted too many easy resolutions, especially the pacifist revisions, in a prison classroom that consisted of students identified by administrators as having "discipline problems."[11]

The apparent value of this otherwise positive group performance was debunked when ex-convict Elvin Johnson, Mitchell's friend and former collaborator in several "theater of the oppressed" workshops at Lorton penitentiary in Virginia, visited the Gossett program for a more pragmatic discussion of some of the same topics we proposed. Johnson, a Black male in his early forties at the time, who had served ten years in prison for a drug-related crime, broke it down in ways neither member of the Cornell team could. When asked by a Gossett prisoner how one could deal with the ever-present threat of violence that resulted from daily challenges of space, such as the stealing of a seat, Johnson noted that you should "just walk away because sooner or later somebody's gonna get 'em if he keeps it up. There's no need for you to fight for the chair because someone else definitely will."[12]

With the guard in the room at all times, conversations never progressed to those unspoken instances where one *did* need to fight. Moreover, even this apparently pacifist solution to overt challenges relied on the surety of violence from others. The irony of prison is that while the panoptic design theoretically eliminates the need for violence to be exerted on prisoner bodies, prisoner survival or relative empowerment always relies upon violence. Johnson's real-world complement to our "theater of the oppressed" exercises illustrated that the collaborative body sculpture of the preceding workshop session did, in fact, include a large amount of "magic." As a counterpoint to the Gossett project's de facto acquiescence to institutional co-optation, Mitchell's expansion of the pilot project to the Austin J. MacCormack Center involved a conflict with prison administrators who were concerned about his role as a "difficultator," the Boalian gadfly who deliberately introduces complications to role-playing scenarios to stimulate critical thinking and problem-solving skills to avoid such "magic." They apparently thought his refusal to assume a judgmental, and thus institutional, demeanor somehow served to glorify violence and drug dealing (Mitchell 2004: 144).

Mitchell has proposed a viable retort to Augusto Boal's skeptical claim that "theater of the oppressed" is impossible in prison since the possibility for revolutionary actions and escape is so remote. Mitchell maintains that "theater of the oppressed" is a viable mechanism for prisoner empowerment. However, our own brief use of this method leads me to an assessment as equally skeptical as Boal's. While many of the graduate students who participated in the Cornell Prison Education

Project continue to write to me about the course's profound impact on their approaches to being organic intellectuals, none of the individual projects were equipped or allowed to conduct the type of social science tracking or testimonial personal reflections of our incarcerated students to even venture a guess on the impact, if any, that our workshop may have had on prisoners' lives. If "theater of the oppressed" is designed to rehearse liberation beyond the merely symbolic, then we failed: none of our prisoner students physically escaped during our workshop, and, moreover, the Gossett prison continues to stand, as does Cornell University. The individual workshops were far too short and ill-equipped to measure the ideological escape of prisoners and facilitators. Even if our goal was simply reform—either of the prisoners or the society that created them and the space to house them—we cannot in good conscience claim success for other reasons: namely, structural exclusions of the classes and groups from which our Cornell students were drawn. In discussing the "Manhood and Responsibility" workshop in his doctoral dissertation, Mitchell concludes:

> The problem is more nuanced when a theatre program like the Gossett
> program is approved by the prison for its positive effects on behavior
> or for promoting "responsibility" as the program name *Manhood and*
> *Responsibility* promises. The challenge of creating and transforming enough
> space for prisoner subjectivity and agency will remain a challenge that
> sits on top of a precarious insider vs. outsider relationship to working in
> prisons. (2005: 36)[13]

In the different yet related context of the Aboriginal prisoner-led prison reform efforts, even Waldram expressed skepticism about the possibilities for success due to institutional bias and the Canadian prison system's lingering colonial function. Regarding the Medea Project, Fraden similarly notes:

> If the final goal of participation in the Medea Project is absolutely utopian
> (and revolutionary)—to create a community that nurtures the best of human
> instincts, liberates creativity, raises critical consciousness, and redistributes
> power—it is not surprising that any account will show the project falling
> short of that goal. (xv)

Left out of both of these discussions, and those in our own classroom, was the nature and degree to which our prison education projects may have enabled the "humane" exercise of imprisonment, the very practice of which we sought to expose and challenge for its essential evil. Following Foucault (1979) and Franklin (1989), Barbara Harlow has eloquently and persuasively argued for the inextricable link between the prison and the contemporary university:

> the prison and the university, while representing "contradictory poles," are also seen to function as complicit parts of the same operational system of dominant state control of dissent and containment of antisystemic challenge. (1992: 12)

On the other hand, few prisoner rights activists or prison educators explore the profound differences and distances between prisoners and university-based activists.

One notable exception is Kenneth McClane, who presents a visceral depiction of this gulf in the epigraph to this chapter. The question is not so much whether or not we are part of the problem or the solution, but what prison work is, and is not, for each person or group doing it in specific historical contexts.

WHAT PRISON WORK IS . . . AND IS NOT

As a sobering counterpoint to the Cornell Prison Education Project's attempt to be accountable to an academic institutional paradigm, as well as personal and political commitments, all of the prison institutions where we taught remain standing, the graduate students obtained academic jobs, the undergraduate continued with a painting career, and I passed my third-year review. Our goal was to help facilitate the deinstitutionalization of prisoners through our workshops and research, albeit with full recognition of the limits and ideologically burdened nature of our interventions. That we pursued this goal by successful negotiations of institutional support is more than merely ironic. After all, how radical could it be if it was done under the auspices of a highly selective and economically prohibitive Ivy League university?

Ruben Navarrette's 1993 memoir, *A Darker Shade of Crimson: Odyssey of a Harvard Chicano*, illustrates the exploitative careerist potential of such institutional "alliances." Navarrette devotes almost half of his memoir to explicating Harvard classmate Jose Razo's armed robbery exploits as the antithesis to his own attempt to deal with alienation, which culminates in a pilgrimage to visit arch-conservative minority pundit Richard Rodriguez and a subsequent parlay of these encounters into a lucrative career as a mainstream newspaper columnist.[14]

The Cornell Prison Education Project, like all prison education projects, must be assessed in relation to this elite institutional context and to other prison "projects" such as Angela Davis's collaborations with George Jackson—which not only involved amorous epistolary exchanges, but revolutionary theoretical meditations that prosecutors allege also included the smuggling of a gun into prison. Several questions emerge. What exactly are we bringing into the prison that will enable prisoner liberation? And what is liberation anyway? Release from prison? Worldwide revolution? Regarding the goals of prison higher education projects, Jones and d'Errico observe:

> Perhaps the most important curricular decision a prison education program can make is to resist the temptation to devise an education appropriate to prisoners. Such an education would be a reflection of, and likely reproduce, the cultural meaning of incarceration. (11)

The successful failures of the Cornell Prison Education Project underscore that it is important to recognize that prison work does not just involve "prisoners," per se, but people who are prisoners. The fact that Jonathan Jackson Jr. withdrew from the course after just two sessions because it was "too close" brought this point home to me. The fact that one of my uncles was incarcerated, released, and reincarcerated during the writing of this book stands as a further reminder of the necessary inadequacy of these proposed acts of "resistance." Even Barbara Harlow, who gave the category "resistance literature" its currency in an eponymous text, disavowed the counterhegemonic valence of the "resistance literature" category that formed part of the title for the course because it was so ideologically inchoate and overstated in even the best of circumstances.

I therefore must conclude that the Cornell Prison Education Project had more benefits for me and the Cornell students who already had the power and privilege to walk out of the institution at the end of the day. Prisoners already knew much about institutions of power, and our interactions with them enabled us to learn from them in ways that further empowered us, not them. This inevitably returns us to the inquiry that animated the course. For even if I still do not know for sure what I was *really* doing there, the most important part of resistance and decolonial transgression is the asking of questions pursuant to taking direct action. Anything else is purely academic. Indeed, anyone and everyone doing prison work becomes part of the carceral exercise of power—even if they never interrogate it. This realization is the point of departure for the real *anti*prison work that must be done.

Pinta/os, Human Rights Regimes, and a New Paradigm for U.S. Prisoner Rights Activism

RELOCATING THE U.S. CARCERAL

As a conclusion to this study, I must return to the U.S. war on terror to map new avenues for intervention into the ever-expanding carceral apparatus. The very draconian measures in the war on terror demand but also enable an alternative, if not altogether new, approach to "prison work" based on human rights regimes. Former president George W. Bush inadvertently provided this impetus on September 7, 2006—five years after the September 11, 2001, attacks—when he confirmed the existence of secret CIA prisons in foreign countries, some of which were legally permitting torture. This revelation, and the U.S. practice of "extraordinary rendition" in which "suspected terrorists" are kidnapped and transported to these offshore prisons, had been an open secret since Seymour Hersh (2004) first reported it in the *New Yorker*. International condemnation over the use of these secret prisons, which Bush and European leaders previously had denied, was compounded by widespread outcries over the widely publicized prisoner abuses at the U.S. Army prisons at Guantanamo Bay and Abu Ghraib, as well as the rapes, murders, and mass executions of civilians by U.S. soldiers in Iraq and Afghanistan. The U.S. war on terror, it is argued, has led to the institutionalization of human rights violations in the United States and abroad.

The intense congressional debate over the proposed 2006 revisions to the U.S. Army Field Manual (*FM 34–52: Intelligence Interrogation*), which governs the use of interrogation techniques, also brought human rights discourses into U.S. incarceration practices. The initial draft of the new manual still did not prohibit practices such as "waterboarding" (near drowning), denial of pain medication, and mock burial, all of which are banned under the Geneva Conventions.[1] It also was to include a secret addendum of other torture techniques until conservative Republican senator John McCain, a POW during the Vietnam War, vociferously opposed it in a July 25, 2005, press release:

> Abuse of prisoners harms—not helps—us in the war on terror, because inevitably these abuses become public. When they do, the cruel actions of a few darken the reputation of our honorable country in the eyes of millions. Mistreatment of our prisoners also endangers U.S. service members who might be captured by the enemy—if not in this war, then in the next. (n.p.)

Although the field manual addendum subsequently was dropped, and some reforms adopted, the final version still does not prohibit all internationally banned interrogation practices and, more importantly, applies only to U.S. Army personnel. Even as President Barack Obama has deemphasized the use of the category "enemy combatant" in favor of civil trials for Guantanamo Bay detainees, his policy shift still promises to preserve the unique treatment of these detainees, who still face the threat of execution. Moreover, President Obama has left intact provisions allowing for "extraordinary rendition," the practice of kidnapping suspected terrorists and transporting them to a third country where no U.S. laws against or restrictions on torture apply.

The rare public revelations of, and dissent over, U.S. penal practices in the war on terror became even more significant in light of the congressional debate that culminated in the 2006 Military Commissions Act, which permits the use of military tribunals to try "enemy combatants." This legislation eliminates habeas corpus for anyone charged and detained for being an "enemy combatant." This constitutional right, a hallmark of modern British and U.S. jurisprudence, permits prisoners to challenge their imprisonment. Former president Bush initiated the Military Commissions Act to subvert the 2005 U.S. Supreme Court ruling in *Hamdi vs. Rumsfeld,* which demanded that detainees in the U.S. war on terror be treated in accordance with Geneva Conventions Article 3, which prohibits "violence to life and person, in particular murder of all kinds, mutilation, cruel treatment and torture" and "outrages upon personal dignity, in particular, humiliating and degrading treatment" (1949).

Such legal debates, compromises, and stratagems to permit torture and extrajudicial detention have, in effect, linked domestic and international standards for the treatment of prisoners. As discussed in the introduction, the U.S. war on crime has made international prisoners of U.S. citizens such as Puerto Rican Jose Padilla. Likewise, the U.S. war on terror has made domestic prisoners of international citizens, almost exclusively Muslim males, some of whom may remain unidentified and held incommunicado in U.S. prisons or its secret detention centers abroad. This application of a legal limbo already had been deployed by immigration detention centers prior to the September 11, 2001, attacks.[2] But the elimination of habeas corpus for U.S. citizens is now formal legal code; worse, it can be cited as a legal precedent, thereby making it potentially applicable to any citizen.

This stripping of both U.S. and non-U.S. citizens of fundamental prisoner rights such as fair trials and protection from torture—which are enshrined in the Geneva Conventions, of which the United States is a signatory—immediately introduces human rights paradigms into the equation. Even Amnesty International, whose Cold War anticommunist bias prevented any critiques of U.S. prisons until the early 1990s, when it began a campaign against the death penalty, has made the link. In its widely publicized 2005 annual report, Amnesty International secretary general Irene Khan described the U.S. prison at Guantanamo Bay as "the gulag of our time." This preliminary intervention of human rights activists has opened a small crack in the heretofore impenetrable myth that U.S. prisons are among the world's "best" (as in Secretary of Defense Donald Rumsfeld's description of Guantanamo Bay concentration camp as a "tropical paradise"). In this context, domestic U.S. prison work can and must be retooled and readapted to deploy human rights theory and practice for "common prisoners" as well as for those who are internationally recognized as "political prisoners." In this new era of the U.S. carceral, the domestic prisoner has become internationalized, and vice versa; our interventions therefore require a new theory of praxis.

PRISONER CLASSIFICATION AS A NEW AND OLD BATTLEGROUND

Prisoner classification has always been a battleground, especially regarding race. Part of the conflict arises from different classification methods used by state and federal agencies.[3] Latina/o prisoners, for instance, are alternately classified as "Hispanic," "White," "Black," "Hispanic: White" and "Hispanic: Non-White." Worse, the U.S. Bureau of Justice Statistics deliberately obfuscates the demographic profile of the U.S. prison population by using different embedded variables from year to year, thus preventing accurate diachronic studies. Examples of these convoluted, incomparable pairings include: "Crime and Justice in the United States and in England and Wales, 1981–96" (October 1998), "Profile of Nonviolent Offenders Exiting State Prisons" (May 2002), and "Crime and Victimization in the Three Largest Metropolitan Areas, 1980–98" (February 2005).

The most politically charged category, however, remains "political prisoner." Officially, the United States has no political prisoners. However, former president Bill Clinton's pardon and release of sixteen Puerto Ricans who had been imprisoned for engaging in insurgent activities to end U.S. colonial domination of Puerto Rico revealed the hypocrisy of such a claim. As noted in the introduction, a decade before Clinton freed these Puerto Rican *independentistas* who had previously been classified as "terrorists"—including those held in "preventative detention" without having actually been convicted of armed insurrection—Ronald Fernandez had succinctly argued that the classification of these prisoners as "terrorist" was a political decision that illuminated, rather than effaced, the fact that they were political prisoners (1994). I further have shown how the provisions of the war on terror—especially extrajudicial detention, extraordinary rendition, and "coercive interrogation"—have exposed a fact that racial minorities have known all along: there were and still are political prisoners in the United States and its neocolonial territories.

The unprecedented exposure of U.S. violations of international laws, combined with the convergence of international prisoners of war with U.S. Latina/os such as José Padilla, confirms an issue that Chicana/o and Latina/o prisoner rights activists have maintained since the nineteenth century: Chicana/o and Latina/o prisoners and incarceration rates must be understood and addressed within an international context. As illustrated in Chapter 1, Modesta Avila's incarceration was a performance of patriarchal privilege that buttressed imperialist occupation and annexation of half of Mexican national territory and the attendant dispossession of Mexican landowners. Other scholars, activists, and prisoners themselves have long argued for the reclassification of Mexican expatriates (e.g., the Magón brothers), Puerto Rican *independentistas* (e.g., Rafael Cancel Miranda), Black nationalists (e.g., Mumia Abu Jamal), and internationalist White prisoners (e.g., Marilyn Buck) as "political prisoners" due the protections and rights delineated in the third Geneva Convention (Geneva Convention Relative to the Treatment of Prisoners of War [1929]). Many of these early campaigns to have domestic prisoners reclassified as international or even political prisoners failed, primarily due to U.S. government stonewalling and the persistent denial of the existence of U.S. political prisoners. But the U.S. government's war on terror has fused old binaries such as local and global "crime," as well as domestic and political prisoners, through catchall terms such as "terrorist" and "enemy combatant." The United States has done so in a clumsy effort to legitimate extrajudicial detainment, torture, and possibly even summary execution.

This new internationalized vocabulary of criminality offers counter-hegemonic opportunities. Indeed, when a U.S. born Puerto Rican, hence a U.S. citizen, can be classified as an "enemy combatant" and held for two years incommunicado without the rights of habeas corpus, and the U.S. Supreme Court can rule, as it did in *Hamdi vs. Rumsfeld* (2005), that a non-U.S. citizen held in the custody of the U.S. military must be afforded both domestic and international rights as delineated in the Geneva Conventions, why can we not reassess the status of all U.S. prisoners within the de facto hybrid domestic/international U.S. criminal and penal system?

In calling for a broader application of the category of "political" imprisonment to enable human rights paradigms in U.S. prison work, I am not naive about the material and subjective conditions in the United States. I know this strategy alone will fail, especially if we are linking prisoner rights to revolutionary critiques of capitalism and U.S. imperialism. The United States, after all, is the world's sole superpower whose people have been sufficiently mystified or mollified into participating in the continued preservation and extension of this empire because of the real and imagined benefits they derive from it. Nor am I insensitive towards the day-to-day struggles of prisoners who rely on appeals to limited but nonetheless tried-and-true domestic civil rights discourses to improve their living conditions and, in some cases, save their lives. The recourse to the U.S. judicial system, however biased and imperfect it may be, is especially important in death penalty cases. Furthermore, I recognize that I am not a prisoner rights lawyer or grassroots activist and thus do not have experience in prisoner rights organizing and litigation.

These caveats notwithstanding, I am nonetheless calling for a refocused approach to what we loosely call "prison work." I propose we readapt the 1960s and 1970s era of prisoner activism, specifically the internationalized methodologies of prisoner rights movements. This move to reclassify domestic prisoners as international political prisoners already is done quite often—but often quite irresponsibly. Joy James offers an important admonition that prisoner rights activists recognize that not all prisoners, especially those who continue to participate in exploitative practices, can claim to be "political prisoners" (2003: 11–14). With this qualification in mind, Alán Eladio Gómez (2006a, 2006b) has noted that prisoner rights movements in the 1960s and 1970s, even those that began as highly localized protests of prison conditions by "common" prisoners, eventually evolved into historical-materialist struggles that not only aligned with internationalist revolutions, but also became part of these revolutionary efforts both inside and outside U.S. prisons. Significantly, Gómez reveals that the U.S. detention facility at Guantanamo Bay was not the first prison designed to facilitate the total physical and psychological breakdown of domestic and international political prisoners. It was the Marion Control Unit in Illinois, which became the heir to Alcatraz after the island prison was closed. In the early 1970s, the Federal Bureau of Prisons transferred "problem prisoners" to Marion "because of their political organizing and activist work in Attica, Leavenworth, McNeil Island, Terre Haute, Soledad, Atlanta, and other prisons" (2006a: 59). Quoting Marion prisoner Eddie Griffin, from a 1977 document published by the National Committee to Support the Marion Brothers and the Task Force on Behavior Control and Human Experimentation of the National Alliance Against Racist and Political Oppression, Gómez adds:

> For inmates, Marion was rumored death: "Whatever existed behind the walls of Marion generated apprehension of a legal form of assassination." (2006a: 59)

Even more disturbing is Gómez's discovery that the Marion prison regime was designed around behavior modification methods taken from those purportedly used against U.S. servicemen taken prisoner during the Korean War. MIT psychology professor Edgar Schein had adapted these for use by staff and senior administrators of the U.S. Bureau of Prisons in a special symposium in 1961. In yet another convergence of educational institutions with prison regimes of control, Bertram Brown, chairman of the National Institute of Mental Health, gave direct encouragement to wardens to "undertake a little experiment of what you can do with Muslims" (Gómez 2006a: 63), then report back for later adaptation to the general prisoner population, especially the political activists relocated to Marion.

After the implementation of these techniques—including forcible administration of psychotropic drugs, isolation and sensory deprivation, arbitrary beatings and sanctions, use of rumors and prisoner snitches, and a selective reward system involving pornography—prisoner organizing coalesced around the immediate need to stop this coordinated use of torture. This activism over prisoner conditions segued into the actualization of broader goals during an era that saw the confluence of third world wars of national liberation, and ethnic and racial minority civil rights movements, as well as more mature anticolonial and even revolutionary struggles within the United States itself. The Black Power Movement, the American Indian Movement (aka AIM), and the ideologically disparate events collectively called "the Chicano Movement" were in full swing at the time. The most important aspect of this era, Gómez notes, is the simultaneous appeal to both domestic (U.S. Congress and various civil rights organizations such as the ACLU, Center for Constitutional Rights, and NAACP) and international bodies—specifically, the United Nations. Through aggressive letter campaigns, prisoners won major concessions from the U.S. Bureau of Prisons by exposing how the Marion prison did not meet the 1957 United Nations' Standard Minimum Rules for the Treatment of Prisoners (2006a: 71). Gómez discusses similar successes by prisoners at Leavenworth Federal Prison, where prisoners also incorporated simultaneous appeals to domestic organizations such as the Black Panthers as well as the Medical Association for Human Rights "that focused on improving medical conditions for prisoners" (Gómez 2006b: 13). Hence, the value of Gómez's archaeology of this important era in the history of the U.S. carceral system, and populist challenges to it, does not arise solely from the prisoners' internationalist politics, but from their international strategy.

It is important to note that the distinction between "internationalist" and "internationalizing" is deliberate yet strategic; the called-for internationalization of U.S. prisoner rights movements through the prism of human rights discourses may not enable prison workers to get beyond reformist civil rights discourses and move towards a truly revolutionary agenda. The latter remains a necessary goal that will require alternative strategies and activities both inside and outside of prison and specific political parties. But there is an immediate pragmatic dimension to the use of human rights discourses that is not inconsistent with the ultimate goal. The appeal to international human rights paradigms and, more importantly, the mobilization of international support can again buttress, if not altogether transform, prison activism: it provides one more tool that will retain a substantial international currency precisely because of the widely exposed excesses of the war on terror. Even capitalist imperialists such as Senator McCain realize that the United States has a human rights "image" problem. The worsening U.S. reputation abroad was compounded by the 2008 revelation that the Canadian government has begun training its immigration civil servants to consider the United States as a country that permits torture.

"THE MOBILIZATION OF SHAME": U.S. PRISON WORK AND THE VOCABULARY OF HUMAN RIGHTS

In discussing what a contemporary Pinta/o human rights praxis might entail, it is important to trace the genealogy of previous uses of human rights discourses by Pinta/os from the early 1970s to the late 1990s. As Gómez has revealed, Chicana/o and broader U.S. prisoner appeals to international bodies and human rights standards as delineated in the United Nations' Universal Declaration of Human Rights (1948), Standard Minimum Rules for the Treatment of Prisoners (1957), and International Convention on the Elimination of All Forms of Racial Discrimination (1969) are not new.[4] Soon after the post–World War II era, when the bulk of the relevant human rights and prisoner treatment documents were created, adopted, or revised, Chicana/o prisoners and prisoner rights activists directly and indirectly appealed to international standards for the treatment of prisoners and for the reclassification of Pinta/os as political prisoners held under colonial occupation. As polemical and problematic as such blanket claims of political status and the attendant use of the internal colonial model may have been, these early prisoner campaigns foregrounded a vocabulary of human rights at a time when institutions for the enforcement of human rights were not yet operationalized. International human rights covenants and institutions such as the United Nations Human Rights Committee did not come into effect until 1976, and did not become a full-fledged human rights movement until the early 1990s.[5] Thomas Risse and Kathryn Sikkink (2002) confirm that

> not until the mid-1980s were all the parts of this structure fully formed and dense—with the increasing number of human rights treaties, institutions, NGOs, increased foundation funding for human rights work—and human rights had become a part of foreign policy of key countries. (31)

Even before the maturation of the human rights movement, the groundbreaking 1976 special issue of the Chicana/o cultural nationalist journal *De Colores*, which was dedicated to Chicana/o prisoners and subtitled "Los Pintos de América," had relocated Pinta/os onto a hemispheric discursive space that enabled them to internationalize Chicana/o incarceration. The cover design by Fernando Peñaloza includes a red, white, and blue watercolor of a perpendicular U.S. flag with the stripes turning into prison bars; behind it stands a Chicano prisoner with a minimalist, pained expression, reaching through the bars, gazing back at the viewer.

The editor's statement, by Anselmo Arellano, proposes the domestic sphere as a site of containment for the always already internationalized Chicana/os who, he notes, are Américanos, or Panamericans:

> Although the central theme of this issue applies to Pintos behind steel bars, it symbolically refers to all Raza who are held captive by the tentacles of monopolistic corporations and other repressive institutions throughout the Americas—North, Central and South. (4)

Figure C1. Cover of *De Colores* 3: 1 (1976), *Los Pintos de América* (special issue).

As noted in the introduction, the terms "Pinto" and "Pinta" are embedded within a critique of U.S. imperialism and global capitalism in the Americas. The domestic and local are simultaneously international and global, and vice versa.

In addition to Ricardo Sánchez's aforementioned "*Tinieblas Pintas Quebradas*: an intro of sorts . . .," poetry by Judy Lucero and other Pinta and Pinto poets, as well as *testimonios* and sociological data on Chicana and Chicano prisoners, *Los Pintos de América* also included a profile of Pinto Eddie Sánchez that adumbrates a potential new era for Pinta/o human rights work today. Eddie Sánchez's story is the epitome of tragedy, but it is not unique: he had been institutionalized since the age of three, when his parents were incarcerated for drug use; placed in a juvenile detention center at age ten after being classified as an "incorrigible"; then incarcerated in an adult penitentiary at age sixteen after being reclassified as a "sophisticated youth"—all without ever having been charged with any crimes. At seventeen he was sent to Vacaville prison in California, the medical facility for the California Department of Corrections. Even though he was repeatedly certified sane by prison psychologists, Vacaville administrators ordered a lobotomy for him as retribution for his activism. To escape the forced surgery/torture, Sánchez wrote a letter to the Secret Service threatening to kill the U.S. president in order to get charged with a federal crime and thus be "saved" by being sent to federal prison. But while he was incarcerated in federal prisons in Springfield, Missouri; Leavenworth, Kansas; and Marion, Illinois, Sánchez was subjected to the behavior modification regimens that Gómez describes. *De Colores* reprinted part of Sánchez's complaints of "inhumane treatment" and legal "torture," including the forcible administration of the drug Anectine:

> The first immediate sensation was a tingling sensation all over my body, like when your foot goes to sleep. The next feeling was a heavy feeling on my chest like somebody had dropped a heavy weight on my chest and all the air rushed out of my body. My eyes closed, but I was not asleep. I could not move any part of my body, and I could not breathe at all. I had heard of the drug before, but knew nothing of what to expect. But I did not think it could be anything like what I was experiencing.
>
> I thought the doctor had messed up and given me the wrong thing, or maybe too much of the right thing. I thought I was dying. I want to say something, to tell him I couldn't breathe. But I could not talk or even move or even open my eyes. Then this doctor starts talking to me. He starts talking about knowing what I'm feeling and that it is not pleasant, but it

was going to happen to me every time I demonstrated bad behavior in the way of violence. I just wanted some air, not no speech about my behavior. I thought, Oh God, this creep is going to kill me sitting here talking to me when he should be giving me air. Finally after what seemed hours (but was only two minutes) he starts to revive me with air from an oxygen tank. (13)

Sánchez's legal strategy involved multiple approaches that sought to expose: (1) de facto criminalization of minority populations; (2) extra-judicial punishment and imprisonment of prisoners; (3) guard use of brutal prison regimens that amounted to unconstitutional "cruel and unusual punishment"; and (4) legally sanctioned and medically supervised uses of torture techniques deemed illegal by international standards.

The American Civil Liberties Union was able to use Sánchez's testimony in successful lawsuits to end the START behavior modification program, but they were never able to save Sánchez from a lifetime of imprisonment.[6] At the time of the publication, Sánchez was facing four life sentences plus seventy additional years of imprisonment for repeatedly assaulting abusive guards, prison officials responsible for administering his torture, and a known informer at Leavenworth used against him as part of the behavior modification program.

Despite this important failure, however, the Sánchez case strategy had important successes in linking U.S. prison standards to emerging international norms for the treatment of prisoners, which led to a provisionally successful lawsuit barring some torture methods. This important linkage between domestic and international incarceration standards was effected through Sánchez's simultaneous appeals for his civil *and* human rights. Concurrent with the dawn of the human rights movement, *De Colores* and the Committee to Free Eddie Sánchez presented Sánchez as the quintessential Pinto: a de facto political prisoner due to the violation of national laws, such as the 1910 Eighth Amendment to the U.S. Constitution outlawing "cruel and unusual punishment," as well as international standards of prisoner treatment, such as the 1948 Universal Declaration of Human Rights, 1957 Standard Minimum Rules for the Treatment of Prisoners, and 1969 International Convention on the Elimination of All Forms of Racial Discrimination.

Other Chicana/o prisoner rights campaigns made similar appeals that linked prison conditions to political persecution. They thus made human rights standards available even for prisoners whose incarceration followed normal domestic legal procedures. This politicization of domestic "common" prisoners coincided with more overtly political prisoner campaigns that also invoked this incipient human rights discourse. These include the National Committee to Free Los Tres, which sought freedom for Chicano activists who had been framed and imprisoned for assaulting an undercover narcotics agent in east Los Angeles in 1973, and the struggle for Los Siete de San Francisco, a campaign to free seven Latinos framed for the murder of an undercover police officer in 1969.[7] Some campaigns were part of multiracial prisoner rights cases, including the rebellions that Gómez documents and others led by the Marxist immigrant rights group CASA (Centro de Acción Social Autónoma/ Center for Autonomous Social Action). On the surface, these 1960s and 1970s prisoner campaigns may appear to be standard grassroots critiques of prejudicial policing, prosecution, and government harassment, which they were. But their importance today, in addition to exposing the long history of racial bias in the U.S. criminal justice system, arises from their implicit and overt invocation of international discourses on human rights that transformed virtually all prisoners in the pre-reform (i.e., pre-1980s) U.S. prison system not into political prisoners, per se, but *internationalized domestic prisoners*.[8]

The category of "political prisoner" in this era anticipated the new classification model developed in the Special International Tribunal on the Human Rights Violations of Political Prisoners/POWs in the USA, held in New York in December 1990. As noted in the introduction, the organizers of the Special International Tribunal sought to expand the use of the term "political prisoner" by arguing that a political prisoner was: (1) someone imprisoned for overtly political activities or (2) someone, including prisoners initially convicted of common crimes, who was subsequently subjected to differential treatment while in prison due to political activism.[9] Pinta/o activism from the 1970s era of prison rebellions appealed to the humanity of all prisoners that used—but did not overstate or overinvest—a claim to the colonial status of Pinta/os and other racial minority and nonminority prisoners. This was not an effacement of their racialized identities, especially given that many prisoners—such as Black liberation fighters and their White allies (such as Marilyn Buck), Puerto Rican *independentistas*, and Chicano nationalists such as Alvaro Hernández Luna—continue to remain in prison precisely because of their cultural nationalist and anticolonial activities. This strategy is apt today. Indeed, in an era in which the U.S. president, the U.S. military, and U.S. law enforcement agencies have freely used the term "enemy combatant" to refer to people suspected of allegedly advocating, without engaging in, armed actions against the U.S. government, troops, or civilian population, activists must be wary of donning the cultural nationalist or internationalist mantle in prisoner solidarity cases. To call a prisoner a "revolutionary" could effectively damn him or her to perpetual incarceration or even execution under PATRIOT Act and related statutes that deprive them of even a minimal recourse to public trials. Even President Obama's proposed shift to civil trials for Guantanamo Bay detainees promises to preserve the special category of "enemy combatant," which carries with it the threat of execution. Past and future anti-imperialist soldiers are always already in danger of being reclassified as "enemy combatants": witness the immediate collapse of the campaign to pardon Assata Shakur after the September 11, 2001, attacks. So we may be able to more successfully use the international language of human rights in tandem with ongoing prison work based on civil rights claims. (Party work, of course, will and must continue pursuant to the ultimate goal.)

I recognize that this redeployment of a vocabulary to "internationalize" domestic prisoners is an old strategy, but it is important to recognize that it has potential new uses now that human rights institutions are becoming mature enough, strong enough, and bold enough to challenge even the United States, as was illustrated by Amnesty International's aforementioned 2005 indictment of the U.S. prison at Guantanamo Bay. This simultaneous appeal to civil and international human rights actually has had preliminary but important successes in delaying the execution of Mumia Abu Jamal, even though it has not resulted in a retrial, pardon, or his release. This multipronged national and international campaign approach was, in fact, the operative model in the groundbreaking Critical Resistance conferences in 1998 (Berkeley), 2001 (New York), and 2003 (New Orleans) that explored and advocated multiple strategies for intervening into all aspects and levels of the U.S. prison-industrial complex. Prison workers really do not have a choice: U.S. prison and broader domestic political conditions in the context of the war on crime/war on terror have become so repressive that this critique of U.S. human rights abuses is not mere political sloganeering, but a reflection of real material conditions. Accordingly, the subjective conditions must also be changed, beginning with our vocabulary and related activities.

The Critical Resistance conferences and ongoing organizing can be seen as part of the human rights movement outlined in Paul Gordon Lauren's *The Evolution of Human Rights: Visions Seen* (2003). Lauren traces the centuries' long efforts to establish and implement human rights protocols, beginning with antiquity, extending through the eras of slavery, world wars, the Holocaust and related Nuremburg war crimes trials, to the establishment of the United Nations and contemporary attempts to apply the litany of standards delineated in dozens of UN conventions, covenants, declarations, treaties, and protocols. Lauren (2003) and Donnelly (2003) note that the human rights movement was consolidated in a collaborative effort between grassroots activists, nongovernmental organizations, academics, and informal groups and organizations involved in specific human rights campaigns throughout the world. This pragmatic approach can be seen as a globalization of the "rebellious lawyering" that Gerald P. Lopez (1992) proposes, and also distinguishes the human rights movement from the state terror movement, which still is primarily a descriptive academic enterprise by social scientists.[10] According to Lauren, human rights theorists and workers have always had the goal of intervening in human rights abuse cases through very practical applications of theory (2003: 233).

Any attempt to deploy human rights discourse in U.S. prison work, however, must be cognizant of the trifurcation of human rights theory and activism into isolationist, anticommunist, and Marxist trajectories. First, with the consolidation of the Universal Declaration of Human Rights in 1948, many countries, including the United States, immediately sought loopholes to subvert these strictures. Their main avenue for subverting enforcement in their own countries has been the national sovereignty clause enshrined in the United Nations Charter in Article 2 (7), which some countries claim protects them from international interventions into their domestic affairs, even in cases of alleged human rights abuses. Other nations have further perverted the UN's stated intent of promoting the rights of minorities in the Declaration of Human Rights and United Nations Charter to claim cultural exceptions. This conflict has emerged in every hemisphere, but has been more fully explored under the rubric of the "Asian values debate." The main trajectories revolve around claims that international statutes such as the Universal Declaration of Human Rights represent an "arrogant universalism" that seeks to impose Western values throughout the world, and equally vociferous retorts that such state resistance to implementation of the human rights paradigm is based on a "morally vacuous relativism" designed to "justify nondemocratic practices" (Bell, Nathan, and Peleg 2001: 4).[11]

The United States also has been one of the most vociferous nations in efforts to blunt enforcement of international human rights and antitorture statutes within its borders or in neocolonial territories such as Puerto Rico. All international treaties, covenants, and declarations must be ratified by two-thirds of the U.S. Congress after they are signed in order for them to become applicable domestic law. To date, the United States has signed, but not ratified, the following international statutes:

- International Covenant on Economic and Social Rights (1976)
- International Covenant on Civil and Political Rights (1976)
- International Convention on the Prevention and Punishment of the Crime of Genocide (1951)
- International Convention on the Elimination of All Forms of Racial Discrimination (1969)
- International Convention on the Elimination of All Forms of Discrimination Against Women (1981)
- International Convention Against Torture and Other Cruel, Inhuman or Degrading Treatment or Punishment (1987)

Furthermore, in May 2002, when former president George W. Bush already had committed to invading Afghanistan and Iraq, and had begun the mass arrests and secret detentions of hundreds of Muslim males under provisions in the first USA PATRIOT Act, the United States took the extraordinary step of removing its signature from the treaty establishing the International Criminal Court, which had been formed in 1998 to oversee the implementation of international laws enshrined in the above international treaties. The United States, in effect, had become a rogue nation. This stratagem notwithstanding, the United States hypocritically deploys various protocols in its unsubstantiated critiques of supposed "human rights violations" in socialist countries, and also to justify its invasions of Serbia, Somalia, Afghanistan, and Iraq. Despite U.S. subterfuge, these human rights standards have become the principal vocabulary for activists in the United States and abroad since the implementation of the U.S. war on terror. The increasing international scrutiny and condemnation of the war, even from U.S. allies, may offer new opportunities for prison work today.

One of the principal strategic mechanisms in the use of human rights and antitorture statutes is the "mobilization of shame": the exposure of specific violations through multimedia avenues and juridical mechanisms such as international courts. The court of public opinion sometimes can be even more powerful.[12]

Human rights scholars and activists have achieved incredible successes since the Declaration of Human Rights in 1948, and these successes—as well as failures—have enabled the mapping of an implementation model.

Thomas Risse and Kathryn Sikkink (2002) identify the various stages that a human rights campaign is likely to follow in what they call a "spiral model." They observe five phases in the targeted state's reaction:

1. Repression
2. Denial
3. Tactical concessions (cosmetic changes)
4. Prescriptive status (i.e., the state's reference to human rights norms to describe its behavior)
5. Rule-consistent behavior

Some might argue that the United States under the Bush and even Obama administrations has been in the midst of a combination of several stages, but definitely not the last. The ongoing efforts to enshrine torture techniques, extrajudicial imprisonment, and outright mass surveillance, harassment, and selective repression within the U.S. legal code correspond to state terror scholar George Lopez's definition of "national security ideology": "the justification for and maintenance of this patterned and persistent violence by government and against real and presumed adversaries [that] rests in the discrete, identifiable, and self-reinforcing dimensions of a shared mindset of governing elites" (1986: 75). Extending Lopez's examination of Latin American dictatorships from the 1960s to the 1980s, I submit that this proto-fascist recourse to such an ideology to justify state terror has transformed the United States into a de facto "terrorist state." The need for a resurgent U.S. human rights movement is thus even more urgent.

TOWARDS A PINTA/O HUMAN RIGHTS PRAXIS

How can these past and ongoing academic and activist interventions into U.S. state terrorism and human rights violations be adapted to mount domestic prisoner campaigns in the era of the war on terror? In this epoch of globalization, the first principle of counterhegemonic organizing revolves around the axiom "think globally, act locally." Risse and Sikkink (2002) argue that "the diffusion of international norms in the human rights area crucially depends on the establishment and the sustainability of networks among domestic and transnational actors who manage to link up with international regimes, to alert Western public opinion and Western governments" (5). They add that "advocacy networks" are needed to coordinate between domestic and international actors seeking to effect a sustainable domestic human rights regime. They have three functions:

1. They put norm-violating states on the international agenda in terms of moral consciousness-raising. In doing so, they also remind liberal states of their own identity as promoters of human rights.
2. They empower and legitimate the claims of domestic opposition groups against norm-violating governments, and they partially protect the physical integrity of such groups from government repression. Thus, they are crucial in mobilizing domestic opposition, social movements, and nongovernmental organizations (NGOs) in target countries.
3. They challenge norm-violating governments by creating a transnational structure pressuring such regimes simultaneously "from above" and "from below" (Brysk 1993). The more these pressures can be sustained, the fewer options are available to political rulers to continue repression. (5)

Although this formulation may appear obvious to veteran activists, this global and local, or "glocal," approach still does not inform all prisoner activism today. This is illustrated by the Innocence Project, a nonprofit legal clinic founded in 1992 at the Benjamin N. Cardozo Law School in New York and dedicated to using new evidence, primarily DNA data, to prove the innocence of unjustly arrested, convicted, and imprisoned people, most of whom are on death row. While this and similar legal clinics and institutes have achieved well-publicized successes that further illuminate inherent injustices in the U.S. criminal justice system, they nonetheless rely on appeals to domestic laws that are even more localized by their statutory contexts. No appeals are made to international bodies, and the Innocence Project takes only cases in which there is clear police or judicial misconduct or error. The prisoners must be "innocent" of the specific crime for which they were charged, convicted, and incarcerated.

This does not mean that this "innocence paradigm" is useless to prisoners who do not deny their "guilt" in crimes that led to their incarceration and inevitably transformed them into victims of inhumane treatment and torture—and thus political or, rather, internationalized domestic prisoners. The legal expertise that such projects bring to bear on gross injustices are exactly the skills that need to be utilized, and expanded, to gain mastery of international statutes that are now at play in all U.S. prisons. We simply cannot rely on U.S. courts as the principal venues for redress, as former president George W. Bush and the U.S. Congress's subversion of *Hamdi vs. Rumsfeld* have revealed. To further illustrate this point, the Innocence Project would not have helped Eddie Sánchez, who was innocent before going to prison but by his own admission was forced to commit, and readily accept guilt, for the crime of threatening the U.S. president in order to escape a torturous lobotomy ordered for his previous resistance to the brutal penitentiary regimes.

If merged with a domestic version of the Amnesty International prisoner campaigns of the 1980s and 1990s, however, I believe the "innocence paradigm" might be effectively adapted to assist prisoners of the war on terror, including "enemy combatants" and potentially all "common" prisoners in the ever more draconian U.S. carceral system. It must be noted, of course, that Amnesty International "prisoner of conscience" campaigns usually function as thinly veiled extensions of Western capitalist hegemony by targeting prisoners in socialist states, with very little attention given to people imprisoned, tortured, and disappeared by Western Hemisphere dictatorships supported by the United States and European colonial powers. Furthermore, it was not until the late 1980s and early 1990s that Amnesty International began to address the death penalty issue in the United States, and these critiques did not coalesce into charges of gross human rights abuses until the 2005 Amnesty International Annual Report cited above. This belated attention to U.S. human rights violations notwithstanding, the Amnesty International "prisoner of conscience" model was highly successful at mobilizing multinational grassroots and institutional (e.g., university and mainstream media) support for select prisoners through its postcard campaigns and attendant teach-ins and public cultural programming that highlighted the given nation's human rights violations. They effectively "mobilized shame" throughout the world to effect local change.

At present, Amnesty International has not embarked on a specific U.S. prisoner of conscience campaign—which raises questions about its lingering links to Western imperialist hegemony—but their tactics have been adopted in important cases that illuminate the possibilities of this global U.S. carceral prisoner approach, specifically the case of imprisoned Black nationalist Mumia Abu Jamal. The multimedia, multi-organizational, multinational campaign to free Jamal has involved the mobilization of Hollywood actors, popular musicians, religious orders, grassroots media, French communists, British antiracists, and a host of community activists who otherwise might never see eye-to-eye. This coalescence has supplemented Jamal's own journalistic efforts to save his life, even though it has yet to result in a new trial, pardon, or even a sanction of the United States for state terror and human rights abuses directly linked to this case (e.g., the conflict of interest involving appeals judges, prejudicial trials, and hostile police-community relations involving the Afro-centric MOVE organization for which Jamal is an advocate).

So, with these constraints in mind, what would a Pinta/o human rights and broader U.S. carceral human rights regimen look like? It might involve all of the above: letter-writing campaigns, postcard blitzes, teach-ins, marches, and other direct actions that continue to be staples of grassroots organizing. It also would further deploy technological innovations such as the Internet and text-messaging in an international context. But in this technologically saturated era, we must be cautious about becoming too dependent on class-exclusive technologies that involve expensive electronic equipment.

Of course, a Pinta/o human rights praxis also must include spectacle. Barbara Harlow has discussed how the popular 1990 Special International Tribunal on the Human Rights Violations of Political Prisoners/POWS in the USA, held at Hunter College in New York, included lawyers, musicians, academics, and activists. This tribunal was highly successful in disseminating a broadened definition of "political prisoners," as previously noted. Part of the success was the presentation of these ideological critiques in populist formats. This was done with even more wide-ranging success during the five-hundred-year anniversary of Christopher Columbus's arrival in the Americas. The Columbus on Trial programming was a series of traveling tribunals that evolved into theatrical, cinematic, poetic, and multimedia satire, farce, and even scatological spectacle—all used to deliver biting critiques of colonialism and its contemporary aftermath. The Chicana/o–Latina/o comedy troupe Culture Clash even produced a highly popular theatrical production and related video skit spoofing "discovery" discourses and their racist subtexts. Significantly, the idea behind the admittedly belated trial was to empower a "people's court" to teach the public about how to understand and address genocide, and, more importantly, to seek redress and prevent future genocide. Even though these locally produced, very loosely coordinated (and sometimes very uncoordinated) "trials" were not binding anywhere but in the court of public opinion, they not only challenged hegemonic discourses, but in many places and among many people, supplanted them.

Such spectacles of shame and satire are not new in prisoner campaigns, as I have shown in my discussion of the multimedia, multigenre, and multinational spectacles surrounding Fred Gómez Carrasco's arrest, imprisonment, and dramatic prison breakout attempt and aftermath (see Chapter 6). And they are never enough in a world where even nonviolent resistance movements inevitably rely on the violence of their enemies to succeed. We cannot afford to forget that Black South African prisoners were not released en masse until the South African apartheid government was militarily defeated on the battlefield by a Black-led, multiracial, multinational coalition of Cuban, Angolan, and Namibian troops in the battle of Cuito Canavale in 1988. The effort to internationalize the domestic U.S. prisoner movement also must involve a variety of alternative strategies and broader goals.

Thus, even as I am calling for a hybrid Pinta/o human rights regimen that already has proven to have some limited successes in their previous incarnations, I must be guarded about suggesting a celebratory prescription for a "new" prisoner rights movement. This multipronged, multimedia mobilization of shame is only one component of a prisoner rights activism that must also involve mass mobilizations and activities not unlike those that occurred during the 1960s and 1970s. The failure to save the life of former gang member Tookie Williams serves as a sobering counterpoint to any overinvestment in the "glocal" mobilization of shame campaign. And despite a vigorous Internet solidarity campaign, Ramsey Muñiz, the former Texas gubernatorial candidate for the Raza Unida Party, is now in his third decade of imprisonment on drug smuggling charges that today would not have yielded even a fraction of the sentence he received. These and other cases confirm that the internationalization of U.S. prison work will not always be successful. Initially, it will rarely work.

Compounding the difficulties in this call to deploy international statutes in a domestic context are governmental stratagems to divest international bodies of their jurisdiction in a given nation. As noted above, the United States withdrew from the treaty establishing the jurisdiction of the International Criminal Court shortly after it began its invasion of Iraq and its expansion of the U.S. prison at Guantanamo Bay. The related Israeli establishment of a team of international lawyers to protect its troops and government officials in the event that they are charged with war crimes for their 2006 invasion of Lebanon or ongoing genocide against Palestinians, including its January 2009 attacks, further suggests that the "glocal" human rights struggle will be difficult. Indeed, both stratagems were undertaken with the explicit intent of preventing the arrest of U.S. and Israeli military and government officials abroad, as was done to former Chilean dictator Augusto Pinochet, who was arrested in 1998 while on vacation in Spain for the violation of the human rights of Spanish citizens. This danger is particularly real for U.S. officials given the practice of "extraordinary rendition," whereby citizens of other countries essentially are kidnapped by U.S. military and paramilitary personnel and shuttled to secret prisons to be tortured.[13]

Hence, while legal machinations and mass mobilizations may not be enough, they are necessary preconditions to renewing and remaking a domestic U.S. prisoner rights movement. The key is to internationalize prisoner campaigns while keeping them local. We must show that the present U.S. carceral system is in fact inhumane and in regular and deliberate violation of international treaties and norms. As the highly successful Critical Resistance activists have shown, there are simultaneous targets, from the massive prison-building boom to the regimens used in the supermax prisons. Another key is to pair the "political" and "politicized" prisoners with the "common" prisoners, as the conditions for both have steadily merged. This, perhaps, is the most important feature of the new U.S. carceral apparatus. The issue at hand is the treatment of human beings, not simply prisoners. Again, the aforementioned recent legislation and the ever-widening scope and ever-increasing draconian nature of the war on crime/war on terror are transforming the entire U.S. prison system, which is making all of those held within it eligible for protections under international statutes. To be sure, it will be a big battle to seek enforcement of international statutes in the United States, and one that will be punctuated by frequent and tragic defeats, most certainly including retribution against activists and prisoners. The challenge, however, is to internationalize the U.S. prisoner. As I have shown in this study, which historicizes Chicana/o criminality while simultaneously mapping counterhegemonic Chicana and Chicano prisoner theories of praxis, a good place to start this battle is with Pintas and Pintos.

Notes

INTRODUCTION

1.   See Donziger 1996 on the war on crime and war on drugs.
2.   This office was closed in September 2003 over concerns about potential civil rights violations, but its provisions migrated into PATRIOT Act II.
3.   This ruling was subverted by the 2006 Military Commissions Act, which eliminated habeas corpus protections for enemy combatants.
4.   See Mauer 1991, 1992, and 2006.
5.   See Gómez 2006a and 2006b on these groups.
6.   Chávez-Ortiz was sentenced to life in prison, which was reduced to twenty years, the minimum for air piracy. See Sweeney 1974.
7.   See Hobsbawm 1965, 1969, and 1973.
8.   Several hundred Pinta/o journals are housed in the University of California Chicana/o Studies Library. Pinta/o writings and drawings are regularly featured in *Lowrider* and *Teen Angel* magazines. Self Help Graphics in east Los Angeles published a catalog of Pinta/o postcards. See Sorell 2005 on Pinta/o handkerchief, or *paño*, art, which also has been collected by the Smithsonian Museum.
9.   See Flores y Escalante 1994, Barker 1953, Webb 1976, and Lipski 2000 for sociolinguistic assessments of Caló. See Rosaura Sánchez 1983 and Arteaga 1994 for transnational theories of Caló. Polkinhorn, Velasco, and Lambert (1986) provide a Caló dictionary.
10. See Foucault 1979 and Rothman 1990.
11. Early twentieth-century positivist criminologist Cesare Lombroso argued that oversized skulls were indicators of a person's predisposition to deviance.
12. See Davis 1998 on the commodification of prisoners.
13. This resistance paradigm is foregrounded in early scholarship on Chicana/o poetry by Ybarra-Frausto (1978) and Chicana/o narrative by Saldívar (1990). See Griswold del Castillo, McKenna, and Yarbro-Bejarano 1991 on this paradigm in contemporary Chicana/o art.
14. See Bentley 1992 on prisoner nomenclature and social structure.
15. Former U.S. Army captain Elam Lynds (1784–1855) institutionalized strict militaristic routines in U.S. prisons, including striped uniforms and prisoner identification numbers designed to eradicate prisoner individuality to facilitate subordination. See Rafter and Stanley 1999: 80–81.
16. See Davis 1981 and 1989.

CHAPTER 1

1. *The People of the State of California vs. Modesta Avila* (1889a: 2). The clothesline reference is recounted by Haas (1995: 1–2), Emmons (1988), Dodson (1988), and Westcott (1990). The actual courtroom transcripts identify only railroad ties and a wagon axle as the obstructions.
2. Ibid., p. 4.
3. All citations are from my transcription of the videotaped inaugural performance on October 10, 1986.
4. See Griswold del Castillo 1990 on the Treaty of Guadalupe-Hidalgo.
5. See Montes and Goldman 2004 for studies on Ruiz de Burton.
6. Sánchez and Pita note that author Frank Norris (1901) referred to the railroad as an "octopus" that sucked the life out of the pastoral rural West (1997: 9). In American romanticist accounts, the railroad is critiqued as a "beast," "black monster," and "hydra-headed monster," while other modernist renditions celebrate the railroad's creation as divine providence.
7. Luana Ross (1998) identifies several Spanish-surnamed female prisoners in her study of Native American women prisoners in nineteenth-century Montana. See Mendoza 2001 and Jennings 2003 for related examinations of nineteenth-century Mexican American prisoner Chipita Rodriguez, the first woman executed in Texas.
8. Haas notes that Avila's brother sold the land to his wife's family while she and other family members were residing on the property. Modesta Avila apparently believed she was still part owner or even the sole owner. See Haas 1995: 90.
9. This headline appeared in the *Santa Ana Weekly Blade*, February 13, 1890 (Haas 1995: 102).
10. According to Haas, Mendelson was the only person who saw the note. He was a merchant who had acquired his wealth by foreclosing on debtors and apparently had designs on the Avila family plot, which he eventually acquired.
11. Haas also mentions this incident (1995: 90).
12. Emmons (1988) and Dodson (1988) note that Avila's child died shortly after birth.
13. George Siposs was a biomedical engineer who claimed credit for inventing the insulin pump. The opera playbill notes that he received musical training in Hungary, Czechoslovakia, Salzburg-Austria, Toronto, and California, where he settled in Costa Mesa.
14. See Barrera 1979 for a materialist assessment of Manifest Destiny.
15. From a personal interview with Joy Neugebauer (2003).
16. This painting by an unknown cast member was provided by Joy Neugeberger.
17. See Emmons 1988: 3. A story and accompanying photo of the reenactment also appeared in the *Los Angeles Times*, August 22, 1988.

CHAPTER 2

1. See Ross 1998, Mirandé 1987, Churchill and Vander Wall 1992 and 2002, Lowe 1996, Takaki 2000, and James 2003 on the role of detention in the racist exercise of state power.
2. From personal interview with Sánchez (1991).
3. Franklin (1989) discusses the rape trope in Black male prisoner writing, and feminist scholars such as Angela Davis (1989) critique it more thoroughly.
4. The tragic mestizo trope undergirds foundational Chicana/o cultural nationalist works such as Rodolfo Gonzales's *I Am Joaquin*/Yo Soy Joaquin (1967) and Alurista's *Floricanto en Aztlán* (1971).
5. In the closing scene of *Lazarrillo de Tormes* the protagonist satirically praises the benevolence of the Church, willfully ignorant of the affair between his wife and the parish priest.
6. See Sommer 1996 on the complex alliances between the metropolitan center and subaltern margins in *testimonio*.
7. This controversy revolves around discrepancies in Rigoberta Menchú's *testimonio* concerning details about the torture and murder of family members, as well as her education. See Arias and Chin 2001 on the Menchú debates.

CHAPTER 3

This chapter is based on previous presentations and publications (Olguín 1989, 1991, 1992, 1993, 2000).

1. "well fuck the law . . . / i'm a city dude, man, / a pachuco from El Paso . . . / i don't believe in god, / society, nor fucking rules . . ." (*HECHIZOspells* [1976a: 81], lines 9, 12–13, 18–19). *HECHIZOspells* subsequently will be referred to as *HS*. All translations are mine unless otherwise indicated.
2. All citations from *Canto y grito mi liberación* correspond to the 1973 second edition, which bears the revised subtitle (. . . *the Liberation of a Chicano Mind* . . .). This text subsequently will be referred to as *CG*.
3. See Ybarra-Frausto 1979, 1984; Pérez-Torres 1995; and Candelaria 1986 on Chicano cultural nationalist poetics.
4. See Moya 1995 and 2002 on Cherríe Moraga's "theory in the flesh."
5. See Hernández Tovar 1984, Mendoza 2001, and Olguín 2003 on Sara Estella Ramirez's poetry.
6. See Gates 1988 and Garner 1983 on the "dozens." See José David Saldívar 2000 on the analogous Latina/o practice known as *cábula* or *choteo*.
7. Sánchez spent nine years in prisons throughout Texas and California for property crimes.
8. See Abu Jamal 1995, Rideau and Wikberg 1992, Martin and Ekland-Olson 1987, and Harlow 1987 and 1992 on the physical abuse and psychological humiliations of U.S. prisoners.

9. See Alarcón 1989 and Cypess 1991 for a genealogy of the Malinche paradigm in Mexican and Mexican American literature.

10. From personal interviews with Sánchez (1980, 1982, 1992a, 1992b).

11. In an interview (1992b), Sánchez recalled that this poem was composed on the occasion of an actual beating of a Chicano Convict by White prison guards similar to the beatings he had suffered. The translation of the Spanish and Caló terms in the last three stanzas are as follows: *también* (also); *del chuco* (El Paso, Texas); *los* (Los Angeles, California); *los perros / lo golpearon* (the dogs [guards] / beat him).

12. The translation of the Pachuco slang present in these stanzas is: "brothers, / when in the course / of pain and motherfuckin' asswhippin's / it becomes imperative to pick up club and switchblade."

13. See Barrera 1979: 184–204 on internal colonialism.

14. The last line of this stanza translates as "to live hurt and anguish and motherfuckin' asswhippin's."

15. The Spanish and Caló translations are: "and my swollen balls / bulging / with the anguish / of my naked soul."

16. These stanzas translate as: "listen to the new song / smile the revolution / beat your drums hard / and burn the nation now . . . / today give birth / to a renewed Aztlán / today give birth / to a social order / and burn out the old motherfuckin' asswhippin's."

17. I first met Sánchez in 1987 at the curbside entrance to a skid row liquor store in downtown Houston, Texas, where he was reciting poetry during a rally organized by La Resistencia and the Revolutionary Communist Party U.S.A.

18. See Howe 1994 and Díaz-Cotto 1996 on the phallocentric premises of Western penology.

CHAPTER 4

This chapter is based on a previously published article (Olguín 1997).

1. See O'Neill 1995 on police reality programming.

2. Some prisoners tattoo teardrops on the cheek to commemorate the number of years in prison, murders committed, or to mourn a loss. See Sanders 1989: 40, 179 n. 4; De Mello 1993: 11; Govenar 1988: 317; and Sorell 2005.

3. Bender (1987) links the epistemological construction of penology to the rise of the proto-bourgeois subject in the eighteenth-century British novel: it pursues a normalized, or re-formed, criminal who is the subject and object of an omnisciently controlled plot.

4. See Butler 1990, Sanders 1989, Mascia-Lees and Sharpe 1992, and De Mello 1993 on tattoos and abjection.

5. See Morín 2005 for statistical analyses of Latina/o and Black prisoners.

6. For further discussion of "differential consciousness," see Sandoval 2000.

7. In the 1980s, the *Houston Chronicle* reported that "dog boys" had been used by prison administrators to entertain elected state officials, an event that later was commemorated with jackets emblazoned with "The Ultimate Hunt." See Mitford 1973, Foucault 1979, Franklin 1989, and Rideau and Wikberg 1992 on forced prisoner labor.

8. Following Chicano prisoner convention, I use "Chicano Convict," "*Convicto*," and "Pinto" interchangeably.

9. Franklin (1989) argues that many White prisoner writers reclaim membership in civil society by using their writing to disavow past criminal activities, which is enabled due to their a priori membership in the racialized hierarchy of U.S. capitalism. In contrast, Black, Chicana/o, and Puerto Rican Convict writers have little choice but to continually synthesize their meditative writings toward a revolutionary theory of praxis because of the impossibility of reintegration into the racially stratified civil society.

10. Tattoo removal methods include scraping, burning, or laser searing, which still leave scars. The most successful way to "remove" a tattoo is to cover it with a new one.

11. Such signs are reported by Salinas, Pardo, and Perez (Mendoza 1993a, 1993b).

12. See Mendoza 1993a, 1993b; Mendoza and Olguín 1995; and Govenar 1988 on Pinto tattoo art.

13. See Foucault 1979 and Franklin 1989 on the prisoner writer as a "bad-man hero."

14. See Govenar 1988, De Mello 1993, and Mendoza 1993a, 1993b on the fabrication of tattoo materials.

15. Alvaro Hernández Luna (1991) notes that Catholic priests smuggled the ink used to make *tatuajes* because they approved of the religious iconography that distinguishes Pinto tattoos.

16. The bilingual neologism *tatuísta* emerged in conversations with Raúl Salinas and other Pintos.

17. Marcos Sánchez-Tranquilino (1991) similarly argues that murals, graffiti art, and stylized *barrio* calligraphy signatures that he identifies as *placas* all function as marks of affirmation and claims to space. See Rubén Martínez 1992 for a complementary discussion of contemporary taggers in Los Angeles.

18. This poem was subsequently republished in 1973 in a Hellcoal Press chapbook entitled *Viaje/Trip*, and in a full collection, *Un Trip Through the Mind Jail y Otras Excursions* (1980), reissued in 2004 by Arte Público Press. See Mendoza 2006 for the poem's publication history.
See Alurista 1971, Acuña 2004, and Muñoz 1989 on the Chicana/o cultural nationalist trope of "Aztlán."

19. These scholars include Tomás Ybarra-Frausto, Joseph Sommers, Lauro Flores, and Antonia Castañeda (then a student), all from the Department of Spanish and Portuguese at the University of Washington. See also Mendoza 2006.

20. Citing a series of *New York Times* articles from 1954, Govenar notes that while this marker served to "reinforce group solidarity" among Pachucos, "for outsiders, particularly Anglo Americans, the 'Pachuco cross' symbolized crime and violence" (1988: 210).

21. Salinas's transformation into an internationalist revolutionary is chronicled by Mendoza (2006) and Gómez (2006a, 2006b).

22. From a personal interview with Raúl Salinas (1994).

23. Raúl Salinas exhibited Mary Jessie Garza's art at Resistencia Books, his bookstore and barrio art gallery. Her work features black-and-white nude photographs covered with brightly colored oil-paint "tattoos" to form what she calls "body altars," a term Salinas also uses for his own *tatuajes*.

24. From a personal interview with Salinas in 1992. See also Mendoza 2006 and Gómez 2006a, 2006b.

25. See Mendoza, Campos, and Maynard 1994 and Mendoza 2006 for Salinas's activities and accomplishments.

26. "La Raza" usually refers to "the People," but the more literal translation of "the Race" also is invoked.

27. See Steward 1990 and Sanders 1989 for the homosocial dimensions of tattoo production. See Sedgewick 1985 on the exchange of women trope.

28. Most of the female figures on Salinas's body were anonymous, except for "Eleanor," the daughter whose name he has spelled across his left collarbone in Old English script (personal interview with Salinas [1994]).

CHAPTER 5

1. See Emma Pérez 1999 on the decolonial imaginary as a gendered and racialized dialectical reinterpretation of salient events in Chicana/o history pursuant to a counterhegemonic praxis.

2. Mutrux and Nakano's screenplay (1992) also informs the one written by Jimmy Santiago Baca for Taylor Hackford's 1993 *Bound by Honor*.

3. See Gutiérrez-Jones 1995 and Fregoso 1993 on the tragic mestizo trope and Malinche paradigm in *American Me*.

4. From personal interview with Salinas (2006).

5. From personal interview with Sánchez (1992b).

6. See Fregoso 1993 on this incident, and Davidson 1974 on the sexual politics in male prisons.

7. Griffith also produced *Martyrs of the Alamo, or the Birth of Texas* (1915), which depicts Mexicans as lecherous villains who threaten democracy and White women's chastity, thereby justifying the Texas war of secession against Mexico.

8. See Keller 1994 on Hollywood genres involving Chicana/os.

9. The citation is quoted in Brauer 2001: 539.

10. According to Fregoso (1993), Olmos revised an earlier script of *American Me* to avoid romantic depictions of the gang leader Santana.

11. See Mazón 1984 on the social significance of the zoot suit riots.

12. The quote is from Olmos's untitled presentation at San Jose State University in 1993.

13. In John Singleton's *Boyz-N-the Hood* (1991), one character refuses to participate in Black-on-Black fratricide and jumps out of a car packed with neighborhood boys on their way to avenge a friend's murder.

14. Sánchez's untitled and undated review is in his personal archives at Stanford University.

15. *Calcos* is Caló for "shoes." Booker T. Washington's *Up From Slavery: An Autobiography* (1901) proposed a self-help, up-by-your-bootstraps approach to Black empowerment that emphasized acquiring vocational skills.

16. In contrast, *Bound by Honor* includes characters who were formerly gang members but now serve as counselors. Allison Anders's *Mi Vida Loca* also features the role of vocational training and counseling as institutional interventions necessary for the reintegration of gang members into mainstream society.

CHAPTER 6

1. Variant B was written by Salomé Gutierrez and recorded by his conjunto group Los Socios on the night of Carrasco's death, August 3, 1974. Original recordings of the four Carrasco *corridos* discussed in this chapter were provided by Gregorio Barrios. All translations of the lyrics are mine.

2. See Morison and Bell 1996 and Ward 1995 on the law and literature movement.

3. "El corrido de Alfredo Carrasco" is also known as "El corrido del Tejas Motel" (Variant A).

4. McKinney (1975) translates line 32 figuratively as "like waiting for water to boil."

5. Ignacio Cuevas, a mentally retarded third Convict who joined Carrasco's plot, survived the shootout. He was later convicted for killing one hostage, despite evidence that she was accidentally shot by police, and executed on May 23, 1991.

6. See Wald 2002 for a teleology of *narco-corridos*.

7. From a personal interview with Cheever (1999).

8. See Hendricks 2000.

9. See Keller 1994 on Mexican and Mexican American stereotypes in Hollywood film.

10. See Rosales 2000 on Gonzalez's political career.

11. This manuscript was provided by Gregorio Barrios.

12. The San Antonio metropolitan area includes more than a dozen inner-city municipalities, including several White majority "cities" within San Antonio that originally incorporated to avoid desegregating their local schools.

13. The daily *San Antonio Express* merged with the evening newspaper, the *San Antonio News*, in the 1970s. The Hearst Corporation purchased

the consolidated *San Antonio Express-News* in 1992, then bought, and promptly closed, its unionized daily competitor, the *San Antonio Light*.

14. From personal interviews with Salinas (1999). Carrasco also was the subject of a book by René Cárdenas Barrios published in Mexico in 1979.

15. The translation of the final three lines is "he died like he lived, / his shoutsong laughing / at social cowardices."

16. The translation of the penultimate line in this excerpt is "a fuckin' state."

17. From a personal interview with Montejano (1993).

18. Barrios's play *¡Carrasco!* (1975) was published in the Chicana/o cultural nationalist journal *Tejidos*.

19. See Broyles-Gonzales 1994 and Valdez 1971 on Teatro Campesino.

20. From a personal interview with Compean (2000).

CHAPTER 7

1. See Camp and Camp 1997: 9–11 on women's incarceration rates.

2. The mandatory sentencing laws implemented by the 1994 Omnibus Crime Bill ensure extended jail time for minor property and drug possession offenses, yet do not include comparable penalties for domestic and sexual abuse.

3. See Bosworth 1999 on women prisoner agency.

4. Chicana prisoner poetry appears in all Pinta/o journals, but the only Chicana prisoner to publish a full collection is New Mexico native Lorri Martinez (1982).

5. See Linda Williams 1992 on gynocritical theory and praxis. See Alcoff 1988 and Moya 1995 on structuralist and poststructuralist feminist theory.

6. Lucero's poems were republished in 1979 by Dexter Fischer.

7. See Cypess 1991 and Alarcón 1989 for diachronic analyses of La Virgen de Guadalupe.

8. See Barrera 1979 and Chabram-Dernersesian 1992 for critiques of the concept of Aztlán.

9. This part of the poem glosses a 1966 ballad, "La copa rota" (The broken glass), by José Feliciano.

   The standard Castilian spelling of the word for "servant" or, in this case, "bartender," is *mozo*, not "moso." In standard Spanish, the command "Sírveme" would be the subjunctive *Sírvame*; "destrosar" would be *destrozar*; "fierve" would be *fiebre*; "obsessión" would be *obsesión*; and "gota a gota" would be *gota por gota*. All translations of Lucero's poetry are mine.

10. The standard spelling of the Spanish word for "humility" is *humildad*.

11. Quetzalcoatl is a Christ-like god of the ancient Aztecs who it is believed will one day return to restore the indigenous people of the Americas to their Precolumbian grandeur. See Lafaye 1985.

12. The standard first-person singular conjugation of the verb "to want" is *quiero*, which Lucero spells phonetically as "quero."

CHAPTER 8

1. Raúl Salinas's "Xicanindio" identity emphasizes Chicana/o indigenous spirituality and historical materialist analysis.
2. This poem is in Salinas's *Un Trip Through the Mind Jail* (1999). See Mendoza 2003 for an explication of this poem.
3. This chapter is informed by a panel I chaired at the first Critical Resistance conference at the University of California at Berkeley in 1998, "Teaching Prison/Prison Teaching," which included course participants Ami Ongiri, Eliza Rodriguez y Gibson, and Annette Portillo.
4. See Schroeder 1996 and Bayliss 2003 on prison education and recidivism rates.
5. Warner (1998) examines the discursive and policy dimensions of refusing to view prisoners as people, which he suggests is a contemporary secular analogue to sixteenth-century debates on whether or not Natives in the Americas had "souls."
6. Cited from the Web site of the National Service Learning Clearinghouse.
7. See Titlebaum et al. 2004.
8. From a personal conversation in 1996.
9. My use of "mixed-blood" and "interracial" corresponds with student self-identifications. These students included offspring of "interracial" White-Mexican marriages, as well as "mixed-blood" offspring of Cherokee, White, and Jewish ancestors.
10. Following the 1996 pilot project, Tim Mitchell expanded the Gossett project and established a companion program at the nearby Austin J. MacCormack (Secure) Residential Center. Both projects continued until 2000.
11. During our initial visit with Gossett staff we pitched our project as being designed to reach prisoners whom standard prison programming failed to "reach." We pledged to work with the prisoners considered to be the "worst," believing (correctly, as it turned out) that institutional racism would result in a class composed of primarily minority prisoners.
12. From a visit to Gossett in fall 1996.
13. See Mitchell 2001 on the ideological negotiations in prison theater programs.
14. Navarrette now works as a columnist for the *San Diego Union-Tribune*.

CONCLUSION

This chapter is based on a previously published article (Olguín 2008).

1. There are four Geneva Conventions: the Geneva Convention for the Amelioration of the Condition of the Wounded and Sick in Armed Forces in the Field (Geneva, 1864); the Geneva Convention for the Amelioration of the Condition of Wounded, Sick and Shipwrecked Members of Armed

Forces at Sea (The Hague, 1907); the Geneva Convention Relative to the Treatment of Prisoners of War (Geneva, 1929); and the Geneva Convention Relative to the Protection of Civilian Persons in Time of War (The Hague, 1949). These resulted in international treaties and were followed by three amendments, subsequently called "Protocols" (1977, 1977, 2005), governing the treatment of civilians.

2. See David M. Hernández 2006 on immigrant detention centers.

3. See Morín 2005 and 2006 on Latina/o incarceration rates.

4. These and related documents have been reissued by the Center for the Study of Human Rights at Columbia University (2001).

5. Andrew Nathan is a scholar-activist in the human rights movement who has taught advanced seminars on human rights theory and practice through the National Endowment for the Humanities. I participated in one of these seminars at Columbia University in 2004.

6. Gómez (2006a, 2006b) notes that START is an acronym for "Special Training and Rehabilitation Training."

7. See Chávez 2002 and García 1995 on Los Tres. See Heins 1972 on Los Siete. See Acuña 2004 and Muñoz 1989 on other Chicana/o prisoner campaigns.

8. See Martin and Ekland-Olson 1987 for a case study of the 1970s and 1980s prison reform movement.

9. See Deutsch and Susler 1990 on political prisoner categories in the United States.

10. The state terror movement is a social science initiative that examines governments, including the United States, as the potential source of terrorism against its own population in the form of political persecution, such as the COINTEL program, anticommunist pogroms, and discriminatory policing practices. See Stohl and Lopez 1984, Lopez 1986, and Homer 1984.

11. See Bauer and Bell 1999 on the Asian values debate.

12. See Drinan 2001 on the "mobilization of shame" paradigm.

13. The susceptibility of U.S. troops and paramilitary personnel to international and foreign prosecution was illustrated by the Italian government's 2006 charges against twelve CIA agents for kidnapping, rendition, and torture of a Muslim man from Italy.

Bibliography

Abbott, Jack Henry. 1981. *In the Belly of the Beast: Letters from Prison.* New York: Vintage.

Abu Jamal, Mumia. 1995. *Live From Death Row.* Reading, PA: Addison-Wesley.

Acosta, Oscar Z. 1989. *The Revolt of the Cockroach People.* New York: Vintage.

Acuña, Rodolfo. 2004. *Occupied America: A History of Chicanos.* 4th ed. New York: Pearson Longman.

Aidi, Hisham. 2002. "Urban Islam and the War on Terror: Amidst Media Sensationalism over the Capture of American-born Jihadis, Few Are Examining Why Urban Youth of Color Increasingly Gravitate Toward Islam." *Colorlines* (Winter). Online edition, n.p.

Alarcón, Norma. 1989. "*Traddutora, Traditora*: A Paradigmatic Figure of Chicana Feminism." *Cultural Critique* 13 (Fall): 57–87.

———. 1990. "Chicana Feminism: In the Tracks of the Native Woman." *Cultural Studies* 4, no. 3: 248–256.

Alcoff, Linda. 1988. "Cultural Feminism versus Post-structuralism: The Identity Crisis in Feminist Theory." *Signs* 13, no. 3: 405–436.

Aldama, Frederick Luis. 2002. "Penalizing Chicano/a Bodies in Edward J. Olmos's *American Me.*" *Decolonial Voices: Chicana and Chicano Cultural Studies in the 21st Century*, 78–97. Ed. Arturo Aldama and Naomi Quiñonez. Bloomington: Indiana UP.

Alejandro, César, dir. 1996. *Down for the Barrio.* Spectrum Entertainment.

Althusser, Louis. 1971. *Lenin and Philosophy, and Other Essays.* New York: Monthly Review Press.

Alurista. *Floricanto en Aztlán.* 1971. Los Angeles: University of California, Los Angeles, Chicano Studies Center.

America's Most Wanted. 1994. NBC, San Francisco. 27 May.

Amnesty International. 2005. *Amnesty International 2005 Report: The State of the World's Human Rights.* London: Amnesty International Publications.

Anders, Allison. 1993. *Mi Vida Loca.* HBO.

Angelou, Maya. 1983. *I Know Why the Caged Bird Sings.* New York: Bantam.

Anonymous. 2001. *La vida de Lazarrillo de Tormes.* New York: Dover.

Anzaldúa, Gloria. 1987. *Borderlands/La Frontera: The New Mestiza.* San Francisco: Aunt Lute.

Arellano, Anselmo. 1976. "Introduction." *De Colores* 3, no. 1: 4.

Arias, Arturo, and Elizabeth Chin, eds. 2001. *The Rigoberta Menchú Controversy*. Minneapolis: University of Minnesota Press.

Armas, José E. 1973. "Memoriam: Poems of Judy A. Lucero." *De Colores* 1, no. 1 (Winter): 71.

Arteaga, Alfred. 1994. "An Other Tongue." *An Other Tongue: Nation and Ethnicity in the Linguistic Borderlands*, 9–33. Ed. Alfred Arteaga. Durham, NC: Duke UP.

Baca, Jimmy Santiago. 1979. *Immigrants in Our Own Land*. Baton Rouge: LSU Press.

———. 1981. *Swords of Darkness*. San Jose, CA: Mango.

———. 1982. *What's Happening*. Willimantic, CT: Curbstone.

———. 1986. *Poems Taken from My Yard*. Fulton, MO: Timberline.

———. 1987. *Martín & Meditations on the South Valley*. New York: New Directions.

———. 1989. *Black Mesa Poems*. New York: New Directions.

———. 1990. *Immigrants in Our Own Land and Selected Early Poems*. New York: New Directions.

———. 1992. *Working in the Dark: Reflections of a Poet of the Barrio*. Santa Fe, NM: Red Crane Books.

———. 1993. *Bound by Honor ("Blood In, Blood Out")*. Script. Hollywood Pictures.

———. 2001a. *Healing Earthquakes: A Love Story in Poems*. New York: Grove.

———. 2001b. *A Place to Stand: The Making of a Poet*. New York: Grove.

———. 2001c. *Set This Book on Fire!* Mena, AR: Cedar Hill Publications.

———. 2002. *C-Train (Dream Boy's Story) and Thirteen Mexicans*. New York: Grove.

———. 2004. *The Importance of a Piece of Paper*. New York: Grove.

———. 2004. *Winter Poems Along the Rio Grande*. New York: New Directions.

Bakhtin, Mikhail Mikhailovich. 1981. *The Dialogic Imagination: Four Essays*. Trans. Caryl Emerson and Michael Holquist. Austin: University of Texas Press.

Barker, George Carpenter. 1953. *Pachuco: An American-Spanish Argot and Its Social Functions in Tucson, Arizona*. Tucson: University of Arizona Press.

Barrera, Mario. 1979. *Race and Class in the Southwest: A Theory of Racial Inequality*. South Bend, IN: University of Notre Dame Press.

Barrios, Gregorio. 1975. *¡Carrasco!*. *Tejidos* 2: 8 *(invierno)*: 29–38.

———. 2001a. "Diary Details Carrasco's Early Start on Life of Crime." *San Antonio Express-News*. Sunday, July 22, pp. G1, G6.

———. 2001b. "The Outlaw King: The Sound and the Fury of Fred Gomez Carrasco." *San Antonio Express-News*. Sunday, July 22, p. G1.

———. 2004. Personal interview. San Antonio, Texas.

Bauer, Joanne R., and Daniel A. Bell. 1999. *The East Asian Challenge for Human Rights*. Cambridge: Cambridge UP.

Baum, L. Frank. 1996. *The Wizard of Oz*. New York: North-South Books.

Bayliss, Phil. 2003. "Learning Behind Bars: Time to Liberate Prison Education." *Studies in the Education of Adults* 35, no. 2 (Autumn): 157–172.

Bell, Lynda S., Andrew J. Nathan, and Ilan Peleg, eds. 2001. "Introduction: Culture and Human Rights." *Negotiating Cultural and Human Rights*, 3–20. Ed. Lynda S. Bell, Andrew J. Nathan, and Ilan Peleg. New York: Columbia UP.

Bender, John. 1987. *Imagining the Penitentiary: Fiction and the Architecture of Mind in Eighteenth-Century England*. Chicago: University of Chicago Press.

Bentley, William K. 1992. *Prison Slang: Words and Expressions Depicting Life Behind Bars*. Jefferson, NC: McFarland and Company.

Beverley, John. 1996. "The Margin at the Center: On *Testimonio*." *The Real Thing: Testimonial Discourse and Latin America*, 23–41. Ed. Georg Gugelberger. Durham, NC: Duke UP.

Bhabha, Homi. 1984. "Of Mimicry and Men: The Ambivalence of Colonial Discourse." *October* 28: 125–133.

———. 2007. *The Location of Culture*. London: Routledge.

Boal, Augusto. 1979. *Theater of the Oppressed*. Trans. Charles A. McBride and Maria-Odilia Leal McBride. New York: Urizen Books.

Bordieu, Pierre. 1985. "The Market of Symbolic Goods." *Poetics* 14: 13–44.

———. 1990. *The Logic of Practice*. Stanford, CA: Stanford UP.

Bosworth, Mary. 1999. *Engendering Resistance: Agency and Power in Women's Prisons*. Aldershot: Ashgate.

Brady, Mary Pat. 2002. *Extinct Lands, Temporal Geographies: Chicana Literature and the Urgency of Space*. Durham: Duke UP.

Brauer, Stephen. 2001. "An Aesthetic of Crime." *American Quarterly* 53, no. 3 (September): 535–547.

Brotherton, David, and Luis Barrios. 2004. *The Almighty Latin King and Queen Nation: Street Politics and the Transformation of a New York City Gang*. New York: Columbia UP.

Brown, Monica. 2002. *Gang Nation: Delinquent Citizens in Puerto Rican, Chicano, and Chicana Narratives*. Minneapolis: University of Minnesota Press.

Broyles-Gonzalez, Yolanda. 1994. *El Teatro Campesino: Theater in the Chicano Movement*. Austin: University of Texas Press.

Bruce-Novoa, Juan. 1980. *Chicano Authors: Inquiry By Interview*. Austin: University of Texas Press.

———. 1982. *Chicano Poetry: A Response to Chaos*. Austin: University of Texas Press.

Bruchac, Joseph. 1987. "Breaking Out With the Pen." *A Gift of Tongues: Critical Challenges to Contemporary American Poetry*, 286–294. Ed. Marie Harris and Kathleen Agüero. Athens: University of Georgia Press.

Butler, Judith. 1990. *Gender Trouble: Feminism and the Subversion of Identity*. New York: Routledge.

California State Legislature. 1974. "Executive Session Senate Subcommittee on Civil Disorder: Gang Violence in Penal Institutions." Los Angeles, March 15.

Camp, Camille Graham, and George M. Camp, eds. 1977. *The Corrections Yearbook, 1997*. South Salem, NY: Criminal Justice Institute.

Canclini, Nestor Garcia. 1989. *Hybrid Cultures: Strategies for Entering and Leaving Modernity*. Minneapolis: University of Minnesota Press.

Candelaria, Cordelia. 1986. *Chicano Poetry: A Critical Introduction*. Westport, CT: Greenwood.

Canfield, Rob. 1994. "*Orale Joaquin*: Arresting the Dissemination of Violence in American Me." *Journal of Popular Film* 2, no. 2: 60–68.

Cárdenas Barrios, René. 1979. *La guerra de los narcotráficos: Once días de angustia*. Mexico: Editorial Universo.

Case, Patricia, and David Fasenfest. 2004. "Expectations for Opportunities Following Prison Education: A Discussion of Race and Gender." *Journal of Correctional Education* 55, no. 1 (March): 24–39.

Castillo, Pedro, and Albert Camarillo. 1973. *Furia y muerte: Los bandidos Chicanos*. Los Angeles: UCLA Chicano Studies Research Center Publications.

Cervantes, Lorna Dee. 1981. *Emplumada*. Pittsburgh: University of Pittsburgh Press.

Chabram-Dernersesian, Angie. 1992. "I Throw Punches for My Race, But I Don't Want to Be a Man: Writing Us-Chica-nos (Girl, Us)/Chicanas into the Movement Script." In *Cultural Studies*, 81–95. Ed. Lawrence Grossberg, Cary Nelson, and Paula A. Treichler. New York: Routledge.

———. 1999. "Introduction: Chicana/o Latina/o Cultural Studies: Transnational and Transdisciplinary Movements." *Cultural Studies* 13, no. 2: 173–194.

Chávez, Ernesto. 2002. *"Mi Raza Primero!" Nationalism, Identity and Insurgency in the Chicano Movement in Los Angeles, 1966–1978*. Berkeley: University of California Press.

Cheever, Cece. 1999. Personal interview. San Antonio, TX.

Chow, Rey. 1995. *Primitive Passions: Visuality, Sexuality, Ethnography, and Contemporary Chinese Cinema*. New York: Columbia UP.

Churchill, Ward, and Jim Vander Wall. 1992. *Cages of Steel: The Politics of Imprisonment in the United States*. Washington, DC: Maisonneuve.

———. 2002. *Agents of Repression: The FBI's Secret Wars Against the Black Panther Party and the American Indian Movement*. Boston: South End.

———. Cleaver, Eldridge. 1968. *Soul on Ice*. New York: Dell.

Collins, Robert E., dir. *Walk Proud*. 1979. Universal Pictures.

Committee to Free Eddie Sánchez. 1976. "The Case of Eddie Sánchez." *De Colores* 3, no. 1: 12–16.

Compean, Mario. 2000. Personal interview. Portland, OR.

Conquistadores, Los. 1974. "El trágico fin de Carrasco." Self-recorded and produced.

COPS. 1993. Executive producers John Landley and Malcolm Barbour. FOX. KTVU, San Francisco. 29 May.

Cypess, Sandra Messinger. 1991. *La Malinche in Mexican Literature: From History to Myth*. Austin: University of Texas Press.

Davidson, Howard S. 1997. "Political Processes in Prison Education: A History." *Journal of Correctional Education* 48, no. 3 (September): 136–141.

Davidson, R. Theodore. 1974. *Chicano Prisoners: The Key to San Quentin*. New York: Holt, Rinehart and Winston.

Davis, Angela Yvonne. 1971. "Letter to Ericka Huggins." *If They Come in the Morning: Voices of Resistance*, 107–112. Ed. Angela Y. Davis. New York: The Third Press.

———. 1981. *Women, Race and Class*. New York: Random House.

———. 1989. "We Do Not Consent: Violence Against Women in a Racist Society." *Women, Culture and Politics*, 35–52. New York: Random House.

———. 1998. "Masked Racism: Reflections on the Prison Industrial Complex." *Color Lines* 1, 2 (Fall): 1–4.

———. 2005. *Abolition Democracy: Prisons, Democracy and Empire*. New York: Seven Stories Press.

De Mello, Margo. 1993. "The Convict Body: Tattooing Among Male American Prisoners." *Anthropology Today* 9, no. 6 (December): 11–13.

Deutsch, Michael E., and Jan Susler. 1990. "Political Prisoners in the United States: The Hidden Reality." *Social Justice* 18, no. 3.

Deveaux, Monique. 1996. "Feminism and Empowerment: A Critical Reading of Foucault." In *Feminist Interpretations of Michel Foucault*, 211–238. Ed. Susan J. Hekman. University Park: Pennsylvania State UP.

Diawara, Manthia. 1993. "Black Spectatorship: Problems of Identification and Resistance." *Black Cinema*, 211–220. Ed. Manthia Diawara. New York: Routledge.

Díaz-Cotto, Juanita. 1996. *Gender, Ethnicity, and the State: Latina and Latino Prison Politics*. Albany: State University of New York Press.

———. 2006. *Chicana Lives and Criminal Justice: Voices from El Barrio*. Austin: University of Texas Press.

Dodson, Marcida. 1988. "Locomotives, Laundry and Legality." *Orange County Times*, Oct. 16, p. 61.

Donnelly, Jack. 2003. *Universal Human Rights in Theory and Practice*. Ithaca, NY: Cornell UP.

Donziger, Steven, ed. 1996. *The Real War on Crime: The Report of the National Criminal Justice Commission*. New York: Harper.

Dowling, Claudia Glenn, and Evelyn Atwood. 1998. "Babies Behind Bars: An Exposé in Pictures." *Life* (October): 76–90.

Drinan, Robert F. 2001. *The Mobilization of Shame: A World View of Human Rights*. New Haven, CT: Yale UP.

Emmons, Steve. 1988. "Act of Defiance Stops Them in Their Tracks." *Orange County Register*, Aug. 22, p. 3.

Ericson, David H. 1989. "Prison Literature and the Question of Genre: The Case of Raúl Salinas." Master's thesis, University of Texas at Austin.

Espinosa, Rudy. 1970. "A Word Para Los Pintos." *El Pocho Che* 1, no. 3, special issue: *El Pinto (Pocho) Che* (December): 57–58.

Estelle, Ted. N.d. *A Forgotten Time Remembered.* Self-published. N.p.

Euripides. *Medea.* 1993. Trans. Rex Warner. New York: Dover.

Fanon, Franz. 1982. *The Wretched of the Earth.* Trans. Constance Farrington. Harmondworth: Penguin.

Feliciano, José. 1966. "La Copa Rota."

Fernandez, Ronald. 1994. *Prisoners of Colonialism: The Struggle for Justice in Puerto Rico.* New York: Common Courage Press.

Fischer, Dexter, ed. 1979. *The Third Woman: Minority Women Writers of the United States.* Boston: Houghton Mifflin.

Flores-Ortiz, Yvette G. 1995a. "Pintas: Policy Implications of Chicana Inmates." Conference presentation, National Association for Chicana/o Studies, Spokane, WA, March 31.

———. 1995b. "Latinas in Prison: A Research Project." Conference presentation, National Association for Chicana/o Studies, Spokane, WA, April 1.

Flores y Escalante, Jesús. 1994. *Morralla del Caló Mexicano.* Distrito Federal: Asociación Mexicana de Estudios Fonográficos.

Foderaro, Lisa W. 2006. "In New York, a Report Details Abuse and Neglect at 2 State-Run Centers for Girls." *New York Times,* September 25, p. A25.

Foucault, Michel. 1979. *Discipline and Punish: The Birth of the Prison.* Trans. Alan Sheridan. New York: Vintage.

Fraden, Rena. 2001. *Imagining Medea: Rhodessa Jones and the Theater for Incarcerated Women.* Chapel Hill: University of North Carolina Press.

Franklin, H. Bruce. 1989. *Prison Literature in America: The Victim as Criminal and Artist.* Expanded edition. New York: Oxford UP.

Freedman, Dan. 2002. "Prison System Could Be Terror Breeding Ground." *San Antonio Express-News,* June 30, pp. A19, A27.

Fregoso, Rosalinda. 1993. *The Bronze Screen: Chicana and Chicano Film Culture.* Minneapolis: University of Minnesota Press.

Freire, Paulo. 1972. *Pedagogy of the Oppressed.* New York: Continuum.

Friedkin, William. 1971. *The French Connection.* 20th Century Fox.

Garcez, Daniel, and Salomé Gutierrez. 1974. "El corrido de Alfredo Carrasco." Del Bravo Records.

García, Mario T. 1995. *Memories of Chicano History: The Life of Bert Corona.* Berkeley: University of California Press.

Garner, Thurmon. 1983. "Playing the Dozens: Folklore as Strategies for Living." *Quarterly Journal of Speech* 69: 47–57.

Garza-Falcón, Leticia. 1998. *Gente Decente: A Borderlands Response to the Rhetoric of Dominance.* Austin: University of Texas Press.

Gates, Henry Louis, Jr. 1988. *The Signifying Monkey: A Theory of African American Literary Criticism.* New York: Oxford UP.

Goetz, Jill. 1997. "Students Lead Workshops at Area Prisons on Minority Writers and Artists." *Cornell Chronicle* (January 16): 1.

Gómez, Alán. 2006a. "'*Nuestras vidas corren casi paralelas*': Aztlán, *Independentistas*, and the Prison Rebellions in Leavenworth, 1969–1972." Conference presentation, *Behind Bars: Latinos and Prisons*, Chicago, October 21.

———. 2006b. "Resisting Living Death at Marion Federal Penitentiary, 1972." *Radical History Review* 96 (Fall): 58–86.

Gonzales, Rodolfo "Corky." 1972 [1967]. *I Am Joaquin/Yo soy Joaquin*. New York: Bantam.

Gonzalez, Henry B. 1974. "Gonzalez: Carrasco Evil Symbol." *San Antonio Express*, Aug. 10, p. A1.

Govenar, Alan. 1988. "The Variable Context of Chicano Tattooing." *Marks of Civilization: Artistic Transformations of the Human Body*, 309–318. Ed. Arnold Rubin. Los Angeles: UCLA Museum of Cultural History.

Gramsci, Antonio. 1971. *Selections from the Prison Notebooks of Antonio Gramsci*. Ed. and trans. Quintin Hoare and Geoffrey Nowell Smith. New York: International Publishers.

Granjeat, Yves-Charles. 1986. "Ricardo Sánchez: The Poetics of Liberation." *European Perspectives on Hispanic Literature of the United States*, 33–43. Ed. Genvieve Fabre. Houston: Arte Público.

Griffith, Beatrice. 1948. *American Me*. Boston: Houghton Mifflin.

Griffith, D. W., dir. 1915. *Birth of a Nation (The Clansman)*. Image Entertainment.

Griffith, D. W., prod., and William Christy Cabanne, dir. 1915. *Martyrs of the Alamo, or the Birth of Texas*. The Windmill Group.

Griswold del Castillo, Richard. 1990. *The Treaty of Guadalupe-Hidalgo: A Legacy of Conflict*. Norman: University of Oklahoma Press.

Griswold del Castillo, Richard, Teresa McKenna, and Yvonne Yarbro-Bejarano. 1991. *CARA—Chicano Art: From Resistance to Affirmation, 1965–1985*. Los Angeles: UCLA Museum of Art.

Gutierrez, Salomé. 1974. "*La muerte de* Fred Gomez Carrasco." Del Bravo Records.

Gutierrez, Salomé, and Los Socios. 1973. "*El corrido de* Alfredo Gómez Carrasco." Del Bravo Records.

Gutiérrez-Jones, Carl. 1995. *Rethinking the Borderlands: Between Chicano Culture and Legal Discourse*. Berkeley: University of California Press.

Haas, Lisbeth. 1995. *Conquests and Historical Identities in California, 1769–1936*. Berkeley: University of California Press.

Hackford, Taylor, dir. 1993. *Bound by Honor*. Buena Vista Pictures.

Hall, Stuart. 1980. "Encoding/Decoding." *Culture, Media, Language*, 128–138. Ed. Stuart Hall, Dorothy Hobson, Andrew Lowe, and Paul Willis. London: Hutchinson.

———. 1981. "The Whites of their Eyes: Racist Ideologies and the Media." *Silver Linings*. Ed. George Bridges and Rosalind Brunt. London: Lawrence and Wishart.

———. 1989. "Cultural Identity and Cinematic Representation." *Framework* 36: 68–81.

Hall, Stuart, Chas Critcher, Tony Jefferson, John Clark, and Brian Roberts. 1978. "The Social Production of News." *Policing the Crisis: Mugging, the State, and Law and Order*, 53–60. Ed. Stuart Hall, Chas Critcher, Tony Jefferson, John Clark, and Brian Roberts. Basingstoke: MacMillan Education.

Hames-Garcia, Michael. 2004. *Fugitive Thought: Prison Movements, Race, and the Meaning of Justice*. Minneapolis: University of Minnesota Press.

Harlow, Barbara. 1987. *Resistance Literature*. New York: Methuen.

———. 1991. "Sites of Struggle: Immigration, Deportation, Prison, and Exile." *Criticism in the Borderlands: Studies in Chicano Literature, Culture, and Ideology*. Ed. Héctor Calderón and José David Saldívar, 149–163. Durham, NC: Duke UP.

———. 1992. *Barred: Women, Writing, and Political Detention*. London: Wesleyan UP.

Harper, William T. 2004. *Eleven Days in Hell: The 1974 Carrasco Prison Siege in Huntsville, Texas*. Denton: University of North Texas Press.

Hawthorne, Nathaniel. 1981. *The Scarlet Letter*. New York: Bantam.

Heins, Marjorie. 1972. *Strictly Ghetto Property: The Story of Los Siete de la Raza*. Berkeley, CA: Ramparts Press.

Hendricks, Bill. 2000. "Crimes of the Century." *San Antonio Express-News*, Sunday, January 16, p. 45N.

Hernández, David M. 2006. "Pursuant to Deportation: Immigrant Detention and Latinos." Conference presentation, *Behind Bars: Latinos and Prisons*, Chicago, October 20.

Hernández Tovar, Inés. 1984. "Sara Estela Ramirez: The Early Twentieth Century Texas-Mexican Poet." Ph.D. dissertation, University of Houston.

Hernández Luna, Alvaro. 1991. "*Testimonio Pintao: La vida de Alvaro Hernández Luna*—Chicano Political Prisoner." Personal interviews with author. July–August.

Herrera-Sobek, Maria. 1990. *The Mexican Corrido: A Feminist Analysis*. Bloomington: Indiana UP.

———. 1999. "The Ethics of the Narco-corrido." Invited lecture, University of Texas at San Antonio.

Hersh, Seymour. 2004. "The Gray Zone: How a Secret Pentagon Program Came to Abu Ghraib." *The New Yorker*, May 24.

Hill, Jack. 1974. *Foxy Brown*. American International Pictures.

Hill, Patricia Liggins. 1982. "Blues for a Mississippi Black Boy: Etheridge Knight's Craft in the Black Oral Tradition." *Mississippi Quarterly: The Journal of Southern Culture* 36, no. 1 (Winter): 21–33.

Hill, Walter, dir. 1979. *Warriors*. Paramount.

Hobsbawm, Eric J. 1965. *Primitive Rebels: Studies in Archaic Form of Social Movement in the Nineteenth and Twentieth Centuries*. New York: Norton.

———. 1969. *Bandits*. New York: Delacorte Press.

———. 1973. *Revolutionaries: Contemporary Essays*. New York: Pantheon Books.

Homer, Frederick D. 1984. "Government Terror in the United States: An Exploration of Containment Policy." *The State as Terrorist: The Dynamics of Governmental Violence and Repression*, 167–181. Ed. Michael Stohl and George A. Lopez. New York: Greenwood Press.

hooks, bell. 1995. "The Oppositional Gaze: Black Female Spectators." *Black Cinema*. Ed. Manthia Diawara, 288–302. New York: Routledge.

Hopper, Dennis, dir. 1988. *Colors*. MGM Studios.

House, Aline. 1975. *The Carrasco Tragedy: Eleven Days of Terror in the Huntsville Prison*. Waco: Texian Press.

Howe, Adrian. 1994. *Punish and Critique: Towards a Feminist Analysis of Penality*. London: Routledge.

Hughes, Albert, and Allen Hughes. 1993. *Menace II Society*. New Line Cinema.

Human Rights Watch Women's Rights Project Advisory Committee. 1995. *Human Rights Watch Global Report on Women's Human Rights, 1995*. New York: Human Rights Watch.

Irigaray, Luce. 1985. *This Sex Which Is Not One*. Trans. Catherine Porter and Carolyn Burke. Ithaca, NY: Cornell UP.

Jackson, George. 1990. *Blood in My Eye*. Baltimore: Black Classic Press.

———. 1994. *Soledad Brother: The Prison Letters of George Jackson*. New York: Lawrence Hill Books.

Jackson, Jonathan, Jr. 1996. Personal conversation with author. Ithaca, NY.

James, Joy. 2002. *States of Confinement: Policing, Detention and Prisons*. Revised. New York: St. Martin's.

———. 2003. *Imprisoned Intellectuals: America's Political Prisoners Write on Life, Liberation, and Rebellion*. New York: Rowman and Littlefield.

Jameson, Fredric. 1981. *The Political Unconscious: Narrative as a Socially Symbolic Act*. Ithaca, NY: Cornell UP.

———. 1991. *Postmodernism: Or, the Cultural Logic of Late Capitalism*. Durham, NC: Duke UP.

Jan Mohamed, Abdul. 1985. "The Economy of Manichean Allegory: The Function of Racial Difference in Colonialist Literature." *Critical Inquiry* 12, no. 1: 59–87.

Jennings, Rachel. 2003. "Celtic Women and White Guilt: Frankie Silver and Chipita Rodriguez in Folk Memory." *MELUS* (Spring): 1–24.

Johnson, Elvin. 2006. Conversation with prisoners at Louis Gossett, Jr. Residential Center. Ithaca, NY.

Johnson, Richard. 1987. "What Is Cultural Studies Anyway?" *Social Text* 16: 38–60.

Jones, Raymond, and Peter d'Errico. 1994. "The Paradox of Higher Education in Prisons. *Higher Education in Prison*, 1–16. Ed. Miriam Williford. Phoenix: Oryx Press.

Kanellos, Nicolás. 1985. "Ricardo Sánchez—Minotaur." Introduction. *Selected Works [of Ricardo Sánchez]*. Houston: Arte Público.

Keller, Gary. 1994. *Hispanics and United States Film: An Overview and Handbook*. Tempe, AZ: Bilingual Review.

Lafaye, Jacques. 1985. *Quetzalcóatl y Guadalupe: La formación de la conciencia nacional en México*. Trans. Ida Vitale y Fulgencio López Vidarte. Mexico: Fondo de Cultura Económica.

Latin American Subaltern Studies Group. 1995. "Founding Statement." *The Postmodernism Debate in Latin America*, 135–146. Ed. John Beverley, Michael Aronna, and Jose Oviedo. Durham, NC: Duke UP.

Lauren, Paul Gordon. 2003. *The Evolution of Human Rights: Visions Seen*. Pittsburgh: University of Pennsylvania Press.

Leal, Luis. 1996. Personal interview. Stanford, CA.

Levinson, Brett. 1996. "Towards a Psychoanalysis of Culture: Sex, Nation, and the Praxis of the Liminal in *American Me* and *The Labyrinth of Solitude*." *Post Script* 16, no. 1: 13–33.

Limón, José E. 1992. *Mexican Ballads, Chicano Poems: History and Influence in Mexican-American Social Poetry*. Berkeley: University of California Press.

Lipski, John M. 2000. "Back to Zero or Ahead to 2001? Issues and Challenges in U.S. Spanish Research." *Research on Spanish in the United States: Linguistic Issues and Challenges*, 1–41. Ed. Ana Roca. Somerville, MA: Cascadilla Press.

List, Christine. 1996. *Chicano Images: Refiguring Ethnicity in Mainstream Film*. New York: Garland.

Lopez, George A. 1986. "National Security Ideology as an Impetus to State Violence and State Terror." *Government Violence and Repression: An Agenda for Research*. Ed. Michael Stohl and George A. Lopez, 73–95. New York: Greenwood.

Lopez, Gerald P. 1992. *Rebellious Lawyering: One Chicano's Vision of Progressive Law Practice*. Boulder, CO: Westview.

López Rojo, Miguel. 2001. *Chicano Timespace: The Poetry and Politics of Ricardo Sánchez*. College Station: Texas A&M Press.

Lowe, Lisa. 1996. *Immigrant Acts: On Asian American Cultural Politics*. Durham, NC: Duke UP.

Lucero, Judy A. 1973. "Christmas Sacrifice." *De Colores* 1, no. 1 (Winter): 78.

———. 1973. "Face of Fear." *De Colores* 1, no. 1 (Winter): 72.

———. 1973. "Jail-Life Walk." *De Colores* 1, no. 1 (Winter): 77.

———. 1973. "A Little Girl's Prayer." *De Colores* 1: no. 1 (Winter): 73.

———. 1973. "Memoriam: Poems of Judy A. Lucero." *De Colores* 1, no. 1 (Winter): 71–79.

———. 1976. "Ocho poemas de amor y desesperación." *De Colores* 3, no. 1: 57–58.

McCain, John. 2005. "Statement of Senator John McCain Amendment on Army Field Manual." July 25. N.p.

McClane, Kenneth. 1991. "Walls: A Journey to Auburn." *Walls: Essays, 1985–1990,* 29–44. Detroit: Wayne State UP.

McKenna, Teresa. 1991. "On Chicano Poetry and the Political Age: Corridos as Social Drama." *Criticism in the Borderlands: Studies in Chicano Literature, Culture, and Ideology,* 181–202. Ed. Hector Calderón and José David Saldívar. Durham, NC: Duke UP.

———. 1997. *Migrant Song: Politics and Process in Contemporary Chicano Literature.* Austin: University of Texas Press.

McKinney, Wilson. 1974. "Carrasco Corrido Stretches Truth." *San Antonio News.* August 6. A1.

———. 1975. *Fred Gómez Carrasco: The Heroin Merchant.* Austin, TX: Heidleberg.

McKinney, Wilson, trans. 1973. Salomé Gutierrez and Los Socios. "The Ballad of Fred Gomez Carrasco." *Fred Gómez Carrasco: The Heroin Merchant.* Austin, TX: Heidleberg.

Martí, José. 1997. *Versos sencillos/Simple Verses.* Trans. Manuel Tellechea. Houston: Arte Público.

Martin, Steve, and Sheldon Ekland-Olson. 1987. *Texas Prisons: The Walls Came Tumbling Down.* Austin: Texas Monthly Press.

Martínez, Elizabeth Coonrod. 1995. "The Mexicano/Chicano Search for Identity in the Films *Los de Abajo* and *American Me.*" *Anuario de Cine y Literatura en Español* 1: 17–28.

Martinez, Lorri. 1982. *Where Eagles Fall.* Brunswick: Blackberry Press.

Martínez, Rubén. 1992. *The Other Side: Notes from the New L.A., Mexico City, and Beyond.* New York: Vintage.

Mascia-Lees, Francis, and Patricia Sharpe. 1992. "Introduction: Soft-Tissue Modification and the Horror Within." *Tattoo, Torture, Mutilation and Adornment: The Denaturalization of the Body in Culture and Text,* 1–9. Ed. Francis Mascia-Lees and Patricia Sharpe. New York: SUNY Press.

Mauer, Marc. 1991. "Americans Behind Bars: A Comparison of International Rates of Incarceration." Washington, DC: The Sentencing Project.

———. 1992. "Americans Behind Bars: One Year Later." Washington, DC: The Sentencing Project.

———. 2006. *Race to Incarcerate.* Revised and updated. New York: New Press.

Mazón, Mauricio. 1984. *The Zoot Suit Riots: The Psychology of Symbolic Annihilation.* Austin: University of Texas Press.

Menchú, Rigoberta. 1987. *I, Rigoberta Menchú: An Indian Woman in Guatemala.* Ed. and trans. Elizabeth Burgos Debray. London: Verso.

Mendoza, Louis G. 1993a. "Re-Reading the Body I: The Cultural Poetics and Politics of Pinto Art—Raúl Salinas." Videographer Cristina Ibarra. February 15.

———. 1993b. "Re-Reading the Body II: The Cultural Poetics and Politics of Pinto Art—Raúl Salinas, Roberto Perez and Amado 'Mayo' Pardo." Videographer Cristina Ibarra. February 22.

———. 2001. *Historia: The Literary Making of Chicana and Chicano History.* College Station: Texas A&M UP.

———. 2003. "The Re-Education of a Xicanindio: Raúl Salinas and the Poetics of Pinto Transformation." *MELUS* 28, no. 1 (Spring): 39–60.

Mendoza, Louis G., ed. 2006. *raúlrsalinas and the Jail Machine: My Weapon is My Pen.* Austin: University of Texas Press.

Mendoza, Louis, Emmet Campos, and Dana Maya Maynard. 1994. *A Guide to Archives of Raúl Salinas.* Austin, TX: Red Salmon Press.

Mendoza, Louis, and B. V. Olguín. 1995. "The Semiotics of the *Pinto* Visual Vernacular: The Political and Symbolic Economy of the Abjected Body." Presentation at the XXIII Annual Meeting of the National Association for Chicano and Chicana Studies, Spokane, March 31.

Menéndez, Ramón, dir. 1988. *Stand and Deliver.* Warner Brothers.

Minh-ha, Trinh T. 1989. *Native, Woman, Other: Writing Postcoloniality and Feminism.* Bloomington: Indiana UP.

Mignolo, Walter D. 2002. *Local Histories/Global Designs: Coloniality, Subaltern Knowledges, and Border Thinking.* Princeton, NJ: Princeton UP.

Miranda, Marie Keta. 2003. *Homegirls in the Public Sphere.* Austin: University of Texas Press.

Mirandé, Alfredo. 1987. *Gringo Justice.* South Bend, IN: University of Notre Dame Press.

Mitchell, Martin (Tim). 2001. "Notes from Inside: Forum Theater in Maximum Security." *Theater* 31, no. 3 (Fall): 55–61.

———. 2004. "Rhythm of the Machine: Theater, Prison Community, and Social Change." *Reflections*: 4, no. 1 (Winter): 136–146.

———. 2005. "Theater of the Oppressed in US Prisons: Eight Years of Working with Adult and Youth Prisoners Examined." Doctoral dissertation. Department of Theater Arts, Cornell University. Draft, November 20.

Mitford, Jessica. 1973. *Cruel and Usual Punishment: The Prison Business.* New York: Knopf.

Montejano, David. 1993. Personal interview. Palo Alto, CA.

Montes, Amelia María de la Luz, and Anne Elizabeth Goldman, eds. 2004. *María Amparo Ruiz de Burton: Critical and Pedagogical Perspectives.* Lincoln: University of Nebraska Press.

Moore, Joan W. 1978. *Homeboys: Gangs, Drugs, and Prison in the Barrios of Los Angeles.* Philadelphia: Temple UP.

———. 1991. *Going Down to the Barrio: Homeboys and Homegirls in Change.* Philadelphia: Temple UP.

Moraga, Cherríe. 1983. *Loving in the War Years: Lo que nunca pasó por sus labios.* Boston: South End Press.

Morante, José E., and El Repertorio Norteña Internacional. "*El trágico fin de Carrasco.*" No label.

Morín, José Luís. 2005. *Latino/a Rights and Justice in the United States: Perspectives and Approaches.* Durham, NC: Carolina Academic Press.

———. 2006. "Latinas/os and Incarceration in the United States: A Criminal Justice Policy Challenge." Conference presentation, "Behind Bars: Latinos and Prisons," Chicago, October 20.

Morison, John, and Christine Bell. 1996. *Tall Stories? Reading Law and Literature*. Aldershot, England: Dartmouth Publishing.

Moya, Paula M. L. 1995. "Postmodernism, 'Realism,' and the Politics of Identity: Cherríe Moraga and Chicana Feminism." *Feminist Genealogies, Colonial Legacies, Democratic Futures*, 125–150. Ed. M. Jacqui Alexander and Chandra Talpade Mohanty. New York: Routledge.

———. 2002. *Learning from Experience: Minority Identities, Multicultural Struggles*. Berkeley: University of California Press.

Moyers, Bill, ed. 1995. "Part 6: Swirl Like a Leaf—Jimmy Santiago Baca, Robert Bly and Marilyn Chin." *The Language of Life: A Festival of Poets*. Audio and video series. Public Affairs Television and David Grubin Productions.

Mulvey, Laura. 1975. "Visual Pleasure and Narrative Cinema." *Screen* 16, no. 3 (Autumn): 6–18.

Munby, Jonathan. 1999. *Public Enemies, Public Heroes: Screening the Gangster from "Little Caesar" to "Touch of Evil."* Chicago: University of Chicago Press.

Muñoz, Carlos, Jr. 1989. *Youth, Identity, Power: The Chicano Movement*. New York: Verso.

Murray, Ixta Maya. 1997. *Locas*. New York: Grove.

Mutrux, Floyd, and Desmond Nakano. 1992. Original script. *American Me*.

National Service Learning Clearinghouse. Web site. May 2004. http://www .servicelearning.org/welcome_to_service-learning/index.php.

Navarrette, Ruben, Jr. 1993. *A Darker Shade of Crimson: Odyssey of a Harvard Chicano*. New York: Bantam.

Neruda, Pablo. 1993 [1950]. *Canto general*. Trans. Jack Schmitt. Berkeley: University of California Press.

Neugebauer, Joy. 2003. Personal interviews with author. Westminster, CA. April.

Newman, Kathleen. 1996. "Reterritorialization in Recent Chicano Cinema: Edward James Olmos's *American Me* (1992)." *The Ethnic Eye: Latino Media Arts*, 95–106. Ed. Chon Noriega and Ana López. Minneapolis: University of Minnesota Press.

Norris, Frank. 1958 (1901). *The Octopus*. Boston: Houghton-Mifflin.

Olguín, B. V. 1989. "Unraveling the Myth of the Minotaur Poet: A Thematic Analysis of Ricardo Sánchez' Poetry." Conference presentation, National Association for Chicana/o Studies, Los Angeles, April 29.

———. 1991. "Unraveling the Myth of the Minotaur Poet: Ricardo Sánchez and the Dialectics of Prison and Poetry." Conference presentation, Stanford Center for Chicano Research, May 22.

———. 1992. "*Echando Madres*: The Political and Symbolic Economy of Dialogism in *Pinto* Poetry—The Case of Ricardo Sánchez." Conference

presentation, "Crossing Borders," First Annual Interdisciplinary
Conference on the Chicano Experience, Pullman, WA, June 12.
——. 1993. "*Echando Madres*: The Political and Symbolic Economy of
Dialogism in *Pinto* Poetry—The Case of Ricardo Sánchez." Conference
presentation, National Association for Chicana/o Studies, San Jose, March
24.
——. 1997. "Tattoos, Abjection, and the Political Unconscious: Towards
a Semiotics of the Pinto Visual Vernacular." *Cultural Critique* 37 (Fall):
159–213.
——. 2000. "*Echando Madres*: Dialogism in Chicano Convict Poetry." *The
Ricardo Sánchez Reader*, 81–106. Ed. Arnoldo Carlos Vento. Eatontown,
NJ: Ediciones Nuevo Espacio.
——. 2001. "Mothers, Daughters, and Deities: Judy Lucero's Gynocritical
Prison Poetics and Materialist Chicana Politics." *Frontiers: A Journal of
Women's Studies* 22 (2) (Fall): 63–86.
——. 2002. "Of Truth, Secrets and Ski Masks: Counterrevolutionary
Appropriations and Zapatista Revisions of Testimonial Narrative."
Nepantla: Views from South 3, no. 2 (Winter): 145–178.
——. 2003. "Barrios of the World Unite! Regionalism, Transnationalism,
and Internationalism in Tejano War Poetry from the Mexican Revolution
to World War II." *Left of the Color Line: Race, Radicalism, and
Twentieth-Century Literature of the United States,* 107–139.
Ed. Bill V. Mullen and James Smethurst. Chapel Hill: University
of North Carolina Press.
——. 2008. "Chicano Convict Writing, Human Rights Regimes and a New
Paradigm for Prisoner Rights Activism Today." *Journal of Latino Studies* 6
(Spring): 160–80.
Olguín, B. V., Ami Ongiri, Eliza Rodriguez y Gibson, and Annette Portillo.
1998. "Teaching Prison/Prison Teaching" panel presentation. Critical
Resistance Conference, Berkeley, CA, September 25.
Olmos, Edward James, dir. 1992. *American Me*. Universal Pictures.
——. 1993. Public lecture at San Jose State University, CA.
O'Neill, Edward R. 1995. "The Seen of the Crime: Violence, Anxiety and the
Domestic in Police Reality Programming." *CineAction* 38 (September):
56–63.
Owens, David Clinton, and Virginia Stem Owens. 2003. *Living Next Door to
the Death House*. Grand Rapids, MI: William Eerdmans Publishing.
Pardo, Mary. 1998. *Mexican American Women Activists: Identity and
Resistance in Two Los Angeles Communities*. Philadelphia: Temple UP.
Paredes, Américo. 1958. *With His Pistol in His Hand: A Border Ballad and Its
Hero*. Austin: University of Texas Press.
——. 1979. "The Folk Base of Chicano Literature." *Modern Chicano
Writers: A Collection of Essays,* 4–17. Ed. Joseph Sommers and Tomás
Ybarra-Frausto. Englewood Cliffs, NJ: Prentice-Hall.

———. 1993. *Folklore and Culture on the Texas-Mexican Border*. Austin: University of Texas Center for Mexican American Studies.

———, ed. 1995. *A Texas-Mexican Cancionero: Folksongs of the Lower Border*. Austin: University of Texas Press.

Parks, Gordon. 1971. *Shaft*. MGM Pictures.

Paz, Octavio. 1985 (1950). *The Labyrinth of Solitude*. Trans. Lysander Kemp, Yara Milos, and Rachel Phillips Belash. New York: Grove.

Peñalosa, Fernando. 1980. *Chicano Sociolinguistics: A Brief Introduction*. Rowley, MA: Newbury House.

The People of the State of California vs. Modesta Avila. 1889a. Criminal Case No. 6, Superior Court of Orange County, October 15.

The People of the State of California vs. Modesta Avila. 1889b. Criminal Case No. 6, Superior Court of Orange County, October 28.

Pérez, Emma. 1999. *The Decolonial Imaginary: Writing Chicanas into History (Theories of Representation and Difference)*. Bloomington: University of Indiana Press.

Pérez-Torres, Rafael. 1995. *Movements in Chicano Poetry: Against Myths, Against Margins*. Cambridge: Cambridge UP.

Polkinhorn, Harry, Alfredo Velasco, and Malcolm Lambert, eds. 1986. *El Libro de Caló: The Dictionary of Chicano Slang*. Revised edition. Berkeley, CA: Floricanto Press.

Powell, Stewart M. 2002. "Lindh may have put FBI on the trail of the Buffalo 6." *San Antonio Express-News*, 24A. September 22.

Prassel, Frank Richard. *The Great American Outlaw: A Legacy of Fact and Fiction*. 1996. Norman: University of Oklahoma Press.

Pressman, Michael, dir. 1979. *Boulevard Nights*. Warner.

Rafter, Nicole. 2000. *Shots in the Mirror: Crime Films and Society*. New York: Oxford UP.

Rafter, Nicole Hahn, and Debra L. Stanley. 1999. *Prisons in America: A Reference Handbook*, 80–81. Santa Barbara: ABC-CLIO.

Ramírez Berg, Charles. 1990. "Stereotyping in Films in General and of the Hispanic in Particular." *The Howard Journal of Communications* 2 (Summer): 286–300.

Ramos, Rubén, and the Texas Revolution. N.d. *El Gato Negro*.

Rideau, Wilbert, and Ron Wikberg, eds. 1992. *Life Sentences: Rage and Survival Behind Bars*. New York: Times Books.

Ripley, Amanda. 2002. "The Case of the Dirty Bomber: How a Chicago Street Gangster Allegedly Became a Soldier for Osama Bin Laden." *Time* 159, 25 (June 24): 28–30.

Risse, Thomas, and Kathryn Sikkink. 2002. "The Socialization of International Human Rights Norms into Domestic Practices: Introduction." *The Power of Human Rights: International Norms and Domestic Change*, 1–38. Ed. Thomas Risse, Stephen C. Ropp, and Kathryn Sikkink. Cambridge: Cambridge UP.

Robinson, Ronald W. 1997. *Prison Hostage: The Siege of the Walls Prison in Huntsville*. Lewiston, NY: Edwin Mellen Press.

Rodgers, Richard, and Oscar Hammerstein. 1999. *Oklahoma*. Dir. Trevor Nunn. Image Entertainment.

Rodriguez, Dylan. 2006. *Forced Passages: Imprisoned Radical Intellectuals and the Formation of the U.S. Prison Regime*. Minneapolis: University of Minnesota Press.

Rodriguez, Luis. 1994. *Always Running: La Vida Loca—Gang Days in L.A.* New York: Touchstone.

Roma, David, and Jonathan Wyche, dirs. *Miami Ink*. 2005. The Learning Channel.

Rony, Fatimah Tobing. 1996. *The Third Eye: Race, Cinema, and Ethnographic Spectacle*. Durham, NC: Duke UP.

Rosaldo, Renato. 1989. *Culture and Truth: The Remaking of Social Analysis*. Boston: Beacon Press.

Rosales, Rodolfo. 2000. *The Illusion of Inclusion: The Political Story of San Antonio*. Austin: University of Texas Press.

Ross, Luana. 1998. *Inventing the Savage: The Social Construction of Native American Criminality*. Austin: University of Texas Press.

Rothman, David J. 1990. *The Discovery of the Asylum: Social Order and Disorder in the New Republic*. Boston: Little, Brown and Company.

Ruiz de Burton, Amparo. 1997 (1885). *The Squatter and the Don*. Houston: Arte Público Press.

Salas, Elizabeth. 1990. *Soldaderas in the Mexican Military: Myth and History*. Austin: University of Texas Press.

Salazar, Armandina. 1974a. "Does Federico Gomez Carrasco Have Rights?" *Chicano Times* 5, no. 49 (August 2–16): 6.

———. 1974b. "Conspiracy Seen to Tarnish Carrasco's Image." *Chicano Times* 5, no. 50 (August 16–30): 4–5.

Saldívar, José David. 1991. *The Dialectics of Our America: Genealogy, Cultural Critique, and Literary History*. Durham, NC: Duke UP.

———. 2000. "Looking Awry at 1898: Roosevelt, Montejo, Paredes, and Mariscal." *American Literary History* 12: 386–406.

Saldívar, Ramón. 1990. *Chicano Narrative: The Dialectics of Difference*. Madison: University of Wisconsin Press.

Saldívar-Hull, Sonia. 2000. *Feminism on the Border: Chicana Gender Politics and Literature*. Berkeley: University of California Press.

Salinas, Raúl. 1970. "A Trip Through the Mind Jail." *Aztlán de Leavenworth* 1, 1 (May): n.p.

———. 1973. *Viaje/Trip*. Providence, RI: Hellcoal Press.

———. 1980. "A Trip Through the Mind Jail." *Un Trip Through the Mind Jail y Otras Excursions*, 55–60. San Francisco: Editorial Pocho-Che.

———. 1992. Personal interview. Austin, TX. May.

———. 1994. Personal interview. Austin, TX. July.

———. 1996. Personal interview. Austin, TX.

———. 1999. Personal interview. Austin, TX.

———. 1999. *Un Trip Through the Mind Jail y Otras Excursions.* Houston: Arte Público.

———. 2006. Personal interview. Austin, TX.

Samora, Julian, Joe Bernal, and Albert Peña. 1979. *Gunpowder Justice: A Reassessment of the Texas Rangers.* South Bend, IN: Notre Dame UP.

Sánchez, Marta E. 1978. "Judy Lucero and Bernice Zamora: Two Dialectical Statements in Chicana Poetry." *Revista Chicano-Riqueña* 6, no. 4 (*otoño*): 69.

Sánchez, Ricardo. 1971. *Canto y grito mi liberación (. . . y lloro mis desmadrazgos . . .).* El Paso: Míctla Press.

———. 1973a. *Canto y grito mi liberación (. . . the Liberation of a Chicano Mind . . .).* New York: Anchor Books.

———. 1973b. "*Míctla*: A Chicano's Long Road Home." *The Publish-It-Yourself Handbook: Literary Tradition & How-To*, 53–70. Ed. Bill Henderson. New York: Pushcart Press.

———. 1976a. *HECHIZOspells.* Los Angeles: UCLA Chicano Studies Center Publications.

———. 1976b. "*Tinieblas Pintas Quebradas*: an intro of sorts." *De Colores* 3, no. 1: 5–11.

———. 1980. Personal interview. Houston.

———. 1982. Personal interview. Houston.

———. 1985. *Selected Poems.* Houston: Arte Público.

———. 1992a. Personal interview. Pullman, WA.

———. 1992b. Personal interview. Stanford University, Stanford, CA.

———. N.d. Untitled and unpublished review of *American Me.* N.p.

———. N.d. "*Cabalgado como bestia.*" Unpublished manuscript. Stanford (CA) University Archives.

Sánchez, Rosaura. 1983. *Chicano Discourse: A Socio-historic Perspective.* Rowley, MA: Newbury House Publishers.

———. 1995. *Telling Identities: The Californio Testimonios.* Minneapolis: University of Minnesota Press.

Sánchez, Rosaura, and Beatrice Pita. 1997. Introduction to *The Squatter and the Don,* by Amparo Ruiz de Burton, 7–49. Houston: Arte Público.

Sánchez-Jakowski, Martín. 1991. *Islands in the Street: Gangs and American Urban Society.* Berkeley: University of California Press.

Sánchez-Tranquilino, Marcos. 1991. "*Mi casa no es su casa*: Chicano Murals and Barrio Calligraphy as Systems of Signification at Estrada Courts, 1972–1978." Ph.D. dissertation, University of California, Los Angeles.

Sanders, Clinton R. 1989. *Customizing the Body: The Art and Culture of Tattooing.* Philadelphia: Temple UP.

Sandoval, Chela. 2000. *Methodology of the Oppressed.* Minneapolis: University of Minnesota Press.

Scheuring, Paul T., writer, and Brett Ratner, dir. 2005. *Prison Breakout*. Fox Television.

Schroeder, Ken. 1996. "Prison Education." *The Education Digest* 62, no. 2 (October): 73–74.

Sedgewick, Eve Kosofsky. 1985. *Between Men: English Literature and Male Homosocial Desire*. New York: Columbia UP.

Shakespeare, William. 1997. *Taming of the Shrew*. New York: Dover.

———. 2004. *The Merchant of Venice*. New York: Washington Square Press.

———. 2004. *The Tempest*. New York: Washington Square Press.

Singleton, John, dir. 1991. *Boyz-N-the Hood*. Sony Pictures.

Siposs, George. 1986. *Modesta Avila: An American Folk Opera*. Dir. Kent Johnson, prod. Joy Neugebauer. Premier performance, Westminster Auditorium. October 10.

Smith, Erin A. 2000. *Hard Boiled: Working-Class Readers and Pulp Magazines*. Philadelphia: Temple UP.

Smith, Kyle. 2006. "'Tempest' Brings Criminals to Tears." *New York Post*. Online edition, March 10. N.p.

Sommer, Doris. 1996. "No Secrets." *The Real Thing: Testimonial Discourse and Latin America*, 130–157. Ed. Georg M. Gugelberger. Durham, NC: Duke UP.

Sophocles. *Antigone*. 1993. New York: Dover.

Sorell, Victor Alejandro. 2005. *Illuminated Handkerchiefs, Tattooed Bodies, and Prison Scribes: Meditations on the Aesthetic, Religious and Social Sensibilities of Chicano Pintos*. South Bend, IN: Snite Museum of Art, University of Notre Dame.

Spivak, Gayatri Chakravorty. 1988. "Can the Subaltern Speak?" *Marxism and the Interpretation of Culture*, 271–313. Ed. Lawrence Grossberg and Cary Nelson. Chicago: University of Illinois Press.

Stahura, Barbara. 2003. "Jimmy Santiago Baca Interview." *The Progressive* (January). Online edition. N.p.

Steward, Samuel M. 1990. *Bad Boys and Tough Tattoos: A Social History of the Tattoo with Gangs, Sailors, and Street-Corner Punks, 1950–1965*. New York: Haworth Press.

Stohl, Michael, and George A. López. 1984. "Introduction." *The State as Terrorist: The Dynamics of Governmental Violence and Repression*, 3–10. Ed. Michael Stohl and George A. López. New York: Greenwood

Stowers, Carlton, and Carroll Pickett. 2002. *Within These Walls: Memoirs of a Death House Chaplain*. New York: St. Martin's.

Sweeney, Joan. 1974. "Latin Hijacks Jet to L.A., Surrenders after Radio Protest." *Los Angeles Times*. April 14. A1, A21.

Takaki, Ronald. 2000. *Iron Cages: Race and Culture in Nineteenth Century America*. New York: Oxford UP.

Taussig, Michael. 1993. *Mimesis and Alterity: A Particular History of the Senses*. New York: Routledge.

Thomas, Piri. 1997. *Down These Mean Streets*. New York: Vintage.

Titlebaum, Peter, Gabrielle Williamson, Corinne Daprano, Janine Baer, and Jane Brahler. 2004. "Annotated History of Service Learning, 1862–2002." National Service Learning Clearinghouse. http://www.servicelearning.org/welcome_to_service-learning/index.php.

Trounstine, Jean. 2001. *Shakespeare Behind Bars: The Power of Drama in a Women's Prison*. New York: St. Martin's.

United Nations. 2001a. "Geneva Conventions. Article II." In *25+ Human Rights Documents*. New York: Center for the Study of Human Rights, Columbia University.

———. 2001b. Geneva Conventions. Article III. In *25+ Human Rights Documents*. New York: Center for the Study of Human Rights, Columbia University.

———. 2001c. "International Convention on the Elimination of All Forms of Racial Discrimination." In *25+ Human Rights Documents*. New York: Center for the Study of Human Rights, Columbia University.

———. 2001d. "Standard Minimum Rules for the Treatment of Prisoners." In *25+ Human Rights Documents*. New York: Center for the Study of Human Rights, Columbia University.

———. 2001e. "United Nations Charter." In *25+ Human Rights Documents*. New York: Center for the Study of Human Rights, Columbia University.

———. 2001f. "Universal Declaration of Human Rights." In *25+ Human Rights Documents*. New York: Center for the Study of Human Rights, Columbia University.

U.S. Army. 2006. *FM (Field Manual) 34–52: Intelligence Interrogation*. Washington, DC: US Army Publications.

U.S. Congress. 1994. Violent Crime Control and Law Enforcement Act (Omnibus Crime Bill).

———. 2001. USA PATRIOT Act.

———. 2006. Military Commissions Act.

———. 2006. USA PATRIOT Act II.

U.S. Constitution. 1865. Amendment XIII, Section 1.

U.S. Declaration of Independence. 1776.

U.S. Department of Justice. 1995a. *Correctional Populations in the United States, 1995*. Washington, DC: Bureau of Justice Statistics.

———. 1995b. *Women in Prison*. Washington, DC: Bureau of Justice Statistics.

———. 1998. "Crime and Justice in the United States and in England and Wales, 1981–96." October.

———. 2002. "Profile of Nonviolent Offenders Exiting State Prisons." May.

———. 2005. "Crime and Victimization in the Three Largest Metropolitan Areas, 1980–98." February.

U.S. Supreme Court. 1966. *Miranda vs. Arizona*.

———. 2005. *Hamdi vs. Rumsfeld*.

Valdez, Luis, dir. 1971. *Actos*. San Juan Bautista: Teatro Campesino.

———. 1981. *Zoot Suit*. Universal Studios.

Van Peeble, Melvin. 1971. *Sweet Sweetback's Baadasssss Song*. Cinemation Industries.

Vento, Arnoldo Carlos, and Luís Leal. 2000. *The Ricardo Sánchez Reader*. Eatontown, NJ: Ediciones Nuevo Espacio.

Vigil, James Diego. 1988. *Barrio Gangs: Street Life and Identity in Southern California*. Austin: University of Texas Press.

Villa, Raúl Homero. 1996. "Of *Corridos* and Convicts: Gringo (In)Justice in Early Border Ballads and Contemporary *Pinto* Poetry." *Chicanos and Chicanas in Contemporary Society*. Ed. Roberto M. De Anda, 113–125. Boston: Allyn and Bacon.

———. 2000. *Barrio-logos: Space and Place in Urban Chicano Literature and Culture*. Austin: University of Texas Press.

Villanueva, Alma. 1977. *Bloodroot*. Austin, TX: Place of Herons Press.

Villanueva, Tino. 1975. "*Más allá del grito: Poesía engagee chicana*." *De Colores: Journal of Emerging Raza Philosophies* 2, 2: 27–46.

Viramontes, Helena Maria. 1985. *The Moths and Other Stories*. Houston: Arte Público Press.

———. 1995. *Under the Feet of Jesus*. New York: Dutton.

———. 1997. "Modesta Avila: Chicana Feminist Foremother." Conference presentation, American Literature Association, Baltimore, May.

———. 2004. Personal interview. Ithaca, NY. Fall.

Viswanathan, Gauri. 1995. "The Beginnings of English Literary Study in British India." In *The Post-Colonial Studies Reader*, 431–437. Ed. Bill Ashcroft, Gareth Griffiths, and Helen Tiffin. London: Routledge.

Wald, Elijah. 2002. *Narcocorrido: A Journey into the Music of Drugs, Guns and Guerrillas*. New York: Rayo.

Waldram, James B. 1997. *Way of the Pipe: Aboriginal Spirituality and Symbolic Healing in Canadian Prisons*. Toronto: Broadview.

Ward, Ian. 1995. *Law and Literature: Possibilities and Perspectives*. Cambridge: Cambridge UP.

Warner, Kevin. 1998. "'The Prisoners Are People' Perspective: And the Problems of Promoting Learning Where this Outlook Is Rejected." *Journal of Correctional Education* 49, no. 3: 118–132.

Washington, Booker T. 2000. *Up from Slavery*. New York: Signet Classics.

Webb, John Terrance. 1976. "A Lexical Study of Caló and Non-Standard Spanish in the Southwest." Doctoral dissertation, University of California at Berkeley.

Westcott, John. 1990. "Railroad's Betrayal Results in OC's First Conviction." *Orange County Register*, May 7, p. 2.

Whitman, Walt. 2006 [1892]. *Leaves of Grass*. New York: Pocket.

Williams, Linda R. 1992. "Happy Families? Feminist Reproduction and Matrilineal Thought." *New Feminist Discourses: Critical Essays on Theories and Texts*, 48–64. Ed. Isobel Armstrong. London: Routledge.

Williams, Raymond. 1978. *Marxism and Literature*. Oxford: Oxford UP.

X, Malcolm, and Alex Haley. 1965. *The Autobiography of Malcolm X.* New York: Grove.

Ybarra-Frausto, Tomás. 1978. "The Chicano Movement and the Emergence of a Chicano Poetic Consciousness." *New Directions in Chicano Scholarship,* 81–110. Ed. Ricardo Romo and Raymund Paredes. La Jolla: University of California, San Diego, Chicano Studies Program.

———. 1979. "Alurista's Poetics: The Oral, the Bilingual, the Pre-Columbian." *Modern Chicano Writers: A Collection of Critical Essays,* 117–131. Ed. Joseph Sommers and Tomás Ybarra-Frausto. Englewood Cliffs, NJ: Prentice-Hall.

———. 1984. "The Chicano Movement and the Emergence of a Chicano Poetic Consciousness." *New Directions in Chicano Scholarship,* 81–109. Ed. Ricardo Romo and Raymund Paredes. Santa Barbara: University of California, San Diego, Center for Chicano Studies.

———. 1991. "*Rasquachismo*: A Chicano Sensibility." *Chicano Art: Resistance to Affirmation, 1965–1985,* 155–162. Ed. Richard Griswold del Castillo, Teresa McKenna, and Yvonne Yarbro-Bejarano. Los Angeles: The Wight Gallery, 1991.

Zeffirelli, Franco. 1967. *The Merchant of Venice.* Paramount Pictures.

Index